IMPLOSION

SEX, LIFE AND LOVE
AT ITS RAWEST

Twenty-three true tales of women's lives
imploding and how they survived

LINDSEY JOANNE BAUER

Cover image and blue-toned images photographed by Sarah Giles

First published in Great Britain 2022 This edition published in 2023 by DB Publishing, an imprint of JMD Media Ltd, Nottingham, United Kingdom.

ISBN 9781780916507

Printed in the UK

This book is dedicated to:
M
(Always Perfect)

It is also dedicated to:
CW: a King Soloman figure in my life
&
my parents
&
all of the important women in my life, especially my daughters,
Helen SB, my other girlfriends, my fellow female colleagues
in academia and the art world and of course,
to all of the women in this book and those
I interviewed as part of the wider book context.

It is also in memory of:
Praxedes Garcia
1976-2022
Praxedes was one of the incredible participants in this book.
For all of us lucky enough to experience Prax's sunshine and bask in it,
her joyful attitude to life will continue to live on, indefinitely

DISCLAIMER

I am unable to share any of my own personal implosions in this book for legal reasons, therefore any perceived similarities between any anonymous true stories contained within this publication and that of my own life (or anyone close to me), are purely coincidental.

In the compilation of 'Implosion', women of all ages, ethnicities and faiths from across the whole of the United Kingdom put themselves forward to me via social media to relay their real experiences. In the process of such an endeavour, it became apparent that there are many relatable universal episodes and it is in the retelling of these, that we can find comfort and strength. This is the purpose of 'Implosion'.

Furthermore, please be aware that in the cases of all the anonymous participants in this book, names mentioned and some details have been changed to keep their identities' private. However, despite any changes made, these anonymous women's stories remain fundamentally the same.

Contents

'It is certain that he who falls can rise again
and not only rise again
but also rise again better than he was when he fell'

– Hugo of St. Victor

FOREWORD

Most of us will have had a point in our lives when things have gone horribly wrong! Perhaps it's just one event which has totally derailed us, say the end of a relationship for example, or maybe it's a series of events, which have gathered momentum and unleashed a metaphorical tsunami, knocking us for six!

Maybe you are trying to pick up the pieces from such a set of catastrophes right now and you have no idea where to begin in order to rebuild your life?

If that is the case, this book is here to support and comfort you. However, even if you're not in that zone, all of the experiences shared within these pages will nonetheless enlighten you as to the variety of trauma which some women have gone through. At the very least, their true stories will enhance your awareness of the human condition so that you can be empathetic and supportive to help all those in need who happen to cross your path in the future.

I've had two episodes so far where it's as though a hand grenade was literally tossed into my life and virtually all of its fundamental structures (especially the aspects which made me really happy), were blown to pieces within a very short space of time. I wish I could share my personal experiences with you but unfortunately due to legal issues, I am unable to. Therefore although my own true stories cannot be included in this volume, instead, in my requests via social media for women across the UK to relate their own life implosions to me, I have found anonymous women who have real experiences that bear similarities to situations that many of us have faced.

I am full of gratitude that these women have let me include their life meltdowns in this book. In fact what I found was that so many wanted to open up and offload their stories because they often become huge burdens to carry; big personal traumas that are so much easier to deal with when the bearer can be transparent, rather than feeling overwhelmed by dark heavy secrets. I can tell you that when a life implosion happens, everything you know and rely upon to make you feel secure, seems as though it's completely spiralling out of control and you're at your wits' end, so to be able to offload stops human beings from feeling so completely isolated and scared.

Sometimes such moments can lead us to feel suicidal because the big picture seems so overwhelming and we can't ever imagine retrieving any sense of normality back and/or we may dread the consequences of our actions. Furthermore, some of you will be suffering huge grief from the loss of a person in your life whether through death or abandonment and that pain is ripping you apart, but you can and will survive this bereavement! This book is here to tell you that no matter how bad things get, there is always, always a reason to dust yourself off and pick yourself up, even if you're in prison as Chapter 1's Lady Unchained was.

All of the women participating in this book have done so with the intention that by sharing their often private, painful stories with you, they can uplift and help you get through whatever situations you too face in your life. I cannot articulate just how grateful I am that all of these participants have stuck with this project throughout as I took so many interviews but quite a few women dropped out for various personal reasons, including the fact that it involves so much courage to share – albeit anonymously for some - the most vulnerable times of their lives with potentially the whole world, so I salute my 23 x incredible participating women for bravely remaining committed to this endeavour.

The idea for Implosion came to me after my last life disaster when things seriously nosedived but as my frazzled brain started to recalibrate, so I began to think that if my life had upended, so must many other women's lives have upended for different reasons and I began to wonder what those reasons could be and how these women managed to rebuild themselves and their futures. I started making investigations and then this book began to materialise and take on a life of its own, until I reached a point where I felt as though I was merely the gatekeeper and guardian of all of these fascinating true stories of women and their trials, but also their amazing strength! Rather scarily, I have used the remainder of my savings to put 'Implosion' through the necessary legal checks and publish it, but if this books helps just one person, then that financial sacrifice will definitely have been worth it.

I've learnt several key things during this project and I'm going to share them with you in the following Introduction, but for now all of the participants are sending you a massive metaphorical hug via these pages (and if you don't need a hug at this present moment, then bank it for when you do! Don't think this is 'lame' too, as honestly you never know when you might need one).

We are all telling you that you CAN and WILL survive anything that life throws at you... and furthermore that you will not only survive, but you will thrive! Believe it!

INTRODUCTION

As you read through each woman's chapter, you will notice that the final paragraphs in every individual woman's true story contain their own insights as to what they have learnt from their experiences, what advice they would give to other women going through similar situations, as well as where they are now in their lives and their future plans. You'll also become aware that some of the professions and implosions feature similarities (i.e, there are a few teachers included and the topics of suicide and brain tumours, etc, pop up more than once), however this project was such an organic one and I 'cast my net far and wide' to gather all the real-life experiences which are included, so this book is, what it is! In time, I hope to undertake a follow-up and expand the diversity of life traumas.

However, I'm also including in this introduction some tips and insights, which I've learnt during the (almost) 2.5 years that I've been working on this project. One of the biggest issues that came out of so many interviews was SEX! Because so many women wanted to talk about this topic, I have given sex its own detailed section at the end of this introduction. It's an insightful read and if you are curious as to how women are expressing themselves in this way right now, you can either go straight to that section now and read this initial part later, or you can work through my research findings in the order they appear… it's totally your choice.

Anyway here's some of the lessons I've learnt from all of my book research which took place between February 2020-June 2022:

FIRSTLY, SOME MISCELLANEOUS THOUGHTS THAT LEAPT OUT AT ME DURING MY VERY FINAL READ-THROUGH

Many couples, and men in particular, often use their phones/laptops as a way of avoiding intimacy. What I mean by this, is that quite often, when women said they wanted to talk to their partners, the latter would be unavailable because they would make themselves engaged on their devices. So for example, some women would find that every evening once the children were in bed and they wanted to talk to their husbands, it was impossible because the husbands would be glued to their phones or laptops.

Another common theme that jumped out from some of the true stories contained within this book, are that when relationships were souring, men would often make autonomous financial decisions with far-reaching effects, such as taking out large secret loans and forging their wife's signature or attempting to purchase a property.

Other common themes include the damage that family secrets do to children. When children are told lies or half-lies (even with good intentions at heart) but then discover the real truths much later on in life, it completely upends their ability to trust their parents and/or adults around them. Honesty is definitely the best policy with your children.

Being a single parent is often portrayed in the media in a negative way, but as some of the true stories show within the book, actually going it solo with your children can ultimately be a very positive experience with good outcomes! It's much better to stride out on your own with your children (even if custody is shared), than to continue to remain for years in a toxic environment which negatively pollutes childhood, because of a fear of breaking-up a family. If there is ongoing, embedded discord within a domestic situation, then at the very least everyone is living in an unhappy atmosphere. If abuse of any kind persists, then the long-term damage is much greater. Staying in a permanently unhappy household results from the mindset of a misplaced sense of duty and brings misery and resentment to all. It's a waste of life.

I need to set out here that I have no personal judgements regarding any of the true stories contained within 'Implosion.' I am merely the literary conduit of each woman's experience. I am not advocating or criticising any woman's decision, whether it be to have an affair, to have an abortion, to flee a foreign country with your children, etc... In every single case in this book (and in all the many differing situations which my female friends and associates in life have found themselves in), I am pro-choice for women in every avenue in life. I think of myself as an empathetic supporter and champion of women.

In a slightly similar way, I want to say that in relating Joy's experiences of her time abroad, I am certainly not saying that what happened to her in particular countries, is resonant of all women's experiences of being in those countries (for example, I spend a lot of time myself in beautiful Italy studying my PhD and I completely love it there and have always had safe, respectful travel experiences all over Italy thus far). Rather I am simply relaying some events which happened to her and which women all over the world experience in their own countries and in many different countries when travelling.

Own your narrative

No matter what has happened to you in your life, do not shrink into a place of fear and shame. Rather, remember it's simply not game over! You have a life to lead and that's a precious gift, so go for it... you can rebuild a life or completely start over! YOU are the Mistress of your destiny!

Fear, guilt and judgement

You have to let all of these negative emotions go. You cannot control what other people think of you, so don't even waste time and energy worrying about this. You will never be able to make everyone like you and you can't ever please everyone, so park any attempts to win people over... just let it go. Learn from everything you experience, grow and move on! Learn self compassion... don't beat yourself up about your fuck-ups... we're only human; sometimes we get things wrong, make a fool of ourselves, allow ourselves to be vulnerable to the wrong people, get ourselves in a muddle... it's all okay! Humans have done this from time immaterial and will continue to do this for time immaterial. Also be compassionate about others and try not to judge.

Shame

This is such a negative emotion that society and others impose upon us, often along with our own harsh judgements. However, you can subvert this and *simply choose to let feelings of shame go*. You literally have a choice: accept shame or let it go. If you give off 'I feel ashamed' vibes, that's how people will respond to you. Rather, if you choose to let shame go and stand proud, holding your head up high, then others have no option but to stop attempting to shame you, because they realise that it doesn't stick to you; you rise above it. Also the way society judges certain situations now, often changes with time, because that is what history teaches us: one century's taboo is another century's flag to fly, to a greater or lesser degree: for example, just think of how homosexuality used to be perceived in the UK. Attitudes change, wax and wane, so we need to have nuanced debates and look at the complex picture of human behaviour before we jump to immediate draconian conclusions based on current irrational cancel-culture notions, which are absolutely the opposite of intellectual thought!

Be strong and don't overthink

With some situations, you may need to find more strength than you ever thought you were capable of. You may find yourself suffering from bullying at the hands of an ex who you have had the strength to leave, or from a work colleague for example, but do not be submissive. Dig deep and find your strength. When we often feel weak, that's actually when we can be incredibly strong! And when your mind starts plummeting into negativity, stop yourself. Stop your thoughts. You may find yourself overthinking a relationship/how a person treats you for example, and these thoughts are taking you to dark places. Distract yourself. Do something positive and look after yourself: what can you do today to show some self-care? It could be as simple as treating yourself to something small or big: a book/candle/new underwear/gym wear/bath oils/a spa treatment/a 10-min meditation etc… take care of yourself! Also see friends who will make you laugh and stop you dwelling on these intense and difficult situations.

Taboos and openness

There were some stories which I had to leave out because either I couldn't get women to come forward or because there are still taboos associated with some of the themes. For example I had a number of different heterosexual married women share their stories with me about totally unexpected lesbian affairs, but all felt unable to take part in this book project. Such affairs are far more common than we think, but these women definitely perceived a sense of taboo around them, more so than with a regular male and female affair.

Two other taboos (amongst others), discussed but for various reasons unable to be included in formal interviews in this book included: Teenagers who verbally/physically abuse their parents and car-key swap parties, but I'm going to quickly write about both of these.

As has been well-documented since Classical times, teens can be both rude and cruel to parents amidst the process of finding their character during their rite of passage into adulthood. Whilst a level of this is normal *to a degree* as teens need to feel they've outgrown their parents, siblings and family homes in order to make the break, equally it's incredibly important for parents not to feel bullied by their kids and for parents to call-out abusive behaviour.

Daughters can often be ageist and misogynistic to mothers, muttering bitchy comments regarding their mum's personal appearance for example, and teenage boys can often lash out physically in temper (but it's important to state that neither of these cited behaviours are restricted to only one gender). However, this type of behaviour often stays within the family home as a dark secret and it's doubly hard if you are a single parent!

Parents do not need to put up with this though and should call out abusive behaviour from their children (for example, if a parent is sent a string of abusive texts from a teenage child, a parent can tell their teenager that if they continue, all of their texts will be forwarded immediately to their Tutor and Head of Year at school; this kind of action can shame teens into realising that their actions are abusive and can also – if followed through – initiate family support. The police can also be contacted if things get desperate).

If your teenager has said to you "you are failing as a mother", you alone will know whether there is merit in what they are saying or whether they are expressing this to hurt you, so acknowledge to yourself whether they are pinpointing a failing you need to rectify or whether they are just projecting their own pent-up frustrations onto you, and if it's the latter, ignore their comments. Try to get them counselling support if they'll take it up – but all you can do, is try! (Also know that this behaviour won't last forever).

Another taboo to mention here which is completely random (but the interview-process brought so many varied topics to the fore and I am citing it as an example of all the many hidden and different secrets that people carry and which affect them, but seem unspeakable), is car-key swap parties and the legacy that these left to children born of related flings. If you have watched film director, Ang Lee's movie: The Ice Storm, you'll be aware that going back some decades, car-key swap parties were most definitely a thing. I know they happened in the county where I grew up but whilst experiences were shared in my book research, these women felt unable to put their stories out there, albeit anonymously, as they felt that the impact upon the parties involved, was sometimes so huge, that they were still trying to process the outcomes themselves: i.e. babies born as a result of picking up a random set of car keys and sleeping with their owner. I met a lady whose parents were not quite who she thought were her parents: her mum was her mum but her birth-dad wasn't her actual dad, he was another guy in a local village.

I'm going to talk about sex later in this introduction as it's still quite a big taboo in the UK, but so is death too. We are so nervous of instigating conversations about it and it's ridiculous because it comes to all of us. Just being able to be open about death, any taboos and getting our angst 'off our chests' is so important, so liberating. For this reason, I particularly love the writing of The Times' journalist, Clover Stroud, especially on her Instagram account. Clover shares her real life feelings about grief, love, intimacy, family stress, everything. She's incredible! When we share our innermost thoughts, others respond to us in kind because they feel liberated to be able to be themselves too.

STORIES WANTED/OMITTED

There were also stories I wanted to feature but couldn't find participants in time, who were able to share their experiences. Thus I wanted to have true stories to tell of prostitution, IVF, genetic illnesses, drug addiction, homelessness, gender transitioning, raising a child with a genetic disease, anorexia and other eating disorders, coping with a sudden life-changing disability, living with a life-shortening genetic disease and so on, but I hope I can gather true stories regarding these for a later book. (I would also love to write a male version of Implosion, so if any men want to come forward with true stories of their life disasters, please do get in touch with me).

Furthermore I also took other incredibly insightful interviews, such as a mother of children who had unrelated, but life-changing cancers; a lady who had a traumatic childbirth and settled into life as a single mum just before lockdown; a woman who had a long abusive boyfriend/girlfriend relationship in her twenties before finally making the break; a woman who went through losing her partner and IVF simultaneously; another woman who'd had a tumultuous time at Greenham Common; another brave lady who escaped horrendous domestic and sexual abuse in a long marriage and another woman whose husband had led a double life amassing a huge amount of debt on drugs and prostitutes... but these women ultimately felt unable to completely let go of their stories, albeit anonymously. Therefore, although I cannot share their traumatic experiences with you, I absolutely respect their honesty and feel humbled from personally hearing their stories.

THE POWER OF FAITH AND SPIRITUALITY

For all those of you who think we live in a secular society, we're actually far more spiritually-conscious and embedded in faith and belief systems than we think. This is regardless of whether it amounts to being fascinated by the tarot, Paganism, Eastern philosophies, traditional Christianity and so on. Religion is still pretty massive in people's lives. Having a foundation of belief can provide much comfort and hope at difficult times, not to mention a useful structure to daily life.

There are many positives to having a belief and these are exemplified by those who minister with love and thoughtfulness within each faith. These people can really sustain traumatised women such as the empathetic and considerate vicars in both Izzy and Nel's stories, along with the compassionate priest who reached out to Lady Unchained. However, as we all know, religion can also be such a negative too at times, paralysing people with fear, shame and guilt, such as inciting some to feel (somewhat incredulously in this day and age): 'if I do [such and such], God will punish me'. However, those who believe in prayer, often feel that God/ some other divine being or force, gives them the strength to cope with difficult situations when they let go of their anxieties through prayer. Overall the aspect of faith and spirituality in people's lives can also be reduced to a question of respect: respect all those with a belief and respect all those who choose to live life without one too.

PERSPECTIVE

We have to remember that all of these stories are told from one perspective and as we all know, the human experience is one of interpretation and subjective individual frames of reference, both of which are fluid and dependent on so many variables.

HUMANITY

Taking the interviews for this book has reminded me of the enormity of the many different facets of our natures, thus the ability of people to cause great harm and hurt to others but then also to be incredibly kind and loving too. The spectrum of behaviour is apparent in the following chapters and as readers we can identify when people get their actions both right and catastrophically wrong! One thing I would say is to please try to be kind. Don't exacerbate people's sufferings!

I've heard of so many examples of people making a truly nightmarish situation a lot worse, for instance, when Lady Unchained suffered horrible racism and threats of deportation in prison, or when Fern's 'friends' snubbed her and started bitchy rumours or when Fern was publicly humiliated by being marched out of her school mid-lesson when she could have been privately summoned to the head's office. These examples are truly medieval. This is no way to treat people in this day and age. Where is the dignity? People are still human beings and deserve to be treated with respect, no matter what.

Just remember when you are aiding an ostracism process or gossiping about someone who is already down or you are marching someone out of their job, you might find yourself at the end of similar brutal treatment one day. Instead, always think: what can I do to lighten their load? All of the women in this book have truly responded favourably to those who have reached out empathetically to them at a time of need and I guarantee that those kind gestures won't ever be forgotten.

As for friends, realise that over time, you will finely hone your friendships and trust the selective process: if circumstances and your own judgement force you to narrow down your friendships, that is okay! Let them go. Don't waste your precious time on people who will never fully 'have your back.' Be strong and walk away. You simply do not need these energy-suckers in your life.

CALLING TIME RE: SHARING

Two of the book participants: Jess and Lizzie reached a point in their stories where their experiences were just too painful for them to continue to talk about and that's fine. I am just so grateful that they were able to share what they could and it was absolutely right for them to end the interviews when they did.

INCREDIBLE MEN BUT ALSO MEN AND THEIR MENTAL HEALTH

In the book chapters, there are some guys featured who let their gender down by their shocking behaviour, but I also want to add that there are some truly brilliant men included too in these stories! One finding throughout the interviews though has been the fact that so many men (particularly of middle age and upwards), attach an old-school-style stigma to counselling and mental health issues, refusing to seek help when they're suffering from stress. Many seem to believe that they have to keep up the stoical stiff upper lip, but this is wrong in this context because often such repressed angst, aggression, gloom, pressure and frustration, gets taken out on their partners/families in various ways. Tragically on occasion, it also leads to suicide.

As a man, you need to know that it is your responsibility to look after your mental well-being and you should prioritise this. It is not your partner/kids/parents' responsibility to prop up your mind! Lose your pride and take the initiative yourself to support your mental health. Because women will not put up with abusive/depressive behaviour forever. We all have a breaking point. As one wise divorcee said to me: "you cannot help a grown man who won't help himself". Wives of men who were abusive at home but charming at work and to others, such as in-laws, articulated how much of a nightmare such situations are, because when these women confided in others about their husband's/partner's behaviour, no one wanted to believe them. Sometimes in such cases though, you just have to hold onto the truth of the situation and recognise it for what it is even if you cannot evidence it to others because that side of a person never manifests itself to them. Just know what you know and don't worry about anyone else's opinion.

I want to add though that also in this book are some accounts of the most incredible guys such as Izzy and Jess' husbands! Whilst writing Implosion, I've heard of some amazing men who have been complete champions of women in all kinds of situations, so I don't want anyone to think that this book is anti-men as it certainly isn't but of course, some of the true stories feature male behaviour that is sadly lacking.

THE BENEFITS OF PROFESSIONAL COUNSELLING

Continuing with my last point but this time addressed to all genders: own *your* responsibility to get help for stress and to work with your own trauma. It's actually selfish not to do this and to try to rely on friends/family instead to prop you up. If you don't ask/say, people assume you're coping and that you're okay. So if you are struggling with anything in your life, make an appointment to see your GP and also get counselling: it's what smart people do. In fact, it's the cool thing to do. Sometimes you may find the first counsellor or even the second one you see, is not the right one for you, but persevere until you find a counsellor experienced and empathetic enough to meet your needs! It's absolutely fine to say if your counsellor is not a good fit and to seek out another.

Also if it's okay for Tom Blomfield, Alastair Campbell, Antonio Horta-Osorio, Bryony Gordon, Ruby Wax, Gail Porter and others, to talk openly about the overwhelming life pressures they've experienced, then it's certainly okay for anyone else to follow suit!

THE POWER OF INTUITION

From all the interviews I conducted, I learnt that we must always, always trust our intuition. I would argue that it's 100% accurate. Literally in every situation covered in the book and also from interviews that I was unable to include, it turned out that an instinctive feeling, thought or gut reaction in a particular situation, whether it was regarding a health niggle/work issue/friends/love/betrayal etc, always turned out to be true. Often we override this because we can't or don't want to believe what our inner voice is saying. However, we ignore our intuition at our peril because it's there to guide and protect us.

I would add as a rider too that in the book, there are women who have used Tarot cards as a way to reach more deeply into their intuition and those readings have often also turned out to be very accurate. I recommend reading Tarot expert, Alice Grist's writings to learn more about this. Whilst to many, the Tarot can seem intimidating and scary, in reality they are not like this at all. Even the 'death' card does not mean death in the sense of someone you love dying, but rather implies the death of something, such as a friendship or a job and so on.

Also on a slightly 'out there' angle, it seems that lots of women have been presented with the same or similar situations in their lives (i.e. similar difficult relationships or issues about boundaries) until they broke the negative patterns/ habits; thus lessons often keep repeating themselves in our lives, until we learn from them.

THE POWER OF EXERCISE

I cannot stress enough just how much of a sanity-saver exercise is. It is an immediate, fail-safe, guaranteeable way to feel a million times better about anything and this process literally kicks in, as soon as you start! Exercise is SO important! It helps you to feel and become physically/mentally strong. It enables you to find clarity of mind, structure and purpose, alongside building a healthy body. It is the most magnificent and transformative tool and comes in so many guises: wild swimming, mountaineering, hiking, gymming, running, dance, yoga, ballet, cycling, team sports, trapeze, etc,… just embrace it! When Lady Unchained (in Chapter 1) was sent to work in a prison's gym, it helped her mental and physical state immensely and she developed a happy addiction to her gym routine, alongside gaining much needed confidence and a toned/strong body!

BODIES

I could write a whole separate book about body image and our relationship to our bodies (I think I will actually write this!) but what I just want to say here is: please, please enjoy your body. Be proud of it. Look after it and get pleasure from it. You never know when it might break down. It is the most wonderful piece of kit you have. It's beautiful – all bodies are. Don't be ashamed of it but rather invest in its care; show it off; value your body. It is actually awe-inspiring and sadly we often only realise this, when something goes wrong with it and it's too late to fully appreciate it. If you dislike your body for any reason, then do something about it if you can but also just be aware that your body is amazing!

MONEY

There is also so much I want to write about the impact of the lack of money in a person's life (conversely the opposite scenario causes its own issues too and I'd love to explore both angles in a future book), but for me Fern's chapter where she talks about what happens when your finances are scarily tenuous all the time and you have to resort to using pawn shops, cash and gold converter shops, early payday loan companies etc, is really powerful! Everyone needs to be aware of how viscerally-stressful, isolating, shaming and time-consuming it is, when you are on the breadline and nobody helps you.

DON'T WASTE TIME IN AN UNHAPPY MARRIAGE/
RELATIONSHIP

When I started taking interviews for this book and telling random strangers about this project, so many women opened up to me and told me how unhappy they are in long marriages and relationships but they feel so trapped by responsibility, finance, pets, children, history, familial expectations, faith, lack of money, social circles, etc. They just don't know how to leave (see Rosie's story). A long-term-unhappy 'LTU' marriage (or an equivalent relationship) really brings you down: some of the effects of an LTU are that you feel depressed, tired, unmotivated, you put on weight, you have nothing to say to each other any more, your confidence erodes, you find each other boring, you don't want to have sex with each other, you find excuses to be anywhere else rather than with each other, you just irritate each other, you want to leave but feel trapped, you feel life is passing you by, you look for affection elsewhere or even simply to be noticed by other people, you stop caring, you don't have fun as a couple any more, you simply exist, your life together drifts, you dread going home, you argue all the time, you don't find each other attractive, you actively dislike each other, you have nothing in common any more and so on. It's a pitiful way to live.

What I would say is when you have tried everything and you know your relationship just isn't going to change and it's making you bitterly unhappy, then don't waste any more time in it until you completely lose yourself and end up really hating each other or just being constantly miserable and/or snappy with each other. Remember listen to your intuition and accept when your marriage is over! Leave before you waste further precious time because otherwise you'll regret it. Find a way to make the break and be brave enough to follow through. There are many examples in this book to help you.

The basic rule should just be that if anyone repeatedly makes you feel bad about yourself (whether that's a friend, boyfriend, girlfriend, husband, wife etc), by not bothering with you, by deliberately trying to make you feel insecure, by putting you down, by playing mind games and so on, then ditch them; let them go. You definitely won't die without them and gradually you'll be so much happier!

FAMILY DYSFUNCTION

What kind of things are normal in families? Well deep family rifts are extremely common (sometimes these are still maintained even on death's door!) and short-term temporary rifts and children that drift between divorced spouses and quite often don't talk to one or other of the parents; also eating disorders, self harm, affairs, abuse of one kind or another, financial disorder, unhappiness, living separate lives and so on… these are all very common issues along with many others! Basically it all goes on behind closed doors.

Sometimes control switches from parents to grown-up children; then from adult to adult (as in partner/spouse to the other partner/spouse) and again control can come from teenagers/adult children to parents – i.e, your children in their teens and beyond, can demonstrate their disapproval at something you do as an adult by completely blanking you for days/weeks/months/years at a time, perhaps occasionally popping up when they need money but otherwise cutting you out of their lives. They can have very clear-cut ideas about what they perceive to be acceptable conduct for parents and be brutal in their rejection of parents who go against their views. From my book interviews and other conversations, I have learnt that this is actually a regular phenomenon. However, you must learn to live *your* life authentically for yourself. Your children – no matter how old – should not be allowed to control you. Otherwise scenarios happen where you find that you never ever live the life you need to live, because you're always worried about being at the receiving end of a family member's judgement and then their punishment. I heard true stories of women in their seventies being afraid of the opinions of their fortysomething children.

Be your true self and give your children time to adapt to how you actually are and if they don't accept you, they don't accept you - but you cannot try to mould yourself for the whole of your life to suit the whimsical and individualist expectations of everyone, including your kids. Be brave. Do your thing.

It has to be said that sometimes when a woman/mother leaves the family home, that her children do not always follow her as she expects, even if the children have been deeply unhappy with their parents' relationship. This can be for many factors – such as the children wanting to stay in the family home, rather than in a rental property (as is often the case for the parent who moves out). Also often the parent left behind, then ups the ante in being a super-parent to the child[ren], so the latter feel a duty to stay and provide company for that parent. There may also be family pets to look after, which the departing parent has not been able to take with them, etc… These are just a few of the reasons, but this still does not mean that if you are desperately unhappy in a relationship, that you should stick it out for the sake of your children because that's not setting a good example either. If you move out of the family home and your children are reticent to split their time between two homes, or they constantly chop/ change the times they're meant to be with you (and they're too old to be 'made' to be with you), then all you can do is keep trying as much as you possibly can to keep your relationship with them as strong as it can be. Just do the best you can. Accept that families aren't perfect and there are many ways to have relationships with your children and show your love, even if you're not with them full-time.

Most families have varieties of dark secrets and dysfunction. Basically I have learnt that pretty much every family has something dire that occurs within it or to it, at some point, it's often just hidden away. Thus we tend to think that other families have the perfect set-up when actually that's so far from the truth!

Suicide

Suicide is viewed with such nuanced complexity by those affected and this comes out in the book interviews. From a historic perspective, suicides in centuries' past, were viewed as acts of murder against God, thus deep shame was projected onto the families of those who committed suicide and so many medieval and early modern families covered up suicides. As a Social Historian, I believe that such long-standing, traditional and completely misguided notions have filtered down somewhat today, so that for some, they still feel a hint of shame regarding a family suicide. I assert that this is why responses and reactions to suicides are so mixed and complex. Whilst some who have had a suicide in their immediate family, view the perpetrator's actions as deeply selfish, others feel very hurt if the word 'selfish' is mentioned in the same sentence. There is absolutely not 'one size fits all' when it comes to responses to suicide, so be particularly considerate when you reach out to anyone who is coping with the aftermath of such a death. Tread delicately but definitely reach out to offer any support you can; do not shrink away for fear of saying the wrong thing, because that's even worse.

A snail and its carapace

We need to remember that we come into this world as an individual and although we often become part of a family/couple and become embroiled in various relationships throughout our lives, often becoming girlfriends, wives, mothers, employees, etc, … we are nonetheless still individuals: autonomous, independent beings. We do not have to morph into our partners/children: we are still unique people in our own right.

Everything we need is inside of us. All the metaphorical tools required to cope with any situation are within us all. Ultimately if push comes to shove, we do not need anyone else: we can manage by ourselves. So know that! If you experience rejection from anyone and you feel alone, just be aware that this difficult time will pass but in the meantime, you can and will cope and survive! If needs be, you CAN get by on your own. You don't need anyone else ultimately. Don't project everything onto one other person or expect someone to rescue you. Be your own beacon. Your own steel core. Just like a snail with its carapace, you too have your own carapace around you. Let it protect you always.

This is important when it comes to the following: within the book are examples of Court Hearings, Inquests, mentions of Tribunals and formal processes that are stressful. If you are facing such official procedures and undergoing associated traumas, then when you need to, withdraw into your shell, become that hermit, but equally do not let life pass you by!

Whatever you are facing, this does not define you! If you are able to, view your upcoming D-Day as though you are climbing a huge mountain like K2 perhaps? Rather than get overwhelmed by the bigger picture, take one step at a time, baby steps: don't look at the top, rather just look at the immediate future, do not fear what is far in the distance because your fears may not be justified.

Have the quiet confidence that you will get through all of this and be stronger and more erudite from the process. We learn and grow from every experience in our lives. Rather than panic, instead grab the support that you need along the way and plan things to keep you happy and to prop yourself up! Continue to invest in yourself. Whatever intimidating process is impending, this does not mean that you should give up taking care of yourself and living the best life you can, as much as possible.

Furthermore, lots of people simultaneously to you, are living with all kinds of trauma for long periods of time, sometimes years. This could be the trauma of coping with cancer and various ongoing treatments; it could be dealing with a sudden bereavement; it could be dealing with an upcoming divorce or court case etc. Many of us spend a chunk of our lives trying to live them whilst also dealing with a traumatic situation – so if this is you – please just know that you are not alone!

So many women are simultaneously facing tough times in the future yet also trying to distract themselves and enjoy life too. I believe this is absolutely the right approach to take! Fight for the right to find happiness, even when stress surrounds you! Try not to be swallowed up by whatever trauma you are living with. Trauma is not the sum total of your worth! For some of the participants in this book, their emotional trauma manifested itself in physical symptoms in their bodies, such as Melissa Todd's painful rash after Adam's death and Charlotte's aches and vomiting, so sometimes physical reactions to stress can invoke even more discomfort, compounding trauma upon trauma, but once again, as far as is possible, find whatever it is that makes you happy or brings a bit of comfort into your life, and go for that!

Happiness

Finally, I truly believe that happiness is a choice! You can choose to be happy! There will always be something to moan about but equally there will always be a reason to smile. Try not to squander your time on this planet because you never know when your time's up! Just aim to be happy! If you're struggling with issues from the past/present that are blocking your happiness, don't wallow. Rather, do something proactive about this. Fight for your happiness! Without sounding too much of a hippy or a 'wetwipe', when you give off and radiate joy, others literally want to hang out with you because they want to absorb some of your infectious positive energy!

...Next ... it's the SEX (AND RELATIONSHIPS) section:

Sex and relationships (warning: graphic content)

It turns out that sex is a massive problem in the UK and especially the lack of it in long-term relationships. Sexual issues featured a lot in the research I undertook. Everyone wants to talk about sex secretly; to know if their sex life and desires are normal or not. Part of this, aside from the fact that sex is just an incredible part of life and obviously produces the next gen (to sum sex up in a very scant and flippant manner), is because everyone wants to feel attractive to themselves and attractive to others at all ages (women in their seventies told me they still want to be found sexy/attractive!)

Feeling attractive is hugely important when it comes to our self worth and also it makes an impact upon others' reactions to us. Furthermore whether we like it or not, our success in the world is impacted by our appearance. This is not a superficial statement. As an academic, I am merely telling it like it is. History demonstrates that those who have been perceived to be attractive throughout time, have been able to use their positive looks to their advantage and as a powerful tool. I attended an Italian Renaissance conference in Florence in November 2021 for my History PhD regarding early modern health and attitudes towards the body and I learnt in a talk about how adult men and women of all ages back at that time fretted about sagging skin and the 'disease of ugliness', thus it is not surprising that yet still today, how we look and the attention we receive according to our appearance, has a huge affect on how attractive and confident we feel.

Women of all ages want others to want to have sex with them; they want to be thought of as sexy; hence why a lot of women (across the class spectrum: including those in elite professions) were talking about wanting to have a 'hot girl summer' – namely, wanting to lose weight, tone up, get tanned and have a glow-up, all in time for the summer in order to manifest their sexual power, receive attention and thus feel validated and fully out-there in this aspect of their lives. No women should feel embarrassed about wanting to undergo this process and enjoy the results!

***

Some of the many frank comments about sex, family life and relationships that came out in discussions included the following:

"I remember one of my brothers trying to tell me about his coke-fuelled threesome escapades whilst I was changing nappies and our lives seemed so different and I thought he'd think I was boring whilst he was having lots of fun."

"After that relationship ended, eventually to get over him - because the loss of him was so massive - I just needed to go through a 'ho-phase'. It was absolutely what I had to do. Just perfunctory sex without any emotion."

"When you feel ambivalent about someone, you're cured. You don't need to hate them to be free of them, you just need to not care and then you know you've moved on."

"The amount of boring dates I went on through the apps, just to try to get over him and a lot of my settled friends actually became quite judgemental and jealous."

"My parents weren't really aware of what I was up to [seeing a married man] and tried to be there for me but they didn't understand because they're just of a different generation where women need rescuing via marriage. I had lots of elderly people tell me I needed a rich older man to look after me! Absolutely not!"

"It was so frustrating because I got completely groomed in anticipation and then he didn't even bother to turn up or send a message. It's so disrespectful when this happens."

"Sex can be so loaded with issues sometimes. Basically I feel that whatever problems you have in your relationship – they get carried over into your sex life or lack of it. For example, generally if there's resentment or disdain for each other, these feelings have such a negative impact on how you respond to one another physically."

"I constantly sneak to the loo at work, so that I can sext him and send upskirt/topless pics."

"When I went to my first sex party, I had no idea how to approach anyone I was interested in, so I asked other women for their advice. The two women I asked, who were probably in their twenties, said that they always said either: "Would you mind if I kissed you?" OR: "I'd like to kiss you", and when they uttered those words, they were never turned down and those kisses led to other intimate experiences. At the next sex party I went to, I bonded with a woman for the first time and told her that I'd like to kiss her and everything happened from there… it was a really intriguing experience. My first time properly kissing and getting intimate with a woman."

"It's a mistake to think that if you're fully absorbed in your children, that your husband will understand if you don't want sex on an ongoing basis, because your husband will know how tired you are and how involved you are with your mutual children; in my experience, husbands might put up with this for a time but underneath, they get fed up and resentful that you're not into sex any more with them and if someone else shows them attention (as happened in my situation), and if that person gets inside their head, then your relationship is doomed. You have to keep making the effort."

"If you get pregnant and decide to keep the baby, try not to be devastated if the father doesn't fall for you and won't commit to you, because if they're not fully invested, then having a baby often pushes them in the other direction, so whilst you hope the guy will stick around, that's a massive gamble. You have to be fully prepared to do it on your own."

***

Many women wanted to express how they felt at living in sexually-frustrated marriages/relationships. To set the scene: I'm going to include a quote that one anonymous woman who I'll name Zoe, wanted to share:

"I had a whirlwind romance, got engaged, married, had twins quickly, then another baby and then I realised, well actually I'd known for a while but I'd tried to ignore, that 7/8 of my sexual desires and fantasies were never, ever going to be met/explored because my husband just wasn't interested and he had his own hang-ups. He thought it was grim and silly if I suggested stuff (dressing up/role plays/sexting and/or sending nudes/using sex toys and porn/trying loads of new positions/spanking/light bondage). He would just get embarrassed or shut down those conversations immediately in a terse tone and he wasn't prepared to compromise. I was so frustrated. Was this it?! 40+ years potentially of marriage with sex 1-2 times per month (occasionally a few more), of 3 positions max (doggy/missionary/me on top) and oral; week after week… take your pick out of that selection! Towards the end, I just went along with whatever was quickest and involved the least intimacy, i.e, not being able to see him. [As part of the book research, it became clear from many women's expressions, that when their relationships were dysfunctional, they preferred to have sex without seeing their partner/ husband so they always tended to have sex with their backs to them because they didn't want to see their faces].

I focused on the kids, work, career plans, socialising, anything not to think about this unexplored part of my psyche. Time passed. I made do. And then one day, I just blurted out that I thought we should try an 'open marriage', so that rather than be unfaithful, I could explore my sexuality and be fulfilled without keeping any dark secrets from him. However, he was appalled. So I didn't change or do anything. I was left in limbo: wondering, missing out, fearing getting to 70, and never having explored this side of my life in the way I needed to. For a while, I became a total frump because I felt what was the point in trying? I wasn't perceived as a sexual/desirable being. After he went to sleep some nights, I'd 'do me' lying with my back to him, stifling any sounds, trying not to let my body shudder in case it woke him up, as he wouldn't appreciate it. One night, I woke up to familiar sounds: he was wanking lying next to me in bed whilst he assumed that I was asleep and it unnerved me because I thought: 'why won't you do that with me? Wake me up and fuck me… this is what I actually want – but I just knew that it wasn't going to happen.'

So I continued to stay put and I made do. However I happened to read some uncensored articles written by brave women who had decided to make huge changes in their lives to live authentically and these true stories stayed in my head and got me thinking. One day when our children hit adulthood and after feeling their censorship over the years too, I decided to let go and explore what was out there because I had read an interview with women of differing ages who all talked about their sex lives and one woman's story stuck with me: she was in her 80s and had only ever slept with one man and she said she 'regretted it' because she felt it probably wasn't very fulfilling but she'd had nothing to compare it with and she had missed out on a sexual journey she should have let herself have. Of course she still could embark on a sexual adventure in her 80s but she didn't feel she had the confidence to try. Her experience stayed with me. I didn't want to be like that woman. I wanted to have fun and build my sexual repertoire! It was the best decision I ever made. When our marriage ended, I was able to go off on and discover a whole new sexual side to myself and that adventure's continuing now. I love it and I'm proud of myself for embarking upon this."

That particular participant was able eventually to recreate a new, thrilling sexual life for herself after suffering a 'desert' for years, so if this is something you also need to do, you can! I'll add some details about this later.

Lots of women are very unhappy with their sex lives and it isn't because their partners demand it too much. Generally it is the opposite: Either sex is often non-existent; infrequent; dull and boring with the same old, same old; a zero-effort routine last thing at night occasionally. Women often feel unable to act out role-plays or discuss fantasies because partners makes it clear they feel uncomfortable hearing these or they simply have no interest/can't be bothered. Some of the latter isn't helped by both parties using their phones in bed, so couple interaction just doesn't happen.

Lots of women expressed that they no longer find their partners attractive; Some couples have fallen into the habit of sleeping in separate beds in separate rooms – especially after children arrive – and the emotional distance between them has grown; Some find their partner has poor personal hygiene; Some have lost their sex drive; Some men suffer with impotence and won't see their doctor or they take erectile dysfunction drugs to have erections but these are taken 'on the sly' and then this secrecy creates anxiety for their partners because these women wonder if their partners still find them desirable?

Many men seemingly make the assumption that their partners are okay with a lack of sex because of outdated 'frigid women' stereotypical fallacies, but actually from the book interviews, it became very apparent that many women are actually pretty thirsty for it and have raw sexual desire which is being squandered, causing distress and frustration. Therefore all it takes is for someone else to come along and light that spark for these women! (This is obviously what happens in some of the book chapters!) Conversely, some sexual desire is automatically curbed because a partner's behaviour causes their spouse to feel turned-off towards them in an intimate capacity.

Whilst many women will put up with a lacklustre sexual status-quo for a period of time, all it takes is for someone with the right chemistry to come along and make us feel desirable again to jeopardise our relationships. Here are extracts from two real women's experiences of such a scenario (these women don't have a chapter in the book but they wanted to share their true tales anonymously in this introduction):

Amber:
"I gave this work colleague a lift and the next thing I knew, his hands were running up my legs as I was driving. The spark between us in the office had been so intense and in the car, it just built. We ended up parked in a deserted lane fucking against the side of my car in the moonlight. It took me ages to get my breath back and I just thought of all the years that I had been missing that and that now I had experienced all of this again, I wasn't going to let it go. I didn't feel guilty about my partner in that moment because he simply wasn't interested in me and hadn't been, for years."

Ruth:
"Geraint was my orchestra conductor. I would leave my disinterested husband at home when it was evening practice, and I'd be wearing frumpy clothes when I left and said goodbye to the children, but then en route, I'd pull into a remote lay-by and I'd strip down to my bra and knickers and then

get changed into an outfit which made me look good; I'd blitz my nails, do my hair, spray perfume, chew mint gum… as much grooming as I could possibly manage in a 10 min car pull-over… but Geraint did begin to notice me and we started talking more and messaging and things developed… We only had an emotional affair before his wife found out (she was also in the same orchestra), but it kick-started my sexual identity; it was so amazing to feel wanted and desired again… "

However, this issue is definitely not one-sided: As part of the contextualising process of my book research, one man told me how he hadn't slept with his wife for 25+ years! They're both successful, healthy, attractive, in professional careers, have a good lifestyle, grown-up children and are financially comfortable. The dwindling and then eventual full-stop of their sex life was never discussed: he wanted it and was having affairs whilst she didn't ask any questions. He thought she probably sussed that he was being unfaithful but she didn't push for answers.

Two other anon women (not featured in the book chapters), smiled as they told tales to me of how one of their husbands had crawled into the dog basket at their home, saying that the dog got more love from her than he did; whilst another woman proudly boasted that she wasn't interested in: "any of that stuff any more" because that side of her life was over now, as she was: "just a mummy". However, not acknowledging the importance of sex and being complacent/dismissive about it, is dangerous territory in a relationship.

Many women told me of erection and libido difficulties their partners/husbands/ boyfriends/dates were experiencing. Younger men too, featured in terms of losing their libido and/or not being able to get - or maintain - an erection. One common problem is men losing their interest in sex and not making any initiatives towards sex but additionally, not discussing it also, thus sex becomes the 'elephant in the room', therefore instigating so many insecurities!

For lots of guys, regular porn use had led them to psychologically associate any sexual encounter with porn, thus many found that when presented with a real female body, they were unable to get an erection or they went soft half way through sex, because they needed either the porn simultaneously or they needed to ditch the real female body altogether and just be able to climax whilst viewing the porn. Obviously the impact on women's self esteem when faced with this scenario, is huge and completely humiliating as women are being cast aside in favour of digital images. This is absolutely not to say that porn isn't a totally enjoyable feature in lots of couples' sex lives, but porn-use is just like anything else that can become addictive: it just needs to be kept in balance.

Also some men have the idea that to make women come, all they need to do is basically just jump on them like an animal and bang away as quickly as poss (the same speedy style is often adopted whilst giving women oral sex too), but whilst a lot of women expressed how much they like a fast, furious fuck, they also want and require some finesse. Quite often women need some time spent on them sexually in order for them to fully relax, let go and be able to reach orgasm but if men just thrust away in a massive rush with zero technique, women are left seriously dissatisfied and sometimes having to fake it!

For a lot of couples, it's difficult for both parties to articulate their feelings and discuss their sexual needs and desires, even when they are both thinking about these. However, for whatever reason, they don't feel they can verbalise them. Thus unspoken dissatisfaction about sex is the silent assassin in a relationship as after all, very few couples want a platonic, non-sexual relationship, so if sex breaks down and stops for a long period of time in a relationship, this often leads to infidelity, as is proven in the book. Both parties in a relationship must be completely aware that by allowing sex to disappear, they are totally making their relationship vulnerable to an interloper.

Many women mentioned that when they tried to talk to their husbands about the latter's lack of desire or erectile dysfunction, these men became defensive and projected it back onto them, they wouldn't contemplate the suggestion of going to see their doctor or a pharmacist and clearly expected their wives to simply accept zero sex. For Fay, in the book, this situation has lasted for over well over a decade and counting. Lots of women discussed how they went into asexual mode for years in their sexless long-term relationships and accepted that this was how their lives were going to be, until someone 'woke them up' to intimacy again.

Withholding sex is sometimes used as a punishment too: One woman's husband wouldn't sleep with her for nearly a year because he was resentful with her for an autonomous decision she had made. At this point in their lives, she was 31 and he was 45. She had absolutely no idea why he was no longer interested in her and began to internalise the situation. Was it her? Was she no longer desirable? She started to doubt her body and lose her confidence? Was he having an affair? Was this going to go on permanently? It was a total headfuck of a situation and began to send her slightly mad until she ended up verbally exploding to him one day and simply demanding: "what's going on?!" and then he said he was still annoyed at the decision she had made all those months ago.

As a country, the UK is so buttoned-up about sex. It's something that when teens discover, is talked about pretty openly and graphically. However, as we get older, in the UK, most people seem to shut down these conversations. Often this is because by this point in life, people are in settled relationships and if their sexual needs aren't being met within those relationships, they don't feel they can talk about this to close friends, because it's a betrayal of their partner and especially so, if their close friends are friends with their partner too.

Also there can be emotional pain involved too, perhaps in thinking that you've been missing out for years on aspects of sexuality that others take for granted, say orgasming, for example. This point is currently being referenced in the 'Leo Grande' film starring Emma Thompson as an older woman who's never experienced an orgasm and so she employs professional help to enable her to climax. From my interviews and also from research published in The Times recently, it's apparent how many women have never experienced orgasm yet after years of sexual activity and also how there are still huge associations of shame and poor body image attached to women in the context of sex.

Many women are afraid to masturbate and explore their bodies by themselves because they've been conditioned to believe that it's wrong and shameful to do this. Hence why Yvette Amos's lockdown interview to BBC Wales went viral because she had a dildo in the background on her bookshelf. One newspaper even contacted Yvette's mother to get her opinion on her daughter's use of sex toys as though it's so shocking that a grown woman would consider her self pleasure?! This demonstrates the immature and repressed British attitude to sex and even more so when it comes to women and sex/masturbation. After all, when boys are little, parents will often giggle about their sons: "playing with their willies" as it's just what boys do, but when girls/women explore themselves (as the Yvette Amos example demonstrates), it's somehow still considered a bit wrong/shameful/dirty in mainstream UK society. Embarrassment and guilt are often foisted upon girls and women for getting to know their bodies intimately but if women don't know every part of their bodies fully and identify which parts give them pleasure, how can they guide their partners to fulfil them and also how can they themselves enjoy them as individuals, as and when they choose to do so.

As part of my historical PhD research, I've read endless accounts of women being sexually shamed in the past often due to religious conditioning and cultural expectations and this continues today in a manner which is not applied to men. It is revealing that two of the women in this book talk of their inner conflict between the demands of their faith and the desires of their minds/bodies. In one chapter, this conflict arises from going to church and then going clubbing on the same day; whilst in the other chapter, the conflict is over a young religious woman who has fallen for her married boss. Women often feel deeply torn between their wish to live fully autonomous lives and their moral/religious selves and others' expectations of them. However, women must be able to subvert the latter and enjoy their bodies and feel sexually fulfilled throughout their whole lives and by themselves too, whenever they want, without any feelings of mortification.

During lockdown, Melissa Todd, who features in this book, discussed how as a dominatrix, she started receiving more enquiries from female clients and my book research made me aware that many (formerly traditional heterosexual) women are becoming much more open-minded to any kind of sexual relationship. Lots of women told me, how post-Covid, they had: "properly kissed" a woman for the first time and/or slept with a woman, unbeknownst to their male partners/husbands, because they felt they had to know what it was like… and they didn't regret it.

In this regard, for sexually frustrated women of all ages, it's important to realise that there is help out there: you can get yourself into this zone by reading erotic literature such as 'The Bride Stripped Bare' by Nikki Gemmell, 'Submission' by Marthe Blau and 'Adele' by Leïla Slimani and be inspired by the sexual adventures of other real-life trailblazing women such as Monique Roffey who charted her own journey in her memoir, 'With the Kisses of His Mouth'. There are lots of online sex forums purely for females to help women navigate their sexual identities and some of these organise intimacy courses and in-person, social events and workshops. Erotic boutiques such as Coco de Mer and others, are there to help women, along with porn made by women for women… Basically, once you start looking to broaden your sexual knowledge as a woman, there is a huge genre for exactly that purpose; you just have to develop the confidence to seek it out!

To all those women who aren't getting any sex at all, as a quick fix, buy yourself a vibrator online and/or other sex toys and re-equate yourself with pleasure and your body. Don't give up and don't feel any shame or embarrassment doing this.

You do not have to live in an intimate-free zone and become asexual for the rest of your days. Take action!

However, there's also so much to talk about too regarding the reality of sex: the stuff that's not shown in the films or written about in books, i.e, you know how it goes: in movies, two people have epic foreplay, then frantic, passionate sex, both come at the same time with all the appropriate noises, spoon afterwards and then fall asleep. BUT real-life sex often has some impish moments that can add embarrassment, anxiety and/or uncertainty into the mix if we're not able to talk about them and feel at ease with all of it. Thus the following are so normal even if they're not discussed: squelchy sex noises (this especially causes some women to worry that they've stretched too much internally after childbirth); not knowing if your partner has come or not and whether they're reliant on any pills; 'fanny farts' caused by pumping air into the vagina via thrusting; the feeling of disappointment but trying not to show it when your partner says: "I don't think I'm going to come… " etc… but this is all normal. It's real sex. We just need to talk about it. Be transparent. Honest. To stop stressing about it all.

Often women stop talking about what they actually want and the variety of sex out there or it's mentioned in hushed tones: blow jobs, anal, bondage, dressing-up, the desire for CNC, masturbation… there is so much embarrassment, fear of judgement, shame, guilt and secrecy attached to sex. There's still nervousness even about the basics of sex: one lady in her sixties (not in the book) complained to me about vaginal dryness. She didn't know about lubricants and she didn't feel she could talk to anyone about it. Another woman (also not featured in the book) told me that she needed to go for sexual counselling to relax enough to have sex again after 2 years of not being able to be penetrated by her husband following an operation on her cervix, because mentally and physically she shut down.

Also it became apparent that issues arise over contraception with some partners having expectations that women will deal with this; sometimes equally women expect men to 'get the snip' but both genders need to negotiate this and discuss it, so contraception doesn't feel a one-sided, onerous responsibility. In extreme cases, a lack of planning/conversations related to contraception, led to different scenarios: namely zero sex or unexpected babies. Both of these outcomes massively impacted on the relationships at the centre and of course, children born as a result.

Separate bedrooms came up quite a lot in many discussions regarding sex and intimacy. It seems many of you crave having a decent night's sleep, without any snoring, and having a space all of your own – not just the bed, but the room around it too – just like elite women in past times, who used to have boudoirs. I completely understand that need for a private sanctuary. Quite a few women I talked to, who have got used to sleeping in separate rooms from their partners (often prompted by the arrival of children and resultant sleeping problems), said that they rarely had sex and had got to a point where it was no longer important to them. The phrase: "I wouldn't miss it if I never had it again" was repeated to me time and time again but these women either ended up, having affairs or being tempted by someone who came along and unlocked their sexuality once again. I'm definitely not saying that separate bedrooms always result in infidelity because there are very positive benefits too (some privacy, undisturbed sleep, being able to do what you want in bed such as reading a novel into the early hours etc), but if you go down this route and you want to keep your current relationship alive, unless you're both happily celibate, you need to make double the effort to keep your sex life going with your partner because without the convenience of being next to each other in the same bed, it's far easier for sex to become neglected and for one or both partners to stray.

A psychological severing regarding sex was also a common result amongst many women who had undergone a traumatic childbirth experience but again, these are all issues that can be resolved. It just takes a visit to your GP, a pharmacist or a psycho-sexual counsellor and overcoming your own embarrassment, because if you don't do this, your relationship may not survive and also you will lose something which is likely to be important in your life and that of your partner.

My interview with Melissa Todd highlights that so much of people's sexuality takes place privately via porn, affairs, sexting, paying for kinky stuff and so on, because people don't prioritise sex and they don't feel they can be more open about it, and that's often with their partners. However, simultaneously many people don't want that side of their lives to be shut down forever, so it's a maelstrom of contradiction; our sexual desires and our sexual lives either go on-pause or go underground, hence the high proportion of attached men/women on hook-up sites looking for a quick fix, for example. Once you embrace that world, dick-pics and sexting are just everyday. After I got divorced, I was deluged by dick pics and it was a whole new learning curve (apt for some dicks!) The assorted dick pics even featured tea towels and pj bottoms sometimes! I realised from all of this, that guys felt extreme pride in showing off their manhood at any available opportunity!

From my book research I also learnt just how many men love receiving sexual vocab alongside explicit images of the female form and women in the process of masturbating. Guys often want to be the recipients of this from a distance to avoid getting emotionally attached. Thus they want to get sexual pleasure from messages and images alone rather than physically meeting up and having a committed relationship and apps facilitate this.

Attached men often also reach out online to express appreciation of a female body and to get a kick out of admiring them, but without wanting anything further. Women who work as Pole Instructors, Personal Trainers, Dance Teachers, Art Models etc, and who post regularly on social media, told me how they all get lots of married men contacting them to tell them how much they loved their uploaded images. These men weren't looking for any kind of relationship with these women, but they just wanted to let them know how much they enjoyed looking at female bodies (other than their wives' bodies) in a 'safe' way. I think I've realised even more how important women's bodies and looks are, to men. Many really need the visual stimulus. Whereas perhaps for many women, our attraction to men and women can be based upon a whole range of factors, such as personality, the ability to make us laugh, a beautiful voice and so on – all of which combined, makes someone really attractive, even if they are not conventionally buff and stunning – however most men really want a visual turn-on.

One of the current sex trends is breathwork/erotic asphyxiation/virtual-choking' to heighten pleasure/get turned on. When I first tried a dating app a while back, in a really early chat, one guy suggested to me that we had a go at choking and if you're unfamiliar with this scene, it's very much a thing out there and loads of women really enjoy it. However, it's always about what everyone is individually comfortable with and all women involved in this always need to make sure they feel safe with the person they're consenting to do this with. It's nuanced because as Danni's chapter (and her comments about 'red flags') shows, there are very fine lines to this kind of behaviour, because any form of choking can hark towards abuse/risk of death/can ring huge alarm bells, so if any type of asphyxiation is undertaken during sex, it must be with the full consent, knowledge and desire of both parties and it's a good idea to have agreed code words in place to know when to stop at any point.

There are aspects of sexuality that we keep hidden from our spouses because we worry they will think less of us because of our needs: i.e., Melissa's chapter discusses men who want to be dominated and lick women's boots (it's very much a thing) or guys who want to dress up as women (this is very common), but worry that their wives will feel disdain for them if they express this to them; there are also a number of women who want to be spanked, tied up, have rough sex – even 'CNC' (desire to be 'consensual, non-consensual'), but they can't say it, because their husbands would be too shocked or because they fear that it's such a tricky area to navigate right now in this time of #MeToo. However, part of the reason 'Fleabag' was so successful, along with 'Fifty Shades of Grey', when the latter first emerged, was because women delighted in an open dialogue around female sexuality and all of our different wants and needs, because in our society, we tend to just feel we can't talk about any of this, especially within older generations.

However, in a long-term relationship (potentially for the rest of our lives), these desires need to find a way to be voiced, even if they can't be fulfilled. If you are with a partner long-term who cannot fulfil your needs and you're unhappy about that and cannot resolve it, then you do have choices and that's fine! It is actually important and totally okay to say that your sexuality is a vital part of your life if that's how you feel. Also if your sexual needs aren't being met, that this factor alone can be enough for you to end your relationship. As a woman, you are entitled to prioritise your sexuality!

As part of my book research, I went to a few exclusive sex parties hosted by different providers in various cities in the UK and further afield, to talk to women who wanted to share their experiences. It's important for me to say that the parties didn't feel sleazy at all but that was also because the venues were beautifully decorated, the behaviour was monitored, the clientele was well-educated and women were very much made to feel safe. I am sure there are sex parties where things get seriously out of hand and women don't feel at ease, however at the ones I attended, I felt in control, intrigued and that I could leave at any time. I enjoyed the sexy atmosphere. The following is a verbal volley of what I learnt: I felt that guys could treat sex as a purely physical release (like scratching an itch) because some would be thrusting away doggy style whilst scanning the room almost to see if something better was out there (although a male friend of mine has said this may not be the case and it might be that this man was thinking that he was not pleasing the woman enough and so was looking for a third person to join them to gain or give greater pleasure). I saw heterosexual couples who were enjoying having sex with each other and others, but I also observed couples, where one person in the couple (and I saw this with both men and women), looked uneasy and insecure at sharing their partner with a newcomer.

There were lots of first-time women of varying ages and sizes at these parties: they were curious about sex and exploring this side of their lives. One of the most erotic visions was two women together, one lying on top of the other on a bed, both wearing beautiful lingerie. In fact, women of all sizes who displayed confidence in their bodies, looked incredibly sexy and I have to say the stereotypical turn-ons of stockings, basques, rhinestone thongs and bras, just enhanced their air of sensuality. It was also empowering to have men approaching women respectfully.

I saw some guys lose their erections and try to reignite them. Maybe for some, sex just loses its mystique when it's all there on a plate; the thrill is in the chase: the lead-up and the anticipation: There were ball gowns, hot tubs, whipping, crystal dog leads with men attached, caviar, floor shows, dancing, frisky nymphs queuing up to be spanked, anything and everything really. The women were incredibly friendly and would stroke your arm and I suddenly saw women in a different light. Often quite a few of them – who were first-timers - would just end up talking to each other as comrades in a situation where they felt out of their comfort zones or just because they wanted to befriend others and put them at their ease. We talked at length and because we were all strangers, women together, we could speak honestly, openly. Women told me how they were a bit bored of the whole dating apps scene, especially combined with covid lockdowns. Rather now they wanted to meet men/women/people in person. Comments regarding organising hook-ups online included "[it's] too perfunctory","like buying a commodity", "there's no mystique" and "guys spread themselves too thin on them". Most women said they much preferred meeting guys organically/in person and seeing if there was chemistry.

A lot of women who attended the parties between their twenties and fifties are really enjoying their independent single lives currently, throwing themselves into their careers, sport, fitness etc… quite a few either didn't have children as a conscious or unconscious choice and were enjoying having fun and living autonomously, sometimes after coming out of long-term relationships and especially post-covid. Many said that they didn't want anything serious right now but just to have fun and different experiences and see what is out there, post-lockdown. The thought of being committed to one person, was not necessarily at the top of each woman's agenda.

It was interesting to see how at the parties, there were often hierarchies in the sense of one man/woman being the one that everyone wanted. When I talked to the guy who was the 'golden boy' at one party, it was obvious that he was very at ease with his status as 'favourite' and it clearly gave him a confident edge and air over all the other men. Likewise with the women and I could see that just to have that public accolade at any age, that you are the most – or one of the most - physically and sexually attractive people out of any group, whether it's politically correct or not, gives the bearer such an advantage in so many different ways.

At these parties I also saw unicorns in action. I'd heard about unicorns before but I'd never met one. For those of you who don't know, a unicorn is someone who joins an established couple to provide a threesome. This can be as a one-off or as a regular arrangement. At one party, I spoke to a beautiful redhead in her twenties who worked in the city by day and then by night, was a unicorn. She had come out of a long heterosexual relationship and afterwards wanted to discover what was out there! Via a specific app, she found a suitable couple and initially met up with the woman in the couple a few times to get to know her and feel safe and then once she felt totally at ease with her, she was then introduced to the guy too and thus they formed a three. In time, the couple split and the unicorn started going out with the woman and hoped for a longer relationship, but it wasn't to be. At the party where I met her, we were talking and then there was a gap in time and the next thing I knew, she'd disappeared. When I next saw her, she was caressing a girl as part of a threesome in a playroom and the two women were heavily into each other and the guy looked a little anxious that his girlfriend was enjoying it a bit too much. Afterwards when I chatted to her, she said that she'd met the couple at the start of the party and they'd mooted the idea of trying this out together, so it wasn't completely spontaneous.

At these parties, I met civil servants, friendly transvestites, long-term married couples with young children, beautiful twentysomethings, a rich array of people… all of whom were very relaxed, warm, friendly and at ease with their sexuality and themselves in general. Single women talked of approaching couples at these parties and asking them: "Can I kiss you?" and they were always told: "Yes".

One of the more bizarre aspects was that nobody who was having sex made any noise… everyone did it silently… Many women admitted to faking it as and when they needed to, in their regular sex lives in general. They weren't citing this for any other reason than to be honest about what really happens. Sometimes they fake it, because sex has gone on for too long and they're not going to come and just want the encounter to stop but they didn't want their partners to feel that they hadn't enabled them to achieve what society presently considers the ultimate sexual goal: namely, climax. Many women that I talked to, felt they could only reach orgasm when they were completely relaxed and had feelings for the person involved. In fact bringing someone to, and achieving, climax can sometimes be far too much of a pressure on both and in the course of my research, I learnt that from a study by Professor Jessica Jordan of the University of South Florida,18% of women regularly fake climax/orgasm as do 16% of men, with on average 4% of both sexes faking it four times per month. Women especially, faked it more if their earnings were greater than their male partners possibly because they didn't want them to feel emasculated.[1] Perhaps if there were more honesty and less pressure on everyone though, a lot of people could actually just enjoy sex.

At the parties, whilst safe sex was absolutely the emphasis with lots of condoms etc, available; in reality in daily life away from such parties, lots of women (and men) hate using contraceptives such as condoms and quite a few women expressed that they regularly take the morning-after pill and have STI checks instead. At the end of these parties, couples just flagged down cabs, caught ubers and went back to their regular lives/children or to hotel rooms with new guests…

In conclusion, from all of this: the parties, the book interviews, the wider discussions linked to the book and otherwise, I think ultimately when people

---

1   *Do Women Withhold Honest Sexual Communication When They Believe Their Partner's Manhood is Threatened?*' - Jessica A. Jordan, Joseph A. Vandello, Martin Heesacker and Dylan M. Larson-Konar, first published 31 January 2022. See SAGE Journals online;

begin wanting to settle down, they hope to find someone who is fixated on them, and only them. We want to be unique to that person. We often hope one person will look to us for their sexual fulfilment; most people I spoke to, don't like the idea of their partners being interested sexually in others or even finding others attractive. We tend to want to claim a person for ourselves, relying on the security of marriage for example, to hopefully add an extra layer of protection to the fidelity between us. But it is very hard to keep a sexual spark and excitement alive in long-term relationships. Even in the most intense affairs, butterflies can disappear once the chase is over and the person who made our heart throb is an established and regular part of our lives but we can progress to being committed and comfortable partners who still enjoy sex and the safety net of each other's companionship - although we have to realistically accept that even the most loyal mate will find other people sexually attractive. This is just normal.

Once the initial sparks have vanished though, if the relationship is lacking (due to complacency/over-familiarity/zero intimacy for example), conflict, inner turmoil and boredom set in and then the tendency to stray/explore is heightened. Some people throw themselves into work/raising a family etc, to keep them out of mischief but they're still vulnerable to attention from others. This is what we need to be aware of: if there are gaps in our relationship and someone we find attractive repeatedly makes a play for us, as human beings who crave attention and to be found desirable, we are quite likely to respond positively towards that temptation.

Overall I think complete monogamy in long-term relationships (think 10 years' onwards) is often an unrealistic expectation, although it can happen. I think it's realistic though to expect at least one or two emotional affairs as a minimum, in a marriage/partnership of several years (obviously with the hope that there won't be a sexual affair).

I don't think monogamy is impossible and I do think long-term relationships can be happy and work (if both parties really, really want them to and invest the energy and time into them), but there will always be huge bumps in the road and times when you feel utterly out of love with the person you are with. But equally if you need to separate and/or get divorced, that's definitely not a failure! It's just a realistic outcome of how people and circumstances morph and change over time. The fact your relationship lasted for as long as it did is a triumph as pairing two individuals together for any length of time is a pretty intense form of chemistry and sometimes it's subjected to outside forces that change the formula and make the results unpredictable.

Whilst I'm on the subject of what causes relationships to wither and die, here's most of the red-flag behaviours that caused my participants and many interviewees to think, eventually, that enough was enough…

- Infidelity (without consent; sometimes once, sometimes persistent – if love was involved, it's so hard to come back from)
- Verbal/physical abuse
- Overt control (including financial control)
- Complacency/lack of consideration/care
- Ongoing immaturity

- Egotistical behaviour (for example, sharing private images with others, to gain status)
- Cowardice (when a person says all the right things, but when push comes to shove, they don't fight for you – i.e., a married man who reneged on a 3-year-promise to his lover)
- No drive/get up and go/constant negativity/boring to be with/doesn't give back any uplifting energy
- Three people in a relationship: this could be an ex-spouse/partner but it could be a parent too. There's nothing worse than having an ex-wife or ex-boyfriend constantly hovering in a relationship or being with an adult who's still emotionally too connected to a parent and always seeking their approval/involvement with decisions/their lives – think Diana Rigg in 'Mother Love'. (From related book discussions, I learnt how one woman insisted that her mum come on her honeymoon with her husband and that connection continued all the way through the marriage until it collapsed with the pressure exerted from the mother; another adult man always asked his mum about any decisions he had to make/told his mum first about everything and his partner just reached a point where she had enough – because it felt infantilising; likewise with a woman who constantly compared her husband to her "amazing" dad… the husband felt he couldn't live up to those expectations. There were ex-partners who constantly reared up in text messages still trying to exert some control/influence over new relationships – which became quite torturous for the new partner – think Daphne Du Maurier's 'Rebecca' for the sense of a presence that may not even physically be there but still exudes a negative energy).

When seeing people/using hook-up apps etc, these were the behaviours that women found off-putting:

- Guys who sext/text loads to get pics, and then don't turn up as agreed, because either they never intended to in the first place; or they cba (couldn't be arsed) or they felt out of their comfort zone or whatever… This was viewed as doubly poor when they were a no-show without even a grovelly message
- The age-old, pull-you-in/push-you-away routine; one minute they message you saying how much they like you, you have the best time, then they go quiet and ignore you, then they ramp up the attention again, you sleep together and then they tell you they're seeing others and you can just be friends (for them to hook up with as and when); Unless it's what you want, most women reported finding that offensive.
- They message you incessantly; you finally reply and then they don't bother to open your message for days or they open it and don't bother to reply but you can see they're online; Women said this was simply rude.
- When guys cast their net wide and far, so whilst you think they're only messaging you – they're actually messaging a whole circle of women simultaneously (but then in fairness, one female book participant was simultaneously messaging 4 x different guys all named Tom… it got complicated for her as she got two mixed-up!)

- When you're going out with a guy but you constantly get the feeling that their radar is on for someone else and however right you are together, he makes you feel you're not good enough (Women spoke of this a lot!)
- Guys who can't drive (women expect it of men as a necessary life-skill and fairly or unfairly, lose respect for men who they have to give lifts to all the time).

Finally, in summary, when it comes to sex, we need to park our British repressiveness. Sex is how we got here in the first place and is a fundamental, important, instinctive and hugely enjoyable part of life for most people. A lot of conversations need to start happening about sex because it's crucial to society and without greater transparency about sex within relationships, these relationships will wither and die.

Okay, so with that huge topic covered just a little, here's all of the amazing women and their true stories... Over to them:

LADY UNCHAINED'S STORY

When you're a good gospel girl who suddenly lands in prison for GBH for trying to protect your sister in a nightclub and then you experience racism…

THE BIRTH OF LADY UNCHAINED

I finally knew that I had adapted to my prison environment when I caught myself walking around the prison yard in circles with all the other women. I had promised myself that I would never do that: walk around in a circle like a hamster-wheel, smoking roll-ups. I normally smoked Benson and Hedges: roll-ups were for chavs, broke people and drug addicts. I was none of the above. I guess I thought I was too good for roll-ups, too good for prison. I was the good girl, the protector, the one you could go to for a good chat, nice food and great company. Now I was the inmate. It's crazy how one decision can change your whole life. Past, present and future.

I remember stopping in my tracks and shouting out: "I am walking in a f****** circle smoking bloody roll-ups". I was known as the drama queen from then on, the joker. I guess it was better than the names they could have called me if I had shown my true emotions. Because in that moment, I wanted to break down and cry, I wanted to ask the judge why? I wanted God himself to come down and explain to me how this was something I needed, or could get through. But instead I laughed it off with my new friends and continued walking around in circles. I was 21 and in prison. This was not how the 13-year old me had seen things in her dreams. In the movies the actress would wake up and realise she was having a bad dream at this point but I was no actress and this was no movie. This is my Unchained story.

BEGINNINGS

I guess I should start from the beginning. I was raised in South East London but born in Uganda, Kampala. I've lived in South East London for as far as I can remember.

To be honest I had to be reminded of the family we had left back home in Uganda. I remember my mum passing me the phone and just saying speak to your uncle, auntie or cousin and that was that. Growing up, when people asked me where I was from, I would say Woolwich/South East London. Basically wherever

I lived at the time, not because I was ashamed of Uganda but how could I say I was from somewhere I really didn't know that well. All the media ever showed was poverty, disease, and death when it talked about African countries such as Uganda. I guess the younger me was grateful that I'd not had to grow up there.

From the age of 11 until around 14 years old, I lived and breathed the church. There were day prayers, evening prayers, church visits and choir practice. I remember on one of our church visits, I met an American guest pastor who was preaching about praying in tongues. Praying in tongues is a personal prayer between an individual and God. I remember thinking that it sounded funny but I really wanted to know how to do it. So every time I would pray, I would pray for God to give me the power to pray in tongues.

Then one day, I had what can only be explained as a vision during one of my group prayers. I must have been at least 12 years old and the vision scared me so much that I started crying during prayers. I was asked by my then-pastor why I was so upset, so I started to explain what I saw in my vision.

In this vision I was standing on a stage speaking but I could not hear any of the words coming out of my mouth, nor could I see any of the audience's faces. Instead there was a bright light covering where the audience was seated. I couldn't even tell how old I was in the vision but I automatically assumed this meant I was destined to become a pastor. Unfortunately that's not what I wanted for my life then though. My church pastor explained that there was more to the vision: that it didn't mean I had to become a church pastor. Maybe I was going to be a church minister instead. But to a teenager, all of the church stuff was becoming boring and my fears of becoming a church pastor or minister, made me mentally separate from the church faster and I slowly started to forget about my vision of standing on a stage talking to an invisible audience.

That vision would later come to light when the only thing I had left was faith and prayer, only this time I would have no choice but to answer my calling.

I may have stopped attending church and singing in the church choir, but one thing stuck with me. I'm not sure when but I'd promised God that I would never go church on a Sunday and then go clubbing on that same Sunday night because this was my faith and those two environments didn't seem to sit well together. On Sunday, 1st of June 2008 my life was about to change in a way I would later only be able to explain through poetry. I was 20 years old and had recently passed the first stages of becoming an independent child-minder through a training scheme organised by my local council. I didn't have any convictions and had never been in trouble with the police but I was intrigued by the whole clubbing scene which was new to me.

I'd been in a serious relationship from the age of 16 years old until around this time and had gone from living with my mum to living with a guy. Now that relationship was over, I was living alone for the first time in my life and starting to rebuild my future, so child-minding was just the beginning of the next chapter of my life.

That afternoon my sister said the plan was to go to evening prayers and then go home to get ready and go clubbing. At first I refused because of my promise to God, surely the God I serve wouldn't punish me this one time, right?

So there I was in church with my sister but I spent the whole time thinking about what I was going to wear that night and how I should do my hair. I remember singing gospel songs but I can only remember one song from that whole 2 to 3 hours we were in service. To go clubbing, I decided to wear a full white mini dress with high heels, which I'm sure I borrowed from my older sister. I wore my instant weave which had to be clipped in (you use your own hair to cover and blend the weave to give it that real effect). The weave was long and curly, falling down my back. I felt good and off we went…

I wish I could say that the night ended with tipsy girl gossip and the exchanging of names and numbers but my clubbing escapade resulted with me in handcuffs and not in a kinky way! Rather, in the way that meant spending a night in the cells.

The fight.

All I can say about the fight was that I defended my older sister when she was attacked by three women. Looking back at it, I realise I may have been fighting for more than just my sister. I think I was also fighting for my place back in the family and to be accepted by them again. See when I was in that serious relationship at such a young age, it had caused a divide between my family and I. A lot of people in my family were not very happy about my relationship. So I went from being the daughter who helped plan family gatherings, to the family member who was invited last. Therefore, when my sister was attacked, what the three women didn't realise was, in that moment, I felt they were attacking my whole family. I had no intention of hurting anyone that night. My only intention was to protect my older sister from getting injured. But in the eyes of the law I went too far. I never knew it was a crime to defend a loved one, so I didn't believe I had done anything wrong. Even when people were telling me to run because the police were outside, in my head, I'd only acted to defend my sister: I hadn't committed a crime. I thought about running for a second, but then I thought guilty people run and I wasn't guilty. At least I didn't believe I was, so I was happy to go outside and speak to the police officers.

When the police officer said I was being charged with GBH, I couldn't believe it. I had only seen charges like this on TV shows such as 'Booze Britain' and crime shows which I used to watch with my mother. I was handcuffed, put in a van and driven away as I watched my sister's face drop through the glass. I could see the fear and panic in her eyes as she realised she would have to be the one to tell our mum that I had been arrested.

I had a lot of time to think in the cell but I can't remember if I slept or not. All I can remember is trying really hard not to read the writing on the ceiling: 'Are you sick and tired of being sick and tired?' followed by some kind of support helpline. I must have read it over 1000 times, each time wondering how I got there and when it would all end?

I was released from the police station on 2nd of June 2008 at some point in the afternoon. The bright light from the sun nearly blinded me as I stood around looking like a typical criminal in my white T-shirt, white jogging bottoms and prison-issue black plimsolls. I'd also draped over me, the blanket which I'd used to keep warm in that cold cell.

My older sister was already waiting for me and I can't remember for how long she'd stood there. We drove back in silence until I asked the big question: "Did you tell Mum?" and my sister's reply:"Yes, she's meeting us at yours". We spoke a bit after that, maybe to get our minds off the topic of mum, as we continued our journey.

When my mum arrived, I wasn't sure how she would react to my arrest and I was scared that I had let her down. But like me, my mum also saw my actions as me trying to protect my sister and she was sure that I would not get sent to prison. But then my case was sent from a Magistrate's Court to a Crown Court and I was now looking at a 3-5 year custodial sentence. That's when everything changed for me: because everyone had been telling me that it would be fine because it was my first-time offence and that because I am female, I wouldn't get a harsh sentence but they were all wrong. Even the Probation Team were asking the Court for a suspended sentence for me, but I could not see past the 3-5 years I felt likely I would spend in prison.

I lost a lot of my identity whilst on bail because somehow the women who came after my sister got hold of my number and started threatening me over the phone, telling me which areas of London I was no longer allowed to be in and what would happen to me if I was seen in those areas. I was seriously starting to lose my mind. I remember one intimidating call when the women rang me and said they were coming to my house. I dashed outside with the phone and screamed into the air: "come on then, I am outside. Where the f*** are you?!" My friend at the time, pulled me back into my flat and told me to start recording the calls.

So I started recording the abusive phone calls and decided to take them to the police station. I tried to explain to the police that I had an ongoing case and was awaiting court procedures to hopefully clear my name against these same women who were continuing to threaten me. I wanted the police to know that if for any reason I was arrested again for fighting before my court case, these threatening calls would be the reason why. However the police officer said the recordings were unclear so they couldn't use them. I was sent away and told I could only bring up charges after my case was dealt with.

I think that was the day I lost all hope in the so called justice system: I was 21 with a serious case pending and 3 grown women out to get me, yet the police weren't willing to help me. The girl I once knew had gone and from that moment on, I no longer believed in justice. I didn't believe anything any more really, because everything I had done with my life up to now, just felt pointless: school, college etc, … it was all for nothing.

The 9th of February 2009 was my sentencing day and I packed a bag with the personal things I thought I might need just as I had done so many times before, whilst on bail. My best friend and older sister were with me and we tried to make small talk to pass the time but the anxiety was way too high for us to keep the conversations going.

My case kept being pushed back later and later in the day, which only made us more nervous. I remember using that waiting-around time to pay off bills and services which I might not be around to use. Before going to prison, I had never owed money for anything.

We spent more time in the Court waiting area than we spent in the Courtroom where my future was decided. It was more or less, in through one door and out in a van, I can't remember everything that was said in the Courtroom but I just heard "two-and-a-half years. Take her away", loud and clear. Everything from that moment on, was a bit of a blur and I couldn't stop the tears from pouring out of my eyes as I was led down to the cells.

Prison X: high walls, large gates, keys I could never hold and women everywhere. Apart from going to an all girls' school when I was a teenager, it had been a long time since I'd been around so many women, even my female friends in the real world acted like mandem: I just didn't get on with women that well and now I had to live with so many of them.

From the moment I got there, I was convinced I wasn't going to make it, and after a few more nights I started planning how I would end it. The screams of other women who everyone had now got used to, only helped fuel my dark thoughts. I started praying with my hand on the Bible, testing God to take my life because I wasn't brave enough to do it myself.

Days before this and whilst still in my induction (which every inmate has to go through when they first arrive in prison), I saw a priest. She was a black female priest and this should have made me happy but it didn't. I wanted nothing to do with her or God. God was nothing to me and he had let me go to prison. He was to blame and she was his messenger so I made no eye contact with the priest, hoping she would walk past me. But she didn't: "God loves you sister", this priest said to me. I can't put into words what I said to her after that comment, but I know it wasn't something I would want to hear. I basically told her where she could go and to take her God with her, adding: "I also have a Quran in my cell and maybe it's time to change my faith". I'm not proud of this moment but you need to understand how low I was by this point. All the other women laughed - some even supported me. But they didn't know that I used to be *the* choir girl and I felt like God should've had my back for all the times when I did go to church.

I think God heard me, because part of me did die in Prison X. In those early days, one morning, I opened my eyes to nurses and doctors standing over me. Then I realised I was on the floor: I didn't know how I'd got there; the only thing I remembered was washing my blue plastic plate fast so I could continue reading the first letter I'd received in prison, from my best friend back home.

I was taken into a private room and asked if I had taken any drugs and if so, what? I was then asked if I had been given anything by another inmate, i.e. a roll-up? The answer to all of these questions was: "no, I have not". The medical staff explained that at one point I had no pulse and I'd stopped breathing. After that inexplicable experience, I started to return to church.

I landed right back in the arms of the same priest who, a few weeks' previously, I'd been so rude to. I apologised for the way I had spoken to her, barely able to get the words out. I couldn't understand how she just welcomed me back so easily because I had been so mean to her. But that's why she was a priest: forgiveness was a fundamental part of her. I was still lost but at least I now had a little bit of my faith back … although not all of it.

I started working within the prison as a cleaner and this was considered a respected position. This role enabled me to start to build relationships with other inmates and officers. I saw many women entering and leaving prison but yes, I also saw many return and I found myself looking down at the women who returned to this hell that I would do anything to leave. I would later find out for myself just how easy it was for someone with a conviction to end up back in prison for the same charge or a whole new charge.

I had fully adapted to Prison X and now started walking around in circles without even thinking about it. This wasn't the routine that I was used to but now I had my own cell, a group of women to socialise with, a job, a few educational courses I'd enrolled upon and I'd started to do other inmates' hair (so they would buy me B&H cigarettes in the canteen), life was starting to get a little better! This wasn't the life I was built for at all, but this was my new home. Unfortunately for me, this was all about to change and not for the better. I was about to lose another part of my identity: one which I had never questioned before.

A knock at my cell door alerted me to my new conditions. I remember thinking 'why do they knock, when we can't open the door?' I answered anyway. Speaking to me through a flap, the officer told me that I needed to pack all of my belongings because I was being shipped off in the morning. I asked the officer where I was being shipped off to and she replied "Prison Y". In that very moment, I felt my heart break. I tried to convince her that this had to be some kind of mistake. I am British.

I remember her looking at me confused. I think a part of her believed me for a second, and at that point in time, her expression revealed her humanity. However, her role as a prison officer was to enforce the rules, not feel sorry for people. So she reminded me that if I refused, I would be sent to the block. The block is where inmates are sent to be punished. There's no TV and you're basically on 23-hour bang-up and only allowed 1-hour a day to do what you need to do. So you're living the pandemic routine without the pandemic. The flap slammed shut, and she left me with the same teardrops that formed the day I was sentenced.

I packed all of my stuff with a flood of tears rolling down my face. I could hear my fellow inmates trying to comfort me from behind their doors. They reminded me of other friends who were already there and told me to make sure I found them as soon as I arrived there. These were the same women I thought could have been lying about their immigration status, now the other women were probably thinking the same about me. But to some of these women, I was the baby and I guess they felt they had a duty of care towards me and to be honest, that only made me cry more.

My journey to Prison Y is one journey I will never forget. It was like we were driving to the end of the world. I knew the officers had made a mistake but no one listens to inmates. I figured that I would have to sort it out when I got to this mystery place. I remember thinking that if it hadn't been for the threat of being sent to 'the block' for refusing my transfer, I would not be sitting in the back of this sweatbox again.

I was driven for hours like a DPD package but the problem was this package had eyes, ears, and a beating heart. And this little heart of mine knew my world was about to fall apart all over again. I remember saying a little prayer when I realised I could no longer see people of colour on the roads we drove past. I am sure I started to count the ones I could see and trust me, they were few and far between. It made me feel unsafe and my fears of being forgotten slowly reached the surface.

That flood of tears from the night before, began forming in my eyes again. There was no thunder or lightning but I could feel a storm brewing. The only question was, would I make it out alive to tell my story or would my story be told in the words of someone else?

We arrived at the massive gates of Prison Y where I saw my first black officer. He opened the gates of the van and it felt as though I was taken deeper into hell. This would be the last time I would see a black officer, yet the prison claims it's designed to care for, and understand the needs of foreign national inmates. Slavery: isn't that what slavery was about? White people controlling black people and trying to convince us that it was for our own good. This was Strike One for me.

Only when I was removed from the van, did I notice that there were two other women with me. I wondered how they felt during our hour's drive? But these women were white woman and I wondered why they had been brought here. I would later find out that like me, they too were born in a different country other than the UK and would soon be facing the same challenges I was about to face.

Strike Two: The reception area had leather sofas and up-to-date magazines: you don't even get up-to-date magazines in the hospital so why were they here? If you watched 'Prison Break' back in the days, then you may have seen me as the guy in the series who kept asking Michael Scofield where the map leads too? Something just wasn't right here and I made sure to tell the other two women to expect the worse. I must have sounded a bit crazy to them looking back, but my instincts are usually never wrong - if just a bit off in parts.

We were collected from reception by a Prison Rep., a Prison Rep. is another inmate who has built up trust to be the person to welcome new inmates. She showed us around our new home with a smile. I remember thinking, she's doing well not to let us know that this is where we've come to die and be erased from the world we once knew. It was scary how beautiful this place was: the only way I can explain it, is like being on death row and waiting to receive your final meal. Being alive, but not truly living for you, rather living through the eyes of others.

There were loads of beautiful stone statues everywhere. It was as though they had never planned for this place to house foreign national inmates. I would later believe this was the reason they treated us so badly, because this place was never intended for black people, especially not foreign national black people. The friends I thought I had lost back in Prison X, started to reappear. They were all shocked to see me as they'd all told me about this place in their letters and hoped I'd never have to join them, but here I was.

One by one the women came and hugged me, making sure to whisper: "Be careful what you say in here", and then as if nothing had been said, they diverted the conversation straight onto another topic. I was led away by my Prison Rep. to the Induction Wing to complete the rest of my induction (until I was fully inducted, I had to eat with my Rep. and the ladies I had arrived with).

Strike Three: In each prison you're given paperwork to sign to confirm who you are, what your convictions are and what dates you are due to be released. As a British inmate, you get British inmate privileges, such as HDC (Home Detention

Curfew), ROTL (Release on Temporary License), and/or an early release date which usually happens 14 days before your expected release date.

However you can only be given these privileges if: (1) you are British; (2) you comply with all the rules; and, (3) do not cause trouble to yourself, others and staff. But in this prison I had none of these privileges; instead I was asked to sign paperwork that had in fact removed all of my British privileges.

When I refused to sign, the Officer tried to convince me disingenuously, that if any of the documents were wrong, I should still sign them and that they would correct them closer to the dates. Of course I refused to sign. I don't know anybody in their right mind who would sign a document with their name on it followed by the wrong information. But I was in prison, I had no rights and by refusing to sign the documents, I was labelling myself as a disobedient inmate. But I didn't care, nothing was right here and my smile was slowly starting to fade away.

In every prison, inmates are placed on the induction wing for at least a week. This is where you learn your new routine and find out what's available to you and how the visit requests' work. Every prison has its own way of dealing with issues, but the only thing I wanted to know was how to get back to South London and become British again, like the rest of my family.

So, you can imagine just how excited I was to find out that all it took to request a move from this hellhole, was to put in a Transfer Application, with the name of the prison I wanted to go to and why. And that's exactly what I did! I put in my Transfer Request, making sure to put more than one prison. I asked to be sent to HMP Z or HMP A. I had friends who had been sent to both and I figured those prisons couldn't be as bad as this place was. Additionally, I hadn't heard of any of my friends at these institutions, being forced to sign the wrong paperwork there. More importantly, they were both closer to home and they were doable for my family to visit me.

Usually it takes days, sometimes even weeks to get a response about any application that an inmate puts in, whilst in prison. I handed my Transfer Request in before I went to work. My prison job at the time was to work in the Sewing Room making clothes like jackets, jumpers, jogging bottoms and basically all the prison-issue clothes that go out to other prisons. I guess Foreign National Inmates are only good for slave labour, because in this prison the waiting list for education was far too long, so our only options were to work in the factories. This didn't make much sense to me back then, but looking back now, why would the authorities spend time and money educating people they planned to deport?

When I returned to my Prison wing after work, there was a reply from Prison Officer H ('P.O.H.'), who was about to become my personal living nightmare. In his response he basically denied my transfer for the following reasons:

1. I was in the right prison to meet my offender management needs.
2. I could meet people who speak the same language as me, if English was not my first language.
3. Prison Y has trained Officers to meet the needs of Foreign National Inmates.
4. I had been confirmed as a Foreign National Inmate.

You can imagine how this made me feel. I was angry and ready for a fight. There would be no more respect from inmate number: A******.

I headed to the library and picked up a dictionary. Maybe I had misspelt a few words and this wasteman was taking me for a mug. My grammar isn't that great: I can admit that and it's still something I'm working on today, but that doesn't mean that I am not British. I guess P.O.H. had never met a girl from South London, but he was about to see how girls from South London roll.

My reply to P.O.H. was straightforward. I replied to every one of his points, starting with meeting people who speak the same language as me. I then addressed the point about having trained officers who meet the needs of Foreign National Inmates, and reminded him that the only Officer he had of colour, was the Officer at the gate who had nothing to do with any of the people of colour inside the prison. I then explained to him that I had been arrested under the same name that I was sentenced in, and how I was sent to prison for fighting, not fraud. Furthermore, I didn't understand why my nationality was being questioned even though I had been cleared by immigration. I told P.O.H. that I believed his prison was trying to kill me and how I wouldn't be surprised if others had died before me in this hell on earth but the prison had covered it up. I was put on Suicide Watch for this comment.

However, I was later taken off Suicide Watch by the Interviewing Officer who didn't see my comment as a threat to take my own life. There were *some* good Officers in this place, the problem was that they didn't have the same power that Mr P.O.H. had. I said a lot of things to Officers that at the time, I didn't have the evidence to prove, but like I said, my instincts are never usually wrong and a lot of those comments turned out to have some truth to them in one way or another.

Once again I handed in my Application before work and continued with my day. This time there was no Application response. Instead P.O.H. came to my wing with another Officer, who I can only describe as his Guard Dog: she was massive! I was finally face-to-face with my slave master. He began by telling me how disrespectful my response to his letter was. I guess noone had spoken to him the way I did, and if they did, he knew exactly how to silence them. I tried to explain that I was only responding to each of his points and found it very patronising that he believed I couldn't speak English because he seemed to understand me just fine now. I reminded him that I had a British passport and all I wanted was the opportunity to be closer to my family, just like the other white inmates in this prison who were British, but had requested to come to a Foreign National Prison because it was closer to their families.

The meeting didn't go so well. In fact, P.O.H. was so upset by everything I'd said to him that he decided he would bark out my options directly at my face: This was the moment I found out my early release date would be on 9th of August. However, it wasn't back to South London, it was back to Uganda, the country where I was born so many years ago!

P.O.H. clarified that there wouldn't be a transfer to another prison but they could send me back to where I'd originally come from: Kampala. "Isn't that where you was born?" he asked. It took everything in my body not to punch this guy in the mouth! Maybe it was the fear of being deported sooner or maybe it was the worry his 'guard dog' would grab me before my fist reached his face. Whatever it was, it turned into laughter! I think it was laughter provoked by fear, because I knew what it would mean for me and my freedom, if I was violent towards this racist man.

Saying that I was British wasn't enough for P.O.H. He had decided that I deserved to be deported. So the best thing I could do was leave the room before things got any worse, but I was stopped by his 'guard dog' once more. Without even looking at her, I turned around to P.O.H. and reminded him again that I was British, and if looks could kill, I would still be doing time now.

My next words to him after that comment, contained a promise that I would come for him when I got out and I would tell the world exactly what goes on under his watch. There's nothing worse than making a threat you truly intend on keeping to somebody who doesn't believe you're being serious and then to make it worse, laughs in your face. I strongly believe he wanted me to punch him in the face and he probably believed that I would, but see from where I was standing, it would've been easier to have kicked him! I already had the twitch in my leg telling me it was ready to balance the score so we could do the world a favour and take out this disgusting excuse of a man. I saw it all play out in my head but I had learnt a lesson and instead I calmly told him to remember my name because I wasn't going to go quietly like the others he had successfully deported. Finally, I promised that I was coming for him!

After a meeting with Immigration where my picture was taken and scanned through a massive machine, within seconds I was cleared as British. So in my eyes I believed this would help my application for transfer, but it didn't so I decided to go on hunger strike. I don't know why, it's not something I'd ever done before but in my head it made sense. If I died here, they would have to explain to the world and my family, why a 21-year-old died under their watch, therefore proving my earlier statement that I felt they were trying to kill me so that I'd be one less person to deport. Again my hunger strike made perfect sense to me at the time but no sense at all to my family, who had to watch me go from a size 14 to a 6!

During a visit from my family (which meant so much to me, knowing just how far they had to travel to see me, and how hard I had to fight to even be allowed a visit in this place), an Officer from the Visiting Hall told me I was to have an interview with an Immigration Officer. I was escorted to a little room where a stranger asked me questions about my identity. I answered all of the man's questions until it got to the parts I couldn't even hazard a guess at, because they related to a time when I was far too young to have had any kind of clue regarding what went on during those years. My mother was called into the interview to help fill in the gaps.

Mum had also brought in my British passport which she'd refused to send in via the post, due to her fears that the prison would claim they hadn't received it. You see a few days, maybe weeks, before this meeting, I'd called my mum in a panic asking her if we were here illegally? She later told me that if the prison could make me question everything I knew to be true and even question her place as a mother, something had to be gravely wrong. The Immigration Officer looked through my passport and asked me where I'd last travelled to, and I proudly responded: "Amsterdam".

The questions continued going back and forth until he asked me why I believed I was being interviewed by him? I responded by saying: "Firstly, we could have done this outside of my visiting time, you guys already cleared me as British. However, an officer in here, P.O.H. to be exact, has decided that he does not believe I am British and for that reason he's refusing to approve my transfer back to London where I am from". The interview ended with the Immigration Officer admitting that he had been on his way home when he was called in to see me by one of the officers at Prison Y, he wouldn't say which one. But he'd been asked if he could interview a woman regarding her nationality to prove that she was who she said she was.

This Immigration Officer said he believed that I was the same person as the woman in the passport so there was no reason why I shouldn't get my Transfer Request approved. I was advised to put in another Transfer Request stating that I had in fact proven that I am British. We finished what was left of our visit and I returned to my Wing and put in my Transfer Request.

This time my Application was approved and I was so happy that you'd have thought I was going home for real, not to another prison. I'd won my war against P.O.H.: I was going back to London, I was British again. I had never once thought that this could be taken away from me. I knew that my country of birth was Uganda but that's not where I grew up. I think the threat of being sent back there, when my family, friends and memories are all here, was what drove my fight.

I now became the woman others sought the advice of, regarding intimidating official paperwork: the 'crazy one' who turned out not to be so crazy after all. My overriding advice to all the women was not to sign anything they believed to be wrong!

I never left the Induction Wing because I refused to settle into this prison. Apart from a few photos on my cell-wall there, I hadn't unpacked from Prison X. I'd never planned to stay at Prison Y this long in the first place! I knew I had to get out of this hellhole, dead or alive.

Once again, a knock on my door by an Officer stopped me in my tracks. He told me that I needed to pack my stuff up, but then paused mid-sentence, when he saw I was ready to leave! "Has someone already told you to pack?" he asked. "No", I replied, "I've been waiting for this day since I arrived". I am not sure if it was the same Officer who came and got me the next day but I was collected for my transfer and walked pass the beautiful stone statues as I departed.

Saying goodbye to the women I'd got to know in the short space of time I was there, however, was poignant. They were all so happy for me. My leaving demonstrated to them, that they too could win their own personal battles. I reminded them to stay strong and to know their Rights as I was escorted back to the same reception where this business had all begun. I remember the Officer deliberately pointing out to me that he'd never seen me smile the whole time I was at Prison Y and I simply replied: "There was nothing to smile about here". He led me to the reception desk where I was to be officially signed out.

My final battle was with a Reception Officer who was clearly trying to be the next P.O.H. asking me what my nationality was? This time I was sure of my answer, after all, I'd already proven that I was British! Right?

"British" I replied. Yet again this seemed to be the wrong answer. I was confused. I wondered if he knew what I'd been through to get to this point, but before I could finish my thought, he asked me the question again. This time I again stated:

"British" but I was beginning to question myself again. I remember the Officer who had come to escort me back to London, also seeming confused. So when the Reception Officer asked me the question for the third time, I just replied "Foreign National".

I was finally processed. I walked with my Escorting Officer to the 'sweat box' (transferral van), which this time, I was so happy to see! In the air, I could smell the cow manure which they used to fertilize the farms with, which they always told us was 'fresh air' (I wasn't used to this aroma back in South London!) I was shocked when my Officer started complaining about the smell, so I told her what the other Officers said to us when we pulled the same face and was happy when she insisted we hurry up and get back to our polluted city air.

After I got into the transferral van, the Officers within, told me I'd be spending the night in Prison Z and should have been made aware of that in advance. I explained that nobody had told me anything and asked why we had to stop off? They explained that the journey was too long for us to make in one go.

I guess when they originally took me to Prison Y like a DPD package, they never thought I would be sent back to the sender: I was placed here either to be deported or to die, whichever came first. These officers had no idea of the emotional journey I had been through. All I could do was thank them for letting me know as I could've spent the night on the side of the road in the sweat box. Regardless, I was just happy to be out of Prison Y!

I spent the night on the Medical Wing at Prison Z. I guess I had too much medication for them to go through so they decided it was easier to keep me on the Medical Wing until my transfer in the morning. I saw a lot of women with serious drug issues on this wing and it was pretty scary. I don't know if I'd ever seen this many women with drug issues simultaneously, during the whole time I had been in prison. That's the one thing I will never forget about Prison Z, that and the fact that the toilet seat was metal, cold, and right by the door without a curtain, so using it made me feel very exposed. But I pushed through all of this because I knew that the next morning I would be going back to London and even though I didn't know what I would find there, I just knew I would be better off!

I arrived at Prison A ready to take on any Officer who dared to fight me! After the Officers I'd dealt with in the Foreign National Prison, I wasn't going to take any shit from any new ones. But the Officers here weren't anything like those racist ones at Prison Y. Instead they smiled and joked in front of me and the jokes weren't directed at me. It was kind of scary: they wore the same uniform but their attitudes were very different. Later on during my sentence, some of the Officers there even empathised with my situation by admitting that they would have done the same thing I did, to protect their sibling, had they been in my shoes. Hearing this, helped me so much. It made me feel human and understood.

This was not the first time I heard white people telling me that they too would've done the same thing. Back in Prison X, one white inmate had actually laughed at me when she found out what I was in prison for, on my first offence. She told me she had been in my situation at least three times before she was ever sent to prison. I wondered if she realised that she was only highlighting to me just how black people are treated in the so-called Criminal Justice System? This made me wonder how many other people knew about this and why they aren't doing anything about it? I decided that one day I would fight this battle but first, I'd have to be released from prison because this wasn't a fight I could win from the inside, not as an inmate anyway.

Some of the Officers here were from South London, just like me and only judged me for my conduct - not my race. Once again I was on the Induction Wing but this time I actually unpacked some of my belongings.

I made new friends again and enrolled myself quickly in work and education. I intended to get a job in the kitchen so I could have access to as much food as possible following my hunger strike, but instead I was given a job in the gym. Although I wasn't happy about working in the gym at first, I slowly became addicted to my gym routine and even trained as a gym instructor while I was there, getting involved with every fitness project that was available.

The gym office slowly became my favourite place in the prison after the chaplaincy dept of course. I remember my first day in the gym when they told me I had to do a fitness test, plus a bleep test, plus 14 x laps around the prison yard and I remember telling them: "I'm not a runner and I'm also a smoker so I don't really play them running games." I was shocked when the Officers replied: "Maybe if you could run, you wouldn't have got caught and wouldn't have come to prison". I was shocked! The other women heard and they all started laughing. This should have made me angry, but instead I started laughing with everybody else and just replied: "Yeah, yeah, I'm walking it". My nightclub fight flashed into my head and I started to imagine what my life would have been like if I had chosen to run from the scene before the police had arrived. I thought about this as I walked around the field, until I was brought back to reality by the gym officers shouting: "At least run the long ones and walk the short ones!"

Our relationship grew stronger from then on and I left the gym months' later with a killer body and legs you could crack an egg on! The other woman started calling me one of the Williams' sisters (Serena and Venus Williams), for a while. I remember one prison visit from my family when I was sitting next to my older brother and we were both wearing white t-shirts and half-way through our chat, my brother looked at my arms and just said "Jesus Christ girl, I think you need to stop now!" We all laughed.

We laughed even more when I saw one of my gym officers was covering a shift in the visiting hall, so I introduced them to her. Now her body was definitely a gym body, and when my family said that I would look like her soon, I was excited! I eventually left my role of working in the gym, not because of what my family said but because I had finally became an 'Enhanced Inmate' and could now work in DHL (the highest paying job at the time). I was still hoping my Appeal would go through and that by some miracle, I would be out by August - before my birthday, or even after, just as long as I was out.

However, I soon discovered that my Appeal had been denied. I called my mum to share the bad news, trying very hard not to let the other women around me see how hurt I really was. A friend came to check on me, she must have heard me cry on the phone, even though I tried not to make a sound, but my whole body felt like it was breaking, so I think I must've given away how much mental distress I was in.

This friend gave me a CD and said that it would probably do more for me than it would for her. She'd also been waiting to hear about her own Appeal, but once she found out that mine had been denied, she said that she had no hope at all, that she would get hers. Usually I'd be quick to tell her to have hope and not to give up but I could barely make it through a sentence without crying. I just couldn't turn it off. The CD she gave me was the 'Mary Mary' album: 'Thankful'. Honestly, it saved my life, and helped me start praying deeply to God again. I started praying for forgiveness and guidance and I began to believe that God must have a reason why I had to stay in this place, and that there was a lesson I still needed to learn.

From that moment on, every application I put in, had to be prayed over before it was submitted. I went from desperately praying for God to help me with what I needed **then and there**, to allowing God to do it **in his own time**. Even though I was still in prison, things were starting to look up for me. I had to celebrate my birthday there, but my friends in prison made sure I enjoyed it. They put their money together and booked me into the salon, so I could get my hair and nails done. My friends and family also made sure I got loads of cards but the best gift was from my 'ride or die' best friends. They ordered me a massive bouquet of flowers and sent them to the prison. I was called to reception to collect them and at first, I thought they were for the officers. When I was told that they were mine, I could've cried. I remember walking through the prison back to my cell wearing a massive smile to match this massive bouquet and being stopped by women every minute to ask about them. The flowers were such a brilliant gesture!

I'd had lots of applications for my Weekend Release being denied, after they'd gone back and forth, but one was finally approved! However on the date of my Weekend Release, I was faced with yet another challenge. For some reason, the Governors didn't believe that I met all the requirements needed to be let out for the weekend. The problem was that my older sister, cousin and best friend had been waiting outside the prison, since very early in the morning to pick me up. They had watched others embrace their loved ones and were constantly on the phone to my mum who was getting ready for my homecoming.

On the other side of the wall I was getting nervous. It was now 12:15pm and the other women were returning from their jobs and education. Officer D had done everything in his power to find out what was stopping me from going home for the weekend. He called so many different Officers to help me but was told to stop ringing because there was nothing else that could be done in my case. He came and shared the bad news with me but said that he would unlock my cell first so that I could run and be one of the first people to speak directly to the governors.

I called my sister and told her that I might not be coming out and maybe it was best that they make their way home, but my sister wasn't having any of it. Before I was locked behind my door again, one of the older ladies in the prison, who I called 'auntie', told me to pray and to remember that only God had the last say. This might sound crazy but it was like God himself was talking to me through this auntie, so as soon as I was locked behind my door, I got down on my knees and I prayed, and I prayed again until my cell was unlocked. It felt like seconds but in reality it had been an hour and 45 minutes.

I used all of my gym training as soon as that door swung open and I took off to speak to the Governors. I was the first person to speak to them on that occasion, so I explained my case in a panic, stating that my 'Outside Probation' and 'Inside Probation' had both cleared me for Weekend Release and that I was on every course set out by Probation. I think the Governors had me confused with somebody else because one of the courses they were talking about, didn't ring any bells in my head, but this happened to a lot of people in prison: people with similar surnames usually got mixed up with other people.

I was told to go back to my cell and would be notified if I was going to be released on Temporary Licence. I walked back, out of breath and wondering if I would ever get to eat my mum's food again. When I arrived on the landing, I was locked behind my door again. I prayed and I cried and I prayed again, until I heard the door unlock. I was allowed to go home for the weekend!!

I didn't care how late it was - I was just grateful! I thanked God for letting me go home and I promised to continue praying. I finally embraced my family and was taken straight to the hairdressers to get my hair and nails done, before going back home to my mum to eat her amazing food.

I remember being given my mobile phone and it started ringing. I had to be told to answer it because in the few months' I'd spent in jail, I'd forgotten the simplest things like my ringtone and how to answer the phone. It all felt weird to me but in a good way. I remember thinking I would never have had the opportunity to do this in the Foreign National Prison. In that place, the only time I would have left would've been to catch a flight back to Uganda. At Prison Y, I would go on to have another four Weekend Releases approved before I was officially set free.

Things in prison were started to look much better. I was finally moved to the Enhanced Landing, which meant less of a lockdown or no lockdown at all, as the rest of the landings had, because we were the trusted ones. It also meant that I could do my own laundry instead of waiting for Friday's laundry day kit change with the rest of the prison. I could do my own washing, when I wanted to do it. I had some autonomy back.

As I was getting closer to the end of my sentence so I started 'Prep for work'. This was to prepare myself for the working world. I looked into youth work and it was as though I was seeing it for the first time. Now my prison sentence started to make sense: I was meant to come to prison to help prevent other young people from ending up here, as I had.

I needed to be in the right frame of mind to see it for myself. I was lucky to have a teacher who believed in me but was also honest with me about my chances of getting back into employment post-prison. She believed that with my attitude, any organisations would be lucky to have me, so we started holding practice job interviews and she taught me how to disclose my conviction to an employer.

The next few months passed quite quickly. It helped that I could go home once a month for the weekend. The next stage was to get approved for HDC (Home Detention Curfew), which would mean possibly being out before the end of the year. A lot of other women had been denied their tag but I still hoped that I would get mine. I'd also applied for Weekend Release over Christmas, however it was denied. I was a little hurt that I would not get to spend Christmas with my family, but it was explained to me that the reason this was denied, was because I had to be in the prison for over a week to be approved for my tag. So if I took a Christmas Weekend Release, the earliest I would be offered a tag, would be in the

New Year, so I accepted the terms and conditions with the hope that I would be home before the New Year.

"A******", I remember hearing an officer screaming out someone's prison number. At first, I didn't realise he was calling my number. See this Officer didn't work on my landing so he didn't know who he was calling. Once my friends and I confirmed that he was calling my number, I went to find out why, and was pleasantly surprised to find out that I could go home!

I remember thinking 'home? Me, now, how?' I didn't understand especially after all my Weekend Release Requests had been denied. I stood at the office door while the Officer made a phone call to find out exactly what sort of release I was getting. My two friends and I waited nervously to find out the outcome.

It turned out that because I wasn't able to have a Christmas Weekend Release, I was given a Surprise Release the week before Christmas, so off I went to Reception for my Weekend Release to surprise my family! I was given money for the travel costs involved and I made my own way home using public transport for the first time in what seemed like forever. None of my family knew I was coming. I remember my mum opening the door and without even looking, walking straight back to the kitchen to continue cooking. So I stood at the door and waited for her to come back. When she returned and saw me standing at door, she just started screaming! Then she asked: "Did you escape?" as she hugged me. One-by-one, my mum let me call my family and friends to let them know I was home for a few days. This would be the last time I would come home on Temporary Licence.

When I returned to prison, I found all of my post was on my bed and some was on the floor. As I went through it, I saw an envelope with 'HDC' (see previous definition) on the front. I opened the letter to find that I have been approved for HDC and would be going home on the 27th December 2009. I called the Officer and asked him to lock my door. I remember him saying: "Did you miss being locked behind your door that much?" and I replied: "No sir, I just need to pray." Once again, I was down on my knees thanking God for the miracles he was making happen in my life. After I prayed, I went and called my mum to let her know that within a week I would be home for good.

I told my friends in prison that I'd been approved for HDC and we screamed in silence because I didn't want anyone to know I was going home. I spent Christmas in prison knowing that within 2 days, I would be leaving. I had my last Prison Visit from my family and we made tribal noises throughout the whole visit! I think in that moment *everybody* knew that we had something to celebrate.

27th December 2009: The day I was finally released from prison had arrived! I stayed up the whole night before, packing and giving away what I could to my friends who would remain behind. I watched people leave to go to Reception to be released and once again I waited and waited for my turn, until I had to ask one of the Officers what was going on because I hadn't been called and was panicking. They reassured me that I was definitely going home that day, but the process was just taking some time as it did for everyone. I called my mum as she'd been at the prison gates for me from God knows what time, to let her know that I was still coming.

When my name was finally called, it was like winning the lottery (I imagine!!) I said goodbye to all of my friends again and walked through the prison yard for the final time, making sure to say my farewells along the way to the Chapel that had heard all of my cries, along with the gym which had made me sweat and built up my powerful abs! I looked at the large gate that I used to dream would open for me and I passed the ghost of my younger self, who used to look at that gate, dreaming that one day, freedom would beckon! That day had finally come and I don't know why, but I screamed out: "Mum I'm coming home!!"

Hugging my mum outside that gate was like being born again: like that first touch from a mother to a child. We loaded my belongings into in the back of the car and started our journey home. We got lost on the way back home and mum said it was because she never had to make that journey again. I think she was nervous for the same reasons I was. We stopped off at a pub for brunch, making sure to call Probation every step of the way.

I finally got to meet my Probation Officer that my mum had now become friends with. He was called Dan. He read out all of my Conditions and one of the Conditions meant that I couldn't go to one of my favourite places. This was the same area where previously, I had gotten into trouble and the patch where those intimidating women, patrolled. However, I accepted it all. I made my way home and opened my door with my own key, for the first time in a year. It felt unreal.

I think everyone thinks that once you're out of prison, you're completely free, but I believe that this is when the second part of your sentence begins. I started volunteering and working with young people and it felt like a dream coming true: all those ideas I'd had in prison finally coming to fruition, but I was just a volunteer; nothing had actually been fixed. If anything I was more broken now, than before I went to prison. See, in prison I realised that I had a lot of issues to deal with; 'Identity' being the biggest one of them all.

Something happened to me in prison; something I couldn't explain. When I was released, to everybody else I was free, that happy, always-smiling person was back. That's what they thought. But the real me was still in prison. This new person they were seeing, was the person who'd learnt how to hide her pain behind a smile. It was as though somehow in prison I'd became two people, but no one really knew what I was fighting in my head. All they saw were fake smiles, until they started to see the abuse, anger and confusion that poured out of me, with the help of some alcohol. To make it worse, my best friend, who was more like a brother (the boy that grew into the man who taught me to love me, for me), died 4 months after I was released. I hit the bottle hard.

But something happened: I remembered a conversation I'd had with him when I was back in Prison A and had realised that there was more to my sentence than had seemed apparent. I'd called him back then and told him that one day I'd be paid because I went to prison and I would help others to prevent/cope with, a similar situation. I remember he laughed and even told his little brother. This was a relationship where we always laughed at each other in a mock-sarcasm way, but the problem was that I took it to heart this time. I started cussing him, I guess in a playful way, but actually really meaning it - if that makes sense. My language to my friend was disconnected because in prison the Officers have the power to terminate any call they think can cause you distress. I remember I called him straight back and before I started speaking to him, I said: "To whoever is listening to this call, this is my brother and this is how we speak to each other. I'm not going to do anything to myself, I promise". I remember him asking me, "What the hell was that?" so I explained why I had said what I had said. This memory is one of the main reasons I continue to do what I do today.

I was glad my brother had introduced me to my second best friend, who was even more broken about our brother-death than I was. He continued to push me until his last breaths' 2 years later, and once again, I was left with a memory. But this time I got to see this brother before he passed, I remember telling him a story word-for-word making sure to re-enact every moment so he didn't miss a thing. See, this time he was in a hospice. I remember him saying to me: "you're actually funny, like proper funny. You can tell a story that can capture anyone from anywhere. You should be on telly or something." I remember replying by saying, jokily: "Come on, obviously I'm going to be on telly soon one day" but this was my brother; he never lied to me, loyalty always.

His reply wasn't very nice, but it was honest and I wouldn't have had it any other way. He said: "So how are you going to be famous? How are you going to be on TV just because *I* know you're funny? Who am I? I can't make you famous". He continued: "You have two eyes, two arms and two legs. I have one of each and I still push myself everyday. Stop talking about it and make it happen". His harsh but loving words, would replay in my mind when I got the call about him passing away.

You have to understand that growing up, these two men shaped and built my confidence and the only time I was truly away from them, was when I was in prison. So for a long time, I blamed myself for removing myself from their love, their truth and their honesty. Many parts of me died with them. Many parts of me also grew after they'd both passed away and only they would understand what I mean by that, because after prison I was arrested two more times for abuse.

I believe I was right each time for the things I said, but again someone with a Conviction is never really seen as a victim. The only reason I wasn't sent back to prison is because each time I was arrested, I'd achieved more goals then your average ex-offender and not only that, but I was building Lady Unchained from the ground-up.

I have to say that I was very lucky to have a good solicitor for the two times I had to appear in Court again. I think it helped that I knew this solicitor from my childhood and she was the lady who had hugged me when I first came out of prison. She asked me if I had ever heard the term 'self-defence of another' used in my case, to which I replied: "What's that?" She then told me that I should never have gone to prison but I was so happy to be out, that I wasn't thinking about how I'd got into prison. I'd even started to forget about the way black people were treated in the system I'd been set free from.

After I was in Court for the third time, I remember my solicitor telling me that she did not want to see me back in front of the Judge and she told me that I needed to believe more in my mission. The truth is, every time I was arrested, I was reminded that even if I was in the right, my Convictions meant that I would have to be questioned as a Suspect, before anything.

What I should say, is that during my time in prison, I would write notes to myself to help me get through the pain, the loneliness and anger of everything I was feeling. I saw those notes as nothing more than a release. For some reason, when I got out, I stopped writing these. Maybe if I had continued to write my angst down, I wouldn't have been arrested so many times after I was released from prison, but this creativity brings me to my platform: Unchained Poetry.

Unchained Poetry is an artistic platform for an artist to talk about their experience of the Criminal Justice System. In the end, it wasn't all the meetings with Probation nor was it my time in prison. It wasn't the second or third arrest or the second time that I was placed on tag or paying the fine I was given. It was the constant reminder through the media, that I was always only going to be an ex-offender and would never break the cycle.

If I was trying so hard to have a successful life after prison, I knew that there had to be other people like me who were trying to achieve the same thing. This is how I came into contact with National Prison Radio and for the first time, I saw people like me, in the radio industry, who were sharing their stories. I then knew that all those little notes that I was now using as poetry, had finally found their intended audience.

All of this takes me right back to that same vision that I once tried so hard to run away from, because now I stand on a stage in front of an audience and I tell my story through poetry. I guess in the end, God was only trying to show me a vision of what would come to pass, no matter how I got there. He had shown me my destiny before I even knew what it would be. So I believe I was meant to go to prison: God had to give me time-out so I could reconnect with his love and start to understand what my mission was. I am not the girl I was, who was sent to prison, but rather I am Lady Unchained: I am the woman who has emerged from the pain I've endured!

WHAT HAVE YOUR EXPERIENCES TAUGHT YOU?

My experiences have taught me many things, but I have learnt that I am stronger than I could have ever imagined. I was born happy and have always fought to stay happy, regardless of my circumstances. I will always fight for what I love and protect those I feel need to be protected. By being sent to prison, I saw and felt just how black women and men are treated in the UK Criminal Justice System and learnt that they will never receive a fair trial. And until we admit that the system is broken and built on the history of black people being enslaved to white people in the UK, we will never see change. It wasn't okay then and shouldn't be okay now. It's a fight I will continue with, needing help along the way, because the history of people who look like me, fighting this same oppressor, end up in prison or dead. So I need people who look like my oppressors to stand with me, and fight with me, because without them, my fight might end up with others having to tell my story.

WHAT WOULD YOU ADVISE OTHER WOMEN IN A SIMILAR SITUATION?

My advice to women or anyone in prison/coming through the UK prison system, is that there is #LifeAfterPrison. Don't let your crime or crimes define your future. Everyone makes mistakes. It's how we learn. Use your mistakes to build your future and help others learn, so they too can grow and avoid the pain you had to endure, just to see another day.

Whilst your oppressors might take your freedom, don't ever let them take your smile. Your smile is your armour: your shield against the negative vibes, the pain and the darkness. Don't sit in the passenger seat to your own life; take the wheel and in doing so, take back control of your journey and your story. As long as you're alive, don't let anyone else tell your story. It's yours to share.

WHERE ARE YOU NOW? WHAT ARE YOUR PLANS FOR THE FUTURE?

Right now I am on a journey to rediscovering the vision of my younger self. I no longer fear my vision: my audience is no longer invisible; it's now my reality. I embraced it in my soul and it allowed my flesh to absorb it. I think of the girl/woman I was before: she was the enslaved me, but through my enslavement, Lady Unchained was born and together, they carry me to places which even the younger me could never have imagined.

I am now a Poet, Performer, TedXLondon speaker, Broadcaster, Radio host for National Prison Radio, Advocate for Life After Prison, Founder and Creative Director of Unchained Poetry: an artistic platform for artists with lived experience of the Criminal Justice System.

MELISSA'S STORY – PART I

Parts I and II: An Oxbridge stripper, actress and dominatrix who falls for a suicidal client

NOTE TO READER

Melissa's story is told in two parts. Part I is the story of her first husband, Adam's, suicide (based upon our initial interview together) and directly following Part I, is an article Melissa herself wrote about Adam's suicide in 'The Blue Nib'; but then Part II is a chapter devoted to Melissa's life experiences working as a stripper, chatline operator and a dominatrix, as this tale is so fascinating too and was begging to be shared! Here's Part I:

***

It's been 4.5 years since Adam's suicide and I never stop thinking about him, the guilt and the trauma of his death.

We met in a strip club called 'The Robert Peel' in Kingston, Richmond, London, where I worked as a stripper. I loved it as I'm a terrible show-off. I was happy to be on stage. Adam came in to watch the performances. He'd been a computer programmer originally but when I met him, he wasn't working.

But then I accidentally became pregnant by another guy, a Canadian, who humped and dumped me and dashed off back to Canada. Because of my pregnancy, I couldn't continue stripping, so I stopped and worked on a sex chatline instead, called 'Cheap Chat'. Adam happened to ring up by total coincidence one night at midnight and we started talking. We basically found each other.

He lived on his own and was a deep thinker. He loved music, films, culture and he was clever, sparky and fun to talk to. He had a real dynamism about him. As a chat-line worker, we were forbidden to meet clients, but Adam and I created a code between us to enable us to meet up. When my son James, was 6 months' old, Adam and I met up for the first time, in person, in January 2002. It was so exciting! He hadn't been in a relationship since the early 1980s and so had been on his own for ages. When I saw him at the local train station, he was really handsome and seemed very debonair. I didn't know it was going to become romantic with Adam but we just clicked. He was so keen to make it work and he was a natural-born father, even though my son wasn't his blood child. Adam was at ease with my stripping too and wasn't judgemental of it.

Adam had been 'in a nut house' (his words) for 2½ years but my intuition told me that he was safe. He was intriguing and talked about his mental health when we first spoke on the chatlines, so he was always very open about his issues. Adam stayed at

my house and every weekend, he would sleep on the sofa as he was so gentlemanly but one day I just ended up coming out with: "what's wrong with you?" because I was so desperate for us to sleep together. So I 'jumped his bones' and we became a thing.

Adam kept his flat and we'd meet up regularly, like a courtship. I kept stripping. I'd actually had to go back to work in this field when my son was 2 weeks' old, as I needed the money. At that time, I was still breastfeeding and had stitches but it was what I had to do as a single mum. Adam was great with map-reading so he would help me get to my stripogram bookings around Hertfordshire, Essex and London. There would be Adam and the baby in the car and we'd rock up at these venues and I would go and do my thing!

The various costumes I had to wear included a nurse, policewoman, businesswoman, nun, etc… my policewoman costume was the most popular outfit. I would pretend to take details of the 'offence' and write down the 'perpetrator's' name in my 'naughty book' before hitting him with a truncheon and squirting him with whipped cream! (Nowadays I hate squirty cream!) I remember having to perform at a house party too on one occasion and we all got invited in. The woman was desperate to cuddle James (my son) as she really wanted a baby. It was a crazy time!

Adam and I got married in April 2006. His mental health issues meant that he didn't want guests at the wedding as he wouldn't have coped with them. Adam couldn't manage social interaction, didn't like any fuss and struggled having people around him. He wanted me at home with him all the time and was dependent upon me. I look back and think I put such a lot of my social life on hold, but when you're in a similar situation, it becomes routine: your normal life.

But it got to a point that whilst I wasn't sobbing, I realised that my life was flat, tedious and grey. My world was shrinking and I needed some excitement. I joined a local theatrical society and took part in a play about UKIP, playing Nigel Farage's henchman. We played lots of gigs and would go to the pub afterwards. I realised then that I needed a lot more from my life and that I had missed being on stage so much. This is when things began to go wrong in our marriage after nearly 9 years together because my new life began to cause friction in our marriage. There were rows and a tense atmosphere. I felt a sense of disapproval and that my life was unravelling but I'd finally reached a point where I hated being constrained, as I was getting a taste of a new life.

Adam needed me more and felt threatened. But other issues surfaced too, for example, I had never met his family and I felt that he was ashamed of me. Also it got to a point where my son James wanted to bring friends home but he couldn't because Adam was unable to cope with anyone else in the house. I started to think about leaving Adam when James reached 18…

Christmas 2015 came and James was in Canada with his dad and grandparents. It was a tricky Christmas. There weren't any massive rows but I could just sense an oppressive atmosphere. I sat on the floor doing a jigsaw puzzle and felt imprisoned as so many of my friends were out at the pub. Adam was on his laptop.

On Boxing Day, we went to the sales and then on New Year's Eve, I went to work for 3 hours (as well as everything else, I also run musical workshops in residential homes). When I came home at around 5pm, I found a note that read: 'Don't go upstairs. Call the police'. Even though his instructions couldn't have been clearer and I knew exactly what they signified, I stood staring at the note, unable to think of what to do next. Eventually I saw a neighbour and they suggested that I do as I was told. So I did.

I heard my voice explain to the 999 Police Operator very calmly that my husband had a history of mental illness and I suspected he'd committed suicide. They told me not to go inside, but to wait on the pavement. I stood there shivering. Soon there were sirens. I'd never summoned sirens before. Two female police officers went upstairs and returned, looking grave, to tell me there was a man hanging in the hallway. I remember how kind they were to me. I was asked to identify the body, but I couldn't so I rang my mum and asked her if she could do it as she's less squeamish than me. She pushed past my husband's swinging corpse to gaze at him, then shouted that he was a bastard. Thus I learnt I was a widow, aged 39.

Prior to meeting me, Adam had already tried to commit suicide by jumping into the Thames but he was fished out. He was pissed and with a friend, so it was more of a cry for help but even so, I knew that the suicide-desire was in him. Adam told me that if I ever got pregnant, he would kill himself. I think he was worried about having a baby who might also grow up with mental health issues. Adam wouldn't have any psychological intervention or take tablets or seek any support when he was with me, because I was his everything. Lots of things had impacted him from the past, for example, he'd been packed off to boarding school when he was little and he'd experienced some kind of sexual abuse and bullying there. He didn't speak about it but I know it affected him a lot. Also his parents had died just before New Year's Eve.

When he committed suicide, Adam put a towel down, to catch any drips. That was just too much for me to bear.

At the Coroner's Inquest, I felt judged and guilty. It was a process that lasted 1-2 hours and although they were actually so kind to me, I felt an overriding sense of guilt. I had to talk about a row we'd had. They read out his medical records and Adam had been to see his doctor just before his suicide but I hadn't known about this, so I felt like a bad wife. The Inquest was the hardest process because it took place in July, so it was 7 months' later and it hurt more as I had just started to get over Adam's suicide, but the Inquest brought it all back. After the Inquest, a policewoman gave me a big hug and said: "now go and live your live", I'll always remember that as such a kind example of sisterhood and that night, I went and got very drunk.

In the following weeks, I was very ill. It was as though it was a physical manifestation of all the stress I'd been under for years and I had to take time off work. I also had to pick up James from the airport after he flew back in from Canada. He suffered with all of this too.

***

When I reflected, I realised that it had actually been really shitty having a 'dementor on my shoulders' as it had sucked all the life out of me. I had been emotionally and financially supporting Adam for years. Adam had never addressed his mental health issues properly. He was constantly trying to cope with life on his own. He found it really traumatic just attempting to review benefits or make a phone call to the dentist, everything seemed a huge deal for him. It used to drive me up the wall. Therefore after his death, there was an awful lot to process and I went through the whole gamut of emotions: from feeling free and ecstatic to desperately guilty, depressed, suicidal and frightened for the future. I suddenly had to do all of the practical jobs in the house but

I got James involved. I told him he was the man of the house now. James and I worked together as a team and felt we didn't need to tell anyone about what had happened to Adam because he never socialised.

I gradually became close to a man named Mr Todd. He was an actor and playwright I had met through taking part in the UKIP play. He was really thoughtful and asked if he could help me. Sometimes we would just sit and play scrabble together. He is really gregarious, so going from Adam to Mr Todd was like switching from one extreme to the other. We just laughed and he lifted my spirits. He's twenty years older than me but he worships me. Mr Todd had never been married before but eighteen months after Adam's suicide, we got married and then we jointly set up a theatre company and pre-covid, we were touring the UK together in his play.

After Adam's death, I was shocked at how people can be with widows. I found that people were a bit frightened of me and they avoided the subject of his suicide, but it suited me when women dodged the topic because often they said the wrong thing. For example, James' grandmother in Canada said: "you mustn't be angry, you must control that." Another woman said: "you should go for counselling" and I felt affronted because I didn't want counselling and felt that I should be allowed to feel anything I felt. Everyone has their own coping strategies. I had talked and sobbed a lot but I reached a point where I had enough of being miserable. I hated being sympathised with. I didn't want to be seen as a victim and judged because my husband had chosen death over me.

I went to back to work quite soon after Adam had died, leaping, singing and dancing with old ladies because there's nothing quite like it, to inspire me or inspire them. I felt as though it was my duty to make them happy! You just have to plaster on a big smile but it works.

I started dating Mr Todd after Adam died but my son James didn't approve and he stipulated that Mr Todd could only stay over for one night a week (my son was being a bit of a prude). I felt that it took ages for James to be pacified, however now he talks to Mr Todd much more than me and he encourages him to see bands and go to gigs. James and Mr Todd basically became friends over the banjo and guitar and when Mr Todd and I got married, James played the guitar at our wedding.

James got his first girlfriend soon after I met Mr Todd and he was able to bring her home and that was a bit of a milestone as that wouldn't have happened when Adam was alive. I mentioned earlier that James and I couldn't have friends over as Adam couldn't cope with other people in the house but Adam didn't really have anything to talk to us about because his world was so limited and I could sense that he was worried about James and I slipping away from him. However, now we could all finally be our true selves.

I'd felt a duty of care to Adam but I wish I hadn't spent so much time with him as duty can hold us back. I wish I'd acted sooner to leave. I still miss Adam though as he was a subtle thinker. I kept his reading books because they felt like a safe thing to hold on to, as there's a little less emotion attached to them.

It's been doubly hard that Adam committed suicide on New Year's Eve because it's meant that each New Year's Eve is such a shitty reminder. However, I've since found my own way to cope on that day and it's by working hard, watching a musical and drinking champagne. All of this helps me to forget the trauma.

Adam was cremated and buried in the garden at our old house at a cost of £4,000. He rests next to our late cat. I moved from there about 3 weeks before my wedding to Mr Todd in July 2017 as I needed to start afresh.

WHAT HAVE YOUR EXPERIENCES TAUGHT YOU?

You're just stronger than you think. It's amazing what you can survive and get through. Having felt so stuck, trapped and traumatised for ages, to be able to come through and be strong and happy is amazing!

Just keep fighting and believe in being amazing! Ruthlessly pursue being happy!

WHAT ADVICE WOULD YOU GIVE TO OTHER WOMEN IN A SIMILAR SITUATION?

Don't feel bad about any survival strategies you adopt to cope. Lean on people. My friend Jenny from Sheffield, messaged me all the time and played online scrabble with me when I was really going through the difficult stuff after Adam's death. This was despite the fact that Jenny has two children, but she made herself available for me. My girlfriends and my mum were amazing.

Writing a letter about what had happened, also was very cathartic. Accept that night-time is always the worst. It's like having PTSD because I would imagine his corpse swinging, so looking at the letter has helped. I feel fondly towards Adam now. I felt for a while that what I had done in trying to look after him just wasn't quite enough, it wasn't quite okay but now I know that it was right at the time and I did my best.

I've realised it's about self care. The need to do anything that makes you feel better: shag, eat jaffa cakes, whatever you need to do… 3 weeks after his suicide, I went and had botox and fillers. It's about being at peace with yourself.

I couldn't read for 6 months afterwards, even though I am a massive reader, but I just had to let it go and find myself again. I gradually picked up an Agatha Christie book and that got me back into reading again…

WHERE ARE YOU NOW? WHAT ARE YOUR PLANS FOR THE FUTURE?

So I met Mr Todd and we got married. I am very happy with him! I run a theatre company and love that. Just before Covid, we were going all around the UK, performing in plays and festivals. I could never have done that before with Adam. I am also the Managing Editor of Thanet Writers. My son James is in a good place also working at a funky hotel, cooking, playing guitar and writing songs. He's happy with his girlfriend too.

BLUE NIB EXTRACT

NOTE TO READER

The following is Melissa's own piece of writing about her experience of Adam's suicide and was created for the Blue Nib. I haven't changed anything. Here it is:

'Bastard corpse identified, I wasn't allowed to return to my house. It was a crime scene now. I sat in the police car watching as they worked their way through all the rooms, looking for evidence of foul play. They asked if I wanted his wedding ring or watch removed from his person. I retched at the thought. Everything he'd ever touched seemed suddenly contaminated, loathsome. We'd been together fourteen years. Raised a child together. That's a lot of memories to want eviscerated.

I went back to my mum's house to give a statement. Where I'd been at the time of the incident, how the day had unfolded. They were nice as could be but I still felt accused. We'd had a row earlier. I'd left the house angry and resentful. What kind of wife does that? What kind of wife goes to work simmering over some petty nonsense I could barely remember, while her husband sits at home, tying a noose?

I went back home the next day. I found his slippers by my bathroom scales. He must have done some calculation as to angles and whether the bannister could take his weight, which astonished me: he was lousy at maths on the best of days. He'd had a beer and a mince pie, and the newspaper he'd been reading lay open on the table. It looked so normal. There was a Christmas tree in the corner of the room, cards on the mantelpiece, and the rope he'd used, lying on the side as if I might want to keep it for a souvenir. I threw it into a bin liner, shuddering. Then the beer bottle, then the slippers, his favourite snacks he'd bought for a special Christmas treat: the idea they'd outlasted him, abhorrent. The pants and socks he'd bought on Boxing Day, still in their packaging. His wallet. Is there any- thing more personal than a wallet, the leather worn thin from his repeated touch? His British library card inside. He'd been so proud of that. I couldn't bear to look at it. I drove ten miles to find a bin that felt far enough away from me.

After that I went home to email everyone that needed to know. The writer in me wanted to send a tidy, coherent narrative. I explained he'd been unhappy since his parents died, that we weren't getting on, that we'd just bought a new business and he was struggling to cope with the stress of that. That sounded plausible, but I'd no idea if it was true. I didn't understand anything, and now I never would.

When I'd finished that, I had to go to the airport to collect my 14-year-old son and tell him what had happened. On that 2-hour drive I went through every emotion, around and around: violent, overwhelming grief, elation, despair, longing, fury. Fury felt best. I settled on that.

For months after his death I sent him texts. You know the first person you think to text whenever anything happens? For me, for years, it had always been him. Now the biggest thing ever had happened and I had no one to talk to about it. Adam was a clever, insightful man, his natural wit sharpened by years of therapy, and his death made me yearn for him as I'd never yearned before. So I would send angry little messages. If only he'd received them, he'd have seen the yearning under the rage, and comforted me. He'd have known what to say. He always did. These were some of the texts:

"Another night spent wondering how long it took you to die, inches from our bed. Cheers for that, prick." Or…

"Boiler's on the blink again. No, don't worry, I'll sort it, you just carry on being dead. In fact I'll just take care of everything, shall I, forever?"

People don't care for angry widows. I was scolded for my rage. I should be weeping daintily into a lace-trimmed handkerchief, not hurling abuse at my dead husband. But angry was how I felt. I went to close his bank account – there's a lot of admin attached to death, I wasn't prepared for that either – and glowered at the teller, daring her to sympathise. She murmured that New Year's Eve was a rotten day to die: I screamed it was a sight worse for me than him, since all the holidays made sorting his affairs insufferably inconvenient. Poor lady. She filled out the forms in silence after that.

I wanted his stuff gone. Everything he'd ever touched seemed suddenly vile. I gave away everything I could, then drove back and forth to the tip all day long. Birthday cards he'd sent me, our wedding photographs. It all got dumped. The sight of his handwriting made me apoplectic. I wanted him not to be dead chiefly so I could smash his face in.

It was me I was angry at, of course. How could I not have guessed what was on his mind? How could I have left the house that day? Why was my love not enough? Why did death seem preferable to a life with me? What kind of monster was I? I smirked sarcastically at whispered sympathy. I wanted to die too. No, death was too easy. I wanted never to have been born. Instead I welcomed the prospect of decades of suffering, stretching ahead of me, dull and unchanging. It was all I deserved.

It was six months before I could read a book or listen to music. I couldn't bear to be made to think or feel. I worked all I could, and when I went home, I drank until I fell asleep. During our 14-year relationship I'd forgotten how to put air in the tyres, fix the printer. These were his jobs. Everything was my job now. I had to relearn how to change a lightbulb.

I developed a peculiar rash, my skin covered in weird pus-filled lumps, so it hurt when I peed or spoke or swallowed. Thanks a lot God, I thought. Yeah, like I'm not suffering enough. People kept telling me to get therapy: I laughed in their stupid faces. Yeah, much good that had done Adam. I wanted to hurt. I wallowed in my grief like a pig in its own filth. Nothing was allowed to distract me from it.

Eighteen months later I moved house and married a man as unlike Adam as I could find, happy go lucky, sociable, sunny-tempered, not the least bit tortured. It worked. I'm happy now. My son is happy too. Took a while, but we got there. I stopped being angry, then sorrow struck in earnest. I miss Adam every day. I miss his brutal wit, the way he could fix anything, the way he could instantly make me feel better. But mostly I miss the happy innocent self I inhabited before he died.

I'm so sorry he's gone. It feels safe to say it now. I will always blame myself. And I will always miss him.

MELISSA'S STORY – PART II

When being a sexual performance artist and dominatrix keeps you sane throughout any life implosion…

NOTE TO READER

Melissa's side-story (and every woman had a side-story), was such a rare insight into an often hidden world, that we ended up having a second interview about this part of her life, just before Christmas 2020 in a cosy Covent Garden pub. I felt that Melissa's experiences as a sexual performance artist and dominatrix, needed their own individual section in the book, aside from the previous part where Melissa honestly discusses the raw reality of Adam's suicide. Honestly, I was really intrigued by this aspect of Melissa's life, because I didn't really know anything about this at all and was pretty much 'in the dark'. Also because women who earn money through sexual acts and performances are generally portrayed in a pejorative manner in the media with those involved, demeaned as victims. However, Melissa's hugely positive experiences show that it's completely naïve to view this genre of work as always degrading to women, as it can be empowering, lucrative and fulfilling, if women are in control of what they do! Anyway, Melissa's experiences here, show that there is a much more nuanced perspective to be aware of, so without further ado, here goes:

***

This aspect of my life began when I was 19 years old and at Oxford University studying PPE (Politics, Philosophy and Economics), and although I was bright, I was incredibly miserable. Back then, I was a shy Essex girl from a state comp. I was very good at writing but not particularly articulate when it came to holding my own with 90-year-old Professors and I just couldn't get the hang of economics. Sometimes no matter how clever you are, any elite university or any university in fact, is not always the right place for you.

I decided to take a year out during my second year at University because I needed to do something different. I learnt to drive, taught aerobics and dance in Greece and anything could've happened. I chanced upon an advert in the Evening Standard newspaper saying 'Dancers Wanted: £600 per night'. I thought it sounded like the perfect job! I was such an idiot. I thought it was a chorus line job and turned up for an audition wearing a leotard and jazz shoes…

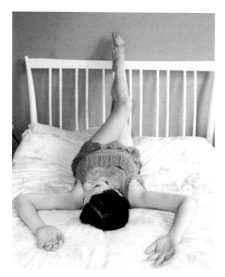

However, what they expected us auditioning girls to do, was to get our tits out on stage and strut about and then walk off. All the other girls were wearing basques, stockings, glitter… I was so out of my depth at this try-out and might as well have been a virgin. However, I also thought, this is brilliant… this is where I want to be!

I really bonded with the other girls auditioning and we were such a mixed bunch. One had started a florist business, one was a backpacker and so on… I had found my tribe. I loved the champagne, the glitter balls, being in Piccadilly London… it was all thrilling. I went to C&A (slightly upmarket former version of Primark), got stockings, 6" heels and re-auditioned. This time, I got the job!

Initially I was dancing at 'The Windmill' in Piccadilly. This iconic club was featured in a film starring Bob Hoskins and Kelly O'Reilly. There was a table dancing bar where clients paid £10 for a table dance in bra and pants, or £20 for a fully nude dance although that took place on stage to prevent any wandering hands. For £30 per hour, men could pay for you to go and talk to them fully dressed and they would ply you with champagne. We would just drink the fizz and chat. I spent hours with famous sportsmen, comedians, politicians, journalists, celebrities, pop stars, actors and so on. One comedian in particular, would tip a lot if I'd had a bad day.

I was there for 4 and a bit months between Sept 1995 and January 1996 but I grew sick of all the talking and competing with other girls. We had a 'House Mother' who was nurturing and who would give us sandwiches, pep talks and do our make-up. There was also our male Manager, who was totally non-lechy but was also very pragmatic so he would check our pubes were trimmed, how we looked in our pants and so on. He wasn't hands-on at all with us physically. Part of the club rules were that we weren't supposed to get clients' numbers or sleep with them.

After a while I became bored though. I hadn't made my targets to give to the club because there were 200 of us girls all circling the men like piranhas: the competition was so great, thus I just decided to walk out. As I walked through Soho, I found myself outside the Soho Strip Theatre and a guy outside called to me: "would you like a job?" I just replied: "yes please" and got it! It was the happiest role! I danced on stage for 8 minutes every hour during my shifts and there was no chatting. I loved it. There were lots of sequins, lace and feathers. I was almost always performing by myself for those 8 minutes and I remember my Policewoman act being very popular. Occasionally there would be a routine with other dancers, so for example a Vampire show. It was art house entertainment with nudity really. It was literally the best 2 years of my life and I enjoyed it so much that I told Oxford University I wasn't going back.

We had a lovely manager, Freddie, who looked after us and was very protective. My working hours were between 11am-9pm and lots of pensioners came in. I had started an English Degree at Birkbeck University so I was reading novels backstage and then every time I got the call to perform my 8 minute routine, I would put my Degree reading aside and dash out on stage. There would be rolled up banknotes under my garter belt. I would be fully dressed and strip, piece by piece, until there was just a feather boa! I had to get creative.

A typical routine would involve 2 songs: after the first song, I would be topless, then I'd take my pants off and ultimately I'd be rolling around nude. I was also always in bare feet: that was my thing. It was fairly dark in the club with the spotlight on the stage. There were rows and rows of red velvet seating with two poles at the front of the stage.

By around 30 years of age, most women stopped stripping and I felt that I should also stop. On the side, I had also started modelling for films and magazines as I have a "nice bottom", so I took part in quite a lot of spanking videos and shoots.

Then the Sunset Strip Club switched management and lovely 'Uncle Freddie' left and it all changed, so I decided to become a stripogram on the London pub circuit instead. I acted out being a policewoman, a nurse and so on. Sometimes I'd be asked to perform my routine in a Care Home on a man who was having his 100th birthday party and on those occasions, I was always worried about triggering a heart attack. I remember performing on Sunday lunchtimes in a popular restaurant chain, with me quietly topless whilst kids ran around… that was pretty bizarre!

Some of the more challenging situations included, on one occasion, having to go into an abattoir which was really difficult for me as I'm a vegan. It was awkward trying to lap dance when the guy had blood on his apron! Another request was to be a 'Health and Safety Executive' and one of the weirdest asks was for me to pretend to be an asylum seeker. This was for a guy from a television programme and he turned out to be a total racist. I didn't take part in those role-plays.

There were so many fascinating psychological aspects to stripping: men are always very calm when they see a pair of tits. Literally, any aggression they might have demonstrated before dissipates when boobs are presented to them. My agent Michelle (who used to strip in her fifties), told me to always use the men's loos and not the ladies' loos, when I was on a pub stripping gig, because women might insult or hurt me, out of sexual jealousy, but men wouldn't.

When I was stripping, I was never self-conscious of my body and the stripping actually saved me from anorexia. Men were always telling me that I was a 'gorgeous goddess' and it was incredibly empowering. No one cared about a belly. We would have a laugh about different breast, vagina, cock sizes and so on. Basically no one gives a toss. Men don't really give a fuck about your body in a frisky moment. So I would just say to other women, just enjoy your body – do what makes you happy and don't forget that there are specialist websites too.

When I had my baby son, I couldn't really strip so I started doing sexy telephone chatline work from home for a site called 'Cheap Chat'. Basically I would dial into the system for 2 hours and then have to talk dirty to different men, i.e. describe a blow job in detail until the caller, came! It cost them 35p per minute. I had all kinds of clients! One man who sounded as though he was in his fifties and was really nice, wanted to pretend he was just a submissive chicken and in our role play, I had to act as a carnivore. He wanted to be my pet, but I was just after him to eat, so I had to make him run around the yard, making chicken noises and then I'd chase him, making all the appropriate sounds, such as: "yum, yum, I'm going to eat you up." I'd have to describe catching him, wringing his neck, plucking his feathers, putting him in the oven with roast potatoes, uncorking the wine. He rang me every day. He would say: "do you feel sorry for me?" and I would reply: "no, you're just a chicken".

I had other men who called and who wanted me to pretend to be a man even though gay chatlines were cheaper, but they couldn't face those. So I had to put on a deep faux-male voice and say I was going to suck their cocks and that it felt so good… I realised that the capacity for human self-deception is incredibly deep. I had to come up with all kinds of props to create the artificial noises that men expected during our calls, i.e., some men liked to hear my boots being zipped up, so I would pull up the zip of a sleeping bag; or other men wanted to hear the sound of a wet pussy, so I would flick my cheek; others wanted to hear me pee, so I had to think of relevant sound effects…

When my baby son James was 2 weeks old and I was around 25 years old, I started doing stripogram work with my childbirth stitches still in (as explained earlier in my chapter about my husband Adam). I never felt unsafe doing this. By this time, I had finished my English Degree. Being a stripogram was such a brilliant and easy thing to do with a baby: £70 (which was quite a lot of money then), for a quick performance and then I'd zoom off to the next. I'd even take James with me sometimes. I would pop James under the bar, give him to a by-standing granny or even incorporate him into the act. If he was crying and my breasts instinctively started to leak milk, I would squirt milk at people! It sounds crazy, but everyone loved it!

But I felt that there was a time limit to doing all of this though. So I started to focus more and more on spanking porn films after seeing an advert in 'The Stage'. I met amazing women making a fortune, doing one-to-ones via a website called ITC (In the Corner). It was then that I decided to become a dominatrix. I got a cane: a little leathery strap and I found items around the house which I could use too on clients: hairbrushes, slippers, a colander, salad tongs, etc.

My first client said I'd got it incredibly wrong: he told me where I was going wrong and what implements I needed. He saw me a few times and gave me lots of tips about props and role plays. Regarding the latter, the most common stories requested were a teacher and a naughty school boy and also a strict aunty. One girl wanted to be my naughty niece who had thrown eggs at a car, so she had to be punished. I soon learnt that dominatrix role plays were basically escape into lalaland.

Clients approach me via email and tweet, so typically, I will receive a message saying: 'I've seen your work, please can I come and see you?' 90-95% of my clients are men but over lockdown, lots of beautiful young women contacted me via twitter too. They wanted to be naughty schoolgirls. Having an increasing number of younger female clients has definitely been a trend that has grown over the last year.

Many clients can't have a punishment that leaves marks because they don't want their partners to see and it's such a cliché but it's absolutely true that lots of my clients are accountants in particular. I also have a lot of lawyers, doctors, surgeons, MPs and actors too, on my books. Often my clients have high-powered/responsible jobs and for once when they come to see me, they don't want to be in charge; it's perfectly understandable that they want to relinquish all that stress and be told what to do for a change! More than 60-70% of my male clients are married and most are in their 50-60s but I see men in their 20s too. They all tend to be creative, intellectual, imaginative - a really nice bunch. The older ones often have teenage children and a bit of disposable income too, so they want to explore their fantasies.

I travel all over the place normally (not in Covid times!) with my dominatrix work, including trips to Mexico, Denmark and America. Also I have my regulars too in Inverness, Norfolk, Bristol, Devon etc! These men pay for my travel, hotel accommodation and of course, my services. I'm renown for hard, accurate caning and I charge £120 per hour, plus expenses. The sessions take place generally either in family homes, hotels and occasionally, in dungeons. If you want to explore this side of your life, go onto the website Fetlife and you'll see that there are venues you can hire and people you can meet. It often becomes an addiction. Twitter is another good platform for finding all things fetish! There's an underground network really, however it has been affected because of the pandemic.

Before I meet someone as a new client, I have lots of email contact first to make sure they're not a nutter or a policeman. If I have any suspicions about that person, I simply won't meet them. When I do arrange an appointment, I have a 'check-in buddy' beforehand, so I'll ring that friend prior to the 'date' and ring them afterwards too, so they know where I'm going and to wait to hear I'm back safely afterwards too. I've never felt in jeopardy though and nothing bad has ever happened to me.

I'll tell you a little bit more about dungeons: With one client, we played for 4 hours in a dungeon (I was paid £480 for this). There's a dungeon, for example, at Gatwick, where you can be suspended from the ceiling; another in Walthamstow has a boxing ring, and so on. There are different areas in dungeons, so you can have medical play with speculums, needles etc. There are also spanking areas, cages, surfaces you can tie people to, sensory deprivation props like hoods… I'm not so great with knots though, I was never a Girl Guide! People from all walks of life get involved in this, there's even a dungeon-owner who's a member of the Chamber of Commerce.

Another role play I get involved in, is 'Spanking School Days' at Whipstock Grange, Portsmouth. These happen every month and adult men pay to attend 'school' for the day and get spanked, slippered, paddled and caned. I normally take part in these 4 x a year. Men get dressed up in 'school uniforms' and have lessons like History, music and so on and then when they're 'naughty', they get punished and attend detentions. All the sex happens in their head. I don't strip off at all, I merely deliver the canings. The most nudity that happens is that the men pull their trousers, pants or boxers down and have their backsides spanked, sometimes their cocks too. The school day includes singing spanking-themed school hymns, having bottles of milk and milk monitors and it has a 1960s' boarding school vibe. There is a similar version in Norway for 'girls'. Women sign up for this but to be eligible, you have to be beautiful, female and young! Most teachers at the Norwegian 'school' are male and I'm the only female that 'teaches'. I teach the girls' music and we sing and then I birch them before we head to the hot tub and sauna!

In terms of seeing clients as a dominatrix, pre-covid I would see 5 x clients a week approximately. I could fit more in too, if I wanted. I generally always see them in a special bedroom at my mother's! My mother has now also become a dom too and she is so popular because men love her age (78!) and authority. She makes more money than me and doesn't even need to advertise!

Being a dominatrix is less about sex and all about play and listening. As soon as I open the door, I'll say: "Right, get here!" There will be scolding, writing lines, gentle caning… sometimes a full hour of caning until a client is bleeding, if that is what they want. I just gauge normally when someone's had enough and I will stop the session. Obviously as mentioned previously, some clients simply cannot have any marks left on their bodies. Caning is my main speciality. My typical look is fifties-style 'Mad Men' secretary.

I'm not into rubber! A popular request is being asked to dress as a Riding Instructor with a whip! I've also been asked to role play being a South American terrorist with an accent… the mind boggles basically… Some men love to have their cocks locked up in a chastity belt and they have to crack the code to get out of it. I so enjoy making someone's sexual fantasy come true. It feels really worthwhile.

So these are some of the things my male clients tell me:

- That sex often stops after having children. It can be a Christmas-only treat, for example.
- Men wish their wives would wear stockings (that's mentioned A LOT!)
- That they wish their wives would beat them.
- That they still love their wives and there is a lot of guilt and conflict in coming to see me. Sometimes they feel heartbroken that they are visiting me and are totally cut-up about it. Some have stopped our sessions early because they have felt tormented about what they are doing.
- Most men are desperate to be faithful, to be someone's king/hero, they don't want to do anything underhand.
- Men often don't feel they can talk to their wives about the sexual aspect of their lives and their fantasies, especially if they want to be a submissive because they don't feel their wives would respect them as husbands if they said they wanted to lick their wives' boots; they feel they'd look idiots, seem hilarious. Any talk regarding sex or desire is shut down and they're told they're "perverts". Lots of men want sex with a strap-on, or to try dressing-up, to be peed on, or to have anal sex too. They basically want to try out lots of different things.
- Some men don't feel any guilt though. Some say that they and their wives never touch eachother and that sex has been non-existent for years or that they have very vanilla sex or can't vocalise what they want, so that's why they can justify seeing me.

I see some clients once a week or a fortnight. Sometimes clients get attached to me: I held the head of one man who sobbed because his identical twins both died of unrelated cancers. Both children were in their early twenties, one had a brain tumour and the other had leukaemia. This man was lost in his own grief and he needed to talk; his wife was lost in her own separate grief and they were unable to share their pain. I have another client who is dying of a lung disorder and likes to be slapped in the face.

These clients don't want normal sex because it would kill the fantasy. Sometimes our discussions are really deep. They feel that there is nothing in their lives for them and they are exploring their inner worlds. Some men will ask: "I hope this isn't too outrageous but can I wear a wig/paint your toenails/kiss your feet?" I won't do racial abuse. I get asked a lot to perform this by men who have suffered it and want to own it. Also there are lots of men who have experienced small penis humiliation and again, want to own it and want me to laugh at their tiny cocks (5" is fine!)

You may be wondering how my son James and my new husband, Mr Todd, feel about my work? Well both are totally fine with my role as a dominatrix. They think it's hilarious and don't have any issues with it. I know some younger people are particularly judgemental about these areas of life and I hear teenage girls being scathing about all porn and feeling somehow that sex is wrong but male domination is not the whole story though. It's not all victimisation.

In terms of whether I find submissive men attractive? Not really, so they wouldn't work for me. I had a fling with a punter about 6 years' ago. It was a little frisson and could've gone further but I stopped it. He made films for me but then it got too serious. He wanted to leave his wife for me, for us to buy a house together and for me to be his dominatrix all the time but that would be exhausting! Sometimes as a woman, you have your period, are tired etc… I've never completely fallen for anyone through my dominatrix work but the men are so keen to worship and admire you. You get to be a terrible egotistical bitch all the time. It does do wonders for your confidence. But in the other side of my work life, I have my 'vanilla' job, where I am a literary editor and there's literally nothing at all sexual about that!

You might have heard of baby role-play? So sometimes I'm asked to do baby role-play work and I hate this! This is when you have to put men in massive nappies (although some women ask for this too). You give them a bottle, a cuddle and I sit and drink a bottle of wine with them. They tend to be big fat men and they just want a mummy! They'll say comments like: "ahh mummy, I love you. Night night mummy". They wear huge babygros with 'I love mummy' on them. When you do this kind of role-play work, you also get a load of Mother's Day presents and cards. If you decide to be a 'mummy' to adult babies, you can buy huge high chairs, give them baths, splash them, get giant rubber ducks etc… watch cartoons together… but I try to avoid this as I'm just not interested in this line of work, but there is good money to be made in it. One lady who does this type of role play, charges £1000 a week. My favourite role play is being a Headmistress but I love hearing all the different ideas that my clients come up with! I had one guy who wanted us to dress in 18th century costumes and he pretended that he had deliberately got his boot stuck in a fencing style and then mysteriously his breeches had also fallen off, so he wanted to be flogged! Which I duly did - with a birch twig! Anything a bit out-there, is amazing!

In terms of my girlfriends knowing about what I do. Yes, they all know and most of them cope with it and ask me for tips. My work has certainly come in handy whenever I've had times when I've been worried about my finances because my punters will always courier £££ to me, because I am their universal panacea. However, I really could've retired at 30 as I've made pots of money through this work.

Diversifying: So I've written a dozen, kinky, spanking-themed short stories as 'Miss Matthews123' on Amazon as I just wanted to be read. I simply follow my imagination and love writing 'out-there shit'! Also I appear on Only Fans as Melissa Todd and sending viewers on that platform, behind-the-scenes clips and one-to-one topless pictures, is a great way to build a new public profile and revenue stream. Relatable videos are popular as clients get to know the real you and I'm now in the top 8%! Over lockdown, I became more resourceful, selling dirty knickers and distanced disciplines via skype, also getting men to write lines to me and send them in the post and finally making customised films on my phone and sending them to my clients.

Finally, I'm just going to add a tiny bit about Max Mosely, the former president of Formula 1. When he had his High Court Privacy case against the News of the World tabloid (which he won), one of my girlfriends was involved in this trial. Max paid all of the girls' legal fees and in turn, the girls turned-up knickerless to support him!

Advice for couples

Talk about what your desires are. Find a way. Watch provocative films/read dirty books together to get you in the mood to discuss this.

If you get shut down though when you are trying to talk about sex and your desires, leave them to it. Maybe you need to explore outside of your relationship? Many men say "if only I could find a sexually liberated woman… " so there are men out there who want this…

Do what you want. Don't be ashamed of anything you need or feel. Explore what you want as you're a long time dead. It just doesn't occur to me to feel constrained about anything now.

Postscript: Summer 2021

I had a fantastic time recently catching up with Melissa and another dominatrix who I'll called Saskia. They talked to me a little more about some of their clients. A man who will pay to spend hours fondling and pampering their feet and then just wanted to come all over their feet! Another man who has a cheese fetish (but it has to be Edam). He wants to be spanked and then to come all over Edam cheese! Another husband who was panicking because his teacher wife had just broken up for the school summer holidays and so would be around him for the next 6 weeks and she was scrutinising him, thus he couldn't go to his regular dungeon and see Saskia… he was asking her how he could possibly cope?

Whilst Saskia normally manages a large city dungeon, she showed me a mini dungeon which she had created in her house, equipped with various items, such as the humbler. Men kneel over and from the back of them, Saskia locks their balls into holes in the humbler. The humbler is then tightened so pressure is applied on the balls and then the humbler can be attached to ankle restraints, whilst simultaneously, kneeling men can be whipped, spanked… you name it…

Needless to say, it was an absolutely fascinating discussion with these two incredible, trailblazing women who are great fun, warm, non-judgemental, erudite, classy and all-knowing! They could teach us all a thing or two about sex, love and life from everything they've heard and experienced thus far…

CHARLOTTE'S STORY

When your charismatic Composer husband is constantly unfaithful…

Blinded with tears, I struggle with my house-keys, working them free from my key-ring. I place them tenderly in the hands of the man I love: his beautiful hands, the graceful, expressive hands I'd fallen in love with years earlier when I'd first watched him conducting the orchestra.

"I don't think you are hearing me" I say: "I am leaving you, Hugo my darling. This time you've gone too far."

There's no anger in my voice, just desolation, the bleak darkness of a grief so soul-shattering, it feels as if it's not me speaking, but someone else from far away.

I put on my coat which was a gift from him. It's a stylish designer coat with a glorious dramatic sweep. I step out of our beautiful home: a house filled with years of memories from our musical life together, into the bitter February cold and I step out of his life.

A chapter in my life closes, and I know in my heart that I will never see him again. Taking a deep breath, I get into my car and begin driving west.

Years earlier, I'd bought a house in the West Country, a nurturing little cottage where I could work undisturbed on my own creative projects. Hugo was intense, a charismatic man twenty years my senior. Life revolved around his brilliance, his talent, his mercurial genius. I needed respite from living in his vortex of chaos, a place to rejuvenate with simple food, long country walks and quiet evenings by the fire with a good book.

It was to the cottage I now planned to go but I'll never forget that terrible drive. It took seven hours: twice the normal traveling time. All the while I continuously repeated the mantra: "keep driving west…keep driving west." I had to stop every few miles, overcome with bouts of crying, unable to drive. After a hundred miles, I drove all the way round a roundabout and headed back east. I told myself that even sharing Hugo with his mistress was better than not having him at all. I imagined throwing myself back into his arms and declaring that I could not live without him, that it was me who was in the wrong. It was me who was being insensitive to his need for intensity. How selfish of me to expect fidelity from a man of such towering ability! Such men should never have to conform to normal expectations. His music was enough; just to live in the presence of his music was more rewarding than any other relationship could possibly be. I would compromise, I would accept whatever crumbs he threw my way. Such were my racing thoughts! Such was my nonsensical reasoning!

But thankfully the mantra - "keep driving west… keep driving west" - worked its power, and for all the struggle and blackness within me, I stopped driving east: I turned back round: I resumed driving west.

Finally, after dark, I arrived at the cottage. For three weeks I sat paralyzed on the stairs, numb with shock, sustained by oatcakes and endless cups of tea. The sense of betrayal bludgeoned my heart to pulp. I could not imagine how I could continue living without Hugo. Everything I knew had blown away. I wanted to chase after the shattered fragments of our love. As news of our separation spread, kind friends sent flowers, chocolates, cards - over a hundred messages of support. Every thoughtful act was precious and healing.

And yet, to my surprise, despite all the pain, a fierce wild flame of unquenchable joy burned deep within me. I had stayed true to myself. Twelve years earlier, I had abandoned cherished values for Hugo. Now I had found the courage to return to the deep principles in my very core.

There were many wobbles during those desperate early weeks, but I remembered Jane Eyre's words to Mr Rochester from Charlotte Brontë's famous novel. Jane is passionately in love but had resolved to leave Rochester because he has lied to her. Her profound and spirited declaration of female self-determination has inspired generations of women. I printed out the words and stuck it on my kitchen wall to help me remain resolute. And there it stayed for the next three years.

But let me go back to the beginning:

As a child and teenager, music was my great love. I practiced my cello for hours, nourished by its rich sonorities, repeating difficult passages over and over until they entered the very marrow of my bones. Music practice felt like entering a magical walled garden, a safe place where no pain could ever intrude, a sunlit garden which no storm could ever disturb. I discovered practice to be the purest of joys: it requires such intense concentration that there is no room for any thoughts of past or future; it exists only in the present; there is just the visceral, primal pleasure of the music itself.

Normal teenage activities passed me by. I was far too absorbed in my music. I never went to discos, got drunk or had bad boyfriends and thus I entered womanhood with shocking naivete. In my early twenties, unfledged and inexperienced, I optimistically married my first boyfriend in a fairy tale wedding with a horse-drawn carriage. I wore a wildly gorgeous silk dress with a long train and an antique lace veil. There were lots of bridesmaids, a centuries-old country church, guests in grand hats, and white lilies everywhere. I was young and eager to please, with no concept of sensible boundaries. Sadly, my new husband proved controlling and cruel. He refused to find work. After four years and two pregnancies, I was exhausted. Most of my once-luxuriant hair had fallen out, my skin was grey, and I was seriously underweight, a pale skeletal shadow of that smiling and sparkling midsummer bride of just a few years earlier. It never crossed my mind to leave the marriage and even if I'd had the courage to do so, my husband never let me out of his sight.

Finally, a day came when he had to attend a family funeral involving an overnight stay. It was the first time we'd been apart in four years. Two friends - a couple with a deep and happy marriage themselves - turned up out of the blue.

"Everyone thinks they shouldn't interfere in a marriage," they declared, "but it's about time someone interfered with yours."

Within a few focused minutes, they speedily bundled me and my babies into their car, filled a bin liner full of nappies and teddies and took me back with them to their big, old, relaxed country house. This kind, open-hearted couple put me to bed in a spacious quiet room, added my children to their own large and happy Bohemian brood, and left me to sleep and sleep.

I now had two adorable healthy sons, a convenient quantity of nappies and a heavy burden of serious debt.

Nevertheless I set to with gusto, determined to support my little family single-handed entirely from my heart, my imagination and my music. I rented a tiny house, and after walking the boys to school in the morning, I rushed home and practiced all day amidst the piles of lego, leaving the breakfast crumbs still scattered on the table. I earned a living by playing gigs of all sorts: weddings, concerts, corporate events and the like. It was hard work, but I loved it. My hair grew back; my health and energy returned. Life blossomed. My growing sons enjoyed a magical childhood with camp fires in the woods and long bedtime stories with hot chocolate and cuddles. Our family motto became "Open House; Open Heart" - the neighbourhood children would come to play and I often found myself cooking for ten or more.

Little by little, I managed to clear the debts and buy a house: the very same cottage which was later to become my sanctuary. What a joyful day it was when I received the keys to my own home. Hurrah! At last I was independent. No landlord held my rice-bowl. The boys were granted music scholarships to good schools. Life was on the up, full of fun and friendships. I felt deep gratitude for my good fortune.

Little did I know that a big change was hurtling towards me, a roller-coaster ride which would consume me for the next twelve years. Coincidentally it began - as it was to end - on a cold February day.

I was now in my early thirties, and on this fateful day I was booked to present a recital in a historic house. After the performance, an older gentleman with twinkling eyes introduced himself: Hugo was well-known in his field, and I was flattered by his compliments. I remember how he made poetic and expressive gestures with his hands as he spoke.

The following week, I received a letter written in a beautiful flowing hand. It was from Hugo inviting me to take part in a recording. He visited me in the cottage to discuss the project, bringing an expensive bottle of champagne, and regaling me with endless entertaining anecdotes about his life in music and his success as an art collector. The recording went well, and Hugo subsequently took me to a concert he was conducting in London. That was when I fell in love with his hands; I adored the way he sculpted the sound of the orchestra with exquisite sensitivity, how he joked with the musicians, displaying exuberant wit and a lively sense of fun.

But he was twenty years my senior, sophisticated, urbane and married! I was a young single mother, somehow managing to earn a living as a musician, but still struggling with shaky self-esteem, doubts about my own abilities, and an oversensitive nature. The thought of any romantic entanglement never crossed my mind.

Nevertheless, this brilliant man began to pursue me with relentless focus, big romantic gestures, enchanting love letters and expensive gifts. Imperceptibly, I fell under his spell. I had never met anyone like him. He had an encyclopedic knowledge of music and art history and continuously affirmed me as a musician. I drank up his praise like nectar.

He arranged a rehearsal in his home but when I arrived, his wife was away. I was bowled over by his atmospheric Tudor manor house, gazing wide-eyed at all the fascinating treasures he had amassed around him. He served me champagne in genuine seventeenth century Venetian glass goblets and I vividly recall the hypnotic beauty of candlelight reflecting in shimmering antique glass. He wooed me with intoxicating promises; he said he wanted to create a cocoon of comfort and beauty wherein I could focus on my creativity and my children, without having to work so hard. He declared that if I would only consent to be his muse, he would be rewarded beyond his happiest dreams. Looking back, to me now, I'm reminded of Hansel and Gretel in the old fairytale: wandering lost and hungry in the dark woods, the little brother and sister stumble across a gingerbread house built out of irresistible sweet things. As they bite into its pleasures, they are unaware of its deadly occupant, the hungry witch waiting to devour them.

When I expressed concern about Hugo's wife, he told me that his marriage had been over for years and he was actually in the middle of divorcing her. I believed him. As he sensed my resolve weakening, his pursuit intensified. He began sending love letters and red roses every single day. Thus it was that seven months after meeting him, I finally consented to go away with him to a country hotel. He assured me that if I didn't feel ready, we could sleep separately; he just wanted to be able to spend time in my company. When we arrived, we were shown to the hotel's finest suite which he had arranged to be filled with flowers. A dozen or more presents were piled on a table, their brightly coloured wrappings reflecting the flames of a roaring log fire. Hugo was so seductive and romantic that I abandoned all my cherished principles and that night we became lovers.

Three weeks later, he left his wife and sold his house, seemingly without a backward glance. One year later, we were living together in an elegant town house by the sea filled with art treasures. Hugo supported my own creative endeavors, and in countless practical ways he helped me juggle the responsibilities of a performing career with being a parent. My own music was flourishing and my confidence was growing. He encouraged me to compose, to experiment with new kinds of music, and to take on bigger challenges. He never stopped his big romantic gestures, and his dazzling wit and humour frequently left me helpless with laughter. He changed my style of dress, buying me sumptuous clothes and sophisticated scent. Time passed. My sons grew up and went off to university. Life was polished, exciting, and passionate.

And yet...and yet...it was also exhausting. Behind his public facade, Hugo had unsettling mood swings. He could be vitriolic about other people. He would be appallingly rude to waiters and doormen, yet wildly flirtatious with waitresses and female receptionists. He would vacillate wildly between thinking he was virtually a god, and tearfully declaring himself to be a worthless waste of space. It tore my heart to see him so deflated and vulnerable, and gradually over the years more and more of my energy was consumed in a desire to heal and protect him. His finances were completely chaotic as a consequence of his irresponsibility at handling money. Hugo had a compulsive need for arousal, getting bored easily, and requiring constant novelty.

And there was yet another problem. Hugo frequently became obsessed with young female musicians. He craved admiration from talented girls. They fed his ego. I never questioned these flirtations: telling myself they were harmless, good for him, and helped to keep him buoyant. He assured me that I was: "Muse Numero Uno" - his first and finest muse, his best beloved. The other girls were simply his secondary muses. We laughed about it, and I felt confident in his love, choosing to befriend these invariably delightful young women, even performing recitals with them. Some evenings when he was sitting in moody silence, and all my efforts to cheer him up were useless, I would text one of his so-called muses, and ask her to send Hugo an uplifting flirty message to try and shift him out of his misery. I did not realize how my accepting behaviour was feeding him, how I was making excuses for him, how his unquenchable thirst for attention was beginning to control my life. I was totally blind.

And then Cindy barged into our lives and finally shattered my rose-tinted spectacles. It was August. I had some work in the West Country and was staying in the cottage, catching up with friends, and enjoying long solitary walks. Each evening, I phoned Hugo to idly chat about our respective days.

"I had a surprise visitor today," he mentioned casually during one of these conversations: "a Canadian singer knocked on my door out of the blue. It was so nice. She's called Cindy and she's a fan of mine. I invited her in for tea."

"Oh that sounds fun." I said, without giving it a second thought.

When I returned home a few days later, Hugo was obsessively playing a CD of a woman singing to synthesized backing tracks, a sort of karaoke. I was surprised: the vocalist couldn't really sing in tune and Hugo had always despised the sound of electronically generated music.

"Who is this singing?" I asked.

"It's Cindy - isn't she wonderful!" he replied, his eyes shining with excitement.

I felt a sudden stab in my heart. This was different from his usual flirtation with a talented new muse. He had always been so discerning - the other girls were accomplished professional musicians. How on earth could he think this sophomoric warbling was 'wonderful'? This was the first time he'd lost his judgment and it exposed him. I knew instantly that Cindy was the proverbial 'other woman'. Whoever she was, she had got under his skin as well as under his bed covers.

Six months of lies and denials followed before he finally admitted that he was having a serious affair. He blurted it out and I actually fainted with the shock. Cindy had returned to Canada to end her own marriage. Worse still, the two of them had decided she would come back to England and live in our spare room as his mistress. Hugo was astonished when I ridiculed the idea. Surely, he couldn't be serious? This was like the 'mad wife in the attic' scenario of some Victorian melodrama!

"But why can't you be like Cindy?" he pouted: "She's so accepting and so forgiving. She's prepared to go and sleep on a friend's floor whenever I want to make love to you instead of her." Yes, these really were his exact words, forever etched into my brain. Even now, it still hurts to remember them. Hugo wanted to keep both relationships. Nevertheless, he reassured me I was still, and would always be, "Muse Numero Uno".

There was another shock to come and this final bombshell was my implosion moment, shattering my illusion that Hugo was a wonderful person. Cindy had three children whom she was planning to abandon in Canada. They were just three, five and six years' old. I could no longer deny the soul-crushing truth - I had chosen to spend my life with a man so selfish and self-absorbed that he could disregard the atrocity of three children losing their mother, merely to satisfy his lust. It was a bitter pill to swallow.

I had believed that being a muse was wondrously romantic, but now the very term sickened me. The words of a wise friend struck home: a muse is a decorative toy, a mere plaything in a position of passivity; she is not a woman in her own right; she must never grow old, or change shape, or lose her beauty. The fate of the muse is always to be discarded.

There was nothing more to be said. I gave him my set of house-keys, I kissed him goodbye. He stood crying in the doorway, unable to believe that I was capable of leaving him. I wrenched myself free. I began driving west.

Thirteen cold Februaries have come and gone since that day of reckoning. The most crushing aftereffect was losing my love of music. My walled garden, my safe sanctuary, was desecrated. When I sat down to try and practice, I was racked with excruciating physical pain like a dagger turning in my stomach. Formerly, I had practiced for hours, but now I had to force myself to sit with the cello for a mere five turbulent minutes a day. Afterwards I would curl up in agony on the floor unable to move, or I'd be hunched over the lavatory, physically sick, vomiting out my distress.

Plunged into despair, I visited my old cello professor in Oxford and wept bitterly as I told him my story. This venerable old gay gentleman listened with deep compassion, and declared Hugo to be a Svengali.[2] It was true: over the years, my love of music had become insidiously bound up with my love for Hugo. I was incapable of extricating one from the other.

The journey back to normality was a slow painful trudge. Healing is never a straight line but a crazy zig-zag with many backward steps. In the first throes of shock, I blamed Cindy, declaring her a manipulative Jezebel. Later, as my anger faded, and my thinking clarified, I realized that she too must have had her own vulnerabilities and pain, for surely no healthy young woman in her 30s would abandon her children on the other side of the world to live with an old age pensioner, however talented he may be?

I'd loved a man who'd never seen the real me, but rather was addicted to the concept of romantic love itself, a man who craved the thrill of infatuation, who demonstrated at the outset of our relationship that he could switch partners without a qualm. His wife, whom I supplanted, and Cindy who in turn supplanted me, were mere projections of his own dramatic fantasies. Hugo - like so many others - used affairs as an antidepressant instead of taking the courageous and difficult path of seeking professional help. It is an old humdrum story occurring across history and cultures. In time, I found that changing my own narrative about the affair helped me find compassion for both Cindy and Hugo.

As for self-compassion, that remains a work in progress. I still feel ashamed and guilty that I was myself 'the other woman' at one vulnerable stage in my life. It took the best part of a decade to disentangle the twisted knot of emotions surrounding the cello and find genuine joy in music-making again.

---

2   Svengali is a character in George du Maurier's 1894 novel *Trilby*, a master musician and hypnotist who seduces and dominates his naïve young protégée to her detriment.

WHAT HAVE YOUR EXPERIENCES TAUGHT YOU?

What have I learned from all of this? No one can tell us how to grieve, for each of us must find our own path. When we have been deeply hurt we must tell our stories over and over again before they start to lose their icy grip on our hearts. I confess I was a sorry bore to my long-suffering friends as I struggled to make sense of it all. Grieving takes a long time, and this has made me more mindful of anyone facing their own turbulent journey afresh. Messages of support and offers of help are small things that mean a lot to a suffering soul.

I've also learned that the art of forgiveness is an essential skill to develop throughout our lives. Forgiveness is hard, but somehow we must find a way to let go and move on with the rest of our lives. The old axiom is worth remembering: resentment is like drinking poison and waiting for the other person to die.

WHAT ADVICE WOULD YOU GIVE TO OTHER WOMEN IN A SIMILAR SITUATION?

To other women, I would advise this: if love feels intense, dramatic, hungry, then run for the hills. Do not look back. Beware the silver-tongued charmer. No one who loves you would expect you to abandon your values. Do not be tempted by his poisoned sweets. His drive towards excitement can mask underlying depression. Choose character over charisma. Find a regular decent guy with friends and a job, a man who gets on well with his family and treats others with respect, regardless of their station in life.

And when you stumble, as we all do from time to time, don't try to tough it out alone: please ask for help. It's instinctive to want to withdraw like a wounded animal, but learning to ask for help is an essential ingredient in your recovery.

Connect with your core self, build sturdy confidence and inner strength. Trust your intuition.

Send cards to others who are suffering. Acts of kindness carry healing magic for both giver and receiver.

I believe in the great regenerative force of nature - the vitality that forces mushrooms to spring up overnight, that ripens strawberries, that opens snowdrops in February. This is the unstoppable power that triggers the greening of the land in Spring as the leaves unfurl, the innate power that pushes a tiny acorn to become a mighty oak tree. This unquenchable Life Force flows through us too. It heals. We can trust it.

We can learn to live with the aftermath of heart-wrenching loss. Like the phoenix, we emerge from grief's dark journey energised and strengthened. We discover that the final gift of grief is Grace.

WHERE ARE YOU NOW? WHAT ARE YOUR PLANS FOR THE FUTURE?

On the whole, I am sure-footed now; I am buoyed up by friends, community, and my love of nature. I feel ready to embark on a new relationship, confident that I won't repeat my youthful mistakes, yet equally content to remain single, enjoying the benefits of autonomy.

OLIVIA'S STORY

When two lives end during lockdown 1: one is weeks' old whilst the other is decades old and both have a massive impact upon you...

Seb and I met when we were at school together: he was 15 and I was 16 and we were in the same friendship group. We got on so well that it was natural for us to progress things and go out together, which we did for 3½ years. Those years equate to such a key age and you go through such a lot at that time: so many changes and experiences with your family, at school, friends, first jobs, learning to drive etc, and you know everything about eachother when you're young. It's almost inevitable with all those stages to work through, that as a couple, you will split up and we did, even though I had originally been convinced that we would be together forever because we had such an amazing connection.

When we first went our separate ways, it was quite bitter between us as our relationship had become pretty toxic towards the end. Seb would say really nasty things to me but I could equally fight back verbally and I did. We had been eachothers' go-to for everything and although the break was mutually agreed, it was still very sour. We both put it off and off for ages but when we finally called it a day, that was it - for a long time. We just didn't speak for 18 months.

We had all this time apart and we absolutely needed this to happen, to discover that we could function without each other. I'd spent 3 years with this guy and now I needed to find myself. I went off to University in Reading and Seb went off and did his own stuff too. Therefore, we were basically off-radar for a year and I heard from my brother that Seb was shagging around. I had mixed emotions about this: it was shit to hear, but what I expected and I went on to meet my next boyfriend. Seb actually was in Reading too for a time working and living with relatives, so I was always aware that I might bump into him and wondered how he would react, but we never ran into each other.

It had been an unspoken thing between us that Seb and I just wouldn't contact each other. I was of the opinion that he hated me and was full of disdain for me. I found that thought really hard to cope with, because he was my first love and as I had no way of knowing what he was thinking, I imagined the absolute worst and it was so hard not seeing him or being able to talk to him after we split up.

I met my second boyfriend, John, in Bristol a couple of months after splitting from Seb and we became attached quite quickly. It was a bit of a summer thing but then it escalated. John and I were together for 1½ years and overall it was a happy relationship but then I lost interest towards the end and I just thought of

73

Seb all the time. We had always been completely drawn to each other. I know it sounds a cliché but we had a really deep connection. I think I was slightly in denial about being over him.

Anyway, after over a year of not talking to each other, my mum asked me if I could get my dad's bike back from Seb and this meant that I had to ring him up. I called and Seb didn't answer. I was bricking it. But then he rang me back! I answered the phone… he was so happy. You know when you can hear someone smiling in their voice? I just could! We started laughing on the phone and spent over an hour catching up. We were instantly back to being the best of friends again and it was as though no time at all had passed. It was such a relief to be on talking terms and Seb and I started messaging each other but innocently.

My boyfriend John was at Uni in Durham and I was in Reading, so I wasn't actually seeing John very often and that physical distance put a huge strain on our relationship. I was honest with John though and told him that I'd rekindled my friendship with Seb. I started to see Seb but I didn't tell John this because I knew it would seem wrong, but nothing dodgy happened between Seb and I. Although Seb would make comments that were slightly sexually charged, we didn't act upon them.

When Seb and I went out together the first time around, he was the centre of my universe. I wasn't mature enough then to know that it didn't have to be so tight but having time apart, had allowed us to become more independent. John meanwhile, found it difficult that I wasn't as needy with him as he wanted the whole 'centre of the universe' thing in a relationship. I remember talking to my housemate asking: "how do I end it with John?" But I couldn't be rushed, I had to make the right decision. John's mum was quite overbearing with him at this point too.

Anyway, because Seb and I had been talking for a few months at this point, I didn't want to see John – it didn't feel right. So initially I told John that I had too much Uni work to do and then when I needed a back-up reason, I added that I couldn't afford to get the train up to see him but he said I'll pay for you. So I ended up going to stay with John but I didn't have the same sexual energy with him and it had never been the same as it was with Seb. I managed to get out of sleeping with John for the length of my stay, by saying that I hadn't had a wax and so I didn't feel comfortable doing anything sexually. I was back in love with Seb and John sensed that things were wrong between us.

John face-timed me a week later and said: "are you ok?" and I replied: "no I'm not happy". The conversation wasn't flowing any more. We had nothing to talk to each other about. I remember just saying: "Can you mute yourself?" when he would face-time me. At the time, I hated the thought of making him feel bad but our relationship had died.

At this point, Seb wasn't at the forefront of my mind but rather it was just really comforting to have him as a supportive friend again and we saw each other with fresher, older eyes. John and I had finally broken up and John accepted it without any issues as he's a logical guy. He would occasionally call to check in on me but not in a controlling or creepy way. He was only being kind. I felt excited to be single but I wasn't thinking about boys. I wanted to feel really liberated to be able to make any decisions I liked, but simultaneously, I'm quite self conscious too so I couldn't just sleep with anyone. I planned to be a free agent with all of my girlfriends at Uni in Reading... and then Coronavirus arrived!

I checked in with my mum and gran to keep tabs with what was going on with them and the world! The night that lockdown was announced, I said to my mum that she needed to collect our 92-year-old granny from Cumbria and take her down to our family home in the South West. Gran lived in a small village and had no intention of staying inside during lockdown, saying: "you can't keep me inside. If I want to go out, I will!"

So mum collected granny from Cumbria and brought her home to the South West and the very next day, my saint-like mum undertook another epic drive to come and collect me from Reading and bring me back home to the South West too. This put an abrupt end to my single days, especially because Seb was back in the South West near me too. I'd had a long dry spell without any sexual desire at all: my libido was rubbish... but then on my return, I was rampant! I was raring to go and there was no getting away from it!!!

Seb and I had had a weird vibe between us for a long time. I met up with Seb and his friend and they were both hammered and Seb drunkenly said to me: "if you ever fancy a shag... " But what we had rebuilt in terms of a friendship was delicate and I didn't want to jeopardise this. However, my cravings got the better of me. I got myself all prepped and I went around to Seb's place whilst his mum was at work, on the premise of just hanging out... I thought he was going to pussy out, so I brazenly took the initiative and said: "are we just going to do this or not?" and afterwards it felt so right. It was pretty great!

And it happened again. Talk about feeding the beast. Stoking the fire.

Seb and I talked a lot and said how are we going to do this again over lockdown? But we'd sneak off to a field and we didn't change the location and laughed at the fact that people would start clocking us, because this added to the excitement. This happened from the beginning of the first March lockdown to early June and we said: "what's actually happening here, as it can't be anything more serious than it is" because I'd be going back to Uni and Seb didn't want to stay back in the South West. We just told each other, it can't be anything more than this because we'll hold each other back and we don't want to get hurt.

But then serendipity kicked-in because my house-plans for my final year of Uni, fell through and I was left in limbo without having anywhere to live, so we both jokingly said why didn't we move in together in Reading. I was more reticent though, because I didn't what to ruin what we had and I was anxious that living together would put unnecessary pressure on something which was already quite fragile, so we put this idea on the backburner.

Seb had been working as a bricklayer throughout lockdown and I was waitressing 50+ hours a week from July onwards. Simultaneously, my granny was poorly. Seb and I were still meeting up and Seb told his gran about us and that we might possibly move in together in Reading. It was an awkward topic to broach as Seb and I thought there might be judgement that we were going back out with each other, let alone thinking of moving in together. We came clean to our families but they were actually quite pleased for us and it affirmed that living together in Reading wasn't the worst idea! So Seb and I started looking for a place together...

Ironically whilst we were so happy together, we'd barely been seeing each other or sleeping together because of our jobs. On the rare times we had sex, we didn't use protection. I have a good female friend and we tracked out periods with an app and found they synced up – pissy shit! This girlfriend and I hadn't seen each other for a while and when we met up, my friend said: "this period's the worst" and I happened to mention that mine hadn't even started. Nothing crossed my mind as to why it hadn't started.

Five days later, my friend asked me if my period had arrived. When I said it still hadn't, she said I should buy a pregnancy test and bring it to her place and take it there. I was thinking 'leave me alone' because I was exhausted from all the waitressing I was doing but I did buy a test and headed over to hers.

I'd just gone to the loo before I went to see my friend and I peed on the stick in front of her, managing to push out a tiny bit! There wasn't any line. I was triumphant! "I fucking told you I'm not pregnant", I said. She replied that I hadn't peed on it for long enough, but I replied: "I did and I'm not". However there were 2 pregnancy tests in the pack so she said I should do another one. I went to work, returned home late and I was shattered so I didn't do one then. The next day I had to drop Seb to work and I was running late, so I did a quick wee on the other pregnancy test at my parents' house with Seb staying over. I put the lid on and a blue line appeared. I was like: "Oh my fucking God!" Seb said: "what's wrong?" He was shocked. I grinned. For some reason I had always thought I wouldn't be able to get pregnant but now I had.

I had to go to work sitting on all of this information. My dad's job involved night-shifts and I wanted to tell both of my parents at the same time: sit them down at the table and divulge. I took a digital pregnancy test at work and it told me the exact date and that I was 3 and a half weeks' pregnant. It confirmed that it was all real but it did help to have a timeline.

I got home and my mum was standing by the front door as I arrived. I just couldn't help myself! I had to tell her. I said: "I think I'm pregnant," and she said: "why?" and I said: "I took a test and it says I'm pregnant," and my mum said: "well in that case, you *are* pregnant". Later she told me that she'd felt she wanted to say: "I'd rather you'd crashed your car", because she knew that I was going to have a really difficult decision to make.

My brother overheard and said: "What?… Are you stupid? How fucking stupid are you?" Later I told my dad and he said: "Right… what do you want to do?" Mum had said the same earlier and I'd replied: "I have to get rid of it".

When I'd had previous chats with my girlfriends and we'd discussed what we would do if we got pregnant, I'd always said that there was so much I wanted to do in life and that having kids would stop that. Now I tried to implement staying this focused in my thinking; I tried not to be swayed by my emotions.

I rang up an advice line and I was put through to several different hospitals. A district hospital in the South West turned out to be the one I would attend for the termination. I had to have a scan first because I'd mostly been using contraception and the foetus had to be dated. I couldn't be scanned until it was 6 weeks' old because otherwise the scan wouldn't pick up the baby. This was confirmed via video chat with an advisor there.

I had already started to notice changes in my body as it was adapting to my pregnancy: my boobs were tender and I was really shattered. I just kept thinking: I'm growing something. One day, I remember being so distressed with the pressure of it all. I hated that I was having to make this decision and it was so hard. It sounds awful as I know so many women are really desperate for a baby but at that time, I wished I could have a miscarriage so that the decision was taken out of my hands.

Seb was struggling too because his mum gave birth to him when she was pretty young also. He'd told her about my pregnancy and she was great with us both but Seb said: "If my mum had had an abortion, I wouldn't be here". Obviously, I heard this and completely understood his view but I knew that having an abortion was still the right decision for me. Nonetheless, however difficult this was for him too, Seb was fully supportive of me although he had a few moments when he found it hard to be. I worried that after my termination however, he would be resentful and would turn against me. I was anxious that long-term he would struggle with my decision.

Simultaneous to all of this, my beloved gran had recently died! Gran had fallen poorly 2-3 weeks into lockdown 1 and it turned out that she had bowel cancer. Initially, she was only given 10 days to live but she was such a toughie, that she surpassed that. She pushed on for another 5 weeks and had a stent put in. I didn't know I was pregnant when she died but it was weird because it was as though gran breathed new life into me as her life had come to an end. It played with my head; I almost felt granny's still here! Gran and I were super-close and when she died, it was still such a shock as even though her prognosis was dire, I hadn't expected her to go so quickly.

I was offered counselling to help me with regards to making the termination decision, but I view myself as resilient and quite stoic so I got myself through it, but I think I might have counselling for this in the future if I'm stuck milling over the repercussions. It's true that not long after gran died, I was really grappling mentally about the baby.

The abortion was going to be completed in one day. I had to go to the Hospital for the scan and then they were going to give me the pills and pessaries to start the process. I had quite an early appointment at 9.30am and Seb, mum and I set off on the hour's drive to get there. We arrived and went into a special hub in the hospital. We sat for what felt like ages, about 40-50 minutes. Then a receptionist said to me: "I'm not going to lie to you, your appointment isn't on the system," but I insisted they fitted me in, because I had email confirmation of this date and I'd been waiting nearly 3 weeks for this appointment and that waiting time, was stressful. The nurse actually worked out that I must now be 7.5 weeks pregnant and I had a brief time window to have the termination because of returning to Uni, hundreds of miles away. She said: "we can fit you in at 12.30pm, but you'll have to go to the maternity ward". I went to that ward eventually and I had to walk past all these pregnant women and newborn babies. It was shit.

I sat in the waiting room for another 40 minutes. Then the process started and I was scanned. There were 2 sonographers and they said: "you don't have to make the decision [to terminate the baby] now", but I knew I had to, because I couldn't go on like this. I was trying to stay detached. They read out the measurements and said: "do you want to see?" I said no. The machine printed out a scan photo anyway and one of the sonographer's said: "I'm sorry, that wasn't meant to happen". It was a headfuck as I saw the picture of my little bean-like baby. I walked back to the Hub and as I headed there, I couldn't help but read the details I'd been given to take with me about the baby: my eyes rested on: 'heartbeat found present'. I think seeing the scan picture and reading about the heartbeat really did something to me and that for a moment, the hospital 'dropped the ball' of care towards me slightly.

Back at the Hub, I asked if they could insert a contraceptive implant into me so that I wouldn't have to go through this again and they did. The type of abortion I was about to have, was where you have a hormone blocker and also pessaries to induce miscarriage. A nurse said: "this is going to hurt so I'm going to give you Cocodamol for the pain". I was a bit anxious as I'd been told the process would just be like a heavy period. A girlfriend who'd also had a termination, said that it was like an: "unholy amount of pain", but all the leaflets downplay this, so I thought that my girlfriend was being melodramatic. I was sent home from the hospital holding a pill in my hand to do this job. It was one of those moments where you think this is a massive decision to make. Do I really want to do it? It was 2pm when I took the pill to begin everything…

Seb was so thoughtful and kind. He bought us lots of sweets so we could have a movie night whilst the whole thing was taking place at home. I had loads of fucking big lady nappies! I didn't quite know what to expect. We were watching a film and I had a twinge of period cramps and I remember thinking 'this isn't too bad'. I projectile-vomited into a bowl and was sick a bit more later. My mum ran me a bath, which helped and I sat in it and then all of a sudden, I felt really light-headed and faint and my hands tingled. I started vomiting. And the pain started and it was unlike anything I'd ever experienced before. It was so animal-like, I couldn't talk. All I wanted to do was let out a moan. I stayed in the foetal position for 3 hours. The pain was borderline unbearable but I couldn't take any more painkillers than I already had. I laid on the cold floor and Seb laid with me. It was a cycle of sleep, pain, sleep, pain. I passed out and that was definitely the best thing.

It was the worst experience I have ever had in my life and not what I expected at all. It's a topic that is shut-down and just not talked about. Women know so little about what they will go through. You're just told if you don't want a baby, you can have an abortion, but it's not as straightforward as just taking a pill and not being pregnant any more. Most people I've talked to, have been shocked when I've told them how it actually was.

My mum was shocked at just how visceral it all was. It's down-played and you're just not told what the reality is. I bled for a month afterwards with big clots initially too, to such an extent that I felt I could identify what they were. Apparently you can bleed for up to 8 weeks afterwards. The really intense pain lasted for 3-4 hours and then it was bleeding and clotting, which later became like a heavy period, with strong pains for a few days afterwards. Overall, I just found the process really traumatic.

The Hospital rang up a few days later, because basically you are given a test to do 3 days after you have taken the abortion pill, to let you know you're not pregnant any more, and the hospital call you to check the outcome. Part of me was thinking: What if I am still pregnant? I had a tiny bit of hope. I wanted to believe I still might be pregnant. But the test confirmed that I no longer was. However, I found myself downloading a pregnancy app to see how far on I would be now if I had kept the baby.

I think about it such a lot as having a baby is something I've always wanted and somehow I thought that it would be harder for me. I have no regrets though, it was the right decision. Although Seb was slightly sad about it all, he was great and I feel I can talk to him about it and also I can talk to my mum too. It weighs heavily on my mind though as I work out how many weeks old the baby would be. My rational brain talks to my emotional brain and tells me no regrets. I always try to convince and remind myself that it was the right thing to do. When it's the baby's due date, I will do something positive, even if it's as simple as lighting a candle as I feel that Seb and I need to mark that date. It will give us some acceptance and closure I think. That's the point we're at.

When I was pregnant and had to wait nearly 3 weeks to have the scan, I didn't drink or smoke etc, because I felt I had to honour the baby and wanted to respect it despite what I knew I had to do. It was such a strange juxtaposition and I know it's different for all women because I had another friend who accidentally got pregnant through a one-night-stand and she went completely mental, partying like mad, to try to get rid of it. She didn't feel the need to protect it as I did. When she had her abortion, it was totally different for her, maybe because she didn't have any emotional connection with the father, whereas my baby was with my partner, so it felt very different.

WHAT HAVE YOUR EXPERIENCES TAUGHT YOU?

Be careful. I wouldn't wish this experience on anyone. It's much bigger than just taking a pill. The psychological aspect is huge. If you can avoid putting yourself in that situation in the first place, so much the better. I have felt an immense sense of guilt. It's okay to put yourself first. I will always think about it. Whatever decision is made, it's made and must be respected, but give yourself permission to think about it. It's a coping mechanism. It's natural to think about what could have been.

I'm so grateful to my parents and Seb. Seb has never once made me feel bad about what happened because he just accepts that ultimately the onus was on me as a woman.

WHAT ADVICE WOULD YOU GIVE TO OTHER WOMEN IN A SIMILAR SITUATION?

Find someone to talk to about it. Being able to offload is such a huge, huge thing. Being able to verbalise, helps so much.

For others reading this who aren't the ones going through the termination: the most insensitive thing you can say would be to give a harsh judgement of what a woman's gone through when she's had an abortion. It would feel hugely isolating. Making someone feel ostracised in a situation where there are lots of unknowns and they feel scared, is cruel.

Where are you now? What are your plans for the future?

So I'll be 22 shortly and Seb will be 21. We've gone through a whole lot of trauma together but it's proven how tight we are as a couple and that there's such a lovely side to him. What happened with losing my gran and having this stressful abortion has been really tough. For example, during the last Christmas, I found it a bit overwhelming seeing gran's things in my family home but not having her with us any more and I also thought about the baby a lot. Everything caught up with me and I felt a bit low. I didn't talk to my mum about it because gran was her mum, so my mum was grieving the loss of her own mother and I didn't want to add my grief to her own. It was quite an emotional time, but having a vision of where I'm going in life, and having distractions, has really helped! Seb and I are living together in Reading now and we're really happy! We've signed our lease for another year. Career-wise, I'm planning to join the Met Police's Graduate Scheme and I do feel very excited about everything!

I know that when the time is right to have kids with Seb, it'll happen and we'll embrace it and in the meantime, I made the right decision, however physically, mentally and emotionally, difficult.

LIZZIE'S STORY

Legacy and shame from your mother's suicide when you're a child...

NOTE TO READER

For Lizzie to be able to tell her story, we agreed to conduct her interview very much in a question and answer format via email, because this was the method that worked best for her and as it was the first time Lizzie had felt able to share this experience, it all felt rather precious and delicate.

I was going to edit Lizzie's responses and turn them into a chapter like all the others but then I decided against that, because I felt it would be tampering with what she had given me herself, which is so naturally articulate and authentic, that it simply doesn't need any tweaking at all. So here are my questions to Lizzie and her heartfelt replies.

Our last email interview ended with Lizzie saying: "I hope it's okay for you. I'm sorry I can't offer more, but it's an accurate reflection of my thoughts."

Here goes with Lizzie's answers to my questions:

Please can you tell me about your childhood, where you lived, what your family was like and your relationship with your mum?

I grew up in a small rural village, with horses and dogs, and on the outside, we probably looked like the perfect family. A mum, a dad, and two daughters (my sister is a year older than me).

It's hard to remember too much about my relationship with my mum. I remember lots of moments of closeness, of cuddles, of affection, of laughter. I have no doubt that she loved my sister and I more than anything else in the world. I hold on to those memories.

There were also arguments. I remember screaming: "I hate you" and: "I wish you would die" more than once, and although I can't remember the exact circumstances in which these words were said, I expect they were triggered either by her drinking (she was an alcoholic), or me being a precocious little brat, or perhaps a mixture of both. I hold on to those memories too, and they hurt more than anything.

Many of the happiest memories involve animals. The ponies, the dogs, the puppies. Animals are what keep me going now as an adult.

What were you like at school?

At primary school, I was very sensitive and clever. I was moved up from year five straight to secondary school because I was ahead of my peers and it was always assumed that I would go to Oxbridge. I often wonder what could have been?

I also excelled at music and played the flute to a high standard. I was at grade 8 by the time I was 13 and again, it was assumed I would have a successful musical future. Again, I wonder what could have been?

If I was told off by a teacher, I crumbled. I still have that awful sensitivity, but I coat it as best as I can.

Did you have any idea as a child that your mum was struggling?

Yes, but I lacked the maturity to fully understand.

Her alcoholism was evident, as was her depression. There were various suicide attempts but I never fully understood and although the rational part of my brain accepts that I was nine years old and therefore of course I didn't understand, the guilt remains.

She was arrested for drink-driving. I found bottles of wine in the wardrobe. I remember the self-harm marks on her arms.

We had family counselling. I don't remember much of it, aside from my sister running out of the room. It really hurts to go back to those years.

Please can you tell me about the day it all happened and what exactly happened?

It was a Thursday in September. I was nine years old and my sister was 11. On a Thursday, I would stay after school for orchestra practice. I would always get the giggles whilst playing music with my friends, and I was giggling … whilst my mother hung from the ceiling.

My music teacher, who happened to live 3 doors down from us, dropped my sister and I off on a Thursday after orchestra. My dad got home from work about 6.

My teacher dropped us off that day and as soon as we opened the front door, we could tell something was wrong. The dogs were howling, and one was on the kitchen table. I remember us shouting: 'Hi mum, we're home! Where are you!' We looked upstairs and in every room but she wasn't there.

There was a note on the kitchen side. It was written in blue marker pen on white paper. It said: 'Girls, don't go in the garage'.

A week earlier, we had been to look at a pony for sale and in our childish naivety, my sister and I had this mad assumption that despite having a field and stables, our mum had brought the pony home to the garage for a surprise.

My sister ran out in excitement, and I will never, ever forget the look on her face as she ran back.

I can't remember the words she spoke, but I will always remember the look on her face.

The phone was by the front door and I sat on the floor whilst she phoned the ambulance. "She's next to me, hugging the dog" are the only words I remember her saying. I assume she must have been asked where I was?

I remember feeling acutely aware of my mum's dead body in the garage. I felt too close to it in the house so I ran out of the front door, but then I could see the garage door, which felt worse, so I ran back inside. I felt completely trapped.

We left the dogs and ran to a neighbour's house, two doors down. Their daughter went to school with us. I don't remember telling them what happened, but I remember, very clearly, sitting in a chair in their living room sobbing, whilst my friend stroked my back.

At some point my dad must have arrived home from work. Someone obviously told him, I guess it was my friend's parents. I left their house and looked down the road and saw the ambulance. I ran into the house and hugged my dad in the hallway and remember him being shell-shocked.

All I wanted to do was go to the field and see the ponies. It was pitch-black and I remember standing in the middle of the field hugging my pony.

That night the three of us stayed at the home of friends. My sister and I stayed in a room together. I closed my eyes and kept picturing mum hanging from different places in the garage. I asked my sister where she was and she described it to me. We've never spoken about that since.

How were you treated by everyone after your mum's suicide?

The next morning was a Friday and we didn't go to school. We walked from the friend's house along the main road to the shop to get sweets. We saw my mum's friend leading her horse down the road: 'Why aren't you at school?' she asked. We casually replied that mum had killed herself. I remember her face.

That night it was the autumn fair at school. I wanted to go. Everyone stared at me: teachers, parents, pupils. I remember running out crying. We were clearly in shock.

What happened next? (the funeral/returning to school/recalibrating as a changed-family)

The funeral took place at the village church. I have a clear memory of walking down the aisle in front of the coffin and the looming, concerned faces of people I barely knew staring at me. My headmaster, people from the village. I felt angry - why were they there, intruding on our grief?

I don't remember much else from the funeral. I think the brain has a fascinating way of blocking some things out but leaving others' crystal clear. I have felt very emotional in churches ever since.

Eight years' ago I attended the wedding of my friend in the same church; the first time I had been back. Everything looked so much smaller and it shocked me. I was okay until we had to sing Jerusalem, the same song played at my mum's funeral. I didn't know how to explain why I was standing there sobbing.

How did you feel during all of this at such a young age?

Although some things are razor-sharp, It's very hard to recall my feelings at that time. I honestly think I was in shock for at least 2 years. I do remember though the hell of starting secondary school and puberty and everything which that rite of passage brought with it. It was as if I only started grieving then.

I have memories of sitting on my bedroom floor night after night, crying until I felt there was nothing left. Piles of crumpled tissues around me. I can still feel the physical pain of those nights, the wracking in my body, night after night.

It affected all of us in different ways. My dad had a heart attack a few years later and nearly died. My sister rebelled; I will always feel guilty that she saw mum hanging and I didn't. Like somehow, I would prefer to bear that pain so she doesn't have to. I feel that she coped better during the teenage years but that her rock-bottom came at university.

What were your family like about it and friends/teachers at school?

I honestly can't remember. Concerned faces, but nothing else.

Did you receive any counselling/offer of counselling?

Again, I can't remember if any was offered. All I know is that I didn't have any and there is no way in this day and age, that would happen. I had a few counselling sessions for an eating disorder (probably related) when I was 17 and that's it.

How did your mum's suicide affect your teenage years and your twenties?

It is really hard to say whether her suicide limited my future because her problems - had she kept living - may have done the same anyway. I have no doubt that she killed herself because she was in so much psychological pain, but also because she felt she was saving us in some way. She did it because she loved us, and that is one of the hardest things to process, even now.

My teenage years were difficult and so were my twenties. I don't feel fully comfortable writing about them right now. Everything comes back to my self-esteem (or lack of it) and it doesn't take a psychologist to work out why.

You talked about your mum's suicide feeling like a "dirty secret". Can you explain?

Imagine the stigma that exists around suicide in 2020, and then rewind 27 years. People pick up on you talking about your dad, but not your mum.

Generally, the conversation goes a little like this:

"Is your mum not around?"

"No, she died when I was 9"

"I'm so sorry. Do you mind me asking what happened?"

(yes, actually)

"It was suicide"

Very awkward silence. Count two beats whilst they consider the appropriateness of the question but can't resist asking anyway…

"Oh that's awful. How, erm, how did she do it?"

"She hanged herself in the garage"

Morbid-curiosity satisfied: horror and guilt on their side, shame on mine.

The conversation would have gone very differently if I had said she died of cancer, or in a car accident.

I have had many, many of these conversations.

How has the loss of your mum through suicide impacted your life as an adult?

I went to university and I've got a career and I'm functioning and I've done okay. But underneath I'm a complete mess because I have never dealt with it. I have an amazing partner but I'm not an easy person to live with. I have a lot of anger.

Every life event – marriage, childbirth – will be marred by the lack of my mum. And because the marriage of my mum and dad was so terrible. I am cynical; I can't see marriage as the fairytale which so many people can.

I am obsessed with animals – dogs and horses particularly – and they are everything to me. They make me feel close to the memory of my mum.

The subject of children is difficult. I am just about to turn 36, which is the age my mum was when she had me. What if I turn out like my mum? I can't do that to anyone else. But what is life without children?

I often think about who I might have been if my childhood wasn't what it was. I could have turned out so much worse. But conversely, I will always feel like I failed by not being the Oxbridge graduate, or the British Orchestra player.

I feel different to other people and that's lonely. I would love nothing more than to connect with someone who lost their mother at a similar age and in a similar way, but I don't have the time in my life to even start that journey.

How have other family members coped? (did your dad remarry, for example? What about your sibling?)

The stress of what happened and bringing up two (difficult) teenage girls alone took its toll on my dad's health and a few years after mum died, he had a heart attack. Luckily, he survived but his ongoing health problems are a constant worry. He has had a couple of relationships over the years but nothing serious. My biggest wish is for him to find someone else and be happy.

My sister has had her struggles and continues to. She has a young family and is a wonderful person but is broken inside like we all are.

How do you feel about your mum now? Have you ever felt angry at her? Or not angry at her, but angry at her actions? - or do you feel empathy and that you understand?

I have felt everything, and I still don't know what the overriding emotion is. I have felt angry at her, but more at myself. I blamed myself for a long, long time. If you told your mum you wished she would die, and then she did, how can you not blame yourself?

Ten years ago, I had a bit of a breakdown (I don't feel I can go into details here) and I felt suicidal. I researched it all, and it scares me to even think about the place I was in then. But even without that experience, I do have empathy. I know that underneath everything, she loved us, and I honestly believe she did it for us as much as she did it for herself.

What have people said/done that have made the situation more/less difficult? How would you like people to be with you (or what would you prefer them to say to you), when they learn about your mum's suicide?

I don't know what I want them to say. Asking how she did it feels very inappropriate, but if the question wasn't asked out loud, I'd know it was being thought about, so in some ways it gets it out of the way.

Something I really struggle with, is hearing people who have never been touched by suicide lamenting how selfish it is. I take it very personally and it wounds me. Everyone's situation is different and to generalise in that way is hurtful and ignorant. I have had some very uncomfortable moments with colleagues and new friends over the years when suicide has been discussed and branded as selfish.

Seeing the comments under social media posts is the worst. When Police forces' post about motorway closures where it is evident that someone has jumped off a bridge, the comments ignite extreme anger and this simultaneously breaks my heart.

What are your feelings about suicide now and people who commit suicide?

I understand why people commit suicide. It is easy to brand it as selfish but the pain that drives someone to take their own life is something, thankfully, many of us will never experience or even comprehend.

I strongly believe that many people who die from suicide didn't mean to die. I am sure that for many it is a cry for help, and especially in young people, I genuinely think some don't grasp the finality of what they do.

I also strongly believe that if my mum could have foreseen the consequences of her suicide, she would not have done it. But I understand that she was very ill, and therefore I do not blame her for the pain she has left behind.

Have you found peace about the situation and does it get any easier with the passing of time or do you have more unanswered questions?

The passage of time helps blur some of the edges but it's a wound that will never heal. I will always be the girl whose mother hung herself in the garage.

I'm also a sister, a partner, a professional and (I hope) a good person, but I will always be defined by what happened when I was nine.

Do you feel that there is stigma attached to suicide? (do you think there is additional stigma associated to a mother who commits suicide and leaves her children as opposed to a father?)

The stigma that is attached to suicide is what makes it so much harder for those left behind.

And yes, it makes it so much worse that it was a mother who abandoned her children in such a devastating way. A mother should protect her children, not ruin their lives by inflicting such trauma.

But she was ill. I honestly believe she thought she was helping us by leaving us. People will always judge her for what she did, but I have to accept that they don't understand and let it go.

What would you want to say to someone who feels suicidal?

That by leaving behind the pain they are feeling, there is a very real possibility that they will be sentencing someone they love to the same pain down the line.

What have your experiences taught you?

Part of my job involves interviewing people diagnosed with life-limiting diseases and I ask similar questions, but I can't answer this.

I suppose the only thing I can think of, is the importance of dealing with things as soon as you can, but to do that, you need the support of others.

And you need money. NHS mental health resources have never been so stretched so going private is the only option for many people.

You also have to believe you are worth it and maybe that's why I haven't done anything.

What advice would you give to other women in a similar situation?

If a woman loses a parent to suicide as an adult, I imagine it comes with different challenges to losing a parent to suicide as a child. Is it a blessing that I was too young to fully understand? Or did that mean I grew up without any proper answers and therefore struggled more? I don't know, and I never will.

I think the best piece of advice I could give would be to access help as quickly as possible. There is so much to work through when a parent takes their own life and it's impossible to do it on your own.

I desperately wish I had received help as a child and as a young adult. I have never had counselling for what happened, and I have always felt too guilty to seek it via the NHS because I am not at crisis point, as so many are, and services are so unbelievably stretched. Paying privately hasn't been an option.

It is hard to offer advice to others because that would suggest I have found something that works, and I haven't.

Where are you now? What are your plans for the future?

I don't feel this is something I can go into right now. As I write, we are eight months into the COVID-19 pandemic, and it feels like another bomb that has gone off under my feet. Thinking ahead is too much.

Note to reader

Just for Lizzie to share this story so publicly is a huge step! She is much braver than she thinks! I am so grateful to her.

ANASTASIA'S STORY

When a dad on the football pitch sidelines, reignites the spark of desire after 3 years of sexual silence but later there's a brutal severing and a horrible confrontation which marks the end of an affair...

I wasn't madly in love with my husband, Max, when he became my boyfriend. We'd gotten to know each other through work, became friends and then started going out. Later, just like so many regular couples, we moved in together and our relationship progressed. There was never a thunderbolt moment rather we just got on and had reached a point where we cared about each other. We must have found one another attractive at that point as we had an active sex life.

Then we had 4 children in quite quick succession: at one point we had 4 children under 5 years: 3 sons and 1 daughter including a set of twin boys. It was hardcore as we also both continued to work – I worked 3 days a week as a doctor in a large hospital whilst Max worked full time as an accountant and we had a nanny to help with the kids. We both commuted to the different cities where we worked, from our home in Bath. Although life was full-on, it felt quite fun! It was challenging but it was as though we were partners in crime: sussing it all out together. We both had the same ideas about raising children which harmonised our approach.

However, Max and I didn't prioritise each other but rather our time was all about the kids and that's how it was for quite a few years. We rarely went out on date nights because we were shattered. We didn't want to ask my dad to come and babysit very often because he was quite elderly and we just got out of the habit of having time together. Our youngest son, Kit, was quite difficult. He was intensely competitive with his twin brothers and when all of the children were together, Kit would just cause problems, kicking the older boys under the dining table, or tripping them up. I could see that he was a real handful when he was a toddler and his feisty attitude was quite cute then, but as he became older, really from 7 years onwards, I noticed that these traits were getting magnified.

Kit was just really challenging all of the time. I think as the youngest, he felt he had to compete with his siblings. Mealtimes became a massive battleground as Kit would simply play up. We tried to send him to his room but he was defiant and refused to go. He was always seeking attention and it didn't matter if it was good or bad attention. Max often ended up chasing Kit around the house trying to force him into his bedroom and we all started to dread the weekends because of Kit's behaviour.

Even now, when Kit's by himself or with 2 of his siblings, he's okay but when they're all together, he just kicks off in some way or another. Kit still dominates everything. Just last night he was calling one of his brothers: "fat" and me: "a 'bitch". I don't really know how to deal with it. Back then though, it was rush, rush, rush all week and then at the weekend, the kids were doing lots of activities:

judo, football and so on. I'd take some kids to one thing; Max would take the others to something else. Then obviously it was back home for mealtimes and Kit's nightmare behaviour. Max started to get angry with Kit and sometimes would pin Kit down on the ground or say he couldn't handle it and go off for a walk or into his study for the rest of the day, slamming the doors as he went. As a mum, I felt I had to try to protect Kit as he was my son and that took priority.

Max recently said that he felt that Kit had split us up but then I think there were other factors in the mix too: Max lost his accountancy job and was worrying about money. He tried new business ventures but these didn't work out and I think he became a bit depressed and would take himself off to bed early every night or go into his study. He started sleeping in the spare room one night after a row and then soon, it became a permanent fixture…

At this point the kids were all under 10 years old and we were in our 40s. I had gotten used to the fact that Max had moved all of his stuff into the spare room. I guess I didn't mind then because I didn't want him touching me or vice versa. At this point, I was tired, had put on weight and didn't have time to exercise. Life was all about the kids and work.

I wasn't getting any attention from anyone else and I remember thinking I can carry on with this situation at home because I don't want the children growing up in a broken home. I said to a girlfriend: "I couldn't care less if I never have sex again" as the desire and memory of it, had all gone. I couldn't even imagine having sex any more and didn't think about it. I didn't feel attractive, confident or happy. But then I would listen to other mums when we went for coffees on my days off, talking about their weddings and about feeling loved-up in their marriages and relationships. I started to feel that I was living a lie and that I didn't want my children to think that what Max and I had, was normal because we were in separate bedrooms and not getting on well with each other.

I met Ralph when Kit and Ralph's youngest son were both 5 and our kids attended the same school. Ralph and I were both fixtures on our boys' football practice sidelines, watching them play a couple of times a week. Once a week was football practice, the other session was the weekly match. Ralph was an architect and his wife was a doctor too who worked really long hours. He could work from home sometimes so he often had the kids. Max and I knew Ralph and his wife in our circle of friends but we weren't particularly close; his wife was very different to me.

Ralph and I gradually got to know each other more because of our respective kids' sports but we would just be with a group of other parents who were cheering on our children and standing around each week, watching them play. Then Ralph started being slightly flirtatious with me in quite a jokey, risqué way. He was a bit cheeky, very personable and clearly at ease talking to women. He would, for example, tap me on the shoulder and pretend it wasn't him, just silly things like that, which made me laugh.

At this point, he was between jobs and had a little bit of time on his hands because he was thinking of working part-time for another architects' practice and then also gradually going freelance, so one day he suggested by text that we had a coffee together. However he said to come to his place otherwise people would talk.

I texted him back jokily: "well okay as long as you don't pounce". He replied: "as long as you don't pounce first". I enjoyed the jokey banter of this but didn't expect, intend or think anything would happen, other than a tiny bit of flirting. So I went over to his. I hadn't undertaken any special fleabag-style grooming because I just decided to be myself and thought we were only going to be sarky with each other – nothing more!

However Ralph turned on the charm and he ended up saying: "you know I've always found you attractive". I didn't know how to reply! I hadn't expected anything to happen. I said something like: "if circumstances were different, I might say the same". This was definitely followed by a bit of an awkward silence as I'd never had loads of confidence with guys or had lots of boyfriends either. Ralph then asked: "Can I have a hug?" and we had a long embrace before he tried to kiss me but I moved so that his lips didn't meet mine.

I can't quite remember what happened next but we must've continued flirting and texting. Although there wasn't a massive spark, Ralph just made me feel good and we arranged for him to come to mine. This time he bought a bottle of prosecco. We ended up having a long snog and it felt amazing. He was such a good kisser. Time just stopped whilst it was happening. All my senses were heightened and I didn't notice anything else… but we didn't have sex then.

Ralph was a constant texter from the minute he woke up, to when he got to work and during the day. He'd text me throughout. I remember saying, teasing him: "are you sending me and your wife these messages in a group text?" but it was really lovely to have all of this attention after not having any from Max for such a long time. It felt amazing to have someone who was so interested in me. One thing that was so special with Ralph was the feel of his skin on mine. I'd never really noticed this with a partner before (or maybe it was because it had been so long since I'd had such skin-to-skin contact), but I loved the feel of his skin. It was so comforting and calming.

At first, Ralph was the one who was really unhappy at home. He hadn't had sex for 4 years. His wife earned a lot more than him and he felt that he was used by her simply to look after the kids. At one point, he said he felt as though 'what's the point of carrying on, would anyone care if I'm not here any more?' We were both stuck in unhappy marriages but we had just found each other. I felt we were both supporting and saving one another. At first he seemed more unhappy than me and we tried to meet as often as we could: I'd use my lunch-hour whenever possible. His family didn't do a weekly shop so he used to pop to a supermarket most days and we'd meet there as it was so inconspicuous.

He told me that he and his wife constantly argued and she let their kids be rude to him, not chastising them and all of this was making him pretty miserable. Ralph said I had given him his confidence back. I never thought I'd have an affair but as it progressed, I was so distracted that I naturally lost weight and felt so happy. He made me feel really good about myself and I fell head over heels in love with him. Ralph told me that I was the love of his life and that we would be together forever. He used to send me text messages full of hearts and kisses.

I didn't think through the practicalities about what would happen with our kids and partners. It would've been a lot easier if our kids and partners hadn't known each other but we were just swept away in a bubble of being in love.

Even within a month of us first seeing each other properly, our relationship got intense! I used to meet him after his gym session on a Monday night and then sometimes on a Tuesday night, he'd skip his football training and we'd go to a random pub in London. I know it sounds like such a cliché, but later on, we started going to local branches of chain hotels just so that we could sleep together. It all seemed such a natural progression. We wanted to be able to relax together. One time we went to a hotel that was about 20 minutes away from where we both lived and the receptionist said: "I hope you haven't come far?" and then realised from the postcodes on our checking-in forms, that we were both from different addresses but a few miles down the road. It was embarrassing, as was checking out at 3am!

In fact it was very soon after we first slept together, that we were professing undying love for each other. The first time we had sex, it just felt completely natural to strip off and sleep with him. He was a normal guy and was so complimentary about me. He just noticed things about me, like he'd say for example: "gosh, that scarf's nice" and he always made me feel at ease with myself. As mentioned before, Ralph's confidence was low and he felt worthless but I was making him feel good about himself. He kept telling me how attractive I was and we'd speak on the phone and Ralph would say: "I'm aroused just by talking to you". It was so exciting to hear this because you stop feeling like this when you're married because you become so familiar with each other.

Ralph and his wife, Catherine, had been together for at least 13 years when I met him. She was very controlling of him: she had access to all his emails and would open his post. It was very emasculating for him. After 3-4 months of our affair, he texted me one day saying: "She knows". Catherine had found out that I had rung him up on the August Bank Holiday and she was suspicious saying: "Why was Anastasia ringing you on the Bank Holiday? That's a family day". He tried to convince her that I had only rung him to see what their kids were up to. But as part of Catherine's detective work, she'd found a receipt for a dress he'd bought for me, which made matters much worse.

When Ralph told me that Catherine was suspicious, I told him that she would now look through all of his phone records because that's what I would do as a woman if I'd been her. I said that he should change his passwords. For whatever reason though, he didn't change these. Sure enough, a few days' later, she did look through all of his phone records and saw that he'd been ringing me but we had already talked through an excuse. Ralph told Catherine that I had been helping him with his depression because Max also suffered from it.

A few days' later, a group of parents including me, Max, Catherine and Ralph, had all arranged to go and see a musical in the West End followed by a meal afterwards and Catherine was definitely frosty towards me but she didn't confront me or say anything. She was awkward with me and looked unhappy, but she didn't know that Ralph had told me that I was aware she was suspicious.

If I had been her, I wouldn't have believed what Ralph had said especially when the phone records showed that our discussions went on for an hour at a time. I just thought 'shit, shit, shit, is she going to tell Max?' but Ralph had persuaded her not to. However, Catherine lay down the law with Ralph: he wasn't allowed to make eye contact with me, speak to me or see me.

Simultaneously, Max began to suspect something was amiss with me: he didn't suspect that anything was going on with Ralph, but just that I might be involved with *someone* because one afternoon when Max's mum was staying with us, I was in my bedroom and talking to Ralph on the phone, when Max burst in to tell me some news that had arrived in the post. Max demanded to know who I was talking to and afterwards, to show him my mobile. But I wouldn't. So he became suspicious and cut up our joint credit card. He went downstairs and told his mum who was then very cold with me. That weekend was pretty awkward.

Thus for a while I couldn't see Ralph. Catherine refused to let him go anywhere that harboured the possibility of us both being there. She was determined to prevent something happening. So we didn't see each other at football or karate any more, but we continued to talk by message/phone.

Ralph said: "I'll get her trust back and then I'll be able to take the boys to football training again". But he also said sentiments that got my hopes up too about our future together, words like: "I'm going to leave her, the ball's in my court." However, on reflection, things had definitely changed a bit with us, Ralph had backed off a little. He seemingly became the loving husband but then between us, it all still felt really positive and within a few weeks, he was back to pledging his undying love for me.

Not long after that, he kept saying how miserable he was and that he wanted to split up from Catherine, but then in the February, they went away just the two of them for the weekend as it was an annual ritual they had. I did think to myself, if their marriage is so bad, how can they be going away? But I had no choice but to accept it. I took my kids off for that same weekend to stay with a girlfriend who'd also had an affair. I offloaded to her and she really understood! By this point, both Max and I had acknowledged that our own relationship was over. I didn't hear anything from Ralph that weekend and I knew I couldn't message him but I also knew that by Monday morning, we'd be able to be in touch again.

Sure enough, Ralph won Catherine's trust back and shortly afterwards, from Spring 2016, we were back to meeting up with each other in hotels, pubs, etc. Ralph got a burner phone so he could call me. Together we felt stronger as we'd been through so much together but the fact we were still going to such lengths to make time for each other, made it feel as though we were invincible, that our love was pure. Our affair continued throughout all of that year. At Christmas, he bought me a necklace with our initials intertwined and I gave him a present of a jacket, t-shirt, jeans... really smart clothes.

However, after that second Christmas, his wife found out again that we were still seeing each other. Prior to this, he'd bought me another dress and I'd taken a photo of myself wearing it and sent this to him via social media. Somehow this photo popped up on their home computer. Once again, Catherine was very suspicious. Ralph tried to say he'd bought them as a thank-you for me and persuaded Catherine that we weren't having an affair but he was once again banned from taking the kids to football and going anywhere that I could potentially be, too. Catherine started looking at the social media platform site again to see if we were both simultaneously using it, and therefore potentially messaging each other.

Around March/April 2017, Ralph and I managed to meet up and he told me that Catherine had managed to get into his social media account and had seen a message from him to me where he had signed off to me with hearts and kisses and she said to him: "I should be the one getting those". I don't know if this actually happened or not though, because from then on, much of what he told me, didn't ring true. I'm not sure if our affair and being under his wife's angry surveillance, was all getting too heavy for him but my intuition told me that he was pulling away from me and it wasn't because I was pressurising him to leave Catherine, because I wasn't, although I did plead with him to be honest to me.

Ralph kept telling me that he and Catherine were going to split up but then weeks went by and nothing changed. My instincts told me that something wasn't right, but then Ralph would reassure me. I just begged him for the truth of the situation but he told me that it was the truth. My own position was that Max and I were barely speaking although living in the same house together with the kids.

But I could tell Ralph just wasn't as invested in me any more. He wasn't texting immediately in the morning and then he started saying things like: "sorry I can't put a date on it" with regards to him moving out of the family home. I got the feeling of being told one thing but knowing that the opposite thing was true. I was being fed information that he knew I wanted to hear but it wasn't necessarily genuine. I wanted to believe him but I just knew something wasn't right. It's tough though when you've lived your life – as far as you know – without people having lied to you, so you feel you can trust people and Ralph was my best friend and my lover so I trusted him implicitly.

Amidst all of this chaos, sometimes I couldn't face going home to my own family, so I would say I had a work 'do' happening. I had to delay seeing everyone back in the house because I was trying to cope with so much in my head. I would sometimes bump into other colleagues I knew doing exactly the same, and they said: "I thought it was only guys who did this to stall time", but no, I think sometimes we all do this.

The uncertain situation with Ralph continued with him keeping me hanging on. So then I did start to pressurise him into telling me the truth but still I had further excuses. I realised that things had definitely changed between us: he was definitely more reticent, not as committed and he made excuses not to see me. Catherine then managed to get Ralph to admit that we had spent a night in a hotel as she'd discovered this somehow. She texted me: 'Does Max know about this?' I just ignored her message. I was getting a bit frantic with Ralph now as the situation was tormenting me. I simply wanted a straight answer about what was happening with us. Ralph said things had changed, but not in the way I hoped and then he stopped getting in contact as much but still he didn't end it with me, although he was evasive.

And then I finally snapped. I'd had enough! I went and confronted his wife one morning at the train station before she went to work; she was standing on the platform with her earphones in and I tapped her on the arm. I couldn't help myself. I felt it was deeply unfair that his wife thought that I had instigated all of this and that she needed to know what Ralph was like; needed to know the truth. At the time, I almost had this crazy, delirious notion that flitted through my head, that we: she and I, could become friends and gang-up against this man who had played us both. We could work through the pain together. It all seemed so unjust that Catherine hated me, when it was Ralph who was behind this.

She said to me: "How could you do this to your marriage? To our marriage? We were friends". We hadn't really been close friends, but I had to tell her: "It was all him. It was bombardment. He bombarded me with texts, emails, messages and I ended up falling in love with him." I didn't tell her that I slept with him and the rest of that stressful conversation is pretty much a blur although I remember Catherine thanking me for being honest with her.

Simultaneously my beloved dad went onto life support as he suddenly became ill. I contacted Ralph but he didn't respond. He was just off with me when I called him and he simply said: "I've got to go". I was so upset and disappointed by his response that I texted him, impulsively saying: "I hope you have a miserable life".

My dad died and the pain and the guilt I felt over that too, were enormous. I used to meet up with my dad but he'd be nursing his cup of tea, asking for more hot water to saviour the moment longer and I'd be desperate to rush off and see Ralph, so I'd be thinking of excuses to get away from dad and now he was no longer here. I felt I'd wasted time seeing a flaky lover, instead of seeing my precious dad. Additionally Max and I split up and he moved out.

In the following weeks and months of 2016, I had to cope with all of this and I cried a lot. I dealt with dad's death on my own: registering it, organising his funeral and so on as I don't have any siblings or other family. It was bleak. It's also just so horrible being dumped by someone who you absolutely, wholeheartedly love! You love them fully and completely and you think you are going to spend the rest of your life with them but ultimately, I couldn't compete with his long-term marriage to his wife, their kids, and their history together.

Occasionally Ralph and I bump into each other now as we don't live that far away from each other, but we don't speak. I still feel pained over it. I'd like to think that there was genuine love there but it just got too complicated and messy.

What have your experiences taught you?

To remember what's important to you. My kids are important. I don't want to reflect on someone who messed me around so much (although of course, I do).

Exercise massively helps: I normally take part in 2 x boot camps each week and yoga once a week too.

Be kind to yourself (whilst I need to be careful with money, I do treat myself too and that makes me feel a bit better!)

What advice would you give to other women in a similar situation?

Try not to fall in love with a married man and don't take everything they say at face value. Be aware of how much they have to lose. He said to me: "she wears the trousers" and when it came to it, he didn't have the balls to leave her and I got hurt.

WHERE ARE YOU NOW? WHAT ARE YOUR PLANS FOR THE FUTURE?

Most of the time, I'm happy and upbeat. Having the kids helps in the sense that life is so busy that I don't get much time to myself to dwell on what's happened.

I'm a lot closer to three of my children and I particularly have a lovely relationship with my daughter but Kit remains challenging and obviously lockdown's made the dynamics tricky too, so for example last night, he got fed up and suddenly rang his dad up and asked if he would collect him? His dad duly did and that was after I'd treated them all to an expensive takeaway and Kit had been rude throughout it. I just thought: 'why do you have to go and ruin things?' and felt really hurt afterwards and sad that all of my children couldn't hang out together with me and we couldn't all just get on but I guess that's how family life really is sometimes and it's vital to be honest about all of this.

Sometimes I am nervous about the future because I am in my early 50s now and feel I am starting afresh and doing it all by myself. It can be hard when I see other loved-up couples, as I can feel like a pariah but then I am not sure if it's possible to be with someone for decades and stay in love, without becoming over-familiar, complacent, disgruntled and even resentful of each other?

Life continues and my financial angst should resolve hopefully with my soon-to-be Ex-husband. At present, we're relatively amicable.

I don't predict any great romantic relationships just yet (I did try online dating but it wasn't that successful and lockdown has put that on-hold for now). However, I would like a significant man in my life! I haven't ruled it out at all and I am ready for it. Overall, I am ready to tackle the next phase of my life and I'm getting through this prelude to that.

I am excited about the future!

PRAXEDES' STORY

When an erudite and exciting businesswoman/divorced mum of 2 young daughters in the midst of moving house, suddenly discovers she's got a highly aggressive form of Leukaemia in January 2020 just before Lockdown 1 and the only possible hope is a very risky stem cell transplant

NOTE TO READER

Praxedes' chapter is particularly brief because she is still recovering from an incredibly intense stem cell transplant treatment and she has only very recently been released from hospital following a relapse. Praxedes gets exhausted quickly so I am incredibly grateful to her for taking part in this book. Here is her story in her own words as emailed to me on 28 February 2021:

CONTEXT (IN PRAXEDES' WORDS)

I've always provided everything for my daughters through my own efforts and through working hard. My girls are very dependent on me so if I'm not around, I always think: what will happen to my daughters? This thought has kept me going throughout my Leukaemia experience because I have constantly thought: 'I don't want to ruin their lives. I need to live. I need to continue providing everything they need.'

WHEN THINGS BEGAN TO GO WRONG

I was about to move house when I started to feel extremely tired. That wasn't like me at all. I had the following symptoms:

- Night sweats: Every morning all my sheets were completely wet
- Chills
- Fever
- Headache
- Pain in my spleen: I could barely eat because of the pain
- Bruises on my legs: I thought I had them because of all the boxes I was packing and the heavy physical lifting, etc, that I was doing, when occasionally I would catch myself

- My gums started to bleed in a way that wasn't normal: One morning my daughter Olympia told me: "Mum, your mouth is bleeding". I checked in the mirror and I had ugly clots of blood coming from my mouth, something I had never seen before!

As a single mother, without any immediate help [Praxedes' closest family lived abroad], I felt I needed to go to the hospital immediately, but I couldn't because we were in the process of moving house! I had to pack everything up, take measurements inside our new flat, make constant trips between it and our former house too, to work out what would fit and what wouldn't. Even though I had been forcing myself to go to the gym, I realised that something was very wrong with me, as I couldn't exercise like before.

I called my GP Practice to explain my symptoms and ask whether it was worth having a GP appointment or whether I should go straight to the hospital? I was told to go to the practice because the GP said: "You have flu" and I responded: "I am 43 years old, I know what flu is like, and this is not flu". The GP prescribed me Ibuprofen for one week (which was actually detrimental for my real condition).

House-moving day arrived! Amongst all the stress with the removals' company and others asking me: "Where do I put this/that?"and cleaning the old house… all my inclinations were that I really needed to go to the hospital. My body felt so weak and I had such a strong headache but I had these huge responsibilities and I just couldn't go to the hospital then.

One week later, once I had unpacked everything and organised all of the girls' belongings and my own, I arranged a sleepover for the girls so I could go to the hospital. After hours of waiting, the doctor wanted to prescribe me some antibiotics but I challenged him and said I needed a blood test.

He didn't want to take any bloods and so I asked him: "What if I have Glandular Fever? The antibiotics will harm me." So finally, I was given a blood test. The only positive thing about having a blood disorder is that they can see it in the blood pretty easily! The doctor told me: "Go home and I will call you tomorrow with the results to confirm you can take the antibiotics."

I arrived home and ten minutes later, I received a call from the hospital, from another doctor saying: "You need to come back immediately, you're going to be admitted to hospital: you have Leukaemia". I went into shock. I started crying and I called my mum who lives in Spain: "Mum, pack and go to the airport, I have bought you a flight that departs in a few hours. I need you! I have been diagnosed with Leukaemia and I need to stay in the hospital, I need you to take care of the girls."

That night in the hospital was one of the worse in my entire life. I had no idea about Leukaemia, I thought it was a type of cancer that only affected children. I couldn't sleep and I was googling about Leukaemia in adults, treatments, and life expectancy. Everything was bleak: my type of Leukaemia (Acute Lymphoblastic Leukaemia) was a very aggressive one with a poor prognosis in adults.

Telling my daughters

Since day one, I have been very open and honest with my daughters and my condition. I think it's best for children to know what's going on and to reassure them that you are in safe hands, and even if it sounds horrible, there is always a solution on offer.

My daughters and my mother visited me the following day. I could see fear in their faces and I knew it was a kind of fear they hadn't experienced before. They were trying to make me feel comfortable but I could see how scared they were. We were all very scared, including me!

My mother is the only person that could really take care of my daughters and help me not to worry about them. Lots of parents at my daughters' school were extremely helpful, inviting my girls for play-dates and even dinner! Good friends helped practically, for example, by driving my mother to the hospital sometimes and I really appreciated that!

THE INITIAL TREATMENT AND WAY FORWARD

I was admitted to hospital for 5 weeks, receiving the first round of a very toxic chemotherapy. It went really well and I started to feel more relaxed. The doctors had a plan that saves 20% of patients and I was determined that I would be in that 20% because I am strong and will withstand whatever is necessary to see my daughters grow! The plan was to have 3 x rounds of chemotherapy and a Stem Cell Transplant.

The success of the Stem Cell Transplant depended on finding a 100% match: a genetic match that might be anywhere in the world. I was positive, thinking that it wouldn't be an issue. Unfortunately no matching donors could be found. I wasn't a donor myself before, because I didn't have any idea about Leukaemia and the importance of stem cell donation. I feel in hindsight that I should've known about the importance of this, but then I know that life is so busy that we can't be aware of everything. However, I felt I had to raise some awareness, not only for me, but for anyone going through any type of blood cancer so I started to contact some charities to see what I could do and DKMS were amazing. A brilliant, erudite journalist named Andrew Billen wrote a piece in The Times and that was really key to getting publicity for this cause. We couldn't find a 100% match for me, but I felt so happy that I managed to encourage so many people to register to be donors. Altruism gives you a beautiful feeling especially when you are really being challenged in so many ways!

THE STEM CELL TRANSPLANT

The transplant was such a cause for stress initially, as I couldn't find a 100% donor match but my consultants said that we could try a transplant from a relative who was at least a 50% match instead. Fortunately, one of my relatives in Spain matched by 50%, so although this presented a lower compatibility than my hospital team ideally wanted, and it made the procedure a bit more complicated, I accepted the situation and was really grateful to my cousin! I just felt so lucky and thankful to be alive and to have the chance to have a transplant.

I really wanted to have the transplant as soon as possible to progress my recovery and move forward. The 'conditioning therapy' that I had to have too, was hard as it involved more chemotherapy, but I embraced it as I knew it was the only hope for a cure. The day of the transplant felt so important but a few days' later, I started to experience the worse fevers ever, and feelings of bloating, etc. The fevers were so horrible that they made me shake in an uncontrollable way as if I were having an epileptic attack.

The first two weeks were very tough. I prefer to leave out the gritty details, but it has definitely been one of the most traumatic experiences I have ever had because it's been so gruelling on my body and my mind. When your immune system is weak, you get infections so easily. I had to be readmitted to hospital many times after I was discharged following the transplant. I had sepsis, an infection that can kill you if it remains untreated.

The Leukaemia and transplant have forced me to face death as a real possibility. When you face death head-on, you don't worry about yourself but rather you worry about the ones you will leave behind. During my condition and treatment, I was constantly thinking: 'I have to recover, I can't die, I can't do that to my daughters and mother, I will ruin their lives.'

THREE MONTHS AFTER THE TRANSPLANT

In the middle of November 2020, three months after my transplant, I was supposed to celebrate the success of the treatment, but instead, I had sepsis again and a very strong pain in my back and stomach. It was unbearable. I was admitted to hospital again and I received the most devastating news. I had relapsed, the Leukaemia was coming back. I started thinking about making a Will and what instructions and wishes I wanted to leave for the welfare of my daughters.

My bone marrow was as delicate as that of a three-month baby and I needed to receive a very toxic treatment to cure the Leukaemia. Amazingly, the treatment worked and all the Leukaemia cells were killed! I couldn't have felt luckier and more grateful. I was in complete remission, but I had to stay isolated in a hospital bed for two and a half months to recover. I spent Christmas and New Year's Eve alone because the Covid restrictions didn't permit any visitors. I managed to cope very well with the isolation. I even feel I developed a variation of 'Stockholm syndrome' when I remember that hospital room as I felt safe there somehow and made it my home whilst an amazing team of doctors and nurses helped me to fight the Leukaemia for a second time.

It's been more than a year since I was initially diagnosed and I'm still trying to recover from all the treatments. I regularly go to the Day Care Unit of the Hospital to receive platelets and I can't wait to recover 100%!! I feel positive!

OTHER PEOPLE'S REACTIONS

I understand some people feel really scared about cancer and they have no idea what to say to help. You can see they have a kind of internal issue that makes them avoid talking about the condition. Some people just want to hear that you're doing great, you're recovering and are out on the other side. But when you're on the side I've been on, it feels like they're thinking: 'please tell me you're finally okay so that I don't need to write to you and ask about how you're doing, any more'. It's as though they have knowledge-fatigue when it comes to you being honest about how you really are. What is helpful is when people accept what is happening and when they understand the whole process. A cancer 'recovery' doesn't end when you get out of hospital, there is always an emotional toll and a full list of medication that you still need to take. This makes you feel tired and miserable. Not all cancers are the same. We can't compare a breast cancer with an acute Leukaemia. Society is not trained or educated to deal with people with cancer.

The most helpful people have always written me more than three words. They have been very understanding, they have listened and accepted that my recovery is not easy. I can't stand the message: "How are you?" and that's it!

If I need to explain to you how I am, then it's going to involve at least ten sentences. I don't like messages like: "You've got this" or "You are an inspiration" because this thing called Leukaemia has actually really got me and I am not an inspiration. I have no choice but to fight for survival. I understand that attitude is key, and I have always had a very positive attitude!

The worse part for me was when I was diagnosed with Leukaemia in January 2020 but then you become more resilient and accept whatever happens next.

I have always been a very strong woman: I am sporty, I eat healthily and I've always had the feeling that I will be okay. When I received that diagnosis, I had the worst night of my life. Even now, thinking about it, makes me want to cry. I had no idea what Leukaemia really was and of course, I googled it and that's when I realised that my diagnosis was bad. My Leukaemia was one of the worst: Acute Lymphoblastic Leukaemia. It's very aggressive and kills you quickly if you are not treated urgently. I remember thinking: 'Please Praxedes, wake up from this horrible nightmare, this is such a nightmare. It can't be real!' However, I am TOTALLY determined to get back to full strength!

WHAT HAVE YOUR EXPERIENCES TAUGHT YOU?

Focus on the now. Don't plan long term. Enjoy every second and if there is anything that makes you unhappy, change it. (I was always such a planner! I still have to rein myself in today). Your family is what really matters. Your friends are important. Feed those relationships and help others. Be altruistic.

WHAT ADVICE WOULD YOU GIVE TO OTHER WOMEN IN A SIMILAR SITUATION?

If you are a controller, try to fix that. We are not here forever and maybe someone else will need to do what you are doing. Ask for help, don't try to do everything yourself. Delegate.

When you receive a devastating diagnosis, cry, let everything out. Don't make a drama or fight out of trying to withhold your shock. For me, acceptance and gratitude has been key. You never know how long you are going to be here, don't make your last days miserable, but instead: shine!

WHERE ARE YOU NOW? WHAT ARE YOUR PLANS FOR THE FUTURE?

After a year of chemo rounds, the transplant, sepsis, moments where I really thought it was the end of my life and had to write a Will and a plan for what would happen in the event I died… also after long isolated stays in hospital, I am very happy and grateful to be alive. My body is still recovering from all of the treatments. I have to come to hospital 3 times a week and I can't work yet, but I hope I will be able to soon. I am not the same person that I was before all of this but I think I am better. Cancer teaches you to enjoy life more!

My hopes for the future are that I would love to continue my work and spend more time with my family. I also can't wait to see and hug all of my friends. I was very touched by the altruism and willingness to help of so many people who I didn't know before. I consider them my friends too. I want to give back to the community now and help others.

Unfortunately I don't want to plan much for the future, because one of the lessons that I have learned, is that it is better to focus on the here and now and to go with the flow.

POSTSCRIPT: APRIL 2022

THE FOLLOWING IS WRITTEN BY ME: LINDSEY JOANNE BAUER (AUTHOR OF 'IMPLOSION')

"I can't wait to get dressed in pvc and go to a party with you… " Praxedes (Prax) said those words to me a few months' ago, when as always, she was desperately staying positive and thinking of better times ahead. This was before her third leukaemia relapse; it returned in her brain, triggering strokes. Still we were always planning parties to go to with all of her girlfriends: reasons to get glammed up and celebrate life once she was back in remission again because she was SO determined to live!

Prax and I first made contact on 10/2/20 over our mutual life implosions. We had loads in common and although our challenges were very different, we really related to each other and she wanted to be in this book, which I had just begun to research then, after being inspired by my own crises.

A few weeks' previously, suddenly, after thinking she might have glandular fever, 43 year-old Prax had been given the diagnosis of having a very aggressive form of leukaemia: her prognosis was that she had just 3 months to live unless a stem cell donor could be found.

Prax was a woman on an urgent mission, especially driven out of a need to stick around for her 2 daughters! Unfortunately a 100% donor match could not be found (all of her friends took the test to see if we were eligible, but sadly we weren't). However, her cousin proved to be a 50% donor match and so he became her dedicated stem cell donor.

Endless rounds of chemo followed for Praxedes and the decimation of her immune system to enable her body to accept the donor stem cells. Then she underwent the actual transplant itself and was completely sealed off in a sterile hospital room for a long period of time only being tended to by gowned-up medical staff to prevent the risk of infection. Prax endured horrendous side effects, more chemo, sepsis, endless infections, 'donor v host' disease (when donor cells become so strong in their host's body that they attack its organs: in Praxedes' case, the donor cells were attacking her skin, hair and eyes).

When Prax died, it was just after she'd been accepted for radical CAR-T Cell therapy in a pioneering hospital in Barcelona and we were all incredibly optimistic for her because because she'd managed to get well enough to leave her London home to fly out to Spain for this. However, ultimately her body had been through enough and not long after she had arrived in Barcelona, all of Prax's friends heard that she'd taken a sudden downturn, whilst surrounded by her family in hospital. We all prayed for a miracle…

But I guess Prax herself was the miracle! Along with being an amazing daughter, friend, businesswoman and mum, she made such a profound and positive impact on the lives of all those she met with her zest, enthusiasm and high energy and in her final years, she did all she possibly could whilst in so much pain and discomfort, to raise awareness of blood cancers and stem cell transplants. We will always, always LOVE her! She will always continue to inspire us!

***

The following are some of Prax's messages to me during the last 6 months of her life which give a real insight into her amazing upbeat nature but also the very real health challenges she faced. Before you read them, I want to add that at her 45th birthday party in August 2021 we talked a lot about some of the difficulties she was experiencing and some of the comments she made at the time included saying how money was a nightmare when receiving cancer treatment because you're too poorly to work but have the same or even increased expenses (such as travelling to the hospital/parking charges etc). Also when you finish a round of chemo, other people don't always understand and they expect you to be dancing, back at work, doing things that indicate you are 'back to normal' but she explained that with something like she was going through, she would never fully be back to normal as she was always going to be monitored and her health could deteriorate very quickly. She was living with a new normality for her and this was so true because on the morning of her actual birthday party, she'd had to go into hospital because she had an increased temperature.

4 September 2021
'Would love to meet… and let's dance!'

1 October 2021
'Love you to the moon!!… Tomorrow I have eye surgery [She included a bonkers'-face emoji here]; non-stop issues. I will do my best to recover shortly and then we will organise something cool.'

7 October 2021
'Hello my love, going through hard times because of GVHD, but my platelets have increased [She included a clapping hands emoji].'

31 October 2021
'Feeling stronger but still dealing with lots of GVHD (Donor V Host disease). I am losing my hair and I can't eat properly. Otherwise I am very happy and motivated with my online Masters in Internet Business. I am studying and taking it very seriously. It's the best decision I have taken in a long time!'

20 December 2021
'Hello my Love! Doing a bit better but my consultant told me today to shield as Covid could be life threatening to me. How are you?'

31 December 2021
[One of Prax's girlfriends and I were going out for New Year's Eve and Praxedes messaged us:]
'Have a fantastic night my sweeties.'
[When we replied that it wouldn't be the same without her, she replied:]

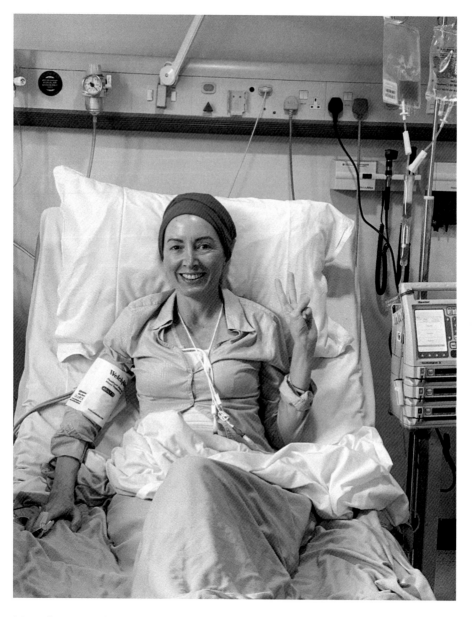

'One day soon after winter hopefully. Enjoy and send a report of the night please [She enclosed a winky eye emoji]'

6 January 2022
'Love you'
2 February 2022
'Leukaemia is back, only in my central nervous system for now. Receiving very awful chemo [Sad face emoji]. I am receiving Chemo and trying to get accepted for CAR-T Cell Therapy

I really need to get better to meet again. Chemo is difficult. Just for the brain. My brain is foggy, [I] lost balance, had a stroke [but it] wasn't a stroke, [was] symptoms of Leukaemia in the brain... found it in time. Quite a strong one [chemotherapy]. Hopefully the last one. On Monday, [I] find out if I can have CAR-T Cell therapy – very expensive. I can't live like that [with Leukaemia coming back] the fact that you are living with constant fear... [this is the] third time I've had Leukaemia in only 2 years. That's crazy. If I am scared, it's because I have reasons to be scared. It's not that I am paranoid, [it's] like it's [actually] happening. These blood disorders – really I hope I am not sounding too repetitive. These are the worst. People don't imagine the magnitude of these types of cancers... like blood cancers with the consequences. They are in a different league. I have some cancer buddies, they have some blood disorders but they don't have a transplant – they don't understand either. I am in touch with someone who had a different type of cancer – he hasn't had a transplant and he doesn't understand. Even people with cancer don't understand how this type of cancer works. I know it's hard for everyone. Before I was sick I had no idea that something like this could exist. Anyway, I am positive, I am strong even if it is hard sometimes to be strong but I am doing my best and I really hope we will start a new period someday soon – the CAR T cell therapy – if I am accepted – is going to be a tough one but I really want to begin as soon as possible because I don't want to be having a normal life and then having to be having chemo again - in this wavelength of major health events – I want to do the therapy as soon as possible.

How are you? Are you happy? How is everything going? What worries you? Are you having issues? I am sending love. I love you very much Lindsey & always because I know you are there. Sending you a big hug.

I will keep you posted about my misery. Hopefully I will start getting good news. It's a hard time but yes there is no other way of doing my best and being strong. Today I was totally [distracted], I realise from my medication that I need to take many medication – one is 9mg of steroids – which gives you energy: I was taking initially one tablet of 5 and four little tablets of 1 to make nine, and I just realised why over the last days I felt I was under the effects of LSD – well instead of taking one milligram tablet of steroids, I was overdosing. Lindsey I did something crazy – that's why I was getting extra bad side effects. I was a disaster. Anyway, yeah let's keep in touch, like this. For me it's much easier than writing. Sometimes I am tired and I don't even have the energy to speak but I will answer when I can, ok? Sending you love. I love you loads. Bye... '

Tues 15 February 2022
'Feeling awful today, migraine and pain all over my body. It's the worst day ever. Will keep you updated. Feeling so bad today. Better days will come soon! I hope you are enjoying life as always!'
28 February 2022
'Just got out of hospital on Saturday. I am very weak but trying to get stronger to go to Barcelona for a new therapy. How are you my darling?'

1 March 2022
'I hope you will publish the book shortly! I had to sell my car. I have paid for British

citizenship for me and my daughters. I have the appointment on Thursday... Sending you lots of love.'

10 March 2022
'So many health exams; wishing I was eligible for the treatment. How was your birthday?'

Our last contact was on 22 March, when she liked a message I sent her but she was too poorly to reply although sadly I didn't know it then.

AUTHOR'S NOTE

I was totally devastated by Prax's death as although I knew from everything she had told me, that realistically the prognosis was probably pretty dire (if I was honest), I guess I was hoping that she would be the exception to the rule; I imagined her to somehow survive everything due to the very strength of her spirit and personality. Praxedes had such a strong and powerful determination to live so I thought that if anyone could make it, that it would be her. I am still processing her death and the incredible impact she made on my life in the time I knew her. She was a powerhouse of a woman; an inspiring exciting female trailblazer. I am so sad she is no longer here...

Any book sales of Implosion will result in royalties to all of my participants and this includes Praxedes' daughters (in the absence of Prax).

Finally, I need to add that Praxedes wanted everyone to try to familiarise themselves with blood cancers and to consider becoming stem cell donors, so please do google blood cancers and what you can do to help. I know that if you can do this, Praxedes would/will be incredibly happy that she has made a difference to so many peoples' lives!

Praxedes was an advocate of the charity, the DKMS regarding this, see: www. dkms.org.uk

CLAIRE'S STORY

Mystery illnesses that shred your twenty-something life

I'm the eldest of two children from older parents in the North of England. My family are awesome but like so many, they can be quite precise about life and their expectations. They want the best for me. This all becomes somewhat relevant as it plays into the importance of my grandad, Billy. He was an awkward old man, but because of him being a generation detached, *everything* we did as his grandchildren, was marvellous and impressive because we weren't leaving school at 14 years' old, to work on the railways.

In my final year of Uni, I had a stressful time applying for my PGCE [Teacher Training Course: 'Postgraduate Certificate of Education']. Exeter was my 7th choice and I had failed 2 x 'Schools Direct' interviews. Things were looking iffy. Then we found out my grandad Billy had cancer! He was in his late 80s and it was spreading through his internal organs rapidly and Billy couldn't fight it. His wife had died 3 years earlier (roughly at the same time of the year that I was going through my undergraduate University final exams).

Billy was my last surviving grandparent and the only person who had ever said that they were proud of me. Anyway, I harassed and applied and got a place at Exeter Uni to study my PGCE! I also received bonus tickets to my Uni graduation because Billy Allen Senior was going to come along too and cheer me on. But ultimately he didn't, because he died in the week before my final exams and I had to cancel the tickets. It was awful.

Summer came. I moved home to my parents in the run-up to the PGCE but something wasn't right. I thought 'grief isn't like this. Surely not? I shouldn't be unable to sleep. I shouldn't feel all hollowed out.' I'd wake up at 1pm, eat lunch, watch TV for an hour, nap, eat dinner, go to bed. My parents thought it was lazy student life. I'd been diagnosed with anxiety in my second year of uni and one of my relatives had been ... questionable. They referred to me hearing voices and did the whole: "everyone gets worried, you need to buck up your ideas" routine.

I went to the GP. Unsurprisingly, I was diagnosed with depression. I took meds and started feeling better. I moved to Exeter, began my PGCE and life was awesome. I was finally doing what I'd wanted to do for so long and I made lovely friends. I went home to my parents again for a week or so at Christmas and then when I returned to Exeter, that's when my mysterious health problems kicked off...

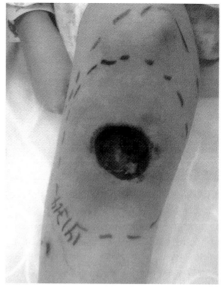

I came back to my student digs feeling a bit off. Sick with a dodgy stomach. I put it down to Christmas excesses. But when my iffy tummy and weird bowel movements continued for over a week, I thought something might be up. I'm talking weird rumbling pain, constantly needing to go to the loo and there being nothing, or just passing liquid poo (not like diarrhoea but actually just liquid – grim fact!) One Thursday after I'd finished being at school on my first teaching placement, I went to the local NHS walk-in centre and gave a stool sample, thinking nothing of it because I'd obviously get a phone call if something was wrong.

I went to school on Friday still feeling like death. I didn't eat all weekend, bar a couple of cups of tea and maybe 4 cookies which my landlady made. By Monday, I was dead on my feet. I could barely stand up straight. I went to school and barely got through my first lesson which was a 'free' [a planning session]. But this was a good thing since I had to make at least 10 trips to the loo and I cried. I felt so poorly that I knew I needed to leave school early to return to my rented place but I had to borrow money for the bus home from Exmouth as I usually got a lift. Once I got home, all I could do was sleep.

The next morning, I went to the GP and explained what was going on. He was puzzled and rang around and discovered that my stool sample had gone missing. My temperature was fine despite me professing to being warm but my blood pressure was a mess, so he insisted on a blood test. I was so dehydrated that my blood couldn't be taken. So I was given multiple cups of water, told to wait an hour and then they could try again. Finally a sample. But when the GP asked who was waiting at home for me and I said: "nobody", he insisted that I wait for another hour in a random examination room. An hour passed and he sent me to hospital.

I went to the hospital and was sent to assessment. They quickly moved me to a little room because I was so much younger than everyone else and they put me on a lot of fluids, asking me also to repeat the stool sample. I contacted my parents to say that I was in hospital. I gave my sample to the nurses and was told off for it not being a 'stool-only' sample, when actually it *was* stool only: this is what my stools looked like: there wasn't much solid stuff happening!

I was eventually moved to a Gastro Ward and had to have a colonoscopy, so I actually got to see my insides, along with a Gastroenterologist. My insides were a mess! My large intestine was mostly ulcerated and it was quickly suggested that I had an inflamatory condition, possibly Crohns, possibly Colitis. I was bunged on a load of antibiotics and steroids. Plus a weird anti-inflammatory medication called Infliximab (I'll come back to this later). I spent the best part of a week in hospital before I was released and then I had to take the rest of the week off. I wasn't officially allowed in Uni, but I snuck in for tea after a seminar day.

After that week off, I went back to school for a fortnight and then on the Friday, I had to return to the hospital for another dose of Infliximab, more blood tests and a lot of steroids. I was on a high dose and had to take calcium to protect my bones. I was permanently hungry and always very blurry-visioned. I got a panicked phone call over that weekend from the hospital, calling me back in on the Monday. My blood tests were off as I wasn't responding to meds the way they thought I should be.

By now it was the week before the February half-term break and I had my first teaching 'observation' on the Wednesday [this can be stressful: it's when your PGCE Director or a similar colleague from the University, visit the school where you are having your teaching placement and they sit in on your lesson, observe it critically and assess your teaching skills]. I was feeling pretty rough. On the Monday, I was given repeated blood tests and I had another colonoscopy. It got to Wednesday morning and I felt awful so I asked my landlady if she could drop me at the hospital. I walked into the 'Infusion Centre' where I usually got my Infliximab and I refused to leave until I was admitted. Within 3 hours I was on the Gastro Ward again. My Consultant said that I had stopped respond- ing to Infliximab and my inflammation markers were raised and my intestine was looking dire! By 4pm, I was ringing my parents saying that I was going to have emergency surgery to remove my large intestine or else it was likely to rupture inside of me! So here I was: in Exeter, 8+ hours' drive from my parents, being told a major organ was going to be removed, but only once the hospital could locate special blood for me, because Infliximab had destroyed my immune response.

On Friday 14 February, I was taken into surgery. When I woke up, my mum was there telling me I wasn't allowed to eat a full jacket potato! I had lines, drips, drains and a catheter attached to me… and now half a jacket potato with no skin. Oh, and a nub of my small intestine in a bag on my stomach.

It was weird. For the first few days, they took my poop away, measuring it to make sure it was working properly. After 3 or so days, I was taught how to change my stoma bag. And it was odd, because I had been at a point where I was happy with my body and now I had this thing attached to me. I was as okay as I could be but it felt as if my agency had completely gone. I had to act. It wasn't like I'd had 20+ years of struggling with meds that didn't work, but rather this was 6 weeks of going from normal to seriously not normal… and I would have to step away from my demanding teacher training. Thus my bursary would stop and I'd have to return to my childhood home for a while. These were all huge unwanted changes for me!

My undergraduate friends were all living their lives, my PGCE friends were all starting to look for teaching jobs but I was moving back to Newcastle to live with my parents. It felt a retrograde step. My mum was awesome, she'd had breast cancer when I was in sixth form and she was very much of the mentality that 'you must do what you need to do to be healthy, just listen to your body'. But another member of my family struggled with it because they had views of what was considered 'normal' by society and that person was worried about me being stigmatised.

So I headed back to Newcastle and life was okay. I decided to go and do some volunteering in a primary school where I'd previously undertaken my preliminary teaching placement, pre-PGCE. I met a nice guy and we went on holiday to the Isle of Man. Whilst there, I bumped my shin when we went to the beach but I didn't think anything much of this and after our hols, I went back to Newcastle. However, something felt off. I convinced myself that I had an intestinal blockage so I went to the hospital and a nurse put a finger in my stoma to check but nothing apparently wrong was detected. But a week later, something really wasn't right as I had a weird spot on my shoulder. I thought it could be a reaction to using a different soap powder or maybe it was the heat as it was early July and the weather was hot.

Then I ended up with a spot on my lower back and it burst (with hindsight, it had way too much pus). My mum dressed my wounds and packed me off to the GP. By this point, I could barely stand up straight. My shoulders had seized up and I walked like quasimodo into the young GP's room, with my mum in tow. The two of them looked at my back. Their facial expressions were hilariously coded. My mum said: "I think it might need some… cream… could you prescribe some cream please?"

The GP replied: "I can't, but I'll book an appointment at the Dermatology Unit tomorrow. They can prescribe cream but if it gets worse in the mean time, go to A&E."

I returned home and new spots appeared right next to my stoma so I dashed to A&E as this meant I had a serious infection! Once in A&E, I was triaged within 20 minutes as my temperature was high. They admitted me as a patient and gave me paracetamol and then…

My life was going to get worse, reader,… I'm just warning you.

I went to the toilet and there was a lot of 'poo goo' (a term used by ileostomy patients to describe the weird stuff your butt makes. It's like it produces a lubricant to help you poo, but obviously I wasn't pooing from there now). I sat in a hospital bay with my mum and I was in a lot of pain and it was coming from my mouth. It felt like my wisdom tooth was being pulled out. I instinctively touched it and it wasn't anything to do with my wisdom tooth, but instead it was a hideous ulcer that had just burst in my mouth. I was admitted and put in a random bed before being moved to a Holding Ward. In the morning, a Mr Price (a Consultant) appeared. He looked at the skin on my chest and at all the spots. They now looked yellow and pus-filled. He declared that I had: "infected chicken pox", needed to go to Infectious Diseases and I was promptly whisked away.

Infectious diseases was Ward 19. A distant ward on the top floor, nigh on impossible to get to, except through elevators. I had to be buzzed in. There was hand wash in the ward, hand wash in the nurses' bay, hand wash before the ward. And the same on the way out but the upside was that patients got their own private en suite, as that's what happens when you're infectious.

I was put on antibiotics and steroids. They ran sample after sample. It got to 11pm. I'd been in hospital for nearly 30 hours and I sobbed to the nurses who were doing the last rounds. Through the sobs, they gathered that no one had looked at my back. So they checked. My mum had run out of dressings so I had been making do with folded-up kitchen roll taped to my skin. By the next morning, things were cranking up. But it still felt like a waiting game.

My collarbone became swollen and hot. My knee was also puffy and bruised with a large blood blister. A decision was made to have plastic surgeons come and look at it. I got up to go and pee and as I sat on the loo, the blister burst! Everywhere! It was like a horror movie. I pulled the emergency cord, crying and apologising that I had made a mess. I was sent to Plastic Surgery to have the wound surgically excised.

When I returned to Infectious Diseases, I had a huge bandage on my knee. Someone from the Dermatology dept. appeared, to look at my skin and then they took a 'dermal punch' from my back (it's like a medical grade hole-punch, to see what was happening). The Plastic Surgery dept. came to inspect my knee and took off all my wound dressings. I waited for the nurses to wrap me back up as I lay on my side, desperate for the loo.

Then my mum walked in to find me in this state. Nobody had told her or me that my knee wound had to be left open. I wasn't aware but when she got home, she cried to my dad that there was no way my knee would heal.

I was now under the care of 6 different departments and I wasn't getting any solid answers but I was told that my condition looked like Atypical Pyoderma

Gangrenosum: an illness only declared when everything else has been ruled out. Or maybe it's genetic. Who knows? The Plastic Surgery dept. said they would let me go home once I was able to change the dressing on my knee every two days. But I was meant to be going home the very next morning. However, that night, the dressing got stuck in my knee wound at 11.30pm, so I received a late dose of morphine to remove the sticky bandage.

At 3am, I was woken by the feeling of something exploding inside of me and I curled up into the foetal position and refused to move. I wasn't allowed to have oral Morphine and had to wait for an IV line to be fitted, so the on-call doctor came and immediately announced she thought she'd missed my vein. Whatever. I couldn't lay flat but they made me lie down and took me for an x-ray.

By 8am, I'd also had a CT scan and been forced to have a catheter because I wasn't peeing; this took 2x attempts and 4x individuals to fit. I deliberately stopped my IV because my wrist became the size of a grapefruit as the fluid pooled under my skin. The medical team insisted I had another colonoscopy and it hurt. Oh Lord, it hurt so much! It got to the point where they had to use a tiny camera because nothing was working. You're not allowed to read your medical records, but if you're not, they shouldn't let patients carry their reports back to the wards with them because I carried my colonoscopy report on my lap back to Ward 19 and of course, I read it! I rang my mum to tell her I was having surgery again. "You don't know that", she stated.

I replied: "Mother, the doctor used an exclamation mark. The opening line was 'This is horrible!' It then went on to discuss a potential rupture".

Slight backtrack: when I had my first lot of surgery to remove my large intestine except a six-inch rectal stump, there was – much to my father's joy - a chance that at some point my small intestine could be hooked up to a rectal stump to reattach the plumbing and make me normal. Well that wasn't going to be the case for much longer and I cried. I cried to the lovely nurse who sat with me for 45 minutes and I drank Horlicks and I raged against the world.

I had been happy. Normal. Only just 7 months ago, I'd turned 22. I'd got through puberty with some stretch marks which were fading but now this: my knee was a hole; my back was a speckled mess; my face was crusty and the nurses changed my pillowcases twice a day because the pus and scabs were everywhere. I had been going to have surgery when the Gastrointestinal dept. had previously released me because I was fine. I'd had keyhole surgery in February but I couldn't now. Even the IV drips I had, left tiny scars. And it all hurt.

My anxiety had always said that I wasn't good enough: I wasn't perfect and now I actually really wasn't! Or that's how I felt. The surgery itself was fairly uneventful. I had a night in ICU, cursing every time they turned me over to stop me getting bed sores. I know it's procedure but I was in for one night and being turned every hour is a pain…

I was sent back to the Gastro Ward and had another week of sitting around, reading, drinking Costa drinks which my mum brought me and being wound-up by my annoying bed neighbour. But then I was allowed to go home! My sister was excited about changing my dressings because she was going off to Uni to do nursing and I was so excited to be out of hospital. But I was on a lot of meds: namely a shedload of steroids.

So I'd been released from hospital. My consultants were still not 100% sure what had caused my illness and I was put on an extended course of Azythromicin. This is a high dose of antibiotic which you're only meant to take for 3 days but I had to take it for a month and have it in different forms at home. One form was liquid, which would only last for 24 hours in the fridge. The NHS won't fund tablets and I can't take capsules as they don't dissolve in my stubby digestive system. I was also on a high dose of steroids. In 2 weeks, I put on a stone and a half. And I hated it.

I hated sitting, feeling achy, waiting for appointments, being mollycoddled by my parents. My hospital stay had seen my back covered in sticky wounds; my face and my knee had exploded; my butt-hole had been stitched, closed and I'd effectively given birth to my remaining large intestine through a c-section. Sitting-up, sneezing, leaning forward and tie-ing shoelaces was fun in a challenging way. Plus my new food and meds was messing with my 'bowel' so my stoma output was a weird consistency and acidity, thus my bag kept leaking. I was now a 22-year-old girl, living with my parents, having to shout for my mum when I had woken up covered in liquid poo. I hated seeing everyone else be 'normal': my sister was going off to Uni; my friends were happy in their graduate jobs; my PGCE friends were teaching and here I was… trapped and getting heavy.

And I was miserable. So I sought to control the one thing I could, which was food. I wouldn't eat breakfast, lunch would be a sandwich and I'd eat half of my dinner. It was soon noticed at home. My dad would stop eating when I did. We'd go for a walk to build my strength up but that was 'excessive' because I was in that zone. We were walking 10k a day. Having the same conversations. Walking the same roads. My mum got annoyed because I was: "ruining my dinner with cake". The reality was… I'd be skipping breakfast, having a coffee and cake with my dad halfway through the walk, then having half of my dinner.

Luckily the hospital kept tabs on me. The Infectious Diseases dept were perplexed and curious about what was going on and they were also obsessively weighing me (their standard procedure as the HIV centre). They noticed my weight plummet below even my sick weight. In about 4 months, I lost about 10% of my body weight. My Consultant asked what was going on with my mum awkwardly sitting beside me, as I explained that I couldn't eat unless I'd justified it; that it didn't feel right to eat; that I hated dealing with my bag and the potential consequences: the smell, the leaks, the bag inflating as I ate and talked; how I'd gone from my fittest and happiest to a little husk of myself. Just before this really kicked-off and my mum found out (maybe 4 weeks or so?) the hospital ran blood tests and my inflammation markers were up. I was meant to return to Exeter after Xmas to restart my PGCE but this marker suggested I might get sick again, so a joint decision was made to push the PGCE course back again. This got me down…

Simultaneously my weird doctor boyfriend dumped me within days of our first date after he'd got back. It's likely that we'd kinda rushed it and it wouldn't have worked but in my mind, that potential relationship had failed because I was a disgusting, fat sticky lump with scars and holes in her face and knee.

So my return to Exeter for my PGCE was then scheduled for after Easter but my brain got sadder. My eating worsened and this was somewhat enabled by another guy I was dating, who had his own food issues. I realise looking back that I was propping myself up and distracting myself from my own unhappiness by dating. I was then moved to a town in the South West for my first teaching placement to make up for the one I'd had to abandon previously. I was on placement 1 whilst the two other trainees there, were on placement 2. I felt very alone and very afraid. I was panicking about getting sick. Also a guy from my original PGCE course that I'd had to abandon when I'd first become ill, was my main teacher in the department which was odd as he was now much more senior to me, having completed his PGCE when I was so poorly. We'd started off at the same stage and now he was leaps and bounds ahead of me.

I was a mess. I wasn't eating or I was deliberately consuming food my body struggled to process in the hope that I wouldn't absorb calories. I would swim on a Sunday morning and then have a cream tea. That was it. My dinner after work was a jacket potato: plain.

Other teachers at school complimented my determination, my resolve, my slim physique: "I'd never be able to wear outfits like that", "you're so slim", "you've got an amazing figure."

I'd never been complimented on my appearance before getting sick. Now people openly commented. I was getting praise for what felt like the first time. And that just fed into it all. And I fell between NHS cracks. I was a temporary resident in the South West. No one had my medical records. I wasn't underweight yet I was at the lower end of normal. I knew this because that was my defence: "I'm not ill, I need to be x pounds lighter to be underweight". I knew my weight daily. I would berate myself if I went above my set number.

My parents visited me around the time my relationship broke down and I discovered that I was being moved to another part of the South West for placement 2 with a teacher named 'M', who'd taught us on my PGCE sometimes. My parents declared I was "skin and bones" and that I "looked like a holocaust survivor". You could see my ribs, my hips, my collar bones, my finger joints. But I only saw that number: my weight. Whilst I was that number, people applauded me.

I moved to another area for teaching placement 2! Life was still messy and I was still struggling with food. I saw counsellors for 2-3 sessions, declared myself: "feeling better" then quit. I dated a guy who loved food but I wasn't loving school so I moved. Again: my 4th address in 15 months. I was going to work with a different guy from our PGCE. Small world! Yet here finally, I found a team who really supported me. And after slightly more than a year, I bought a flat.

I had dated, been unhappy, been panicky that I couldn't find happiness, that other people couldn't fix me. I declared that I was going back to counselling for real this time. And I took up sport. Not a normal sport: I started Roller Derby and I was awful. I couldn't stay up or stop. Or turn around. But we were all awful. And everyone accepted that I was this awkward ball of anxiety because they were too. It was interesting being in a female-dominated environment where people were willing to openly accept someone different. That I could talk about being ill, but also people could share their insecurities, imperfections and health issues. People were willing to discuss their trauma, their gender identity and their fears. And watching people of all sizes, ages and identities' skate – which was often something they'd never done before - was awesome!

I kept seeing my counsellor and doing therapy properly. I made notes, thought carefully about what was causing my unhappiness and did things I enjoyed. I walked a lot, read and skated. I swotted up about anxiety and depression and tried to break that negative cycle of thinking. I got to a position where I was willing to come off my antidepressants and cope with my own brain. I found myself acknowledging sadness and panic, but I was able to push it aside and not let it control me. I could let the sadness come and then let it drift away.

I was eating and I was cooking. Partially because I started dating after about 6 months of focusing on just me. And my new guy liked food, but hated cooking. He didn't care about my bag or my weird scars: he was absent-minded in a way where he didn't notice things. The first time he stayed at mine, the seal on my bag exploded and he stripped the bed without even thinking.

My focus became being healthy and strong so I could skate better. I knew I was getting heavier but I was happier as it was serving a purpose. I had to go back on my meds, but as I realised I was unhappy in that teaching job at the time, thus I took the decision to increase my medication dose while I looked for a new job and settled into that.

And life's not perfect. It's not easy. I have really negative patches but I know they'll end. I know it'll be awful for a week or a month and I know I'll settle back down. I worry a lot, the state of the world right now [during the beginning of lockdown] is terrifying for me. I'm scared of getting sick, of letting people down, of not doing enough, of other people's actions, of being irritating. I sometimes seek approval: I worry my anxiety and negativity will push people away. But it is a part of me that I can't change, but it is something I can mostly manage.

I took one day off for mental health reasons and that was when coursework and chaos at home kicked off. It was officially written up as 'sleep deprivation'. I always have the panic of telling employers about how I am, but no one has ever reacted negatively.

I've had to accept that my changeable mental health is part of me forever, like my changeable physical health is. I may be one of those people who always needs medication to pootle along. And I still get insecure about my appearance, about my bag, about my weight. It's not helped by little comments people can make such as: "you'll be needing your fat clothes soon"; "you know you've put on X kg since we last weighed you (a doctor). And I have sad moments that I am not stereotypically 'attractive'. I'm not like people in adverts or instagram. I have a weird external organ and kids sometimes think I'm pregnant. Some of my trousers give me a muffin-top and I wear high-waisted underwear that covers my bag but they're either Spanx or made for grandmas or are like a billion quid! I know I have lots of clothing that I've kept that won't fit me and that at some point, I'll have to try them on and then send them all to a charity shop... and then I'll probably cry.

But equally I have moments where someone compliments something I've done. I know if I wasn't eating, I would not be able to skate. I know if I'd done my teacher training in one go, I probably wouldn't be living where I am and teaching in a sweet school.* Overall life is pretty good!

What have your experiences taught you?

That the pressure you put on yourself to be perfect, will break you. That you can't be perfect and you cannot assume perfection from those around you.

Also that disability can be challenging, especially hidden disability, where people don't know how to support you or how to say things.

*I love teaching but acknowledge the pressure and mechanics of it: diluting everything down to stats and seeing kids as numbers. That was really driven home when we were treated like smucks by the government [during the Covid lockdowns] regarding school shutdowns, results, reopening and the political and media campaign against teachers. I want to teach so much but teaching doesn't always feel how I want it to be.

What advice would you give to other women in a similar situation?

I think for me, seeking professional counselling support and giving it the space to work has massively helped. It might take shopping around, as it were, to find a counsellor or therapist that you click with.

Also take the space you need. There is no shame in taking a break, having a 'mental health day'. If you force yourself to be performing all the time, you will break.

Where are you now? What are your plans for the future?

Now I'm oddly settled. I own a flat. I have a good job teaching History at a lovely school and they are super-supportive of my health issues and have been awesome during the whole Covid business.

And after 3 or so years of umm'ing and ahh'ing about doing an MA, I finally applied and got accepted!!

I have an awesome partner who keeps me grounded. He's great at looking after me when my brain goes weird. And my health is fine: literally nothing has gone wrong since July 2014. (I had a scare in December, because I had stomach pains for like 3 months… it turned out I'm now lactose-intolerant too but I can cope… !)

FAY'S STORY

A controlling husband, a 14-year affair and sexual desire in your seventies

How you feel when you're in your seventies about

LOVE AND INTIMACY

Four years' ago, for my 72nd birthday, I had a trip to the South of France with my family and I fell completely head-over-heels in love with a guy in his forties! I was in the hotel lift by myself, going back up to the apartment that my husband and I were sharing, when I met this mystery man. I had just come out of the pool and I was still in my swimming costume and wearing a 'cover up' over the top of it. In that lift, a man started smiling at me to catch my attention and we both clocked each other and started laughing. It turned out that he was one of the Hotel Managers and prior to being there, he had worked on ship liners and at a hotel in Morocco, so he had lots of fascinating stories to tell. We immediately clicked and it was as if we had known each other all of our lives.

He was very Spanish, completely at ease with women and he simply opened up to me: the conversation flowed. He told me he had slept around a lot and later invited me up to his flat. I wanted to go but I didn't. At this point, all physical intimacy with my husband had stopped a long, long time ago and I truly missed it so I was severely tempted, but I still resisted going. I never even found out this man's name but the connection between us was so powerful. During that holiday, I spent all of his lunch-breaks with him and I don't even know if my family noticed that I was gone so much or how distracted I was?

One day on this holiday, I was in the pool and he walked past me in his trunks. I have never before (even during my long affair with another man), or ever since, experienced the same physical excitement that I did then, of seeing this guy. I felt sheer lust. He really sparked intense sexual desire in me.

And I could tell that he had really fallen for me too: I am flirty and bubbly and have a huge appetite for life which he brought out of me. We had a lot of fun chatting and laughing together. Our age difference was completely irrelevant.

Another time whilst I there, I saw him waiting for me by the entrance to his apartment. Later when I didn't go to up to his flat, he found me and asked: "why didn't you come? I wouldn't have done anything against your will" and I regretted not going. Then towards the end of my holiday, his family arrived to visit him. A women in the hotel kitchen walked towards me and just gave me a pointed look that made me realise that she just knew something was going on between the Manager and myself.

My birthday took place whilst we were over there and this man sent me a card and a bottle of wine. I just couldn't believe the effect he was having on me! It made me realise that no matter what age we are, we all want to be desired, to be loved and I was now in my seventies and experiencing pure lust but it was frustrating because it wasn't being sated.

After we had returned to England, later, that Christmas, he was still in my head! I sent him a card and it was as though I was possessed, besotted… I had fallen completely in love and it had come totally out of the blue! What I have learnt during my life is that the best experiences come in this way, when you least expect them.

This episode made me reflect on my life and my romantic relationships…

BACKGROUND TO MY LONG AFFAIR: MY CAREER, FINANCIAL CONTROL AND MARRIED LIFE ABROAD

When I was in the first training period as a teacher in the 1970s, my husband Paul, told me that I wasn't 'allowed' to work with men and he went ballistic about the fact that I might be, but I challenged him and said: "this is ridiculous. Our children will be taught by men and women; you can't expect me to be in a school without any men," but it was clear to me that he had deep insecurities and was jealous.

Later when I undertook further educational training, Paul didn't want me to do it. It was such a huge effort as simultaneously I was juggling our 4 children too and work. Meanwhile, Paul had just taken on a new role as a Partner in a Medical Practice and I think he felt threatened by my career ambitions so he simply said a flat: "no" to me progressing to become an assistant headteacher and ultimately a headteacher.

To make matters more difficult for me (and I know this probably sounds unbelievable to younger generations today), he wouldn't let me use our car to travel to the school where I worked and I just accepted that. I didn't have the money to buy a car for myself so I had to use a public bus to get to the school where I was doing my training, which was an hour away from my home. Therefore, I had this long arduous journey but I had time off during teaching periods, so I took all of my training books and luggage into the staff room and studied there. Additionally I stayed at a B&B next door one night a week to give me more study time. It was an enormous task but I fought so hard for my career. I had to pass some additional exams but I was there to succeed and I did! One day, Paul suddenly appeared at my school unexpectedly. He was checking up on me, but there was nothing for him to discover, because he soon realised that I was simply studying![3]

Paul was a wonderful father but for many decades, he had authority over me as his wife. I married him when I was 18 years old. He was keenly into amateur dramatics and so was I, he was also a Christian and that made me feel safe. We met

---

3   I admire my granddaughters because they have a much more equal marriage than I've had. They will say things to their husbands like: "I'm going on a hen weekend soon and you'll need to arrange childcare" and they just do it.

in the September and by the following April, we'd got engaged because I thought of him as a decent and honest man and it was what you did back then, in terms of life plans! Paul's mum had died when he was 19 years old, not long before he met me, so I think I became a mother figure to him.

Not long after our wedding, I was expecting our first baby, Stephen, but already Paul had taken off abroad, independently of me to further his medical career (he'd been working in medicine at a hospital in London where we were living, but he'd been ambitious to practice it abroad). Back then it wasn't normal for men to be present at the birth anyway, so I'd backed his decision and encouraged him to have this adventure, although I missed him massively and obviously it wasn't an easy situation for me as a new bride, but I accepted it.

I had a horrible birth delivering Stephen on my own whilst Paul was away. I tore a lot and needed stitches and then had a haematoma afterwards. To recover, I stayed with my parents. They paid for everything: the pram, and so on, because Paul didn't send any money back home to me. When the baby was 6 weeks' old, I went abroad to join my husband and I have to say that despite his earlier absence, he was fantastic with the baby. After a little while out there, I undertook a foundation teaching course to gain a qualification. Back then, if you worked for the British Overseas' Department for 36 months', then you could go back to the UK for 6 months' leave, and that's what we did and whilst there, I took my formal teaching exams in London. Paul had thrown himself into our family life and he was supportive of what I was doing as it meant that I would be earning money but via working with primary school children I am convinced that he thought this would be a cosy career for me and one where I was unlikely to meet many men and potentially stray.

On reflection, I can now see that limiting my access to money throughout the early years of our marriage was my husband's way of ensuring that I was dependent on him. We have an old friend, Tom Price, who we met abroad when I was 21. We caught up recently and Tom said that he remembered Paul telling him back then: "Fay's always asking why we don't have any money? Little does she know that we're living off her salary because I'm saving all my wages up secretly" and Paul had laughed about this and my gullibility. When Tom told me this, it really upset me because it took me right back to those early years when Paul had my unwavering support and I felt I had been an utter fool to have placed all my trust in him, whilst he slyly enjoyed my naivety. To me, it demonstrated a total lack of respect and equality early on in our marriage. Paul doesn't know that I'm now aware of this. Basically, I didn't have any financial security back then and for a long portion of our marriage and I felt trapped. I feel that one of the biggest mistakes women can make, is letting men be in full control of the finances in married/family life.

We left London after our 6 months' leave came to an end and we returned abroad, I applied to work in an international prep school but I didn't get the post. However, I was offered another position and one where I had to teach music too. Paul didn't object to this because it meant I was gaining an income again in what he considered to be a 'safe' environment without men around. My employment really helped our financial situation. By this point, we had spent 7 years abroad but where we were living was becoming unsafe as civil war was about to break out. We passed armed members of the militia every day on our way to work. Our neighbour worked for the government and he came to tell us that we should leave because the situation was dangerous and only getting worse. Before he even confided this information, he made us close our curtains and windows because he was so frightened of getting caught in the process. He chose to stay on and fortunately he was okay.

Things were getting to a stage where we were having to make big decisions about our family's future. By the early 1970s, life in the country where we were living abroad, was getting really dicey and we decided we had to leave, but the process of getting out was tough. We had to show a tax form for everything we had purchased there. Without producing these receipts, we couldn't leave, but somehow we managed to find them all and depart. Coming back to the UK, was definitely the right decision and we breathed a sigh of relief.

It was an epic move, but we headed back to England and the North. Paul got a job in a Hospital whilst I started teaching the violin and also became a teacher in a primary school too.

Teaching had always been in my family as my father had been a Headmaster and a woman I worked with, encouraged me to actually make the leap from being a teacher to a Headteacher. In my thirties, I threw myself fully into the additional training which I needed to do to achieve this and I was so ready for the challenge. Age wasn't an issue: another lady I came to know started her teacher training at 40 and is now an executive Head of 3 schools!

My implosion affair

I met Mr X at my Amateur Dramatics ('Am Dram') group when I was 39 and he'd moved nearby for his job as a Finance Director in the public sector (that's all I feel I can say about his career out of respect for his privacy). Mr X's wife had left him years' before and he had 2 grown-up children, who he never confided in, regarding our relationship.

I couldn't help but wonder what had happened to his wife, why she had suddenly taken off? Mr X wouldn't really discuss her and it was obvious that at one point, they had loved one another, but I was able to piece together that she'd had mental health issues, I think probably post-natal depression and possibly even PTSD following childbirth because she'd suffered an injury during labour which hadn't been fully repaired, which led to her bowel opening up whenever she needed to have a wee.

It's bizarre how our affair started out as there wasn't any real attraction between us at first. Paul was in the same Am Dram club as Mr X and myself and for some reason, one night Mr X gave just me (not Paul), a lift home from a rehearsal and our affair just started from there. It was so lovely to have a man interested in me: someone who saw and respected **me** as an individual again!

The three of us acting in the same productions, added a frisson and Paul didn't pick up on the chemistry between Mr X and me. At the time I was studying for another qualification in teaching leadership but I would go and see Mr X on my days off and seduce him! He was totally willing and it went from there. We met up at least once a week and it was so exciting but also made me feel conflicted because obviously it was very deceitful and went against my faith, which has always been important to me and it was important to him too.

It was life-enhancing to be listened to and supported, for what felt like the first time in years. Mr X told me he loved me and asked me what I wanted from him. I remember saying: "I don't want an affair, I want to marry you", but then when it came to the crunch, I couldn't leave my family. The crunch came in a brutal way: a while into our affair, when Paul still didn't know about it, Mr X rang Paul up and told Paul that he loved me. Mr X was trying to force the situation and force me to choose him and of course, everything kicked off then. After Mr X told my husband, Paul threatened to kill Mr X by sabotaging his car.

I begged Paul to have counselling as he was struggling to cope with the fallout because during my affair with Mr X, (like lots of people who have affairs), I tried to act normally throughout at home and I had interacted with Paul as I had always done but Paul couldn't square this. It really played on his mind. He said to me: "I cannot believe you have been so deceitful. You've always been so honest." He was utterly shocked that I could have two sides to my personality. Just as he had two sides to his personality when it came to how he was with me and our finances: telling me one thing but doing something else behind my back: He could be like that, but hadn't anticipated that in another capacity, I too was capable of deception and acting autonomously.

Paul rang up my dad and told him what I had done, as a way of shaming me. Later, my elderly grandmother rang me and told me that she understood what had happened but that I was "destroying" my parents. She said she didn't blame me, but she couldn't condone my behaviour because of my children and the fact that it was having such a negative impact on everyone. When my dad died not that long after, I remember saying to my grandmother that it was my fault, but she said it wasn't; my dad had had a minor stroke previously but he just hadn't told me about it because he didn't want to worry me, but again the guilt kicked in hard.

I was harshly judged by one of my daughters because she was seventeen years' old at the time she found out about my affair, and she worshipped her dad, who made a 'cry for help' suicide attempt because of it (he took an overdose). This daughter turned up at the school where I was now an Assistant Head and she hit me in a corridor, out of disgust, saying: "how can you be so selfish?!" She was shocked and couldn't get over the fact I'd been involved in a sexual relationship because like lots of teenagers, she didn't want to think of either of her parents having that dimension to their lives. There was a level of jealousy aimed at me from her, along with her sense of my disloyalty to all of them. Additionally, she couldn't fathom my dishonesty as I was a deeply-committed Christian. However, little did she know that her beloved brother would also have an affair in the future and that she would completely support him as his marriage broke down as a result, because later in her maturity, my daughter realised how unhappy her brother had been to have the affair in the first place.

In terms of my husband Paul, he did let go of my infidelity and miraculously, wasn't suspicious of me nor did he hurl it back in my face. But although I had done a U-turn with Mr X, I was still really in love with him. He considered me so much and we got on so well but if I'm honest, his wife's departure played on my mind a lot when we were together and I was torn between my love for him and my loyalty to my family. After I made the choice to remain with my husband, my affair with Mr X unbelievably, somehow still continued… but then he retired from his career and he made a huge decision.

His decision was to move a long distance away from me. He said he needed to physically separate himself from me because I wouldn't leave Paul. This was my implosion moment! It was an absolutely devastating blow to me! Because he had been my lifeline! I was working lots, the children were hardcore, and he was there *for me* and I loved him so much. I didn't feel like that about my husband any more. I had fallen completely out of love with Paul but I just couldn't break up my family home. A sense of duty and my beliefs stopped me from following my heart. However, I still needed Mr X and I know that sounds selfish but he was my support and when he moved away, I pined: I missed him terribly!

One of my sons said to me years' later: "you'd have been bored mum" as Mr X was 17 years older than me, but I didn't ever think of the age gap. Unlike my son, I didn't see him as "boring", I just saw Mr X as an adventurer. After Mr X moved away, we had a period of time when we didn't see each other but ultimately we kept in touch via phoning. The affair still continued and the physical side of it reignited too. I would travel for 5 hours to see him on my days off as I needed him and what we had together. I loved the way he made me feel so valued and respected. He also made me laugh, which was so uplifting. We were very compatible intimately as well and this was important. All of this combined, literally kept me together. My affair – bizarrely – kept me happy and sane.

In my marriage, even from the beginning, the intimate side of our life together had never been wonderful, right from the very beginning. I hadn't had any experience in this way before I got married, because the 'rule' back then was, no sex before marriage. No one talked about it. When I was a student and before I got married, I suggested to Paul that we went away for the weekend, got drunk and explored this part of our lives together but Paul wouldn't and I respected his decision because I felt as though I would be going against my parents and also there was the risk that I would get pregnant. However, once we got married, sex wasn't ideal as it hurt at the beginning and it put me off really. Paul was just as inexperienced as I was and so it was all a bit perfunctory but furthermore, I just didn't fancy him.

Mr X was the first person I made love with, other than my husband. So for over 2 decades until Mr X and I started our affair, Paul was the only man I had ever been intimate with. I married Paul because I knew he'd be a steady man and father, but I always wish I'd had more sensual experiences. If this had happened before I met Paul, I don't think I would have married him as on reflection, I feel that marrying him was a mistake, but all of this happened as were coming into the Swinging Sixties and before the pill.

The affair with Mr X happened for several reasons including, not feeling valued, loved, noticed or sexual but rather, feeling demeaned and financially trapped. I talked earlier about the difficulties Paul imposed on me when I decided to pursue and then further a teaching career and his insecurities regarding me having male colleagues. However, in terms of pushing forward my ambitions, I was completely single-minded: I did feel conflicted and guilty as do so many women. Yes, I wanted to train to go into teaching leadership but I was always conscious of the time element with regards to my family. For a while, I worked for a local charity in their Education Department so that I would be more physically present for my family, as opposed to taking a more demanding role in a prestigious independent school further away. But although I gained lots of useful experience, I became bored because having worked in hectic environments, the pace of the local charity was too slow for me. Ultimately I moved to a big state comprehensive to increase my experience but it was tricky because even getting to this workplace was complicated because of the transport issues mentioned at the outset of this chapter.

At one point I had to move into nearby B&B accommodation again and only had a few pence to my name. In his efforts to thwart my career plans, Paul even said to me: "I'm going to bleed you dry", but another male friend told me that he would help and he would give me the money to get by initially. Later, I was able to open a bank account in my own name and start to save some money. Since then, I've always had my own money so that I am financially strong and I have choices. This made such a difference as I hadn't had access to Paul's money and so for such a long time in my marriage, I felt financially trapped. I want to say to women now: know your worth as a woman and have your own financial means!

Mr X took away the lacklustre feeling from my life but ultimately he respected my situation and because he was close to his own kids, he could understand how important my family were to me. My conscience kept dragging me back to my family and in a way, I'm glad it did. The affair with Mr X gradually fizzled out after 14 years, by which point, I'd worked my way up in my career to be an Assistant Headteacher and so I felt stretched and fulfilled in this respect. With Mr X then, I felt that we had grown apart and had less to talk about but we decided that we should meet one last time.

We both mutually felt that it was the right time to end the affair but we had the most incredible passionate session together the last time we met and I still felt that he honoured and respected me. However, then I returned to my marriage 100%. I'm sure I'll have to answer for my affair one day, but even now, after all these years, I don't feel any regret about it because it came at a time in my life when I desperately needed it, Mr X kept me sane and happy.

After the affair ended with Mr X, I settled back into marriage and stayed with Paul. He's never disgraced me. Overall, I think I'm glad I stayed with him but I can't stress how having my own financial safety-net changed everything for me as it felt so empowering. Paul and I have had wonderful times together, but…

…I've enjoyed flirting with other men since Mr X, but nothing else. However, when you're in your seventies, you still want to be fancied, to have someone find you attractive. Paul has said to me: "you're a little old lady now" and that makes me angry as it's his attempts to denigrate me and put me down. There's a young man I see through the Am Dram club and he gives me massive hugs and I love that. No matter what age you are, you always want to be attractive to people and to be attracted to, people. Some people meet their true love and don't feel this need to be attractive to others but most do (additionally, some mighten ever meet that one special person that gives them butterflies).

When I turned 60 years' old, Paul stopped sleeping with me because he had prostrate problems and he wouldn't go to the doctor about this (due to embarrassment, I think). So since that age, I haven't had sex with my husband or anyone else. This is difficult for me as I know what it is to be loved. So I self-pleasure. I know that other older couples are also in this sexless situation and if their partners won't seek help, then I want to say to them, for goodness sake, masturbate too. But these are issues that are considered taboo. We don't talk to our friends about it.

For the last 15+ years, I feel I have just been expected to put up with a marriage without intimacy. It's just become an unspoken rule and part of that is Paul's arrogance and pride; men do not address the fact that, let alone their needs, women have needs too! We're not all frigid once we've had kids, as the media quite often portrays. Denying one's partner intimacy, long-term, is downright bloody cruel. I would still go into a physical relationship now. I have often thought about going onto a website to find someone else but I haven't yet because I worry about safety. I don't know how/where a woman (or a man) of my age would start on this kind of 'journey' and not be taken advantage of.

Paul seems happy to have a platonic relationship and he's in his eighties now, but the lack of sex is a huge problem for me. When I think about this aspect of my affair with Mr X and how it felt to be desired, it makes me feel nostalgic as it was amazing to be wanted in this way. He both really respected and desired me. Even as our affair was fizzling out, the intimate connection we had between us, was still powerful, even on that very last day when our hearts were sinking as we knew it was over, but our love-making was still special.

What have your experiences taught you?

If you're going to have an affair, don't feel guilty. Misbehave, enjoy it. You're an adult. You know right from wrong. Sometimes you need to be deceitful to 'survive'. I have felt I have an obligation to stay married to Paul because of our children (but that decision has not been made through love).

Also in a marriage, I firmly believe that mutual respect and equality are essential.

Additionally, be who YOU are! I was a trailblazer in terms of pushing for my career when it was expected that I would take much more of a back-seat and be at home raising the kids, whilst my husband rose through the ranks, I accept that this was rare for my generation. I was an adventurer (my mum was an adventurer too) but I needed to be *that* person – it took me a while to stride out and make a stand for my career, but I'm so glad I did!

What advice would you give to other women in a similar situation?

Give yourself permission to make whatever decision is right for you and stick by it. The worst thing that happened to me was when I kept getting chest pains and was having treatment and it made me fearful that something much more serious was going to happen to me, so I reflected on my life.

I'm sorry but I don't feel guilty for my affair. I acted against my conscience but I needed it. I loved every minute of it. No man had ever made me feel like that before. Falling in love/lust can happen at any time. You can be eighty years old and really tumble head over heels for someone. We can have very strong judgements about situations and other people's behaviour but none of us ever know how life can shake us up and how our high principles can be challenged, so my advice is always to try to park your judgements and instead, just be empathetic!

WHERE ARE YOU NOW? WHAT ARE YOUR PLANS FOR THE FUTURE?

I still perform in my local acting club and I love it. I am active, busy and really full of beans. I am also a successful artist/painter. I regularly go hiking (which surprises people) and I enjoy this so much. I'm generally a very happy person except for the sexless part of my marriage which feels like a punishment for my affair (I still may go on a website in order to have some physical intimacy which I crave, but I am anxious about staying safe and not being exploited).

On the flip-side, I love having my great-grandchildren and watching them develop. I'm definitely a family person. In our anniversary cards now, Paul will often write to me: "you are the most wonderful wife, mother and grandmother" and **I am** a good wife, mother and grandmother. If Paul died, I'm not sure — even now — what our financial situation is, but the difference now is that I am financially safe on my own merits because unbeknownst to him, I have money! It's such a safety net.

Finally, I've been protective of Paul getting Covid, so I must love him, deep-down, mustn't I?

IZZY'S STORY

When your baby dies inside of you at 20 weeks during the pandemic lockdown and you have to go through a normal delivery but it's anything but normal and there isn't a happy outcome…

I discovered that I was pregnant either at Christmas 2019, or in early January 2020. My husband Kris had been saying to me for ages that we should have a second baby but I was reluctant because I feel really ill when I'm pregnant. I suffer from bad morning sickness. Also when I had our first child, Hugo, 2 years' ago, the pregnancy was Consultant-led, because I'd previously had some cancer cells lasered-off, so there was an uncertainty as to whether my cervix would open or not.

Hugo was a happy accident. I'm not sure how it happened?! - we even thought it might be down to pre-cum! I was Head of History in a comprehensive school back then and having a baby wasn't on my periphery. Kris wasn't keen either and none of our friends had babies. I was 28 years old at this point. However, my mum had had 6 miscarriages and one had been when she was 24 weeks' pregnant. She'd coped so well and all of this just made me ponder, so we decided to press ahead with having our first baby!

Our son Hugo was born and for his birth, I went to a midwife-led maternity Unit in Hospital A. If you needed a doctor, you had to go to Hospital B. With Hugo, they thought he was distressed, so they wanted to transfer me to Hospital B and pause the contractions but I didn't want to be transferred, so I managed to push him out in Hospital A, before I was transferred. Baby Hugo was fine. I was given tea and toast and a few stitches and I felt amazing. At the time, I was given pain relief but as the day progressed with me in Hospital A, the pain increased enormously and I felt really poorly. My intuition told me that something wasn't quite right especially when I ended up crying out with the pain. I'd had gas and air for the birth but this was almost even more painful than the birth. I ultimately told a midwife about it and she asked to examine me and it was so excruciating: I couldn't even open my legs… I was diagnosed with a Haematoema. I was drip-fed Diamorphine and Hugo was put in an incubator. Later the pain did actually became worse than the birth itself!

I was rushed to Hospital B and Kris had to follow in the car. The doctor took one look at me and said: "give her morphine, give her morphine". I had wind and kept blaming Kris because I didn't realise it was me. I was totally out of it. The Doctor who was tending to me was a fit guy and I didn't want to put him off me!

I was given a 'Spinal Block' which meant I could kind of feel but then I couldn't! My Haematoma was the size of a golf ball and the staff didn't know where the bleeding was coming from and so they couldn't stop it. At one point when I was partially out of it, I heard the staff say to me: "we'll bring Kris and Hugo in, to say goodbye to you".

I later discovered that they had contacted the on-call Consultant by phone and he had told the team to clean me up and then 'pack me' internally with loads of padding. I was put on a high dose of morphine and antibiotics. I was so out of it, that I wasn't thinking of the consequences. It was stressful for Kris too and he was completely knackered. He had to change Hugo's nappy for the first time and in a panic, he asked the nurse if she would do it, but she insisted Kris had a go, which he did!

I struggled with breastfeeding as Hugo wouldn't latch on properly. I didn't realise it but Hugo had tongue-tie but I was a bit limited in my ability to be mobile because I was on a catheter. A trained breastfeeding support lady came to talk to me about breastfeeding for 40 minutes and it was a lot to take in. I had three nights by myself in the hospital and one of the doctors took one look at my birth battle-scars and he declared: "it looks as though Mike Tyson's been at her, down there!"

I kept trying to breastfeed and one day when I was attached to a breast pump, my dad just turned up! Things turned a corner when a young 18-year-old volunteer midwife told me about nipple-shields. They were a complete game-changer! They were so helpful. Like a nipple extender... finally Hugo could latch on! It was amazing! (Midwives aren't really allowed to advise nursing mothers to use nipple shields but new mums should definitely be aware of them! If you're struggling with breastfeeding, try them). I breastfed Hugo for nearly a year. I didn't really have any problems afterwards with breastfeeding.

I realise there's such a pressure for new mums to be ecstatically happy and walking around parading their new baby but sometimes it's not quite like that. For example, it took me at least 5 months after childbirth before I felt ready to have sex again and also I was really constipated for 2 weeks after the birth. I just couldn't poo at all. I took Lactulose to ease this situation and then promptly puked up after necking half a bottle of it. I didn't really know what was wrong as you're not examined by a midwife, health visitor or doctor a few weeks down the line after a birth and so you feel embarrassed, because you think everything should be fine. Ultimately a doctor prodded her finger up my arse and told me I had piles. I felt traumatised! During this time, some really lifesaving podcasts that helped me whilst I was in this zone included: 'Happy mum, happy baby' with Giovanna Fletcher and also 'Sex, drugs and lullabies'.

After all of this turbulence, I didn't want to get pregnant anytime soon. Hugo wouldn't take a bottle until he was 11 months' old and so we couldn't go out. I just wanted to ride my horse and get fit again. Hugo was born in 2018 and by the end of 2019, we started trying for a baby again, I got pregnant in the first month of trying and so Kris was convinced he had super-sperm!

Second time around, I felt a lot more relaxed. My midwives were going to review whether I should have my next baby at Hospital A as opposed to Hospital B, as now my cervix had opened, I only needed 2 scans and they expected me to have a normal birth. I thought everything was okay. My 12-week scan was fine and I was given a due date of 22 September 2020. My biggest issue at that time, was wondering whether we should find out the baby's sex. I felt really nauseous but this was common for me. I ended up drinking quite a lot of diet coke at this stage as that was one of the few things I could stomach, but overall I was blasé. The time came on 29 April 2020 for me to go for my 20-week scan and I had to go on my own because of the whole Covid situation but I was totally calm about this.

I decided that at the scan, I would get the hospital consultant to write down the gender and put it in an envelope and then Kris and I could decide if we wanted to know.

When I was 16 weeks' pregnant, I had heard the baby's strong heartbeat and just before my 20-week scan, I felt a kick and a big lurch in my tummy, so there were no red flag warnings of what was to come. Once I was in the sonography room, lying down on the couch, with gel on my tummy, I looked to the screen excitedly to see the first images of my baby. Despite my full bladder (which was necessary for the scan), I felt relaxed but then the Sonographer went quiet... and then she said:

"I'm really sorry but I can't find a heartbeat". (This was my implosion moment).

I was so shocked! I looked at the screen but the baby wasn't moving at all. I knew something was clearly very wrong because in previous scans I'd had, my baby had been so active. I couldn't believe this could be happening to me and I just lay there. I felt a bit stupid that I hadn't known the baby had died. A colleague of the Sonographer came into the room and both were wearing face masks because of the pandemic, but this just made it all more morose and clinical. The colleague confirmed what I had been told earlier: "I'm really sorry but I have to confirm that the baby has died".

I was trying to hold it all together. I just kept on feeling stupid. How did I know not this? I was told that I would be talked through the process of what would happen next and I feared that I would have to sit in a waiting room with all the pregnant women waiting for their scans, but I was shown into a side room and I rang Kris. I burst into tears. He wondered what on earth was wrong and I just rattled it out: "there's no heart beat, the baby's dead". Kris burst into tears. I rang my dad and said "I know it's lockdown, but please can you look after Hugo because I need Kris with me. I don't want to hear the options by myself." My dad drove to our house to look after Hugo and Kris drove to Hospital A to be with me. I phoned my sisters too and got hold of my mum, who also cried, because she'd lost babies previously so she could identify with me.

It was so depressing being in that side room. It felt like a funeral parlour with all the bereavement leaflets and tissues. I kept thinking 'how am I going to tell people that I'm not pregnant". I asked my mum and she said: "don't worry about it right now, just think about you." The midwives allowed Kris to come and see me. They then told us that we'd be sent to Hospital B where I'd be told my next options. At that point, I just wanted and expected a 'D & C' type procedure.

That day felt poignant in so many ways: for example, it was the first day, I'd put maternity clothes on and I felt a fraud now for wearing them. Because I felt I wasn't entitled to. It was such a headfuck as the night before, I had felt kicks. My mum said: "have they definitely got it right?" But having seen enough live baby scans when I was pregnant with Hugo and my earlier one with this baby, I knew that what they said was true. The midwife gave Kris the paperwork for us to take to Hospital B, 40 minutes away. The last time I'd been to that hospital, I'd delivered Hugo, whereas on the journey there this time, I found myself deleting all my pregnancy apps on my phone.

When we arrived at Hospital B, we had to go to the delivery suite and tell the receptionists that I was a 'Snowdrop lady' and they would know that this meant my baby had died and that I had to deliver it. I remember not wanting anyone to see me. I was shown into a little side room. Again it was full of bereavement leaflets and I could hear a baby crying on the wards. All of my morning sickness had suddenly gone. I felt as if I was looking at someone else and experiencing their life, not my own.

I wasn't given options. I was just told what would happen. The Head Midwife said that they would start off the induction process and I really hadn't been expecting this or wanting it. I'd just hoped that I would be put under general anaesthetic and the baby would be removed without me knowing a thing. But I took a pill on that Wednesday to start the labour. I returned home and then had to go back to the hospital on the Friday. It was a totally weird experience. I was asked lots of questions, such as whether I was allergic to anything?

I asked the Head Midwife how often babies die like this, because it's just not spoken about. She said a few a week and that was just in Hospital B. It made me think that this is happening every week to lots of women in hospitals all over the country (all over the world too), but it's just not talked about. All those women and men having to deal with the physical experience of the process and all of the resulting emotions. It was huge. How could this not be spoken about?

Going home that day, having taken the induction pill, there was a package on my doorstep. It was more baby clothes. I couldn't bear to look at them. On Thursday lunchtime, I was desperate to ride my horse, just do something normal. I phoned a friend who's a midwife in Derby. She's caring but also really knowledgable and practical. I'd had no further information about what would happen to me during the induction process and I needed to know, so I could brace myself. I still didn't know if it was going to be like a 'normal' labour.

My Derby midwife friend said I'd be given a lot of forms to fill out and she told me that I would be asked if I wanted photographs of the baby? Also handprints/footprints and if I wanted to hold the baby? My mum recommended that I held the baby as she hadn't wanted to see the babies she lost, but then she regretted this later. She said that I wouldn't get the chance to see the baby again.

I found myself googling what a 20-week-old dead baby looked like and however macabre that sounds, I just had to know what I was going to see. I walked past 2 live-birth delivery suites to get to the 'Snowdrop Rooms'. The kitchen, toilet, bathroom and other adjacent rooms were separate from the facilities for parents whose babies were still very much alive. We were asked lots of questions, such as did I want to be tested to see if there was a specific reason why the baby hadn't survived? Did we want a postmortem? What parts of the baby did we want to be tested and later, would we consent to those parts being donated to science?

In the delivery suite for Snowdrop ladies, everything had been donated by other parents who had lost babies during pregnancy like me, so in one sense, it was sweet but in another sense, it felt really morbid. There was a radio playing in there all the time too, to drown out the sound of babies being born.

I was given more tablets orally, then a vaginal pessary. My contractions started in earnest. It was just like it was when I was pregnant with Hugo. All afternoon, I had flashbacks to what had happened when I was giving birth to him, but the difference was that he was alive. It was so hard to acknowledge that this baby wasn't. My midwives said: "you're coping so well. You're so strong", but I was just trying to get through it. I asked for gas and air. There was obviously no need to worry about the baby so there was no monitor to check for the baby's heartbeat because that had already stopped, the midwives were just taking care of me.

Kris was so good. He helped me by being at my side and we just watched Netflix. My waters broke and I was really upset. I was a bit frightened at that point because I didn't know what was going to happen. It was nerve-wracking. This was the one moment that really got to me: my body was going through all of this labour for nothing.

The midwives said: "if you get up now to go for a wee, take a bedpan with you, as the baby could just fall out". That made me anxious. I did have 2 wees during this time, but I was afraid to look down in case I saw a foot poking out. Fortunately the baby was quite settled inside me and it didn't fall out.

My contractions stopped and I had a kindly doctor looking after me. I tried to push the baby out but the baby was lying sideways and the doctor said: "I'm going to have to help the baby out." My legs were put in stirrups and I was puffing on gas and air and the lady doctor delivered my baby with her hand. It was a little baby girl (but we didn't know this at the time).

This doctor said: "I can see why your baby hasn't survived. Her cord has wrapped itself around her neck 6 times, really tightly". She explained that it's sometimes normal for the cord to be wrapped around a baby's neck 1-2 times and for the baby still to survive, but to survive when it was wrapped around 6 times was impossible. I was a bit relieved to hear this but I was so worried what my baby would look like.

Also I blamed myself. I wondered whether it was because I had stopped taking pregnancy tablets or whether it was because I'd drunken diet cola… I thought everything through so many times… but I was told that what had happened with the cord is really rare. I don't know if that made me feel better or worse. It took the doctor ages to get the placenta out and then there was a massive anti-climax. The doctor said: "I'm so sorry". I remember saying to her: "I know it's not easy for you either." This process had taken all day. It was 11pm at night and our lovely doctor talked to our baby as if she were a real live baby and that really helped.

At the time, we couldn't tell what sex she was as she had stopped growing at 17 weeks when the nutrients were no longer reaching her properly. She had a flap of skin which made it hard to recognise her gender but we were told that she was a little girl. She was very much a perfect tiny baby girl. I remember observing her perfect fingers, even her fingernails. Looking at her wasn't frightening or scary. It was more a case of us marvelling at the perfectness of her feet. Both of us held her and took photographs of her and the midwives helped so much. They put a little hat on her, wrapped her in a blanket. They have 2 teddy bears also: one is for you to keep and one is for the baby to keep. Additionally, the midwives then put her in a tiny sleeping bag-type outfit to keep her warm.

They checked me physically and also made a point of checking the baby too, and again that made everything feel so much better because it showed that they valued her and gave her dignity even though she wasn't breathing. Those midwives were fantastic at being able to switch their personas from being with mums, dads, partners and live babies next door to caring for parents with non-living babies in our suite. We were able to be with our baby all through the night too, which was comforting.

After delivering our baby, I found myself covered in blood and diarrhoea because the drugs they give you to start the birth, make you evacuate everything. I remember thinking 'this is a bit shit.' Literally. My body had gone through the wringer. Kris hosed me down and he was fab. There haven't been many things we haven't gone through. If you don't find moments to console yourself at times like this then life becomes impossible.

I just knew that giving birth to her was a job that had to be done. Having a cuddle with her helped so much and having the photographs of her with us, hugely benefited us too. I realise that having 2 days to see the baby and having laboured to deliver her, was better than having her clinically extracted from my system.

I think it was the best closure because if I'd had a surgical removal, I would have struggled more with mental health issues afterwards. That time with the baby helped Kris and I to be at peace with what had happened but it was incredibly difficult too because we had our son and this was the daughter we'd hoped to have, to complete our family. I overheard Kris talking to the baby. He made the effort to go over to her. She was in a little basket which kept her cool. The midwives then put us up in a made-up bed and we ended up going to sleep for a couple of hours.

Later we were asked if we would like a funeral for her. She would be going off for a post-mortem and then when she came back, we could decide. They also asked us if we wanted professional photographs taken of her. I said yes. They have arrived since, but neither of us have felt able to look at them yet. We also have models of her feet and hands and we have kept her little hat and teddy.

Kris and I were relieved to come home. We thought we had managed the worst part. Lockdown felt a bit rough and Hugo sensed that something wasn't quite right but he's not like having a full-time baby. We've felt some trauma over lockdown but I've tried to stay really busy, especially in the garden, painting our fence, planting etc. When I was pregnant and had really bad nausea, I couldn't do very much but that left and so later in lockdown, I actually felt physically well, so I just threw myself into being outdoors and Kris focused on keeping his business going.

We had a Bereavement Midwife. She was so lovely. She said: "all I want to do is give you a hug" and said that she would keep us in touch about what happened next after we left hospital. About ten days' later, she texted me and said: "can I give you a call?" Normally she would have come over to see us, but because of lockdown, she had to speak to us over the phone instead. The baby was back from the Postmortem. She then told us that the lab had confirmed that our baby was a girl. Some people said to me: "maybe you were so ill because something wasn't right", but that wasn't helpful.

We decided we wanted to give our daughter, who we named 'May Elizabeth', a funeral and part of me thought that I was being over-dramatic because May wasn't full-term. But if you don't hold your own funeral for your baby, then your baby will be cremated with lots of other babies who have also died and that really upset me as it reminded me of the holocaust. So we said we had to give her a funeral ourselves. Funeral directors don't charge anything in these situations, so it was literally just the cost of the flowers only. It was poignant to hear from them how this happens quite a lot. As always, Kris was amazing and helped so much with this. The whole process was more complicated because of lockdown. However, we felt much better knowing that we were giving her the send-off she deserved.

Our local vicar was really warm. Again he confirmed what the funeral directors had said, namely that as a Vicar, he dealt with this situation a lot but people don't talk about it. To enable him to judge how we wanted him to conduct the service, he asked us some questions including how religious we were? How we wanted him to dress up – i.e., in layman's clothes, or in his dog collar and a jumper or in his full robes? He was fantastic. He sent us an email with comforting scriptural verses in it and we took a middle-road approach. There were only going to be 5-6 people attending the funeral but we wanted to tell everyone about it so it would end this taboo.

I don't know what I expected from the whole funeral experience but all the professionals involved, treated us with dignity. My mum wrote a poem about our baby that the vicar read out at the funeral and we played Eric Clapton's 'Tears in Heaven' written for his young son who had died after accidentally falling out of a tall apartment block. Additionally, we found a beautiful song by Ed Sheeran called 'Small Bump'. He wrote it for friends who had lost a baby at 20 weeks too and as soon as we heard the lyrics, the song fitted our feelings, so we wanted to use it. The service wasn't too depressing. The funeral director had put May into a wicker basket and a florist made a bouquet of pink and white roses for her.

Kris asked me if I wanted to see May in her willow coffin? I looked in and saw that the funeral director had put teddy bears and unicorns in with her. They had done everything they could to soften the experience. Although I was sad, it was the right thing to do. I don't feel bad about the way we dealt with it. If we didn't have the funeral, I would have felt guilty. The next stage is to collect the ashes but I cannot bear this endless sadness about her. I need to look into the legal terms for example, whether she can be buried in a graveyard. Kris' brother and sister-in-law came to the funeral and supported us and Kris' brother carved a tiny urn. It's amazing how some people surprise you with just how fantastic they are. Kris carried May's wicker coffin and I just thought what a special man he is. It also really helped us having Hugo there because he kept us busy.

We called our baby daughter 'May Elizabeth' because she was born on 1 May 2020. We didn't want to give it too much thought. We didn't use the names we'd planned to use for our baby. When we first found out that our baby had died we didn't want to name her, but the whole process in hospital made me change my idea, made me realise it was different. I read a book called 'Ask me his Name' by Elle Wright, which was about how she felt when her baby died 4 days after his birth. She talked about wanting people to say his name and that she shouldn't feel bad mentioning her own son's name. I also felt why shouldn't I talk about my second child?

We found we were able to talk about May and that what happened to her actually brought us closer together as a couple. But I also didn't want this experience to define who I am either. I didn't want to be thought of as a hysterical woman, because I'm tough and didn't want to be seen as a victim. (My brother committed suicide when I was nine years' old and so previously, I have felt that I had to be strong for my half-brother).

Kris has been amazing. He helps with Hugo and has demonstrated such a lovely side to him. If he hadn't opened up, I can see how it could have gone the other way but he's been open and not afraid to show his feelings. We've got through all of this by supporting each other.

WHAT HAVE YOUR EXPERIENCES TAUGHT YOU?

That life is precious and that even though you feel that you can't deal with a situation, it's amazing how much inner strength you have. You can actually cope with any situation. It also proves whether you're with the right person or not.

I also really appreciate Hugo. Having him gives me such a different perspective on work, babies, this pandemic too.

WHAT ADVICE WOULD YOU GIVE TO OTHER WOMEN IN A SIMILAR SITUATION?

Trust your instincts and don't be afraid to ask questions.

WHERE ARE YOU NOW? WHAT ARE YOUR PLANS FOR THE FUTURE?

It's okay to want to try for a baby again. After our second baby died, I thought 'when can I try for a baby again?' A relative suggested that we were trying too soon but we still want another baby. We're not replacing May. I'm pregnant now and trying not to focus too much on being pregnant and also I'm trying not to be petrified of the scans. The baby is due on 28 Feb 2021.

Listening to podcasts has also helped.

I am going to go to my GP and ask to be assessed because I'm struggling to get the support I need over my pregnancy fears. I feel I can contact the Bereavement Midwife again if I need to and she will help. I haven't felt sick with this pregnancy and for a while, another relative wondered whether the baby was still okay and they articulated this to me. They didn't think before they said it and they didn't mean to upset me. It's just been such a hard situation for everyone.

Part of me wants to get back on the pregnancy train again. You have to put yourself back out there and get rid of your fears. Get out of the fear bubble.

Kris and I are personally stronger as a couple. We realise how precious life is and how much we want another baby. We had to have a first scan with this current baby we are expecting, at 8 weeks. Kris was allowed to come along this time and everything was fine, including the heartbeat. We had another scan last Tuesday, as I had reached 12 weeks. Our male Consultant was so lovely and just joked: "come on, let's find these triplets", to cheer me up! Reassuringly, he will be with us all the way through my pregnancy this time.

I couldn't bear to look at the screen this time after what I saw previously, but all was well, and it was nice. The heartbeat was strong and powerful. I have to take aspirin now and my Consultant/midwives regularly check the blood-flow to the baby.

The Postmortem results came back for May, and aside from the umbilical cord that was twisted around her neck, there was nothing else that they could find that was wrong with her.

POSTSCRIPT

After the trauma of losing their second baby during lockdown 1, Izzy and Kris went on to have a very healthy baby girl in February 2021 and Hugo's adapted as a brilliant big brother. I'm so happy for them all.

ABBY'S STORY

When your fiancé calls off your wedding, sleeps with a mutual work colleague and then later, when you have finally married and had two children, he sleeps with your best friend…

I met Tom when we were in our late teens. We were both working at the same restaurant in a city - I was studying Physiotherapy at the University there too, so I only helped out a few eves a week in the Restaurant to earn a bit of extra money. Tom was fun-loving, an absolute idiot and he tried his hardest to woo me but I was in a long-term relationship with another guy, so I ignored Tom for ages. Bizarrely, prior to meeting me, Tom had also been thinking of becoming a Physio.

However, I realised that I couldn't fight my feelings and ultimately when I became single quite quickly, Tom and I started going out. Not long after, we moved in together. I was head over heels in love with Tom but I had applied for some medical placements abroad and Tom was also going to an English University to study to become a physio. Whilst I was away on my first placement, initially we stayed together but as time progressed and because of work pressures and the huge distances that separated us, we reluctantly decided to be friends instead. But I ended up having to return to the UK earlier than I'd expected to deal with an important family issue and Tom and I happened to bump into each other again. I realised I still really loved Tom and we got back together. I was able to end one of my Physio placements earlier than intended.

I had also been planning to apply for some kind of Physio role in Europe so that I could travel, but I got a position in the closest district hospital to us instead so that I could stay with Tom. Meanwhile he had qualified as a Physio and started working at the same hospital as me. In terms of our working lives and the positions we were employed in, I was viewed as more senior than Tom and I also earned more than he did, however, overall at the time, this didn't cause any issues and we ended up renting a small barn conversion in a sweet village about 30 minutes away from the hospital. It was a happy time!

It felt natural as a next step to get engaged and we planned our wedding! However, a few weeks before the Big Day, Tom just panicked and said: "I can't do this". He didn't say "I don't want to be with you" but he just expressed that everything had got too much for him and he felt overwhelmed. When I reflect on this now, I can understand his reluctance a little. Basically, 18 months' before our wedding, my maternal grandfather had died and so my mum threw herself into organising my wedding to Tom as a form of distraction from her own grief.

Mum's plans meant that the event was becoming a wedding we didn't really want, certainly not Tom.

When Tom told me he didn't want to get married though, it was so humiliating. We had bought so much already for the wedding and also we were still working together at the same hospital. I took it really badly and we went our separate ways. I stayed in the barn conversion and Tom moved out. Eventually though we started talking again.

I went away for a break on what should have been my honeymoon and a couple of young female European Physio students who were on placement at the hospital where Tom and I both worked, stayed in my barn whilst I was away on holiday. When I returned, one of the students said some things and I suddenly realised that Tom had slept with her, and it would have been the week just before I'd gone away. Tom and I weren't officially together when he slept with this student, so it wasn't an affair but it felt like such a kick-in-the-teeth as it was so close to us breaking up and near to the time when we should have been getting married. After all the twists and turns of our relationship and me being totally in love with him, I felt that it demonstrated a complete lack of respect. Obviously, it all blew up and the Physio student left her placement early and moved areas.

I had made plans to go to America for the summer holidays to see my best friend and her husband, who had relocated there and to have some fun. However, Tom worked his magic on me and persuaded me not to go. So instead of me being in America that summer without him, Tom and I drove across France together, camping in a romantic Jack Kerouac way, which was exactly the vibe that Tom sought to create in his life as he was desperate, deep down, to become a serious painter (he was good at art). We knew that the experience would either make or break us as a couple. When we came back from our French trip, we decided to give our relationship another go and we even decided to get married!! We were both fully on board this time!

My parents didn't approve of this decision but Tom and I went ahead and planned the wedding ourselves. Tom had issues with the town where I had grown up and which wasn't too far away from us. My ex-boyfriend was based near there and Tom used to wonder if I had slept with certain people who lived there, so instead we decided to get married in the quaint village where our rented barn conversion was. I wanted to take my childhood town out of the equation for Tom.

We also moved together into a cottage that a local barrister rented out cheaply to us and we planned our wedding. My parents learnt about the wedding when they received the invite and I wasn't sure if they'd come as they'd didn't approve of Tom. However, when Tom read through the vows and became emotional, my dad saw this and felt that Tom was truly sincere, so dad said that he would give me away after all at my wedding.

All of the villagers close to the church where we were having our wedding, knew our backstory and they wanted to help us. There was a beautiful tithe barn nearby, so it was suggested that we could use that for free for our reception and the locals made our cake, decorated the church and the tithe barn for free too. Meanwhile the pretty rose-clad pub a few yards away, prepared delicious food for our big day and they even donated some drinks – everyone was just so kind! My parents had lost lots of money on our previous wedding which had been called-off before, so we had to pay for everything this time around, but it was perfect!

After the wedding, we stayed in our rented cottage and continued to work at the hospital in our respective roles. We were really happy! Tom wanted to go into a specific area of physiotherapy that would enable him to earn more money, so he applied to a University an hour away from us, to undertake further training.

I had been trying for a year to get pregnant but nothing had happened and we both really wanted a baby. However, subconsciously, the fact that Tom was studying so hard, actually took the pressure off us and I fell pregnant! Simultaneously Tom started painting too, pursuing his dream. He completed his additional Physio course when Freddie was born. There wasn't a job at the Hospital though where I still worked and where Tom had been before, for him this time around though, so he got a position at a private sports' physio clinic 45 minutes' away.

I had to return to work quickly after having our baby son, Freddie, because I was the main breadwinner but my mum helped me with him. At the time, Tom seemed happy and he was a good dad to Freddie who was a fantastic baby. I was happy too. If we'd stayed in that perfect little bubble, maybe life would have continued to be good?

However, I had a long commute to and from my mum's daily, both before and after I worked at the hospital, to drop Freddie off to mum and I just became exhausted. In addition, nobody else in our village had young children and as much as I loved the village, I wanted to move back to my home-town where my parents lived, so that we would have childcare support on our doorstep and also so that Freddie would have friends there. This was vital as Freddie was nearly 2 years' old.

So I found a house to rent in my home-town, not far from the sea. Tom was reluctant but I said I had to do it because I couldn't cope with all the extra driving every weekday to drop Freddie off. Tom reluctantly agreed but it was probably the beginning of the end for us because of his insecurities about me being back amongst my former peers and boyfriends. That house move did fundamentally change him because Tom felt he had a lack of control over that decision because I had basically made it. So then he metaphorically 'threw his toys out of the pram.'

Not long after, everyone just assumed we weren't together because we weren't pictured together and he was never with us. I didn't end up actually seeing any of my old friendship group that I had grown up with either, rather all of our village friends used to drive to see us, including one couple Clare and Rob, who we socialised with a lot. But Tom and I were suddenly under more financial pressure as the rent on our new property was three times more than our village rent had been, but I worked hard and paid it. Tom wanted us to try for a second baby but I had an upcoming conference to go to in America, so I wanted to postpone baby plans.

Simultaneously, I had begun to sense a shift in Tom's attitude towards me also. Although he had finished all his training, he struggled with the role. He pushed against boundaries and censorship, and I sensed that he developed close attachments to sports' physio patients that he worked with for long periods of time. These didn't become inappropriate but I knew he found it hard to keep a distance from his patients/clients.

I got back from America and Tom made a remark in front of his sister and brother-in-law that we couldn't try for a second baby because I was too fat! They had asked when we were thinking of having another baby and Tom said: "until she's fit enough to do a 100 push ups, we can't have another baby." There followed nervous laughter as my in-laws thought that Tom was joking and I played along with it, by getting down on the floor, there and then and literally banging out 100 push-ups. I did fall pregnant again very quickly though with our daughter, Ruby, who was born by caesarean section and who was poorly afterwards. Tom again, seemed happy at this point: he had wanted a son and then a daughter, and now he had both.

It was the Queen's Jubilee year and it was quite a monumental year for us too: our close friends from our former village, Clare and Rob, moved to Portugal and we became friendly with a new group of families but particularly one couple: Ed and Ruth. Tom got on really well with Ed because just as Tom wanted to be a successful artist, Ed desired to be a credible musician and he brought out Tom's fun side too. A cheaper house became available the other side of Ed and Ruth's fence, and Tom really pushed for us to buy it and move there, which we did. It wasn't in such a nice area and we had to gut it but it was our first proper home. Tom even converted a shed at the end of our garden for his painting! After taking maternity leave, I returned to work and was promoted,

Socially, life got exciting as not only did we get on well with Ed and Ruth but their young children got on equally well with ours and so we all did a lot together as two families. However, Tom seemed increasingly detached from us as a family, particularly because he was involved in a lot of sport: this meant that he was out two nights a week, training and then he was also out on Friday night and a lot of the weekend too. Alongside this, there was also his art. At this point, it felt like his heart wasn't properly in our family life.

At 2am on the first day of a new senior role for me in the hospital, Ed sent me a text saying: 'I think Tom and Ruth are having an affair'. It was a huge shock and I challenged Tom. He denied it but I knew that he was lying. I was so stressed because of starting the new position, so I was under increasing pressure.

My mind churned over everything: for example, after Ruby was born I had wanted Tom to have a vasectomy because I'd nearly died after Freddie's birth and Ruby was poorly herself in her early days, so I felt that I was 'done' after having two babies via c-section, but Tom had refused to have a vasectomy. He'd said: "what if we don't work out and I go on to have another relationship?" When he said this, I knew he'd been having doubts about us as a couple…

I went through a week of hell because Ruth and I had been so close and whilst Ed refused to talk to me, Ruth wouldn't leave me alone out of guilt. Ruth initially denied it but I just knew that something had been going on. In fact, even my mum had been saying for the previous 3 months, that she was convinced Tom and Ruth were having an affair. Tom continued to deny it and he had deleted everything from his phone.

I had to know, so I confronted Ruth. She confessed and said that it had been going on for just a couple of months and that it was a: "meeting of minds." Ruth felt that she and Tom had an 'emotional connection'. Almost immediately after the truth came out, Ed and Ruth put their house on the market and they promptly moved far away from us. Tom stopped seeing Ruth but this was a massive rupture in our lives because our children lost their friendship with Ed and Ruth's kids who they were so close to. Also I was devastated to lose Ruth as a friend but even more hurt by her betrayal of me. In addition I knew that deep-down, Tom was sad because he'd lost his friendship with Ed. Overall as a family, what had happened between Tom and Ruth had caused a massive loss to us all. It also affected our wider friendship group as we had all been so close and did a lot together, I pulled back from the group for a while and two of the women asked me if it was "because of Tom and Ruth?". I just cried. The group were lovely to me though and generally, none of the girls in our friendship circle are still in touch with Ruth and that helped me.

One of the hardest things to confront was thinking of all the intimate details I had shared with Ruth feeling that I could trust her. So for example, I had confided to her that after having Freddie, I used to panic about getting pregnant and I didn't 'get on' with the pill and Tom refused to use a condom, so on one occasion I had to go to the chemist to get a 'morning after pill' and I felt like a slut.

Despite everything, Tom still denied the affair. His parents asked me if we: "could get over it?" but for me, the trust was broken and Tom did nothing to try to win it back. Tom blamed me for the breakdown of our marriage because we weren't sleeping together and hadn't been for a while, because of our respective issues over contraception and my fear of getting pregnant. Tom refused to address that contraception was as much of a duty for him, as me. He just assumed I would take the precautions. In hindsight, when I reflected on Tom and Ruth's affair, I realised that when Tom and I stopped sleeping together, that this was a big turning point in our relationship, but at the time, you ignore it. Tom had started sleeping on the sofa for 3-4 years before he left and he would tell our children that it was because I snored. Basically when the sex stopped, the nastiness started.

How I would describe Tom in our relationship and family life then, was that he just became 'absent'. Our relationship became more and more terse. For example, I'd arrange to go shopping with Clare when she was on a visit back home, and then about 10 minutes before Clare arrived, Tom would start an argument and then tell me I couldn't go out with Clare, because the argument wasn't resolved. I felt that this was Tom's way of gaining control over my day. His 'digs' at me weren't related to finances but they were always about my weight and the way he talked to me in front of people was degrading and humiliating although in other ways, he was okay, for example, he did his share of the cooking. Tom told me that he wanted someone who was more intellectual than me: a woman he could talk to about politics and other topics.

One evening we were all invited out but Tom didn't want to go so I tried to talk to him and he said that he was going to stay in because he was feeling down, so I went out and told our friends that Tom was a bit low. However, when I got home, I discovered that Tom had actually gone out himself around the town and then he'd posted a load of photos of his escapades on social media for everyone to see. I felt humiliated.

Simultaneously, Tom was made redundant from the sports' physio job he was working at and he got a post at a hospital instead but his heart wasn't in it. He left that position too. I kept thinking of a girlfriend of mine who had been killed a few years' previously in a sailing accident. Before she'd died, she'd told me to: "get out" of my marriage and now I felt I was finally ready to do this. I asked Tom to leave but he refused.

I had to attend some training through work and it included a safeguarding module. My implosion moment came on the second day of training, when the session covered domestic abuse, featuring verbal abuse, coercive control and so on. We were shown a film about it and there was a trigger-warning given beforehand but I thought I'd be fine, so I was blasé. However, as the taught session continued, I started crying and I remember saying: "they're describing my life" and it was horrible to feel a 'victim'. I kept thinking how have I let myself get in this position as I'm normally so strong. One of my colleagues said he hadn't realised I had been going through this.

That domestic abuse film was my wake-up call because I realised that although I had never been hit by Tom, I had been suffering from verbal and psychological abuse. I thought about how he had denied his affair with Ruth, how he had mentally withdrawn from my life and all the times he had picked-on my weight, my intellect, my friends and how he would engineer situations so I would have to cancel events, such as going on holiday, going to a wedding etc. He would gaslight me and try to blame me, say it was my fault, not his. All of this behaviour really played with my mind.

Alongside realising what had happened in my marriage, it was also an incredibly difficult time because my friend died in the sailing accident but I hadn't really grieved at the time and furthermore my gran died too, so it all caught up with me. I started making mental plans to leave Tom but I felt that I couldn't get a divorce because nobody in our family had been divorced and I was worried about the impact on the children. Then one day I came home from work and Tom had just left! His wedding ring was on the mantelpiece. There was no letter or anything for the kids. I phoned him and asked him if he'd left and he said: "yeah, I'm at my mum's".

I called my own mum and told her he'd left. I ultimately ended up collapsing in a heap of tears on my hallway floor and my friend came over and took me back to hers to look after me. Tom didn't see the children for 3 weeks and then eventually we both sat them down together and told them that we were separating. Otherwise, everyone had just assumed we weren't together anyway because we weren't pictured together and he was never with us.

After that, I felt like I was going through the motions and my prime focus was to make sure the kids were okay and that I could pay the bills, keep the house and keep my job. I was now in charge of a range of Physio services, so there was lots of pressure on me. Tom hadn't ever indicated that he felt emasculated because I was the main breadwinner. Rather, I feel that me earning the wedge of our household income gave him a licence to feel relaxed. When he did earn 'decent' money, Tom would contribute to the bills, but his earnings were more his own.

Since Tom left, during the past few years, we've been through a difficult divorce. I've not had a relationship since and I probably won't ever marry again. The last few years have been about making sure my finances and career are good. In fact the latter has surged ahead. I absolutely love my job and I need to shore up my finances for the children to give them economic security because Tom won't contribute anything. My parents have moved closer to be near me and they help with the children, although I have to make sure that they're okay too as they're getting to that stage in life when things can go downhill, but overall, we're all doing fine!

WHAT HAVE YOUR EXPERIENCS TAUGHT YOU?

Trust yourself, know yourself. I'd lost that ability.

Also don't take any shit. I had to rediscover myself as a strong woman. You're an okay person, you're not a bad person for breaking up your family.

Now I can breathe and sleep better. I have the freedom of having my life back and I look forward to the future positively! I felt trapped before. Ending my marriage was actually a physical thing to do, a weight was lifted off my chest. I feel a lightness about me now.

It's down to you to take responsibility.

WHAT ADVICE WOULD YOU GIVE TO OTHER WOMEN IN A SIMILAR SITUATION?

Trust your instincts. People will be telling you what to do – but do what is right for you. Believe in your strength. You can do this but also don't be afraid to lean on people too. I didn't lean on people because I didn't want to involve people but sometimes we all need scaffolding. Take advice. Make the break if you need to and just accept it all - because nothing is as bad as what you're going through.

WHERE ARE YOU NOW? WHAT ARE YOUR PLANS FOR THE FUTURE?

My kids are amazing. Also I have the most wonderful friendship group! My friends are amazing and their husbands have been so supportive too and their perspective has helped. One of them, who used to be friends with Tom, said that he really understood why I couldn't take any more and that really helped me because he'd always been loyal to Tom, so for him to understand where I was coming from, made me feel more validated.

Out of our female group of 14 girlfriends, half have since left their husbands. They had similar circumstances and after Tom and I split, these women started confiding in me. Another of our group hasn't worked outside of the home, since having children and her husband is the breadwinner, so she doesn't feel strong enough to leave, but we need to empower other women who need to leave and put together a package to help them to do this, because women can feel so trapped. For example I didn't realise I was at rock bottom until I was on that Safeguarding course, because we become so conditioned to bad behaviour. We think it's normal.

Also we have to realise that sometimes our former husbands won't ever accept that they did anything wrong. One night during our divorce, Tom let himself into our home. I thought someone had broken in downstairs, not realising it was him. At 2am I found him lying naked on the sofa and he arrogantly said: "do you fancy it?" and I replied: "absolutely not", told him to leave and then just wanted to bleach the sofa. I had to face hard truths too, such as the fact that whilst Tom was having his affair, he also took out a £35,000 loan behind my back in both of our names against the house, forging my signature to pay off his debts. I've just had to deal with all of this.

Tom's had lots of relationships with other women since we split and is currently undertaking an art course. Whilst initially our children didn't want us to get divorced, they've accepted it now.

I realise that I won't ever be taken to the cleaners again financially. Basically the only thing I'm missing from my life right now is a penis but knowing I was able to leave my marriage will hopefully empower other women too, to know that they can leave a bad relationship!

JANE'S STORY

…when you don't ever 'get over' the death of a much-loved parent

My beloved dad, Lesley, was the youngest of 7 children born in Devon. His father worked in the navy and he was away a lot and his mother worked hard to try to bring up the children. There was very little money and the children were often hungry. Dad's parents died when he was a young man and he was very involved in their care.

My dad became an engineer and was offered an opportunity to manage an engineering works in the South West where he met my mum, Joan. Mum had experienced a very traumatic childhood. She had been born illegitimately, at a time when this was very stigmatised. She was raised by her grandparents, who she thought were her parents, until a child at school informed her otherwise, by calling her a 'bastard'. Mum didn't know what that child was referring to, so of course, she asked her family and the whole story came out: the woman she thought was her sister 'Maud' was actually her mother and Joan was the result of Maud's affair with a married man. After discovering all of this, Joan carried such a lot of shame about her birth for the rest of her life. Joan's grandmother had assured her that when Maud was later married and settled, that she would come and collect Joan but even though Maud did marry and have more children, she never came to collect Joan. That was a huge let-down and rejection to my mum. Also Joan's grandparents were strict Victorians and they used the horsewhip on her when they felt she needed disciplining: one example of this was when Joan was little and messing around with embers from the fire, her grandmother quickly shoved her hand into the fire to teach Joan a brutal lesson about not playing near a hot fire! The punishments were extremely harsh!

My childhood

I always remember being very well cared for by both of my parents, who each had a strong work ethic. Mum was really house-proud and liked order and despite having an extremely tight budget, she managed to keep on top of all the bills and save money too. Dad was very practical and could turn his hand to anything. He loved the challenge of fixing things. However, he wasn't so good at balancing the books. Because of mum's childhood, which I was not aware of until my early teens, she made it very difficult for me to get emotionally close to her. She put a barrier up and was often moody and depressed but wouldn't or couldn't explain it. Bottling up her experiences when she was young really affected her entire life.

With my dad, it was very different! Dad was always a glass half full (or more!) person. He had a great sense of humour and loved playing practical jokes. He was a great teacher, and was very open and always easy to talk to without judgement. For example, if I made a cake whilst my mother was out, then when she returned, she would immediately notice the flour on the floor before seeing my cake. Furthermore she would be worried about the cost and be critical. Whereas dad would immediately praise my efforts. Sometimes if the cake wasn't quite right, he would ask me how I thought I could make it even better next time. He was full of encouragement for me.

When I look back, I was always really close to my dad. He was just such a warm and cuddly person. I remember him saying once that he had promised himself that if he ever had children, he wanted them to have a happy and secure upbringing and that he also wanted to be close to his children. I can testify that he achieved that!

There had been tuberculosis (TB) in my father's family. TB is a contagious infection caused by bacteria that mainly affects the lungs but can also affect any other organ and can be life threatening. When I was three, my dad had pneumonia. After that, he developed TB. Obviously my mother was very worried about him but she never really explained anything much to me. In those days, parents didn't really open up and talk to children about important issues that were happening in their families. Children just observed what was happening around them and had to draw their own conclusions. My dad was suddenly sent away to a sanatorium in Bristol for 6 months and I was heartbroken as it was a long way from where we lived. From having dad around at home so much and being an only child who had endless love and affection from him, suddenly my dad was gone. I think even at that age, I realised how fragile life can be. During that time, I saw dad very little. Occasionally I was allowed to go and visit him. I couldn't understand why he wanted to be there rather than at home. Eventually he returned, but his health was never the same. Lots of hospital admissions followed over the years.

Despite his TB, dad was always upbeat and had great empathy when anyone was sick. I remember having lots of ear infections when I was at pre-school and when he came home from work, he would gather me up and give me a cuddle. Even though the pain of my earache couldn't simply be magicked away by this, dad gave me a great feeling of being safe and secure.

Growing up in England in the 1950s and 60s, I caught the typical infections that children later would be vaccinated against. So as a child, I had measles really badly: I had a high fever for a week and was so poorly for a further couple of weeks (the man I married years' later was so ill with measles when he was little, that he was hospitalised and it really affected his eyesight for a long time). Yet the care both my parents gave me was so reassuring. Mum did all the practical stuff for me whilst my dad gave me the hugs, telling me that I'd soon be better. He always had this way of wrapping his arms around me and making me think everything would be okay. Although I knew he wasn't well and that people died, dad continuously returned from his hospital trips, so I suppose I always expected that he would do this.

As I was an only child, dad and I did so many things together: cooking, making air-fix kits and playing games. Many evenings we would play card games, etc. Mum loved the piano, so when she was feeling up to it, we would sing songs too. Whereas dad was always the same old dad, mum was very fragile inside and often down in the dumps. When she told me about her illegitimacy, she genuinely thought that I wouldn't want anything more to do with her. The shame of it for her, was huge! The trouble was I could never change her mind and she couldn't let it go and move on. Also counselling wasn't a thing then in a rural village, so she couldn't go and talk to a professional and release all of the mental baggage she carried. Hence I always gravitated to dad because he was constant, the same, easy to talk to, a good listener and he would always try and see something positive out of a negative situation.

Nothing changed after I got married in my late teens. My dad would often pop over at lunchtimes as he and my mum lived about 20 minutes away. We always had a big hug and a chat. Because of her ongoing anxieties, my mum would never dream of coming over without a formal invitation but dad would just rock up. He could literally chat to anyone and immediately put them at their ease and there would always be laughter. That was until early 1980…

One afternoon I got a phone call to say that my father had collapsed and stopped breathing whilst he was out working. Fortunately the man he was working for, performed CPR on dad and brought him back to life. Dad was taken to a district hospital in the south west and placed in Intensive Care. I went and picked my mum up and we drove to the hospital. No one said very much: it was a heart problem and the consultants were running tests. Dad, although looking grey, said: "don't worry, I'll soon be home" and he seemed stable and positive.

Mum, my husband and I, visited him again the next day. The hospital still weren't saying very much as they were endeavouring to get to the bottom of what was wrong with him. Dad kept trying to reassure us in his typical manner. I just had a bad feeling that the hospital knew more than they were letting on.

On the Thursday morning, I just felt I should go and visit dad in the afternoon. But mum and my husband persuaded me to wait until later when we could all go down together. I nodded off to sleep as I was tired (my children were 4 and 6, so they were always lively). Then suddenly I was aware of the phone ringing. I felt really cold because immediately I knew that it was bad news. Apparently dad had been chatting with the patient in the next bed when dad just died. Later the doctor told us that dad simply: "went". The alarms kicked off and the crash t eam came but they couldn't bring him around. We later found out that dad had originally collapsed at work due to having a tear in his aorta, which totally ruptured on that Thursday afternoon. We then understood why we hadn't been told what the consultants suspected, because at that time the hospital couldn't fix the tear.

Dad had died and I simply hadn't been prepared for that. He had told us that he would come home and he always came home! I just couldn't get my head around it. My beloved father had died! And then came the guilt. If only I had asked the hospital more questions. At least we would have known. We could have been more psyched. We could have stayed by his side. The worst guilt was that I hadn't visited him on that Thursday afternoon when I felt I should have. If I had gone, then I would have been at his bedside but instead nobody from his family was there with him in his last moments and I just cried and cried. I had so many mixed emotions and I was inconsolable.

I tried to soothe my mum but my own heart was breaking. The glue of our family was gone. My father, my brother and friend all rolled into one, had just left me. Who was going to make it all better now, especially for mum? I never did. Mum died five years later. She just didn't want to go on. Not even her grandchildren could fill the void. The same void in my heart opened up for me when my dad died and no one else has been able to replace it.

I don't think death is the end of it. I do have a strong Christian faith and I believe I will see my father again in an incredible afterlife, but I still have a hole in my heart. It's because for all of these years, I have so missed his presence in my life and in the life of my own family. I cried for dad for several months, every day, mostly whilst on my own. Early on after his death, everything was so raw. Something would trigger a memory and emotion would overwhelm me. There were countless questions I should have asked dad about, but after he died, it was so hard to know that I'd not have that opportunity again.

So many funny things happened after he died that he would have loved to hear about. One of the saddest things is that my son Antony is so like my dad and is interested in many of the same things but Antony was only six years old when his Grandad died. I feel my son has missed the opportunity to learn from such an encouraging teacher about all kinds of things. The two of them would have got on so well as they have the same temperament and sense of humour. Both could talk to anybody. It feels like a wealth of experience has been lost for now. My daughter Harriet too has missed out on all the affection her grandad would have lavished on her over the years. She was only little at the time of his death. She loves baking so the two of them could have created masterpieces together and had lots of laughs. I think Harriet would also have been very close to my mum as my daughter loves clothes and girly things, just like my mum did.

As a grandmother myself, I realise that older generations can add a very vital dimension to the lives of our grandchildren. Whilst parents juggle all manner of tasks and jobs to provide for their children, we grandparents can indulge our grandchildren and love them dearly. We can devote exclusive time to them. I certainly love all of my grandchildren and any time that we can spend together. But whilst this is wonderful, again there is a huge sadness as my own children missed out on this. No one else can fill that particular role.

It is said that time is a great healer. This is true. Initially loss brings so much raw pain, but I found that as time went by, I began to think of dad without crying as much, although it's also equally true, that I do still well-up when I talk about him sometimes, because grief isn't necessarily something that moves through the transitional linear stages that one assumes, but rather it can be a fluid, changeable process. I haven't 'gotten over' the death of him, rather I have had to learn to try to adapt to him not being physically present with me although he's mentally present with me. I think of him every day but generally my memories of him are happy ones full of laughter. This has all taken time: there is no short cut.

In terms of a dead loved one's physical possessions: some people feel you should get rid of the items that remind you of the person who died and who you miss, but I didn't. I couldn't initially. Although in time, I gradually let some items go. The last thing I gave away of dad's, was a beautiful green Harris tweed suit and in which, he'd always looked so smart. Whenever I saw the suit hanging up in our spare bedroom wardrobe, I could only picture my dad in it but after a few years, I just woke up one day and thought that the suit would be ideal for someone else to wear. I knew that dad would have liked that, so I gave it to a charity and I was ready to make that decision then.

I think that we can also keep our late parents/loved ones, alive by trying to live by their good principles. For example, mum was feisty and had a great sense of the need for justice. She would be fearless in standing up for what she believed in and what was honest and upright. My children often laugh at the true story of my mum dashing out of our cottage with a hot poker to confront a man who flashed at me when I was playing outside as a child! My mum wouldn't take any nonsense, the flasher took one look at my petite but sassy mum brandishing this weapon with intent and he immediately fled! As for dad, he was so warm and loving. He always made me feel safe when I was with him. He was generous, kind, approachable and such a good listener. I could talk to dad about anything. Something else that was special about him was that he was always telling me how much he loved me. That is a lot for me to live up to, but I keep trying. I really think that love is a perfect bond of union and it brings joy to the heart of those who are around such people.

Finally, I just want to end my chapter with a poem I wrote about love during lockdown:

LOVE IS LIKE CLOTHING

Love is like clothing that wraps
itself around you
Like a garment once secured,
Love is unbound.

It is like the warm coat in the icy
wind of disappointment or sorrow
Or a waterproof for when the
rain of torment and the
persecution of hail beats down
on you

It offers the glowing protection
like the sun, from the cold
world that would tear your
garment undone

This garment of love is
beautiful and bright. It radiates
warmth and light

It is roomy enough to share
with others, family, friends and
brothers, even those who
would resist its appeal

This garment of love is
generous, warm and kind to all
that wear it

From where did it come?
My Father gave it to me. It is the
most precious of gifts and its
cost was very dear
I will endeavour to wear it close
to me every day

WHAT HAVE YOUR EXPERIENCES TAUGHT YOU?

That you can continue to live and love well despite a huge loss. You can process the pain and the experience of living with that person or people so that in time, they sit on your shoulders metaphorically, but in a comforting way. Over the years, I have come to appreciate my parents more and more, for what they taught me by instruction and example. Their courage in the face of adversity has been inspiring: dad coping with his unpredictable and worrying health prognosis and mum dealing with the thought of losing him and coping on a really low income and often as a single parent whilst dad was in hospital. However, despite all of this, they made me feel secure and so loved. I try not to think about losing them at relatively young ages, rather I look at what they achieved despite the adversities they suffered. My dad had so much illness but I remember his bravery, calmness and consideration for others, even when he was in a lot of pain. I remember mum trying to manage our household and working so hard at lots of cleaning jobs that she would often take me to, when I wasn't at school. Additionally, she was great at caring for others and was scrupulously clean and tidy.

So when I think of mum and dad now, I think of the positive and upbuilding aspects that I loved and admired about them both. They have inspired me to try and do the best I can. I don't dwell on the sad or bad times. My mum used to do that a lot. She would say: "if only I had done that differently". However, my dad used to say that it's a waste of energy to focus on what is past because it's gone and you can't change it. Rather to learn from it, to make the present and future better through your experience. So I try to be more like my dad, with my glass half full or more. I try to move forward, not dwell on past mistakes, but learn from them and move on. I remember their idiosyncratic ways, i.e., mum was always so house-proud. I can't say that I am as diligent with housework as my mum was, but 'Rome wasn't built in a day' and I do have such funny, happy memories of the dreaded 'spring clean' when mum insisted on every room being turned out and 'properly' cleaned. Dad used to hate it. You would hear them going on about why the wardrobe had to come out and be cleaned and polished, including the wall behind it. Dad would say: "no one ever sees it". That would set my mother off. It was so funny. She would retort: "it's about being thorough, doing a job properly." Memories like that have helped me to process the pain and make my peace with the loss of my dad and the loss of them both.

WHAT ADVICE WOULD YOU GIVE TO OTHER WOMEN IN A SIMILAR SITUATION?

Something else to remember is that just when you think you are coping well, something can trigger a memory that can make you cry. For example, when I saw the film 'The Railway Children', the scene where the eldest daughter goes to meet her father from the train after he has been released from prison, and she calls out to him as she runs towards him, was so painful for me to watch as I felt the tears well up. However, they weren't tears of sadness but of joy for the father I loved and still love. That love for him is still as strong as ever. Finally if I can do half as well as my parents in the way of my relationship with my children and grandchildren, then I think I will be happy.

For anyone going through the loss of someone, it will get better if you let it. It takes as long as it takes, so be patient. Don't let anyone dictate to you how your grief should go. It's like a river, it will find its own path. Let it navigate itself. Dwell on the happy times, laugh about the fun times. Even looking at photos get easier. Think of their lives, achievements and characters. The grief we have been through, can help us to empathise with others going through similar experiences.

WHERE ARE YOU NOW? WHAT ARE YOUR PLANS FOR THE FUTURE?

41 years after my beloved dad passed away, I feel that the hole in my heart is gradually healing as I fill it with happy memories of him and I accept that it is all part of the process. My faith has been invaluable in this as has prayer and my church community. My own family have always been supportive. I've told my children and my grandchildren such a lot about both of my parents so that even though they're not alive and my children didn't know them for very long, their characters and personalities are well known to them. When my children comment: "I bet Gran or Grandad would have loved that", it says it all.

I have a rich, full life with my family, friends, hobbies and my church and I take comfort in my memories of my parents.

ALICE'S STORY

When someone you admire professionally starts to cyber-stalk you...

I first met Robert in 2014 in London, where I worked for a leading arts organisation. His performance company were hosting a series of scratch shows across London and Europe and they were the official residents at my workplace for 3 months. During their stay in London, it was my job to be the first point of contact on site. It was a happy productive time and I admit I was a little awestruck by this group who had a huge entourage around them.

Robert's company were given the freedom to travel the world playing to different crowds whereas my own humdrum existence in the corporate world, didn't allow me to indulge in my own creativity. I had a boss who routinely bullied me, I was £30,000 in debt, I had colleagues who were cliquey and I yearned to escape it all. So it felt exciting to be included in the planning and staging of their shows as they were a much younger, dynamic group. I only saw them every two weeks but when I met the group, they were polite, professional and friendly.

In my capacity as a freelance journalist also, I attended their show after-hours' party with my husband and 20 other people. I provided the company with a glowing theatre review and Robert was delighted. He told me: "you're the best" remarking that he was smiling so much from my review and that he had even shown the review to his mother. Robert graciously gave me flowers as a thank-you before they left for their European tour and we connected on social media because of our shared experience. However after a period of time, I stopped posting because of my own insecurities. I felt inadequate and as though I had nothing of note to share, whilst the members of this group seemed to be appearing in festivals, winning awards and earning lots of social media coverage. Robert intrigued me because he was much younger than me, came from a completely different background and he mixed with a group of people so unlike those I associated with. He oozed success and confidence.

I made the mistake of sending Robert a rather fawning fan letter which my husband knew about and had no problem with. In hindsight though, I feel it was a huge error of judgement on my part, and totally out of character for me. My letter didn't mention anything about Robert's personal life or his relationships, but now I think it seems sycophantic and cringe-worthy: it was a wannabe-writer bowing down to an established artist. I talked about how I was inspired by him after meeting him in London. He has been the creator of many art festivals and started his career when he was young with a group of friends. I admired him as an entrepreneur. He was a breath of fresh air as I had never experienced a theatre company working in my building before. Robert was good looking, young, charming, articulate and everyone wanted to talk to him. I got used to seeing him and his colleagues come into my workplace and Robert was the friendliest as he was the founder of the company. I wrote in my letter to him how much I liked his shows and unlocking the codes and clues of his work. I put the line 'everything is perfect' (which he referred to later in a social media post). Robert nevertheless gave me a sweet response and I thought nothing more about it; he was used to receiving lots of attention from men and women.

However not long afterwards, Robert and his interactive friends decided to play games with my identity to grab my attention online: baiting me and playing with my emotions for 'scientific research' on google. I suddenly began to pick up several cues through a dozen links to content under my full name, which I hadn't created. Despite us parting on good terms without any acrimony, I just knew that Robert was behind this as he was the only interactive artist I had communicated with. Robert also referred to a line from the private letter which I had sent to him, on a social media post. I soon discovered that the man I met was entirely separate from his alter-ego as a bad boy provocateur. I felt disgusted with myself for engaging with him. Over time I found he had done the following with my identity:

- My LinkedIn page duplicated with the words 'revenge' and 'porn' with a model wearing a t-shirt saying 'ugly woman'.
- My full name on a German chat line
- A playlist created under my name linking it to his, under a search engine platform. Some of the lyrics were explicit and misogynistic, with the 'N' word in rap lyrics, and mean-spirited lyrics told from a female perspective, which included the line from a pop song which said: 'I guess I'm just a loser..'
- A fake blog and twitter account with my married name as 'the author'. The blog lifted content from my Facebook and social media pages. My ghostwriter referred to me, 'for fun' as one who was 'matronly' and 'googling people I once knew and feeling jealous of their achievements'.
- A game with my full name as a character, accompanied by unkind commentary: 'With her parents letting her down and with her life feeling so alone, she doesn't want other people to feel that way.'
- A poetry track under an album he created with a friend which had my date of birth and time of birth as the 'track title'.

Robert's public postings on social media didn't hide the fact that he was behind it all. He mentioned: "harassment through humiliation," admitting that: "some of my ideas are based on jealousy, fear, anger and spite." and the 'desire to needle someone.' He was derogatory towards middle-aged women like me and cited the story from Chaucer's Canterbury Tales of 'The loathly lady', whilst sarcastically referring to a middle-aged woman's sex life on his company page. I thought all of this was extremely disrespectful and unprofessional. I couldn't understand why I was being treated with such contempt and I was devastated.

I tried to kid myself that his opinions didn't matter as he wasn't a friend, relative or co-worker, and I wouldn't meet him again but I was horrified because I was hurt and I didn't want others - including my partner, bosses, friends or potential employers - to see the click bait. I slowly turned from being a fan, to despising him as he was cold and indifferent to my distress. Robert emailed me saying: "I'm offended you would think I would do that. Why would I? If you have a problem, go to the police." But there were so many clear clues between the pages of his blog posts, one of his social media accounts and that of his boss and partner. I found more 'games' under my name online. Despite the company's denials and indifference from the men involved, I found my name, images and work linked to their individual names under another search engine.

Over the last six years, I admit I have handled things incorrectly but all within the law. I rose to the bait, angrily attacking the fake blog in my name. I tried in vain to turn the other cheek, to 'forgive and forget'. I thought if I introduced myself as a human being in a 'kill it with kindness' approach, there might be a sense of shame, or an effort to be polite. I donated to their charity with a promise of a present and an acknowledgement (I waited 9 months for a company postcard) and I tried to appeal individually to those closest to him (but was met with a cold shoulder). I was resorting to everything I could possibly think of in an effort to end Robert's behaviour.

Robert's boss appeared to mimic and mirror my actions on one of his social media accounts, whilst giving a self-pitying performance on another online platform referring to his own poem on stormy seascapes; the latter was a topic I had covered in my own poetry and company blog. I realised that this was becoming a futile, toxic game of one-upmanship and I was getting sick of it. The laws in England are diabolical [new online safety regulations in the UK are being timetabled as this book goes to print]. The University I worked with then, also sympathised, but said *unless the university is in disrepute,* they couldn't get involved. During my birthday week, yet more games appeared under my name online. However, those involved all played dumb, and acted as though they didn't know how to help. Ultimately, I had to post a public complaint on another global online platform to put an end to it.

This kind of online stalking makes you question your sanity and judgements. You feel you are becoming paranoid but then again because of the ongoing behaviour inflicted upon you, any such feelings are completely justified. Last year I saw both men observe me outside my workplace, from the opposite side of the road. Once was when I entered my place of work; the second time, Robert's boss was standing near the traffic lights. Our eyes locked but I coolly walked past. I've also seen Robert pass by me with his head bowed down, to undertake business in another building. I know that a couple of my work colleagues have relayed information to Robert and his boss and they are in on the joke because there are insider references on social media accounts that only these work colleagues would have known about. These colleagues have linked to Robert and his boss via social media. I simply don't understand their mindset. In the real world I've not been in a confrontation with anybody at work, yet they feel they have the right to steal my identity and social media content to continue with their weird, cruel 'scientific' experiment.

In 2020 after much futile wrangling between parties, I had no option but to officially post something on an online forum to officially distance myself from this 'homage' which was something I really should have done years ago. The two men (Robert and his boss) have remained strangely defiant. Their name is easily found on social media next to my name and all of this feels like unfinished business. We remain digitally (and mentally connected), yet there's a lot of toxicity between parties. There's still a fake social media account in my name which I've had problems proving to a third party, is based upon me. However, I guess one positive thing is that Robert and his boss stopped writing as me a few years' ago. Also I've noticed that some of Robert's 'helpers' have since switched their social media accounts to 'private'. But this dystopian experience has been something which has very much been a part of my life for what feels like a long time now and has really caused me so much stress, uncertainty and confusion. I still remain on high-alert for anything that is posted about me or aimed at me.

Ultimately I guess the biggest revenge is for me to be successful in life so that I can rise above all of this. I am now starting a postgraduate programme at a prestigious University and I have managed to be commissioned for freelance work too! Also the most important thing for me is that I have a wonderful husband who has been understanding of my feelings.

What have your experiences taught you?

I've reflected a lot upon the whole situation. Robert did give my life some excitement and a way to escape the monotony of the everyday. I still work in the same place which has not been helpful sometimes. My husband is older than me and is more savvy than I am. He's seen me distressed and said: 'you've been conned' and that's not easy to hear. He met Robert at the aftershow party where Robert was extremely nice towards us both. My family and friends have all been supportive and it helps that my colleagues, counsellors and other figures, including my university, know my story. My older sister commented that Robert's parody blog is like a: "cruel mirror" and that I was probably flattered with the extra attention he gave me.

I have learnt not to write another 'fan letter' to someone who I don't really know. Also that the best revenge is success. Use the humiliation (including the put-downs and innuendos) as a stepping stone to become powerful in your own right! Subvert it!

What advice would you give to other women in a similar situation?

That sometimes you need to block people on social media and for me, limiting my visibility. However, that's a bit difficult as one who wants to write publicly. I do feel that there should really be far more regulations in the UK about this kind of harassment. I see a lot of websites to help young people - but it appears that a cruel parody of a person is still allowed in the public domain.

Where are you now? What are your plans for the future?

As mentioned earlier, I am now at a prestigious university focusing on a humanities' course and I have joined societies that will enable me to pursue various personal goals including my desire to become a published writer. I feel incredibly positive about my future.

JESS'S STORY

Discovering you have a tumour behind your eye and it's your second cancer diagnosis...

About 15 months; ago, I began to feel really unwell. I was constantly exhausted and seemed to start every day feeling really under the weather but I couldn't pinpoint what it was. I work in a very busy reception/year 1 class as a Teaching Assistant and we were in the middle of an intense summer term, so I just kept putting it down to that. As we got closer to the long school holiday, I was feeling worse and worse. The fatigue was crippling and I constantly had a bad headache.

In addition, a couple of times I had a 'funny turn' at work. I remember the first time, I was talking to a colleague in the staff room and it was as though he just started swaying and I couldn't focus on him properly at all. The more I tried to concentrate on him, the more unwell I started to feel. I felt so hot, as though I was going to self-combust if I didn't rip off all my clothes and immerse myself in cold water (obviously not appropriate in a school staffroom!) I then felt sick and very faint. I ended up lying on the floor with my feet on a chair with very kind people holding ice-packs to my neck, face and feet to try to cool me down. The second time this happened was after a swimming trip with my class. I started to really overheat and feel sick, dizzy and disorientated. Again, I struggled to focus visually and ended up on the floor again with my icepack friends!

About a fortnight before the end of term, I noticed that my right eyelid kept swelling up, it was particularly bad in the mornings but I put it down to being so tired and also wondered if I had perhaps become sensitive to the eye-cream that I use (I am always very careful with my eyes as I had long suspected that I have an auto-immune condition called Sjogrens Syndrome). I have had severe dry eyes for years as well as a dry mouth, spells of fatigue and joint pain. Five or six years' ago, I was referred to an Ophthalmologist after I was waking every night in severe pain because my eyelids were welded to my eyeballs. After going back and forth to the specialist for several months, I eventually saw a Consultant who asked me lots and lots of questions, not just about my eyes but about me as a whole person. He did a 'Schirmer's Test' which measures tear volume in your eyes by placing paper strips into your lower eyelid for 5 minutes. Mine came back with 0% tears in both eyes and was actually quite painful to remove as the paper strips had stuck to my eyes. I also had to do a spit test where I had to spit as much as I could into a tube to gauge my saliva production. Again not terribly productive. After talking some more, he said he would like to get a colleague to come and see me as well to get another opinion. After answering all the questions of the second consultant, they both agreed on a symptom-based diagnosis of Sjogrens Syndrome.

I was then booked to return to the hospital in a month's time to discuss everything further. Having never heard of it, I went home and researched Sjogrens Syndrome as much as I could. So much of what I read, was very familiar to me and I scribbled down lots of questions that I hoped to get answers to, at my next appointment. So I duly arrived at the hospital with my list of questions and was shown in to see the consultant. It was a different person to the one I had seen before and he was quite abrupt and obviously running very behind with his clinic. He did a few cursory eye tests and said he would see me again in 6 months. I said that I would like to ask some questions about the Sjorgrens and he looked at me and said: "you haven't got Sjorgrens. If you had Sjorgrens, your eyes would be red", and that was literally it. I remember feeling really anxious and upset but I couldn't just walk away without trying to do something so I asked to speak to a nurse to see if she could look up the name of the consultant that I'd seen before who had been so thorough. Unfortunately she informed me that the previous consultant was a locum who had been with them for 6 months and had now returned to his hospital: "up country." So really for the next few years, that was that. I was now classed as someone with severe dry eyes, I was seen once or twice more at the hospital but then signed off with eye drops to use day and night to rehydrate my eyes.

Anyway as the last couple of weeks of term went by, my eyelid seemed to be swelling more and more and I often felt that my eyes didn't feel like they were working in sync with each other. It almost felt like a conscious effort to make them focus together. A few days into the summer holidays of 2019, I made an appointment to see my optician. I discovered that I could have a free emergency appointment with them on the NHS. When I went, I had to fill in a form describing the symptoms and how long they had been going on for. I think I must have put 3 weeks because I could only see the optician if I'd had the symptoms for more than a month. The lady I saw was very nice but she said that I should try using drops to help with the dry eyes and they could sell me a heat-pad and wipes to treat Blepharitis. I explained that I felt it was more than this and that I was already using eye drops all the time and I had a heat-pad at home that I was using daily but that it wasn't making any difference. I also really didn't think it was anything to do with Blepharitis. Anyway, I eventually left after being told that if the symptoms hadn't improved in the next week or two, to come back (cue: much internal screaming and metaphorical hair-pulling).

The following week, I made an appointment to see my Doctor, although when I arrived I was seen by a Nurse Practitioner who prescribed me some different hydrating eye drops to try. I again attempted to say that I didn't feel that this was what was causing my eye to swell and that I already used eye drops all the time, but I was given a prescription and told to come back again if it didn't improve. Unsurprisingly, I made another appointment a week later, specifying very clearly that I wanted to be seen by a GP as I was really worried about my symptoms. I was still feeling so unwell in myself too. I was exhausted all the time. I was on my summer holiday from work but all I wanted to do was lie down. Everything hurt and my vision was intermittently either really dire or okay. I felt as though I was wading through treacle and I was frightened.

When I went to see the GP, she said that we should try some antibiotic drops in case it was an infection. Now I'm honestly not the sort of person who goes around disregarding everything that professionals tell me, in fact I'm quite the opposite but this just felt wrong to me. I'd had no signs of infection in my eye, no gunk, no pain, just this swollen lid that was now starting to make my face look wonky. I did explain this to the GP but she said that the drops would be 'worth a try'. Honestly, I've never felt so miserable. I had this feeling in my gut that something was seriously wrong but I couldn't get anyone to take me seriously.

My experiences of having Ulcerative Colitis and Cervical Cancer previously

At this point, I want to stress that I'm really not a hypochondriac. I do know what it's like to be 'properly' ill because I have a backstory: I was diagnosed with Ulcerative Colitis: an inflammatory bowel disease, in 1996, when I was 23 years old, which had affected the whole of my large intestine. This resulted in me being practically housebound for long periods of time as the panicky rush to the toilet (anything up to 40 times a day), was not conducive to a lively social life. Then in 2007, at 34, I was diagnosed with Cervical Cancer and was offered a fertility-saving treatment at one of London's main hospitals. As someone who has spent their whole life in a small seaside town, this stay on a huge ward in London was almost as overwhelming as the cancer itself. Instead of a hysterectomy, I underwent a radical tracholectomy and my lymph nodes were removed from my abdomen. The operation itself involved removing the cervix, the base of the womb and the top of the vagina, then joining the womb and vagina together with a thick stitch to act as a false cervix (this is a very simplified version of what was a seriously complex operation).

I had lots of problems after the operation. I lost control of my bowels on several occasions post-op (hello again Colitis), but because they had to rule out C.Difficile. I was put onto strong antibiotics (which would send my Colitis into overdrive), and I was put onto an isolation ward until the results for C.Difficile came back as negative. This is another example of me knowing my own body but not really being listened to (although I understood the clinician's need to rule out C.Difficile). Ultimately, it turned out that I had a huge blood clot in my stomach, which was why I was struggling so much to be 'up and about' after the op.

About 10 years later in 2017 aged 44 years, I had to have a hysterectomy as I was having huge problems every month when I had a period. On my second or third day (at its heaviest), my period would abruptly stop and I would be in terrible pain that gradually got worse and worse until I would suddenly start gushing blood again (it was as if it had been stuck). After explaining this to my Consultant (who was almost like an old friend after many years of seeing him), he decided to try to dilate the hole where the stitch was, so that the blood would be more free-flowing when I menstruated. I was put under anaesthetic for this process. However, when my Consultant went in to look, he was unable to even locate where the entrance was because of the huge amount of scar tissue that had formed over the stitch. He felt the only way forward was an operation that nobody at the hospital had performed before, classed as a 'post-trachelectomy hysterectomy'. So it was with huge trepidation and fear that I went into hospital to have this procedure.

The catastrophic, life-threatening bleed-risks with this surgery were apparently very high which didn't feel great to be honest, but I had trusted this amazing Consultant for a long time and I didn't seem to have many other options. Anyway, I'm here writing my story, so I obviously came through it, not mentally or emotionally unscathed by any means, but with a body that recovered and still works reasonably well…

BACK TO MY EYE ISSUES

…That's been a bit of a story detour, but I just wanted to explain that I know what it's like to have gone 'through the mill' with serious health issues and that's why I knew something was seriously wrong regarding my eye in Summer 2019. Thus continuing with my eye problems…

Needless to say the antibiotic eye drops made no difference at all, apart from stinging like hell when I put them in. In desperation, I had recently joined an online Sjogrens Support Group and had posted a picture of my eye to the members, asking if any of them had similar symptoms? Several people came back saying that my eye looked serious and I should get myself to the nearest eye hospital whilst others posted pictures of how their eyes sometimes became swollen during a flare-up. I had also seen several posts from members of the Group who had paid privately to see a Consultant in Swindon who had a special interest in Sjogrens. By this time, I was desperate to know what was wrong with me. Was it Sjogrens Syndrome that was the cause of all of my problems? That day I bit the bullet and rang the secretary of this Consultant to see if I could make a private appointment with the latter? Thanks to a huge stroke of luck, they'd had a cancellation for the following Monday morning (3 days away), so I made arrangements for my husband and I to go to the appointment together and stay overnight so we wouldn't have any potential travel issues on the way.

I was very nervous going in to see the Consultant. What if she told me I was imagining it all? However, she was absolutely lovely . She asked me so many questions, checked my eyes, mouth, joints, etc. Then she had a really good look at my bad eye, getting me to go through different exercises. She diagnosed me with Secondary Sjorgrens. You either get Primary Sjogrens or Secondary Sjorgrens, which follows another auto-immune condition, in my case, the Colitis. She also told me that although swollen eyelids could be a symptom of Sjogrens, my case was presenting differently. My eyes were asymmetric with my right eye sitting lower than the left and the double vision I was experiencing on an upward gaze, was also not a symptom of Sjogrens and so I would need to see an eye specialist.

I came away from that appointment feeling a little more positive! The relief of seeing someone who actually listened and seemed to take my symptoms seriously, was immense. This Consultant was also going to put everything we discussed and her diagnosis, in writing so that I could take her letter with me as required, to other clinical meetings. She also ordered lots of different blood tests for me to rule out other conditions that she suspected may possibly be causing my additional eye problems such as the asymmetry and the double vision. I suddenly felt like I had a way to move forward. I remember going out to the car park with my husband and breaking down into floods of tears because of the tension and fear that had been gradually building up inside of me. I'm exceedingly lucky on the husband-front at least, as he is so supportive and my absolute rock and he just held me tight, probably for ages in hindsight until I'd finally pulled myself together and we could get on the road and head for home.

As it turned out, the journey home wasn't without incident. We were on the motorway and I was really struggling to see (don't worry, I wasn't driving). I was having to make a conscious effort to try to focus on anything and it really wasn't working. I can only explain it as feeling like my eyes were working independently of each other, with my right one a good second behind the left and the more I tried to focus, the worse it got. This was more than a visual disturbance and it was terrifying. My husband ended up driving us to the nearest A&E. Although as expected there was a quite a long wait, they were brilliant. I was initially seen in triage, then by a Doctor, followed by a second Doctor, before being sent to the Eye Unit, to see the emergency Consultant there. He gave me a thorough examination and was concerned with the asymmetric nature of the appearance of my eyes and my vision itself, so he referred me to be seen by the Ocular Plastics Team within the next fortnight.

This time-frame meant that I would be back at school then after the holidays and I knew that I should call the headteacher to explain what had been happening but I absolutely hate feeling like I'm letting anyone down and anyway I kept hoping that I would miraculously start to feel better and be able to get back to some sort of normal. Suffice to say, this didn't happen and I had to take some time off from work as apart from anything else, I wasn't safe to drive because my vision was so unpredictable.

When my appointment with Ocular Plastics came around, my anxiety was really bad. I'd stupidly looked up a couple of conditions that had been mentioned and was convinced that I had one of them that matched a lot of my symptoms (desperation does strange things to people! I've always stuck by the 'don't google your symptoms' line of thought, but once I'd started, it was a bit of a downward spiral).

I was given a simple eye test first and then I underwent other varied tests. I'd also taken a photo along with me of how I normally look, 'pre-wonky-eye' so they could see the difference. In one of the tests, I had to look at a spot on the ceiling for as long as I could and randomly this was one of the most upsetting tests as I was unable to do it for more than a few seconds with my right eye as the eyelid would fall down over it. The Doctor told me to keep trying, which I did but it was making the eyeball itself ache intensely and I just couldn't hold my gaze there. When she'd finished all the tests, the Doctor wanted to get the main Consultant to come and look at me, which she did and she duly asked lots of questions and I had to retake some of the tests. She then said that within the next fortnight, she wanted me to see the hospital Ophthalmologist, have an MRI scan and to have more bloods taken and then to return to her. I felt relieved that some sort of plan was being put into motion but fearful of what the outcome might be. I duly had my blood tests and made an appointment with the Ophthalmologist, but I didn't receive any calls about my scan so felt that I should chase it up.

I rang the hospital and was redirected several times before being told that my referral for a scan had been put into the wrong pile, apparently onto the PET scan list and that they would make sure this was rectified and I should get a call in the next couple of days. Three days later I rang again about the scan as it was now less than a week before my appointment and I'd still not heard anything. I received yet another apology as there had obviously been some confusion over this scan and they could give me a slot for the following week, 2 days after my appointment with the Consultant. I again explained that I needed the results to be there for my appointment and was told that they would call me back that afternoon.

Frustratingly, I ended up calling them again later in the afternoon as they hadn't called back and it was a Friday and I didn't want to be left in limbo over the weekend. Now don't get me wrong, I am not knocking the NHS at all as I have received fantastic treatment from them over the years and continue to receive that care now but sometimes when you're at a really low point and feel like you don't have any fight left in you, it's at this time that you have to fight your hardest to make your voice heard above all the others. You need to move on from being just another number and name on a piece of paper to being 'that pain in the arse' that keeps calling and badgering until you get noticed. Anyway this time I was asked if I could get to the hospital within the next 2 hours which thankfully I was able to do and I finally got my scan.

The following week I arrived at the hospital filled with fear and trepidation. As always in these situations, I had my husband by my side, holding my hand and metaphorically keeping me together. Where would I be without this man by my side? That's certainly not a scenario I ever want to contemplate! When we were called through to the consulting room, I was shaking like a leaf. We exchanged pleasantries and took a seat and the Consultant said: "Let's get a good look at these scan pictures, shall we?"

Even before she spoke, I could see that something didn't look right. She talked me through what she could see. Sitting above and slightly behind the eyes are the Lacrimal Glands. On my left eye it looked like a perfect, almost-crescent-moon-shape, which was how it should be. On my right eye however, the Lacrimal Glad just looked like a misshapen blob. She told me that this was why my vision was distorted and why my eyes were asymmetric as the gland was pushing the eyeball outwards and downwards. She felt it could be one of two things, either an idiopathic swelling which arises spontaneously and of which the cause is unknown, or the other possibility was a Lymphoma. At this point, I was almost blinded by an internal neon sign flashing the word 'cancer' at me in big, bold letters... flash, flash, flash... CANCER, CANCER, CANCER, over and over again. At this point, I looked at my husband who was suddenly very pale.

My husband and I seem to have this weird, non-verbal communication thing where a look just says it all. I was thinking: 'if it's cancer, I don't think I can do this again... I'm not strong enough', but he knew what was going through my head and he gave me a look which said: 'we've got this, we've got each other and you're such a strong woman, we'll get through it together'. I think it's at this point that I relinquished control over my life a bit and allowed him to take the reins more firmly. And this is how I cope in times of huge stress. I simply have to step back, albeit unconsciously and just go through the motions of whatever follows.

In this case, that was the Consultant asking if I could come back in 2 days' time to have biopsies taken from the Lacrimal Gland and could we stay on that day to have pre-op checks made in the afternoon? Afterwards, my husband and I went out to the car park to extend our parking ticket and I just felt numb. We sat holding each other on a bench and we talked for a while, lurching between thinking: "it's probably the idiopathic thing and they'll give me steroids for a while and it will disappear", to: "oh my God, what if it's cancer again?"

I remember my dad ringing me to see how it had all gone and I broke down when I heard his voice. I explained what the Consultant had said and then my poor dad got really emotional and couldn't speak any more so had to pass the phone to my step mum. It's strange how at these times, different emotions pierce the numbness: right then it was guilt: guilt that I was upsetting all the people I love the most. I know none of it was my fault but that didn't make the guilty feeling any easier to bear. I thought the following: 'I should just have said the appointment went fine', 'I shouldn't have said anything until there was something concrete to tell him', 'I shouldn't have answered the phone until I was in control of my emotions'. The 'should have, shouldn't have' options went on and on until I tied myself in knots. Anyway over the next few months, guilt tucked itself into my mind comfortably alongside fear, frustration, anxiety, anger and vulnerability and guilt was along for the ride for the foreseeable future.

Two days later, I was back in hospital for the biopsies under general anaesthetic and I returned home later that evening looking like I'd done ten rounds with Tyson Fury. I now had hourly iced compresses to the eye area for the next few days, followed by a fortnight's wait for the results. The following week crawled around as slowly as the previous two had, with me trying to go through the motions of normal life. I was still feeling cripplingly exhausted all the time but I forced myself to go for a cuppa with a friend and for a short walk with my husband, because sitting and looking at a phone that didn't ring was driving me slightly doolally. Eventually Friday rolled around and at lunchtime, that call came. My worst fears were confirmed as my Consultant gently told me that yes I had a cancerous tumour in the Lacrimal Gland and she would now be passing my care onto the Haematology Department and I would hear from them over the next few days.

As promised a few days later, I received a call from the Haematology Department offering me an appointment. I remember sitting in the waiting room looking around me, feeling more and more agitated. I don't know if this was the first time that it had properly hit me. Everywhere I looked, cancer was there, from the posters on the wall for cancer support to racks full of leaflets and booklets with information on all different forms of cancer. There were patients coming and going for chemotherapy treatment, some looking really unwell and others chatting away like they were waiting for a bus, pulling off itchy, woolly hats and rubbing their bare heads. I remember thinking how brave and amazing they all were but how I wanted more than anything, not to be a member of this club. The longer I waited, the more unsettled I felt: "please will you just take me home?" I asked my husband, who just looked at me and smiled, 'not an option' being the unspoken answer.

We were eventually called through to meet the Consultant and a specialist cancer nurse. They were both fantastic, very caring and patient. I remember asking why, if I had cancer, I was being seen by Haematology instead of Oncology and I was told that it was because Lymphoma is a blood cancer. I didn't know this and felt stupid for not knowing it, but I just couldn't bring myself to research my illness before, as I was terrified of what I would discover. Throughout the next half an hour, we were given lots of information and asked several questions. The next step would be to go in for bone marrow biopsies so that they would be able to glean more information and also to see if the Lymphoma was present in the bone marrow itself. They also told me that I would be treated with radiotherapy.

I almost think the worst thing about this whole process is the waiting, particularly once you get a definitive diagnosis. For me anyway, it was a case of 'right, we know what's wrong so now we just need to start treatment and get better' but it doesn't work that way. I tended to work myself up to the next appointment only to then have another 2-4 week wait before the next one. Bearing in mind this whole journey started in July 2019 with my swollen eye, it was now October 2019 and I had got my diagnosis but as I was later to discover, there was a whole lot of waiting and anticipation in front of me as my radiotherapy wasn't going to begin until February 2020. In lots of ways, I was lucky as my cancer wasn't extremely high grade or aggressive but living through such a long period of stress and uncertainty was exhausting and life-altering in so many ways.

A few weeks' later, I was back at the hospital for my bone marrow biopsies, feeling very nervous about the procedure. I had to lay on my side and was very grateful to have a nurse sitting with me, holding my hand and talking to me. I had two consultants by my back preparing all the slides, needles and local anaesthetic. One of them was pushing into the bones at the bottom of my back on the right side of my pelvis, finding the best place to go in with the needle. My anxiety ratcheted up several notches. Then he was putting in the anaesthetic, which although felt uncomfortable and stung, wasn't really painful. We then waited a few minutes for it to take effect before he started to retrieve the biopsies.

I found the taking of the bone marrow fluid really uncomfortable but bearable although it did feel like it took a long time. When it came to taking out some of the bone, they told me that they would warn me when they were going to do it and it might make me jump but it was really important to stay as still as possible. I was already shaking but making a huge effort to control it as I could feel myself freaking out as to what might happen if I moved involuntarily. When the scraping started, to extract some of the bone for the biopsy, I cried out. It was really painful and I started to feel sick and could feel panic welling up inside me. The nurse was brilliant and she kept talking and breathing with me. I felt such relief when they told me they had finished.

I was really surprised to see the samples, when I had pulled myself together. There were 2 glass squares with about 10 slides on each, all with samples on and a little pot containing fluid with a cylinder-shaped piece of my bone within. I thought it would be a little chip of bone so was amazed to see this perfectly-formed sample. It was as though an apple-corer had been used! We came away with an appointment to return in 3 weeks for the results. I remember my back feeling very bruised for a while after. When we returned to the hospital 3 weeks later for my appointment, we were told that I had Non-Hodgkins MALT Lymphoma. The Consultant said that there was low level Lymphoma within the bone marrow which my husband and I were both quite shocked about. We'd felt it was more of a ruling-out process and had pretty much convinced ourselves that it would be clear. So this felt like another big knock to us.

We also discussed an appointment to have a mask made for my radiotherapy and it was at this point that I just burst into tears. This fear had been building for a while, probably since they told me that I would need radiotherapy. I am hugely claustrophobic: I don't like lifts, small spaces or anywhere that I can't easily get out of and the thought of lying on a table whilst someone covered my face with a mask was utterly horrifying. I couldn't see how I was ever going to have this treatment without it resulting in a complete meltdown. My nurse was as lovely as ever and tried to be as reassuring as possible. She even went to the other end of the hospital to fetch an old mask for me to look at and to explain how everything worked. Whilst in some ways, this was helpful, when she showed me the bolts that attached the mask to the bed, I just went 'completely into myself'. How could I not have realised that the mask holds your head tightly to the table so that you cannot move at all? Of course, I hadn't realised that I would have to keep as still as possible. It just hadn't crossed my mind that this was how they absolutely ensured that the radiation was directed exactly to where it needed to be.

By the time my mask fitting appointment came around, I had given myself numerous mini lectures! I had to be stoical. Nothing bad was going to happen, I needed to remember to keep my breathing slow and steady. Other people managed to do this all the time. Millions of people around the world were going through far worse than this, etc. My family and friends also boosted me along, telling me how strong and brave I was and that I could do this as it was what was going to make me better. So I went along and was nervous, but in a relatively positive mindset.

My husband was allowed into the room with me where I would have my mask made. We sat together while a nurse explained everything step-by-step. They had put a plastic sheet into a warming bath of water to make it pliable. I then lay down on the table and when the plastic was ready, they laid it over my face and proceeded to stretch it out over my face and mould it to my features. Then they fastened the clips to attach it to the table and my goodness, I certainly had to tell myself to breathe as it felt so tight. As soon as they had it where they wanted it, they started putting cold wet cloths and fans onto it to harden it as quickly as possible. I just concentrated on the feel of my husband stroking the side of my hand until they unclipped the mask. I actually felt like I had coped quite well and was still feeling reasonably positive when we went out to the waiting room to wait for the mask to fully set before having it on once more to have my scans. We had to wait for nearly 2 hours and during that time, my positive, upbeat attitude began to wane somewhat.

Obviously because of the scan, my husband couldn't come in with me this time, although they did allow him in whilst they got me ready. I lay back on the table, gripping his hand while they checked over the mask. Then they put it over my face and pushed it down to click it into place. I couldn't believe how tight and restrictive it felt. It was like having my head in a vice and each time they clicked it down, they were squeezing it tighter and tighter. The mould was pushing uncomfortably into my eye sockets and it felt like someone was holding something very firmly over my mouth. I was trapped. I could feel my panic building and I tried to focus on something else, anything else, but it was futile. When my husband had to leave the room, I wouldn't let go of his hand. I was gripping it so tightly, he practically had to prise my fingers off. I knew that at any moment he would be gone and also that the people who were setting up my scan would have to leave the room too and I would be alone and totally trapped with no way of moving or escaping. My heart was pounding, absolutely banging out of my chest. I couldn't breathe properly. The tightness around my head, my mouth in particular, was unbearable. I tried to ground myself and think of my happy place, but I couldn't find it.

I was suddenly feeling extremely hot. I attempted to let out a slow breath but it just exacerbated the heat inside the mask and made me feel sick. My God! What if I was sick? I would choke. It was at this point, I completely lost it and was overcome by complete and utter panic and I started to scream out: "You've got to get me out, get me out!" The nurses came rushing in and unclipped the mask and took it straight off but I was hysterical, crying uncontrollably: "I can't do it! I can't do it!... What am I going to do?" The feeling of panic and the loss of control completely engulfed me and I was gasping for air. Someone had fetched my husband and as he came in, I clung to him like I was drowning and he was the only one who could save me.

I'm afraid that at this point, I am going to leave my story – this story - where it is. I know that I'm ending it mid-flow and it's not particularly positive and heart-warming but it's still such early days for me and revisiting everything in such detail has been difficult. Reliving what was such a traumatic time for me, has caused my anxiety to skyrocket. So in short, to finish up, I will say that with a huge amount of support, I did manage to get through my course of treatment. It was exhausting, not helped by the daily 130-mile round trip, but I did it and I am now recovering. In some ways, I count myself as very lucky to have had my last treatment just 3 weeks before the country went into lockdown because of the Coronavirus pandemic and I feel so much empathy for other people who had to continue their treatment in the midst of all the pandemic uncertainty.

WHAT HAVE YOUR EXPERIENCES TAUGHT YOU?

Throughout my treatment, I needed something sensory to distract my mind each time I had to have my mask on. I asked the nurses to play music and also to keep talking to me over the speakers whilst the radiotherapy was happening. I had a small soft toy that I held in one hand and stroked with my thumb as it felt a bit like my cat. In my other hand, I held a fidget cube, which I used to click one of the switches to, in time to the music. These small props helped massively to focus my mind away from the claustrophobic feelings.

Don't be afraid to accept drugs that are offered. I took Lorazepam to get me through the initial few sessions and then, as and when I needed it. Some days, I felt I could manage without; some days, I couldn't.

Sometimes you hear from people who've had a cancer diagnosis that once they get through their treatment, that they really grabbed life by the horns. That it was a real turning point for them: they went off and ran marathons and climbed mountains and if that was right for them, then that's amazing. But I didn't personally feel like that and I sometimes felt like perhaps it was because I didn't have that fighting spirit or I wasn't brave enough, but actually now I know that it's just as okay not to want to do those things, as it is to want to do them. I'm happy curled up with my family watching a film or having a walk on the beach. It's absolutely okay just to be yourself. Just because you've had cancer, doesn't mean you have something to prove.

WHAT ADVICE WOULD YOU GIVE TO OTHER WOMEN GOING THROUGH A SIMILAR EXPERIENCE?

I think that it would be difficult for me to advise anyone as everybody's experience will be so different. But one thing I've learnt along the way is to take each day as it comes. Particularly at the beginning when you've first received your diagnosis. I initially tried to look at everything in front of me (like having the bone marrow biopsies, scans, the process of having the mask made, having the mask bolted to the table, thinking of the radiotherapy itself, etc) as a big picture. This was completely and utterly overwhelming and I felt like I was unable to cope and kept breaking down. Once I started to approach things step-by-step, I gradually felt more able to cope and slowly move forward. I remember feeling terrified of having the bone marrow biopsies but my mantra became "by teatime, this will be another thing behind me". Normally I would research everything to the eighth degree, but this time, I didn't want to know other people's horror stories or otherwise. I just found it easier to approach everything blind and just deal with it as it happened.

WHERE ARE YOU NOW? WHAT ARE YOUR PLANS FOR THE FUTURE?

I'm taking things one step at a time, but I am incredibly grateful for my amazing family!

NEL'S STORY

When your paramedic husband's PTSD tips him over the edge...

Every day I have a constant reminder of my husband Del, because he bought me a Golden Retriever puppy as both a combined Happy Christmas and Birthday present for my December birthday. Despite the fact that Del was a clean-freak, he completely relaxed with our dog! But having this lovely pooch is poignant because it brings up memories of Del every day, yet he's no longer with me...

***

In November 2012, Del was the first on the scene one morning at 7.30 to a Road Traffic Accident (RTA). A cyclist had been hit by a van and when Del arrived, the cyclist was someone he knew. The poor man later died at a hospital in Cornwall.

Weeks later, in January 2013, Del was meant to be on a break and was on his motorbike when a call came through via radio to say a man was lying unconscious on a road. Del was nearby so he said he would help and he headed to the area. The guy was young, just 22 and he'd also been on a motorbike but had been going too fast and had lost control. His motorbike had slid out from underneath him and he ended up going under the wheels of a Clearflow lorry. Del hadn't been warned about the severity of the accident, so wasn't prepared for the graphic sight that awaited him. To make matters worse, an off-duty fireman criticised Del and another paramedic that arrived, saying that they hadn't handled the situation correctly. Del didn't tell me about this accident, I only found out because he'd put his uniform in the wash and I could see it spinning red because of all the blood...

PREVIOUSLY

Del was originally trained as a 'blood biker' when he became a Paramedic and he had such a kind heart. He was a fit guy at 5 feet 10 inches tall and in his spare time, he undertook loads of fundraising for Marie Curie and other charities. These events included sponsored motorbike rides, climbing Mount Kilimanjaro, swimming from Padstow to Rock and so on. He was a Freemason too and always tried to give back to the community and other people, even after he'd witnessed the cyclist's crash which started to badly affect him.

However, it wasn't just the two incidents of the cyclist's death and the motorbike crash that affected him, because Del was also facing bullying at work with someone he regularly came into contact with. This person was 'difficult' with him and used to verbally undermine Del, so much so that this was picked up by a policeman who noticed it during a work call-out. That policeman said that he would back Del up if Del wanted to make a complaint about it. Looking back, I think Del began to lose his confidence with the stress of these events.

After the motorbike crash that he assisted with, Del became a different person. He attended 'a job' at a Cornish Leisure Centre and the local fire brigade went too and for some reason Del fell out with them and they put in a complaint about him. Also at a nursing home, a lady had fallen and hit her head and Del rushed in to help her but he didn't take his bags with him which contained all of his kit, because he didn't feel that she was poorly. However, not taking your kit can potentially be an immediate Disciplinary matter. The next day, the lady was vomiting and a complaint was made about Del. He was away on holiday when he found out that he was going to be put through a Disciplinary procedure for this and he started to panic as he thought he was going to be dismissed from his job.

I had just started a new employment role working at a major hospital in the south west. It was July 2013 and the beginning of a weekend when I was meant to be participating in a Marie Curie fundraising classic car event at Trewithen Estate the following day, helping out at the bar. Before I left, I happened to be googling something on our home laptop and in the browser history, I saw that Del had been researching 'Death in Service payments' and also, 'Suicide'. I had to confront him about this and he was offhand with me but I couldn't leave him at home after what I had discovered, so I made him come with me to Trewithen and he pinkie-promised me that he wasn't going to do anything regarding suicide! Nothing would happen!

Del had a friend who supported him and this friend invited Del for a drink but my husband felt that I was monitoring him, asking me: "Have you got me on suicide watch?" However the signs weren't great: he was waking up every day at 4.30am. Del had been signed off work from May 2013 due to PTSD from the motorbike crash and he lost a lot of weight. I didn't know where to go to access help for him. Previously, Del used to attend lots of spin and body pump classes but now he didn't want to go any more. He just lost all interest in it. The last body pump class he went to, he suffered his first panic attack.

Then Del bumped into someone with whom he had a close relationship with, at a leisure centre, but this 'friend' turned his back on him and Del had no idea why. Del came home and cried and wouldn't return to the leisure centre. I messaged another of Del's friends to try to help him because I was at my wits' end regarding what to do with him as Del had always been strong but now I felt unable to reach him. I have to say that I felt that the Service Del was employed with, didn't help at this point. Personally, it seemed a bit of a 'closed boys shop'. They didn't get Del a referral for counselling because they said they thought his GP had. In the end, the GP organised this and both the GP and the counsellor were great but there were long gaps between appointments.

On Thursday, 15 August 2013, at 4.30am, Del woke me up and said "I know what's wrong with me. I've got a God complex. I think I can cure everything but I can't". I remember replying: "I can't cope with this, you're either up or down. It's 4.30 in the morning!" I had to be at my hospital workplace by 8am, so I told Del to get some chamomile tea and listen to some mindfulness clips which we had. He did actually get up and do this and wasn't in bed, stressing. I went back to sleep and before I left for work, Del promised me that he would be okay. He was due to go to the GP that day and to have another counselling session but when I got home at 5pm, Del wasn't at home.

I called my mum in case she had heard from him and then I noticed 2 x letters on the mantelpiece in the living room (one was addressed to me and one was addressed to Del's GP). They were suicide notes. I tried calling his friend Phil, and I called his best friend John, they were paramedics together but they didn't know where Del was either. I called the police too and they were brilliant. They tracked his car to 'North Cliffs car park' which wasn't that far away. Del's keys were in the ignition but there was no sign of him so the police started searching for him. It had been a lovely sunny day and Del would have been wearing his shorts and a t-shirt but now I thought of him getting cold as the evening arrived. The Search and Rescue Team and Lifeboat crew were also all looking for Del but they couldn't find him.

The next day I was panicking as the weather was grim and although I just knew that Del was dead, I was still worrying about his lack of warm clothes. But I did know that he'd gone and I knew this because of his letter and because of the kind of person he was. I knew that this wasn't a cry for help. One of my friends, Peter, is a Vicar and he organised a beach vigil for Del. Hundreds of people turned up and Peter waded out to sea with notes in bottles that people had written for Del. Lifeboats continued to search for him. A kind Police Officer named Jim searched for Del even before his shifts began.

I wasn't speaking to some of Del's circle at all then and they were complaining that I wasn't passing on information. At this point, Del was still classed as 'missing' and the Police led an active search for 48 hours, directed by a CID Officer, Jo. My boss, who was married to a Policeman who coincidentally knew Del, was so supportive of me as I had to take time off work as sick-leave whilst this was unfolding.

For two weeks I had no idea what had happened to Del. He was still officially missing but on Sunday, 1 September 2013, a guy was out bird-watching and he caught sight of some rocks at North Cliff and could see what looked like a body. He called 999. The body was Del and he'd obviously jumped off the cliffs. Where he had jumped, his body had been partially-submerged by the sea so that's why nobody had been able to find it for quite some time. On that Sunday at 8.15pm, Del's friend John told me that his body had been found.

That particular evening, there was a beautiful red sky. Afterwards, I always named skies like that, a 'Del-sky'…

But then the devastation set in…

When Del committed suicide, simultaneously I had also been looking after my mum and she felt so guilty because she was the last person to see him alive and she hadn't noticed any difference in him. Mum had no inclination that he was going to take his life. Thanks to the multiple traumas that Del had experienced, at the age of 46 he was no longer with us. My mum continued to feel guilty about this.

Del's friend, Steve, identified his body but the Coroner wouldn't release Del's body until dental enquiries had been undertaken. Meanwhile, the Ambulance Service started a 'Serious Incident Review' into his death but I had some issues with the manner in which this was conducted. I felt that some of the comments they made were unfair. It did help however, to talk to Del's Line Manager as initially I had struggled with some aspects regarding Del's work but later he and his wife became two of my favourite people.

Monday, 23 September 2013 was Del's funeral. I didn't hear anything from any of the officials of the Ambulance Service for a long time and when I eventually did, a senior executive said to me: "Nel, you're not the only one who is grieving". I wanted to hit him because there was such a lack of empathy! On the other hand, the Chief Constable for Devon and Cornwall Police, Shaun Sawyer, rang me and was so lovely, amazing actually. He said: "I've read Del's records and I've have him back tomorrow". That personal touch from such an important and busy professional, massively helped!

The Inquest into Del's death happened on 1 December 2013 and it was hideous. The Coroner read out the whole of the post-mortem report and I cried because I heard everything: details I didn't want to hear: the decomposition of Del's facial bones for example. At one point, the Coroner said: "do you want a break?" I said: "no" as I had to get the process over and done with, but the Coroner, (I felt, insensitively) replied: "good, let's just carry on".

I had to go back to work the following day because I was new to my job and I was worried about losing it but there were so many things going on in my life, for example, someone said to me: "Why are you organising his funeral. You're not his proper family". I was his wife! After returning to my job, I found that I couldn't cope with the long hours it entailed and my mum (who was living with me), couldn't cope with me being out as much, so I changed roles from being a Ward Clerk to a Receptionist organising patient transport, for 3 days a week, which enabled me to have more time with my mum.

In July 2014, my God-daughter, Morwenna, and I, flew to New York for a break and it was a brilliant experience as she's like my surrogate child (I lost a baby conceived with Del, years before during pregnancy and this was obviously a huge blow. I don't have any children so that's also why Morwenna is really special to me). When we'd had the beach vigil for Del when he was missing, Morwenna stayed with me pretty much all of the time and has been so supportive of me. In the Big Apple, we had cocktails and pizza at 11am some days and it felt so good to kick back at convention after all of the stress of the previous years. However, when I got back from New York, I discovered that a local hospital had put a care package in place for my mum who had become poorly in my absence. I spent 2 weeks' sleeping beside her on the floor so that I could keep an eye on her as she was 82 years old and had been through so much too recently!

Mum cried a lot about not recognising what was wrong with Del before he took his life. I feel that people don't realise the impact that suicide has on those remaining as there are so many feelings of guilt and unanswered questions that torture those left behind. In May 2016, mum and I were on a shopping trip and when we returned home, mum fainted. I carried her indoors and although she'd always worried about her weight, now she was tiny. Things didn't look good. I dialled 999. Mum died in her sleep because of a lung condition (COPD) but she had an ambulance crew and her GP beside her, so at least that gave me some comfort that everyone had done all that they possibly could to help her!

Afterwards, I fell into a void. It was so tough not having mum around as looking after her had been a distraction following Del's death and she was great company for me. Now it was just me and my dogs. The following Monday came and I couldn't face work. I was signed off for 2 weeks and I went sailing with friends but my life now felt pointless and empty. I even worried about my own sanity as I actually felt suicidal. My friend Liz and her husband Steve were brilliant though and came to my rescue: they rallied around, listened to and supported me.

The hardest thing was feeling like I was 'just existing'. I returned to work and soldiered on, putting on a brave front. I didn't like being asked how I was, as it was 'too deep', so I would say that I was fine. I didn't want people to pity me. Some friends (both genders), my dogs and wine, got me through this time. Having the pups to walk made me organise my day along with having to go back to work. I now work 3 days a week from 8-4pm in the Trauma Unit of my local city hospital coordinating the discharges and transfers of patients and organising their care packages, so this role makes me feel purposeful. After Del died, I felt I'm not a wife, and then after my mum died, I was no longer a carer either and I felt useless - but with my job, I am *useful*. Also I've started getting up early to go running with the dogs before work, and that helps gives my life structure too!

I AM getting through all of this.

WHAT HAVE YOUR EXPERIENCES TAUGHT YOU?

Just enjoy life. It's not forever and not everyone has the opportunity to enjoy it but there's so much to love in life, even when you think there isn't.

Try to be aware if you're falling into traps to help you cope with a bad situation, for example, if you're drinking too much, etc. Just be aware.

WHAT ADVICE WOULD YOU GIVE TO OTHER WOMEN EXPERIENCING A SIMILAR SITUATION?

Talk to friends and keep reaching out. I felt a burden sometimes but proper friends understand and if they are genuine, they will be there for you.

Also go and have a different experience: get away! So in 2013, it was my 50th birthday and Del and I were going to go to Borneo but we obviously couldn't go. However, I went with another friend in 2015 and we had an amazing time seeing Orangutans!

WHERE ARE YOU NOW? WHAT ARE YOUR PLANS FOR THE FUTURE?

I'm going through a bit of a blip because I'm coming up to the anniversary of Del's death but overall I'm looking forward to life, travelling with friends, going to music gigs and planning treats in the future!

DANNI'S STORY

When the man you think will protect you, turns out to be who you need protecting from… escaping over a decade of domestic violence at the hands of a policeman

Chris was a Police Officer in the town where I lived and I was a divorced single mum, planning to become a paramedic. However, at that time, I was working as a bartender covering some shifts and that's how Chris and I met as he would respond to incidents at the bar in his professional capacity and so we started talking…

Chris basically love-bombed me with lots of texts and attention. Initially for me there wasn't fireworks but it was hard to resist his concerted efforts to win me over. I found out that he was also divorced with 3 step-children and a biological daughter. Lots of people warned me off him but because of my character, that only served to push me closer to him. Chris put a lot of pressure on me to move in with him quite quickly and my gut feeling was that it was too soon, but I didn't want to lose him so we moved in together six months after we met. Thus in our household, ultimately, was Chris, myself and my two children, Freya and Nick. Chris' children would come and stay too every other weekend although his daughter stopped coming when she reached 16. At this stage, there were definite red flags but I ignored them…

After three years' together, we had our son, Freddie. Even in the early days, Chris was quite aggressive. There were a couple of incidents where I felt his aptitude for violence and rage: for example, when we argued, he would push me very roughly and get extremely angry, putting his face right in mine and shouting directly at me. He was also the same with my son Nick. One incident really stood out for me: it was when I was 8 months' pregnant with Freddie and Chris went away for the weekend in Basingstoke on a police training course. He attended with another female colleague that he was close to and I felt uncomfortable about it all. I had asked him not to go as I hadn't been very well whilst I was expecting, but he was insistent. I checked the browsing history on his laptop and it revealed: 'looking for sex in Basingstoke'. I challenged him but he joked it away. Nonetheless, we had a big row about it. Despite me being heavily pregnant, he wrestled me to the ground and looking back, this was a red flag!

Freddie was born with a kidney condition and needed to be in hospital sometimes because of this but Chris just wasn't interested. There had been a police complaint made about Chris because of a special police scheme which he had started. This scheme meant that he was earning more money and it was also affecting the business of a local man who was doing something similar professionally. He said that Chris was effectively pinching his clientele so an investigation was launched about Chris' scheme. This resulted in him spending loads of time on his computer replying to emails related to this complaint. Therefore, I had no help from him with Freddie and I knew he missed my attention being focused on him instead of it having to be divided between him, Freddie and my other children too.

Chris didn't cope very well with family life and having a baby. Paradoxically, whilst he loved to show Freddie off in public, at home in private, it was a different story: he was disengaged and just didn't support me, for example, he would never get up in the night to help. Basically he went into a depressive mode with me and things gradually declined.

Another 'red flag' incident happened when Freddie was about 6 months' old. Chris and I were meant to have a weekend in Budapest with Freddie whilst Freya and Nick were at their grandparents. But we missed our flight and Chris had a huge 'tantrum' at the airport and security had to be called to calm him down. We ended up going to a hotel in the Cotswolds instead but there were lots of horrible arguments and during one, he grabbed my thumb and pulled it so hard, he ruptured a ligament. Afterwards, I had to have plastic surgery on it but I told everyone who asked, that I'd had a fall at work.

I realised that I was attached to a man who liked to be the centre of attention. Chris had an idea to get involved in a special fundraising event and I supported him and raised hundreds of pounds to help him reach his funding target. I even drove all the children thousands of miles to meet him in another part of Europe at the finish line. As a 'Master of the Grand Gesture', Chris then proposed to me with 400 other event participants looking on. I just felt I couldn't say no, so I accepted. However, my intuition was making me nervous… it told me that I was making a big mistake.

Not long after we set off to have a family holiday staying in an apartment with a balcony. But there was a gap on the balcony and I was worried that Freddie might fall through so I vocalised my worries to Chris a few times but he perceived it as me nagging at him. Ultimately he became very angry and punched my arm incredibly hard. I was really shocked and ended up with a severe bruise. One of my stepchildren even noticed this a few days later and said: "what's happened to your arm?" but I made up an excuse because I just rationalised Chris' behaviour as the result of his tiredness and stress but deep down I remember thinking 'oh my God'.

We returned home to our small cottage but life with him continued to be stressful because he was always falling out with colleagues and my friends didn't like him. By this point, I was working for the Ambulance Service but I hadn't qualified as a Paramedic yet. We started planning our wedding. I wanted it to be a quiet affair but Chris wanted a 'big do'. Our actual wedding day was very disjointed. All of his family ended up in the pub next door to the hotel where we were and my family and his just didn't mix at all. At the start of the evening reception, he went missing for 45 minutes and he said later that it was because he had an upset stomach but I am convinced he was with another woman and I just stood around in my wedding dress thinking 'where is he?'

Once we were married, Chris' anger and abusive behaviour just got worse as it manifested itself more physically. I tried to stand up for myself but he was much stronger than me so we'd end up with lots of broken items in the house such as smashed pictures etc. I would try to protect myself so I scratched Chris in self-defence. He really couldn't cope with Freddie and he was always trying to start an argument or be very defensive, so I felt as though I was constantly walking on eggshells. If the kids played up, he would say: "they're your kids, you deal with them". In addition, our relationship with other people locally and his colleagues was becoming fraught so we decided to move an hour away within the same county. Around this time I also had to have a hysterectomy and came home from hospital with 200 stitches but once again, Chris didn't help at all.

Chris went onto raise more money for charity by taking part in a funny sketch and making it public. However, whilst some in the police really admired Chris for doing this, others simply didn't approve and felt it was inappropriate for the Police to be involved in something like this. However, Chris relished finding himself in the maelstrom of attention. Random women now sent him messages and some were slightly sexual. It resulted in him constantly being online replying to these dms and to be honest, I found it all a bit difficult to cope with.

Christmas came around and I took the children with me to my parents, which was a few hours' drive from our family home when I got a call from Chris and he asked me to go outside to speak to him, in private. My heart was pounding. He said he'd been suspended from the police because he'd got involved with another member of the police force in a very inappropriate way, which due to confidentiality, I am unable to provide details of but Chris was suspended and then sacked. He told me that he and the female involved had met up several times and now she was stalking and blackmailing him. I was devastated about it all. At the time, it became public knowledge and we ended up moving house and then because of this, Chris couldn't get a job and so over the coming months, he tried starting various businesses but they all failed and amidst this, he also accrued debts with people and then he began a new hospitality venture, renting a premises to run it from.

By this point we had been together for 14 years and previously I had even had to declare myself bankrupt as I had used whatever money and credit I had access to, in order to keep us afloat financially as a family and to bail-out Chris! So I was now desperate to get out of our marriage but I had no idea how to, as money continued to be such a nightmare and I felt physically, mentally and emotionally trapped.

Simultaneously I was working as a Paramedic and Chris' abuse towards me continued. There were numerous instances where he was violent and very aggressive towards Nick especially. I would put myself in between Chris and Nick to protect my son and Nick learnt to withdraw. I tried to protect my children from the worst so if Chris started getting aggressive, I would tell the kids to go off into another room. I didn't know it at the time but they would all go to one room together as a group. Freddie would sometimes try to put himself in the middle of Chris and I to protect me but he was obviously becoming really affected by what he was absorbing as we started having lots of problems with him. He was 10 years' old at this stage and was a very angry child, having witnessed lots of violence and aggression but what was going on in our household, somehow became 'normal'.

Lots of people saw how bad it was before I did and many simply didn't like Chris. I also suspected he was having an affair but I couldn't find any proof and it was driving me a little insane. My gut told me this was happening but because I didn't have any evidence when I confronted him, Chris would call me a 'psycho' and say that it was all in my head and make me feel that I deserved his anger. He made life so difficult for me then. So for example, as a Paramedic, I was working night shifts and needed time in the day to sleep, but Chris would deliberately disturb my rest so that I was exhausted all the time. I was also helping Chris out with his new hospitality venture to help save money and support him. Looking back it was a mad time. I would contact all of Chris' creditors to agree payment plans as Chris wouldn't do this and sometimes I even paid the Staff wages out of my own money because Chris couldn't pay them. However, Chris was asking all of my friends and family for money too, generally behind my back. Whilst I knew about some of this, I only discovered the full extent after we split up and then I was upset to learn that they all thought I knew about the borrowing and they believed that he was approaching them with my blessing too.

The violence, extreme acts and aggression continued. One day, Chris pulled a knife out and threatened to kill himself. This wasn't the first time he had threatened this as he'd done so previously after he had been sacked from the police. Back then, he went missing for a while and left notes for the kids but then he reappeared. It was just Chris' way of trying to be in control. However, he would always bring people around because Chris had the 'gift of the gab' and a lot of people got swept away by his charisma.

At the same time as Chris starting his hospitality venture, I had actually asked him to leave our home as I wanted time out from our relationship. He was always threatening to leave anyway. This was a constant theme. Chris actually did go to stay with his dad then and our kids (who were all still at home then), said to me: "don't let him come back". This was the closest I got to making the break with him, but Chris pleaded to return and I let him. The children accepted my decision.

In the middle of one day a few years' ago, I started feeling unwell. I had a headache, a bleed in my eye and the whole of the right side of my face was numb. The people I was with at the time were concerned and wanted me to go to hospital but I wasn't 'thinking straight'. I drove home and called my doctor. I was sent to A&E, was scanned and given the diagnosis that I had suffered a stroke. This resulted in me having to take time off work. I had to attend quite a few neurology appointments afterwards and I always went on my own to these as Chris wouldn't accompany me. However, this caused difficulties and incurred extra costs because I wasn't allowed to drive due to the stroke so I had to take taxis to all of these appointments.

I still had some facial symptoms whilst I recovered but these disappeared after 3 months. The fatigue was ongoing but my stroke experience fundamentally changed my mindset. I reflected on how Chris had been whenever I was ill or laid a bit low and how this would be another trigger point for his aggression, for example, when I was pregnant, had the hysterectomy and also when I'd had an inflamed gallbladder. On each of these occasions, Chris wouldn't help me in any way.

That summer, I applied for a promotion with the Ambulance Service. It was the position of Clinical Supervisor and the role was based at a site nearly 2 hours away from our home and I was successful! I think subconsciously that I thought this was a way out of my toxic marriage because throughout all of these years, the aggression had continued. It was simply a constant theme and now especially with Freddie too, there was never any peace in our home: just always screaming and shouting. Freddie now stood up to his father and that made Chris' behaviour worse. He wouldn't look after him whilst I was away working and he started drinking really heavily either in bars and then he'd come home and vomit in the bathroom without clearing it up. My son Nick was having to look after Freddie when I was working, as Freya was away in her first year at University.

At this point, the violence really escalated and I began to think that Chris would actually kill me. We had really bad wrestles where he would punch me, get me up against a wall in a headlock or a choke-hold. As a former policeman, he knew all the ways to restrain me. Although once before in 2011, he had given me a black eye and I'd gone to work with it and everyone had queried it in concern (I'd told them all that I had slipped in the bath), generally Chris was really cautious not to hit me where resultant bruises would be visible. Previously his punches were never aimed at my face, but rather they would be directed to the top of my arms, legs and parts of my body which would be covered up. However, Chris had started to become less careful where he landed his hits, so this was a red flag to me that he was really losing it now because he obviously didn't care how visible the damage from his assaults was. I would take photos of the bruises he gave me but then delete them later because he would gaslight me, remarking: "well you scratched me. You're the one who's violent". I actually still have the photo of the black eye though as a reminder of how bad things were. Although my colleagues then kept trying to ask if I needed help, I remember shutting them down because I didn't feel I could talk about my personal life. Later, one of my work friends told me that no one believed the excuses I gave at the time.

Chris took out four loans in my name without me knowing, totalling £40,000, which he personally guaranteed by forging my signature. At this point, he wasn't paying his staff their wages and money was also really tight at home to the extent that we could hardly afford to buy any food. It also became apparent that Chris had become emotionally close to a female member of staff and over that Christmas, he refused to come home and stayed away for a number of weeks. I found a card from that employee to him with lots of hearts and kisses in it and I learnt that she had also bought him an expensive bottle of whisky. After that, I didn't trust him or this situation at all. My eldest daughter Freya walked in on them in an embrace.

The following months after my stroke was particularly awful. One evening he ended up pinning me down on the floor as he began to assault me. The kids were all out. Afterwards, I had a lot of bruising and I was physically in pain. Somehow I managed to get out from under his grasp and he went off to work. I would be angry with him for an hour and then due to the dysfunctional dependency I had on Chris, I would chase after him sending him texts asking him to call me despite what he had done. He'd created this controlling relationship where I felt that I couldn't manage without him and I had got to the point where I felt that I was worthless, a nothing. I didn't feel I could leave, because Chris always said that no one else would have me and I believed that this was the best I was going to get.

My son Nick had started to stand up to Chris verbally but Chris would push him around physically and mentally by belittling him and calling him a: "stupid little boy". Chris was intimidated by Nick and Freya's academic abilities as he had a chip on his shoulder about not going to university. Freddie turned to his siblings for support, often ringing Freya at University for example, to have a listening ear from someone who knew exactly what was going on.

We were so broke. Our eleventh wedding anniversary came later that year and it was so stressful at home but Chris liked to perform grand gestures for weddings and birthdays in order to tell everyone about them. I told him not to do anything because we simply couldn't afford it. However, I woke up on that morning and he said: "Come on, get up, something's planned, I've sorted something out". He drove us to an airport: he had booked flights for an extravagant day trip but I was stressed because I was worried where the money had come from to do this. Chris told me not to spoil it but I just felt it was morally wrong to be having an expensive time when the kids didn't even have any food at home as our financial situation was so dire. It was just horrible! We flew back later that day and Chris got us an Indian takeaway. Freddie, Nick and Freya (who was back from University) had laid the table in advance as they were 'in' on this surprise meal but again I was just thinking it was so wrong.

The next day, I woke up and Chris was screaming at Freddie and Freya and then he and Freddie got into a physical fight. He pushed him up against the banister. Freddie's yelling was so loud! The next thing Chris was sitting at the table on his laptop and something clicked inside me and I said: "you just really need to go", and I remember how he calmly closed his laptop and weirdly said: "alright then". There was no fight, no arguing and he literally left.

Freddie tried to get in touch with him because Chris had a hold over him. Chris texted Freddie to say that he was sleeping on the streets but this was a lie. He was actually sleeping inside the cabin in our boat. We had a camper van in our garden and Chris asked if he could stay in it and then in the daytime, when I was at work, if he could go in the house? (but Chris actually ended up sleeping in my bed). I said yes, because it felt like it was the dutiful thing to do. Although I felt quite adamant that I couldn't properly be with him, I thought I loved him. Looking back though, I know that I let him use the house out of loyalty even though he didn't deserve it because once I'm loyal to someone, then they always have that.

Chris asked to borrow £100 from me and he went off to stay with a family member who lived away from us. At this point we were still speaking on the phone but I suspected that Chris was seeing someone. I had a shift at work and was driving to start it, when the children called me because we all had a shared Spotify account and a random woman's name came up on this shared account. I asked Chris about this and he said that she was just a friend but I knew immediately this wasn't the case and I called him a liar.

The following day, I was driving Freddie up to Leeds and Chris was meant to be starting a new job that he had got in the city where we lived, but we couldn't get in touch with him. I received a phone call from a member of his family who asked me if I was ok? I said: "not really" and explained that Chris and I had split up and that I suspected he was having an affair, but was worried too as he was meant to start this new job and we couldn't reach him. Chris' family member then denied that Chris was having an affair and said that Chris was actually on his way up to London to live there.

I was devastated. How could I tell Freddie that his dad had left for good without even telling him or saying goodbye? We drove all the way up to Leeds where we stayed with Freya who was in her University halls there. That journey was the hardest thing ever. I was in pieces. I spoke to Chris that night. Three days after he'd left having not told anyone he was leaving, he posted a picture on social media of him cuddling up with a woman and that's how we all found out about the new affair he was having. It was a double kick in the teeth and for Freddie especially too. He tried to call his dad and Chris would hang up on him, shouting.

When we returned home from London, we were met on the doorstep by bailiffs. One was really aggressive and I had to call the police, who changed all the locks on our house and put something over our letterbox too. Chris had racked up debts of over £100,000. I collapsed with chest pains and was taken to hospital by ambulance.

You might wonder why I didn't open up and tell other people about what was happening? But you don't tell others what's really going on because you don't want to burst their bubble of the way they perceive your family. You just don't feel you can discuss these matters. Also often when you do try to confide, some people look at you with distaste and disdain and simply don't want to discuss it. So it all becomes a dark hidden secret. Family life looks normal on the outside but inwardly, it's toxic and horrid. Before we split, Chris' drinking escalated and I started drinking a lot too. In the last few years, people sensed tension around us so maybe that's another reason why some backed away. He would make jokes at my expense in public and I started to get braver and do the same to him too but only in public.

I've reflected a lot upon what happened but back then, Chris would ring me all the time if I met up with friends. He was always chasing me to know where I was and initially I found this flattering. In hindsight, I think the biggest key to dealing with something like this, is not to keep it a secret but I also think that due to religious conditioning (my mum is a Catholic), I was told that family business is family business, you don't ever discuss private family issues, not even with your doctor, rather everything should stay within the family, hence it becomes this nasty tangled mess.

There is a high percentage of domestic violence within the police because they are trained physically to deal with violence and they are used to controlling people as part of their job. Additionally for some policemen, being abusive gives them a power trip but also simultaneously some use it because they are trying to cope with the stress and PTSD caused by some of the issues they've faced in their line of work, so it's a complex picture, but this doesn't mean that abuse can be condoned. This whole experience has made me think of other careers where professionals may become more violent in their home lives due to the nature of their work, for example, prison officers, those in the services and so on. It's made me realise that we need to check in with their partners!

Chris would never apologise for his outbursts and violence. He simply used to pretend they hadn't happened and the weird thing was that we would carry on normally afterwards as though that were the case. We would just focus on practical domestic stuff. Also throughout all of this and right up until the end, we continued having sex and whilst he was very selfish in bed, he wasn't abusive sexually. Looking back, it's quite weird how detached we were but I think that can be a common feature too and I just compartmentalised it. It didn't cross my mind to withhold sex, I just did it.

Just before I started planning how to finally end things with Chris, I began to think more about the choke-holds he performed on me. It's an action like a strangle. I've done a lot of safeguarding training and strangulation is a massive red-flag as a precursor to murder. On a DASH Form which is used for domestic assault assessments by regulatory bodies, one of the questions is: 'has the person ever strangled you or tried to strangle you?' If yes, it's a massive red flag for serious domestic violence. Towards the end of our relationship, Chris was using the choke-hold on me more and more and Freddie let it slip, that Chris had even used it on Nick.

My daughter Freya was really clever at defusing aggressive situations and would always back down with Chris but Freddie and Chris' fights were getting worse: there was real anger there and often they felt out of control. Chris' ex-wife said to me that he'd been violent with her but when I'd originally heard this, I thought it was 'sour grapes': she was trying to slur him because their marriage had ended. It didn't help that Chris said that she'd been violent to him, but later on, I realised that she must've been speaking the truth. Other issues Chris caused, included deliberately sabotaging any family trips and get-togethers with my own family. If he did come after I'd begged him to, we would all be on tenterhooks. My family detected that things were not good between Chris and I during the last 5 years of our marriage but they didn't say anything until it was over.

After Chris left to be with his new woman, he prolifically uploaded information onto his social media accounts knowing that it would reach the kids and I. I blocked him and filed for divorce on the grounds of unreasonable behaviour as I was advised that if I cited adultery, it could be disputed and take longer, however, I did mention his adultery too and Chris admitted this. He basically 'didn't give a shit'. His family rallied around him and I tried to rebuild my life. Initially I felt incredibly lonely, thinking 'what the hell am I going to do?'

Freddie was put under CAMHS (Child Adolescent Mental Health Services) and wouldn't go to school or out of the house. He wanted to move to the area where I had got my new job. Simultaneously, my work was really helping me. My close friends were incredibly supportive and some opened up about their own problems but no one close to me had been through the same issues. However, I slowly started to put together the pieces of my life. The following year we made plans to move away to live permanently in the city where I had my new job so that I would be closer for work. My son Nick decided to live with his dad (my first husband) so that he could finish college nearby but Nick was happy about all of this!

I met a new guy through the ambulance service and this grew into a relationship. I'll call him Ben. Ben has been a big part of me being able to rebuild my life. He has shown me that I am worthy of love and that a man can be a strong man and yet not dominate women. Ben makes me feel really good about myself. I can talk to him about anything whereas with Chris, lots of issues were off limits. When Ben and I talk about topics, if we disagree: we discuss it, there's never a horrible argument. With Chris, very quickly there would be screaming. If Ben ever does anything wrong, he will say sorry and I do the same. It's so lovely and refreshing not having to be on tenterhooks all the time.

Freddie is an ongoing concern because of what he witnessed. He has PTSD and is having specialised therapy. Freddie disclosed the violence to CAMHS before Chris left and those agencies have reiterated to me, that it wasn't my fault. Nick and Freya have nightmares too about what they've seen and heard. There's a huge amount of guilt attached to this, regarding my kids. There's nothing I can ever do to explain that. I just have to understand why I couldn't leave Chris for such a long time. I started seeing a specialist counsellor for trauma a couple of months' ago to help me process it all.

I am now renting my house, have a fulfilling job and a lovely relationship. My divorce from Chris has been finalised and we are trying to sort out a financial settlement. My closest friends remain the same with me. I am not ashamed of telling people my story.

WHAT HAVE YOUR EXPERIENCES TAUGHT YOU?

Trust your gut.

Listen to the red flags and really take notice of them.

I don't think that people fundamentally change. People can grow and learn but if someone is fundamentally a controlling and dominant person, I believe they always will be.

Victims don't have to be shrinking violets. People who now know what happened to me say: "but you're such a strong woman" and I do normally fight my corner/stand up for my principles and yet the abuse still happened to me. Abuse can happen to anyone (man or woman), in any walk of life and/or economic situation.

WHAT ADVICE WOULD YOU GIVE TO OTHER WOMEN IN A SIMILAR SITUATION?

The minute someone is violent to you, tell someone! Once you say it, it makes it real and you can't lie to yourself about it.

Love does not look like abuse. Nothing about abuse is love.

Build some financial savings of your own. Make sure you keep some money back. Even if it's only enough to stay in a hotel or a B&B for a few nights so that you can escape if you need to.

Where are you now? What are your plans for the future?

I feel like I've got myself back My oldest friend said that to me recently. Before, Chris always had to be the centre of attention, I wasn't allowed any attention. Meeting my lovely partner, enjoying work and feeling safe is so good. Feeling safe is actually a massive thing. I can go to sleep and know that I won't be woken up by a raging drama. I didn't get to this point too, by having Ben by my side, but I got to this point by myself. I can be on my own if I need to. I love having Ben in my life and he makes me feel safe, but I know I don't need a relationship to cope.

My kids are generally in a much better place. They've learnt a lot from everything. Freya is very picky about men. She's certainly a lot stronger than I was at her age. If there are any red flags, she's all over them. Nick is very mindful of toxic masculinity too. He's not aggressive at all and took one of his friends to town over his behaviour when he noticed some worrying signs.

I've got lovely friends and I'm happy living in a new area despite the lockdown. Ben and I are hoping to move in together after Christmas but there's no rush, I'm much more patient now, I just take things slowly.

A massive weight has come off my shoulders. I didn't realise until I left my abusive marriage, how much pressure and strain I'd been under on a day-to-day basis and how many people I'd lost in my life. Life feels a lot lighter now. I used to watch a comedy previously and I couldn't laugh before or cry because I had become numb and emotionless just to survive, but then it all comes back.

My experiences have made me want to reach out and help others. I feel much more physically and mentally healthier, my biggest challenge is working through the guilt about exposing all of the abuse to the children and not leaving sooner. But my Trauma Counsellor said that our subconscious mind is stronger than our conscious mind and when I question myself: 'why didn't I leave?' she says "you're talking as if you had a choice, but you didn't" - because I couldn't leave until I felt absolutely that I *had* to leave and I had the confidence to leave because before, I just didn't feel that I could end my marriage. By leaving, you feel that you are going against everything that's inculcated in you as a wife and mother. You always feel intrinsically that you should stay with your family and keep it together so it sometimes has to be a catalogue of events and then one final huge 'tipping point' that pushes you to leave, before you actually have the strength to make the break. You realise at this point that if you don't quit your horrendous relationship, then the ramifications will be too awful to contemplate. I have to say that I felt relief when Freddie disclosed the violence to CAMHS because it took the whole stressful situation out of my hands. (I just want to add here that the CPS – Crown Prosecution Service - won't take on domestic violence cases if they are over 6 months' old, if the CPS cannot be sure of a conviction).

LYDIA'S STORY

When you've grown up in a very strict faith and your first love is your older married boss... but then his wife tries to befriend you and predictably it all goes horribly wrong...

A song came up on my Spotify playlist recently and it instantly took me back to that turbulent but totally intoxicating time. Although it's over 20 years ago now, it still hits a raw spot to recall that experience properly because the pain at the end was so great. I actually don't know how I survived it at the age of 20 as it almost broke me. The love I felt for that man and all the accompanying headfucks which that situation gave me! That episode in my life took me to the absolute pinnacle of happiness... literally euphoria... and then again, it also took me completely to the depths of despair!

When it was over, I felt suicidal. I remember getting in my car one bleak, stormy February day and just driving and driving, heading to the wild sea. I drove to some rugged cliffs and stood and watched the raging water... but I wasn't ready to jump; I wasn't ready to quit life... somehow I had to get over this person who loomed so large in my mind. It took me moving hundreds of miles away to Oxford to begin a new life, to gradually break his hold over me...

When I was recently looking back through my diary from the time of my relationship with him, I saw that ten years after our affair had ended, I had re-read my written entries in that diary and I had scribbled in the margins: 'I miss you so much even now, wherever you are, no doubt carrying on being the same charming flirt you've always been. What I would give to see you again and for us to talk and catch up and laugh. I miss you so much. You left such a big legacy Seth.'

For a while, I lived in hope that somehow we would at least reconcile and I tried to take comfort in the fact that *had* we been together, my life would have been no life at all as I would always have felt completely paranoid that he was having an affair with someone as he seemingly couldn't help himself. He needed to know that *every* women desired him. I remember him asking me as we were about to sleep together for the first time, if our mutual female work colleague Amelia had ever said she 'liked' him?! By that I knew he meant he wanted to know if Amelia fancied him? Honestly, his timing!!! And I knew immediately then that he was completely bad news but I just blanked it out of my head because I loved him so much. However, this man's massive charisma and his impact on my life at the time, was so huge and the way I felt for him, was so overwhelming, that when he was no longer in the picture, I felt such grief and such a massive loss as though my life was over. What was the point of anything now, because all of the colour and fun had literally, completely drained away…

Over lockdown (the first Covid one), out of curiosity I searched for him on social media. I can't reveal his actual name so I'll call him Seth. He has quite a lively and open profile on one site and I found myself scrolling through it, feeling horribly guilty and stalky for doing so, but I felt the need to check-in somehow, to see how he is, what he's been up to, and to acknowledge/reconcile how I felt about him now. I know loads of people do the same, even though they try not to. I only do it very occasionally, so I don't feel so bad and during the lockdowns, I heard how checking-in on former lovers became quite a thing as most people had more time to sink into nostalgia and become introspective.

And yes, I could still detect what I had originally seen in him: that huge attraction, that magnetism, his lust for life and his presence: it came through in all of his photos and warm comments: he was still so open, full of life and fun. I saw photos of his family and they had all grown up… life had moved on for them all. But now I felt happy for him, for all of them. I didn't feel bitter or pained about it any more. Instead, I felt a fondness and a peace and this is the gift of time: that it takes the rough edges off stressful experiences.

WHEN I WAS 20

I'd been invited to the baby's head-wetting party: the third baby of my handsome boss! Or rather the fifth baby of that man as the first two were with his former wife; he'd actually been married three times. He had a history. At the age of 20, whilst I wanted a baby one day, I wasn't fawning over them at that time, whereas mentally I couldn't help fawning over my boss and felt so incredibly guilty for feeling like this, but he had awoken something deep inside of me…

There had been such a huge overwhelming attraction the first time I saw him! I literally couldn't get my breath back as his physical presence was so powerful! When I reflected on this moment many years' later, I couldn't help but acknowledge how much of a life-changing experience it is, when you have an immense headrush due to a person's aesthetics that you're rendered mute because your mind and body react in a completely involuntary way: you simply can't control either! To put it bluntly, they are so fucking delicious that you just want to leap on them!

As I've got older and experienced more in life, I've discovered that not everyone is lucky enough to go through this monumental thunderclap emotion ever: they settle for comfortable relationships, namely just 'getting on' with someone, growing to find them attractive and then becoming partners. Maybe this is a healthier alternative? But my relationship with Seth was based on pure lust, I guess. He was so unbelievably gorgeous and beautiful in a strong masculine way, that he stopped me dead in my tracks. My heart literally skipped a beat whenever I saw him. At the very moment I realised we both felt the same, I knew this dynamic would change the course of my life.

***

THE FIRST TIME WE MET

There'd been a lull in my hectic morning at the Post Office where, aged 18, I had my temporary summer job. It was just a regular weekday and I was standing, daydreaming, behind the counter staff, Lauren and Esme, waiting to collect some letters I'd sent to the printer when I found myself completely mesmerised by a tall, well-built man who'd walked in. He had an athletic muscular physique, jet black hair and an extremely handsome face with a strong jawline and as I would come to know so well, onyx-black eyes that bore right into you and which contained a hint of danger. I could tell immediately that he had an edge to him.

I guessed he was in his thirties and I couldn't take my eyes off him as he looked so out of place. I felt he belonged on a film-set as an actor, not in my small childhood town in the home counties: it felt completely bizarre. He reminded me of Sylvester Stallone in his prime with an overwhelming presence to boot: this man was just incredibly masculine. I was completely bowled-over because I had simply never seen anyone this attractive before.

Although I was so naïve then, floozy-like thoughts immediately inspired me to make up an excuse to walk through the customer area of the Post Office purely so that I could walk past him and see if he noticed me… or at least noticed me a *little more* than I already knew he had done (because I just sensed that he had), when I was standing behind the counter staff. Sure enough my plan worked: as I walked past him, he paused from speaking to Lauren, to turn around, clock me and smile. He then muttered: "hello" softly, in a strong Scottish accent. God, I was instantly smitten! Who was he?

His voice immediately served to make me like him even more because I loved particular accents: Russian, Italian, Eastern European, and of course, Scottish. I gave him my biggest beam and said quietly, coyly: "hi", suddenly feeling a little bit vulnerable and shy as I wasn't used to being the focus of such an intense gaze and I felt out-of-my-depth with him as he was a total 1000/100!!! We both looked at each other for a few seconds and then I turned away to walk towards the door to head to a shop and buy a bottle of water.

A few minutes' later, when I walked back into the bank with a bottle of flavoured water which I didn't even like, my hot man was still at the counter and we both exchanged glances and smiles. Once he'd left, I couldn't help but ask the other staff who the mystery guy was. Lauren said: "It's Seth McPherson. He's the Manager of Steepleheston, that huge Elizabethan estate. It's owned by this really wealthy family who also own other estates around the UK, but Seth normally comes in here on the days you don't work".

Lauren paused and then added, reading my mind: "He's good-looking isn't he?" she then took a breath again, before adding: "but he knows it. Overall, he's okay though."

I was pleased and intrigued! If Seth was a local businessman, that meant there might be other opportunities when he could just pop up into my mundane life but I didn't really elucidate this to Lauren as I was pretty quiet back then and I was also very religious. I had led a very sheltered life in the countryside living on my grandparents' smallholding, pre-social media (my parents had separated and gone off abroad for different reasons, when my two older brothers and I were very little, so we were raised by our grandparents). The year before, I'd learnt to drive, changed my job, broadened my set of friends and begun to feel a little more confident, and realised – just a little – that men were beginning to respond to me and I liked… no actually, secretly, I *loved* the attention I was getting. At the time, I didn't mind if Seth seemed arrogant, because looking like that, he had every right to be. He was a real alpha male.

But then Lauren added another downer: "He's married with children" and I remember piping up and saying, grinning, "that's a shame!" Lauren had replied that she felt sorry for his wife because women always fancied Seth and flirted with him. I thought at the time that I wouldn't want everyone after my husband as it would make me so insecure but then I also chided myself, 'don't be so ridiculous. He's totally out of your league. And he's married!' and I hated myself for even thinking – for a fleeting moment – that there might ever be the possibility of some romantic liaison with him because I wasn't a homewrecker. I definitely wasn't *that kind of girl*. I was decent, upright and had good morals but… but there was just something overwhelmingly attractive about him…

***

Over the coming weeks, Seth came into the Post Office more and more on the days I was in there and I found myself looking out for him all the time… but maybe I was just imagining this? Did he provoke this reaction in all the women he came into contact with, because however religious I was, I literally felt like I just wanted to drop my knickers for him!!

However, although I experienced the sensation of butterflies in my stomach whenever my eyes alighted on him, during the gaps in-between, I was preoccupied with my faith which took up a large part of my week and I slipped back into sensible thinking that: (a) he was married; and, (b) he wasn't a member of the same religion as me. I would never ever let myself fall for a married man. What would my grandparents say? It went against everything I stood for.

My religious upbringing had been intense. It was a branch of strict Christianity which was all I'd ever known and it gave a lot of structure and depth to my life. However, I was struggling with some aspects of it as it was incredibly black and white. My grandfather had a senior role of responsibility in the local church, which he shared with other more established male members of the church too. Therefore granddad always felt a level of accountability to be seen to practice literally what he preached when it came to his own life and his family's life too. My grandmother too was also fully involved in the religion but my older brothers had stepped away from it. However, with all the zealous fervour of an early teen who's found a cause and a mission, I'd been baptized in these beliefs at the age of 13 and now I needed to stick to the Christian vows that I'd made. If I broke them, then potentially my grandparents and other friends in the faith would not be able to have any contact with me..the stakes were high.

Some of these vows included: no sex before marriage; to always put God first; to spend time with others in your faith and not to marry an unbeliever or hang-out with unbelievers; not to seek to be overly-educated or involved in a career that would lessen your time for your faith; not to smoke, masturbate or get divorced unless on the basis of infidelity and there were other strict rules too.

When I was younger, these codes of conduct hadn't been much of a problem because my faith was all I really knew, although I quickly broke the no-masturbation rule aged 10, but I felt then, that this 'naughtiness' was just between God and myself. Later on, it was either touch myself or go off the rails with an older student, Harry, who I liked at school when I was in year 11 and he was in the upper-sixth. I knew I liked guys and kissing because I'd had a sweet and innocent boyfriend/girlfriend relationship with a boy named Zack at Primary School between the ages of 9 and 10 and I'd been absolutely devastated when he and his family emigrated to Canada. We were even pen-pals for a while and are still in touch now. However, I could be a good Christian girl and reign-in all of my desires as long as I felt I had a sense of purpose, had at least one close female friend, had some social events to go to and that there were some yummy guys out there who were also in the same religion as me.

But then things changed. I changed too. I began to see the nuances in life and although I left school as soon as I could, skipping A-levels because of my faith, to undertake part-time admin roles in order to spend part of my week being heavily involved in my church, my brain was actually really clamouring for academia and adventure. I needed more than my parochial life. I needed more than for my world to be so black and white.

In addition, my best female friend Sophie, moved away from the area, so ultimately within my church, I was just surrounded by older people, many of whom were married or elderly and I felt isolated from anyone of my age who shared my beliefs. I also realised that I was quite a colourful person both physically in the choices of tangible things I liked, and metaphorically, although I kept this pretty much to myself. I really fell for Harry because he just seemed so at ease with himself. He chivalrously often helped me to carry all my school bags and home-economics' cooking onto my school bus and impressively, he was a really talented, self-taught classical guitarist. However, when I mentioned Harry to my grandmother, she told me I needed to forget him because of my religious beliefs and so obediently, I distanced myself from him and nothing further happened with Harry, other than that we talked and then he left the area to head off to Uni. Meanwhile, I continued to focus on my devout religious life and gradually put him behind me…

However, I still struggled with my life as religious 'socials' with teens my age from other congregations of my faith, were few and far between and of course, they were very tame events without alcohol or cool music and there was always a parent around to act as a chaperone! But then, a pretty blonde, Vanessa, moved into my church after relocating to my area from New Zealand along with her three children and non-believing husband and she took me under her wing. Vanessa and I went on shopping trips and to the cinema and she sensed I needed a mate after Sophie's departure. Simultaneously a few other mature women, also mums, reached out to me too.

Having female company (albeit with older women), definitely helped ease the massive void I experienced when Sophie relocated, although these newer friendships were completely different to the girlish one that my friend and I'd had. I felt that these females had their children and husbands to help keep them on the straight and narrow and they had already navigated their teenage years, getting safely out to the other side. Or they'd discovered religion once their hedonistic teens and twenties were spent. These women weren't obsessed by sex or the lack of it, as they pretty much all had a vent for this need if they so desired, as apart from one woman who was now a single mum, they had their husbands to sleep with as and when, and I figured from what little I knew, that they were probably sick of being bugged for it. Sex was something that could taken or left whereas I was a late starter and very curious about sex.

It's human nature that when something is forbidden but so hyped, then in one's mind *that* something becomes an even greater source of fascination. I tried to blank all of this out of my head though because I'd made a promise to myself, my grandparents, church and God, that since I'd been caught in the midst of 'getting-off' with a year 10 student at the beginning of secondary school, I wouldn't even be kissing anyone until I was engaged to be married (to someone in my faith), let alone sleeping with anybody. I'd only just recently discovered what a load of slang terms for sex actually meant, as up until that point, I'd been so naïve. But life was beginning to open up in this way to me even though I felt so out of the zone.

I was reminded of my unworldliness when I overheard my boss, the Post Office Manager, Simon - the least unsleazy man I knew - joking with Robert, an Assistant Manager, that a fellow employee had a lot of 'lead in his pencil'. It had taken me a little bit of time to work out what they were referring to and whilst I was quietly shocked, I was relieved that I was gradually beginning to catch up with this new and exciting, forbidden side of life as I guess my religious upbringing made me feel like I was half convent girl + half Amish!

The fact that I was expected to marry a fellow believer - especially when there wasn't anyone suitable in my congregation or those nearby - gave rise to my expectation that I was going to be single for a long, long time, living a virtuous, nun-like life! This was a pretty disappointing, boring prospect but I threw myself into other stuff: wholesome church activities, job hunting for when my temporary role at the P.O. came to its natural end and arranging my next visit to see Sophie! I'd just squeeze in a little bit of flirting wherever the opportunities arose and get my kicks that way! Or that had been my plan before it was derailed…

***

The following day, I was in my local town's job centre when my gaze was instantly averted to a card reading: 'Part-time Personal Assistant and Receptionist wanted for a Historic Country Estate'. My eagle eyes scanned the few details listed and then I stopped dead in my tracks as I knew exactly where this position was likely to be based. After all how many holiday resorts were there around my neck of the woods? Despite my lack of life exposure, I'd picked up on a tiny frisson of interest between Seth McPherson and myself and I'd hesitated, wondering if I should get the job details? But then the pragmatic part of my brain kicked in and started telling me not to be so stupid. It could be the perfect job and anyway, I probably wouldn't get it and even if I did, nothing – *absolutely nothing* – would happen because as I kept reminding myself, Seth was married and I had my beliefs and my whole life was immersed in them. So I queued to get the rest of the info and that evening, I filled in the application form, made a special effort with my accompanying letter and then walked down my grandparents' farm lane, to pop it all in the red postbox, crossing my fingers!

***

A few days later when I was back working in the Post Office, my direct telephone line rang and I knew immediately that it was Seth before he even spoke. My heart immediately somersaulted! I was invited to an interview. But then the doubts crept in: 'I don't stand a chance' I thought. 'Why would he employ me? I've only worked at the Post Office for a short while. I haven't been a P.A. or a receptionist before. I left school without taking A-levels because of my beliefs. He'll be inundated with highly qualified applicants.'

However, I was still pretty blown-away that I actually had a job interview lined up and I tried not to let myself dwell on how gorgeous Seth was. I told myself that I hadn't applied for *that* reason. I did have quite a will of iron then and youthful self-righteousness, so I refused to let myself dwell on Seth.

Besides, there were a few other things going on in my life then. My grandparents had put their house up for sale and I thought that the estate agent, Tim Shipley, who came out to take the details, *liked* me a tiny bit because ever since he'd come out to my family home, Tim had made a point of standing at the window of his shop, whenever I was passing and he would smile at me. Walking past his estate agency more often than I needed to in order to get his attention, became a bit of an obsession for me. We also used to regularly 'bump into' each other in a bakery in our nearby town and we'd acknowledge one another with a nod, but we wouldn't really speak, however it felt as though there was a spark developing. This was 'meeting my needs' to be found attractive by guys without breaking any rules!

Tim was the same physical type as Seth: the whole tall, dark and handsome cliché but Tim looked as though he was in his mid-twenties maybe? He was a dead-ringer for a young Charlie Sheen and drove a blue Vauxhall Astra. I quickly memorised his registration plate so I could clock wherever he was driving. Tim and I didn't wave at each other: we just looked out for one another. I knew he was a decent guy and the reason I had this insight was because he was extremely sweet to one of the elderly ladies, Rosemary, in my local church who was selling her house through Tim's firm. He had offered to get Rosemary's shopping when she had the flu and didn't have any family to assist her and when I heard this, I was really touched. Rosemary told me how she'd given Tim some of our church's religious leaflets and he'd politely accepted them. That story did something to me: to know that a guy I really liked and found handsome could be so kind and gracious to an older, vulnerable person was just a good sign of an intrinsically lovely man!

However, I just kept thinking that I couldn't look for anyone outside of my church, any 'non-believers' and also I was pretty sure that Tim had a girlfriend anyway: a bespectacled, petit, red-haired librarian type, but I still couldn't help but enjoy being noticed by him. Having not had a lot of male attention in the past apart from the odd one or two and lacking confidence in this respect, Tim's interest bolstered my self esteem.

But I parked Tim in my mind because I had my first family-free trip abroad: to PARIS!! It wasn't quite how you'd imagine it though because it was cheap, involved a long coach-trip and it was with other members of my faith so there was definitely not going to be any wild parties but it did make me feel that despite not going to University, my life was opening up just a little. Although Sophie had moved away, I felt that I too was beginning to do interesting things; I wasn't going to be left behind to wallow.

***

My interview as Seth's PA/Receptionist at the holiday resort went well and I wrote in my diary afterwards: 'Seth is lovely but I don't think he will be such a softie as Simon.' On Seth's desk, I saw a stylish black and white photo of him and his wife. I remember not being able to stop looking at it. The following day was my last one at the Post Office and I was given cards, gift vouchers and best wishes! I knew I'd miss everyone there as they'd helped me to find my feet at the beginning of my professional life and I definitely felt more confident than when I had started, but from now on, I was actually unemployed and it felt scary.

I'd received some inheritance money which would help me financially for a few months but the pressure was on for me to find work but then lo and behold, Seth called to offer me the role of his PA/receptionist, which of course, I accepted! And then I found myself wondering what I was letting myself in for? I thought of my interview with him: his piercing dark eyes staring at me from across his desk.

***

The following Monday, I spent the whole day absorbing everything involved in my new role as Seth's PA and sometime Receptionist and I met most of the other estate staff. An attractive woman with a funky copper pixie cut and casual clothes, popped into Seth's office where I had a desk too. The woman had a toddler wedged on her hip and she was introduced to me as the Creche Manager and also Seth's wife: Susie! She was bubbly and I smiled back, saying a more reserved hello. Susie seemed nice! Also I could immediately sense the dynamic between her and Seth, because as galling as it was to admit, they did seem a very well-matched couple.

As the days progressed, I began to get to know my new boss and relax. We'd be working together mainly in silence in his office, with the door shut to everyone else. He'd ask me occasional questions and sometimes he'd start to sing a song (I never knew which ones they were but he liked stuff from decades before). On my third day in, he was giving a really dodgy rendition of a tune which made me laugh and I remember instinctively frowning at him in a sarcastic way, which he grinned at and his face had then lit up in a playful manner: "don't you like my singing Lydia?" he said laughingly. I could tell he felt that I was a challenge and he wanted to draw me out of myself...

I'd smiled back and told him that it sounded as though he was in pain and he'd raised his eyebrows at me and beamed, telling me how cheeky I was! I was a bit speechless. Working together was so much fun. I was bemused and intrigued by Seth because he was just so unlike any other man I'd met, anyone in fact. As time went on, his sense of humour and charisma became more and more apparent: Seth just knew how to create drama, a sense of atmosphere and fun just by walking into a room and making everyone take notice of him. Even in my first week of working for him, I felt I was blossoming in his presence. He made me laugh a lot and I regularly defaulted to simply smiling at him and he'd reciprocate back and then I'd feel awkward and look away back at my computer screen and one of his handwritten letters which I was typing up.

This was long before the days of the #MeToo movement and so behaviours were very different then. It was probably in my second week of working for him that he pinched one of my mint sweets and proceeded to suck it really provocatively in front of me: "mmmm" he said, visibly demonstrating his pleasure… and making groaning noises… or was I imagining that this was what he was doing? … but his eyes were almost closing in rapture. I remember shaking my head at him. I wasn't quite sure if Seth was trying to imply something risqué in that gesture or whether I was overthinking it in my sex-deprived state or whether he was just trying to wind me up as my elder brother used to do, but one thing was for sure, I was massively enjoying the banter we were sharing, which definitely had a minxy edge to it.

I would respond to Seth's juvenile humour by mock-acting my disapproval as a stern secretary, peering over my glasses at his childish jokes, improvised tuneless trilling and occasional bad language. After an upbringing of sensible religious restraint and serious responsibility, now being able to have such a lot of fun was definitely welcome! I loved it and felt that I was beginning to come alive! Just to have a laugh with someone young, worldly-wise and handsome was all I really needed at that moment in time, to feel 18 years' old as opposed to 80!

Not long after I started my job there, I spent a day working in reception with my colleague Amelia who was sassy, acerbic and comical, when Seth strolled in, asking: "right, "who's going to make me coffee?" I'd dutifully jumped-up like a proverbial cat on a hot tin roof and said, "I will!"

"By the way girls", he added: "we'll be going on a trip next week." My heart had lurched because: (1) my grandparents probably wouldn't approve; and, (2) I was supposed to be going to Paris then. But Seth read my face: "don't worry Lydia, it won't affect your Paris sojourn. Basically the three of us are being sent to the Edinburgh estate to have a day's festival training. We'll be going up on Monday lunchtime and returning late on Tuesday night, so you'll need to pack your pjs, but you'll be back in time for your trip".

I'd never had to go away for a job before. Prior to my Post Office job, I'd waitressed and acted as a data inputter in a very boring role for another company and so suddenly I felt a little bit important and validated for the first time in my life. We'd be clocking up the miles and then I'd be back for a day before trekking off to Paris. This was the life I'd wanted, needed, for ages, rather than the same old, same old, every day. But a voice had niggled in my head: 'don't forget your priority lies with your faith'.

During the week preceding the Edinburgh/Paris visit, I lost a fax, made some errors on a database, got told by Seth to drive more slowly around the site and developed three unsightly spots on my chin which merited a mention in my diary as did the remedial face pack I used, to try to get rid of them. I instinctively tried to hide them by regularly placing my hand in front of my chin hoping that Seth wouldn't notice, but he was sharp: "Lydia why are you talking with your hand in the way?" he'd ask me, smiling, knowing exactly why. I would feel my face redden. Ugh. This man – I realised - already knew all of my vulnerabilities. He was sharp. I felt he could read my mind…

Simultaneously, I also seemed to be passing Tim's estate agents a lot more and was bumping into Tim on the local streets and a momentum there, seemed to be building too. The smiles between us were intensifying and I thought of him more and more. He'd now started waving to me from the shop window and I'd glance in more explicitly… it felt like progress. Surely it was only a matter of time before something actually happened with him?! I finally felt that my interior life, away from my family, childhood and religious beliefs, was really beginning to heat up and it made me feel both wired and nervous. A tiny part of me desperately wanted to subvert the boundaries.

***

The drive up to Edinburgh was entertaining to say the least. Prior to heading off, I'd visited my great-gran in a Care Home and it had been quite depressing as she'd barely recognised me. I sat next to her in a stiff upright armchair for 20 minutes before one of the assistants helped her to remember that I was her great-granddaughter. Witnessing her decline made me want to fill my life with fun and our trek up to Edinburgh was certainly that! Seth sped up the motorway in his sporty Audi with me in the back seat and Amelia in the front. He played songs from loads of bands I'd never heard of and I felt that I was receiving an initiation into a far more sophisticated music repertoire than I had. When Seth used his mobile phone whilst driving, he was clocked by the police and pulled over but as ever he ultimately charmed them too and they let us continue on our way.

Wearing Armani Shades, Seth was a bonafide poser: a guy who didn't give a fuck and quiet, bookish me found this so attractive because of the almost Amish-style modesty I'd been used to, along with having zero self-awareness. I remembered dressing up to go to church once in my early teens and my granddad had told me to put something less colourful on so as not to draw attention to myself, but here was someone who actively sought to draw attention to himself and I found it totally exciting! Additionally, Seth was completely in touch with just how attractive he was and his popularity, and he played on this. As 'The Streets' sang in their hit song, he was fit and he knew it, but Seth literally didn't care! His self-ease could have been so off-putting but it wasn't. Instead, every time he was around, life felt fun, unpredictable and joyous. It was intoxicating.

My boss regularly looked up in his mirror at me sitting in the back of his car and we caught each other's eyes. I remember smiling from ear to ear! Hours' later, we arrived at the Edinburgh resort and after depositing our overnight bags in a nearby lodge, we headed to the site restaurant. It wasn't particularly busy but a heady mix of alcohol plus Seth and Amelia's easy familiarity with each other, made the evening buzz. I felt so new to all of this and as the night wore on, an exhilaration overtook me but then I also felt slightly uncomfortable and out of my depth, especially when Seth said after sinking a few pints: "that waitress could spin pineapple rings around her nipples". I knew that the shock I felt at such a blatant sexual reference, immediately registered on my face and he noticed this, saying with a smile: "don't be such a prude Lydia. I'm just joking. But they could do with having someone who looks a bit friendlier serving in the restaurant though, couldn't they? She's a bit frosty." He laughed again cheekily and Amelia joined in.

I did too this time. It was true, the waitress was giving 'please piss off. I'm tired' vibes and it was impossible for me not to feel a camaraderie with my colleagues.

We ate Dover Sole and finished off with coffee and brandy and I tried to stand up but as a total drinking novice who'd already downed a Southern Comfort and lemonade alongside 3 glasses of wine in quick succession, my legs felt like they belonged to somebody else and Seth and Amelia had to help me to the room that Amelia and I were sharing. Then Seth disappeared and I thought that was the last I would see of him that evening, which I felt both reassured and disappointed by. Wearing my best pink satin pyjamas, Amelia and I chatted drunkenly with each other and then there was a knock on our door…

The knock resulted in Seth sitting on a chair in our bedroom with his feet up on the end of my bed. We all chatted and laughed. The alcohol had definitely relaxed me and I was far more at ease. For all my naivety, I mentally acknowledged that there was a definite edge between us and wrote in my diary of how he was giving me 'bedroom eyes.' We attempted to make hot drinks but we were all so hammered, we couldn't measure the coffee out properly… after a while, Seth said: "I'd better go, it's probably a bit inappropriate for me to be in here in the first place". That night, I dreamt of both Tim and Seth.

After a tour of the Edinburgh resort the following day and a training meeting between Seth, Amelia, myself and the staff there, the long drive home began and my boss jokily told his wife on the phone in earshot of us: "make sure you're wearing your red underwear when I get back Susie." As soon as he said this, Amelia and I both shook our heads in mock disapproval but inwardly I felt slightly piqued, jealous even. For all his risqué bravado, Seth was demonstrating that he was happily married and had an active sex life and on one hand, I was glad, because I could safely have an ego-boosting flirt… BUT on the other hand…

Although I knew there was a spark between us, I was adamant that I wasn't going to put my religious, straight life in jeopardy and I really liked Seth and Susie and their children and I was enjoying my job too! Everything was well in my world for once and I was no longer hankering after Sophie's new exciting Bristol life, but I was actually feeling comfortable in my own skin for once. I didn't want to ruin anything.

Two days later and Paris beckoned. Seth thought I was going with a group of sassy girlfriends rather than on a Christian trip and I wanted him to believe this. I hoped he'd think I was embarking upon a bit of a hedonistic weekend so I could see if I could detect just a tiny hint of jealousy but then I felt bad for even thinking like this. However, my instincts were correct, because his final comment to me before I left, was: "Don't go kissing any Frenchmen Lydia. With your beliefs, I expect you to behave yourself", and he was remarkably serious for once.

Church companions or not, Paris was amazing and when I came back and resumed life, working as Seth's PA continued to be exciting! There was never a dull moment and he was such a dynamic source of energy. I'd never met anyone like him and I was developing intense feelings for him…

FAST FORWARD A FEW MONTHS TO MAY

"Lydia come on, don't be so shy", Seth said to me. "Come and wet the baby's head with us!" (He'd become a dad again: fifth time around. He now had 3 children with his third wife Susie and 2 children with his first wife).

"I don't know if I can make it", I replied, feeling awkward because I'd have to go by myself as none of my religious friends would accompany me. By now I was familiar with Seth's reputation as a bit of a player and I'd fallen a little bit in love with him, so I was trying to be cautious.

"Yes you can", he muttered in his soft Scottish lilt "Just come for a bit. One drink, that's all".

I intuitively knew that it was a bad idea but I was desperate to go. I felt nervous about fitting in but it was in the local pub and the whole team of staff were going, plus partners, kids etc. It would be a lively mix and I didn't want to seem anti-social. Susie was going too, and Amelia and her solicitor husband, Rich, so why was I feeling anxious?

Was it just my religious conscience kicking in? Making me feel dubious about the company I was now keeping which felt dangerous compared to my usual positively-puritan network by contrast. I remembered passages from the bible and my granddad telling me: "remember the Apostle Paul's advice to the Christian congregation at Corinth: 'Do not be misled. Bad associations spoil useful habits.' At my church meetings, this verse was repeatedly pointed out but the interior me was balking at it because I wanted some FUN and to see some of the world, live a bit! I knew that I was bored of being perceived as the quiet mousey one: I wanted to have a richer, more vibrant life and so on this occasion, I just decided to override the angel on my shoulders, bin my social unease and head along to the pub with my colleagues.

As I chose my outfit, I felt nervous. I'd only had my job as Seth's PA for 8 months and I still felt a little like an interloper. All the staff at the estate were such a tight-knit team having worked together for a long while and there was an incredibly easy camaraderie between them all but already I'd grown in confidence too and was gradually becoming more worldly-wise and feeling a readiness to question life and my upbringing a little. Inwardly I was in conflict because I recognised that I was having really strong feelings for my handsome, gregarious boss and these were impossible to switch off but for all kinds of reason, he was a headfuck and of course one of the main reasons was that he lived on site with his wife Susie and their children. Also the fact that Susie was employed at the estate too meant that she was ever present.

Seth had got under my skin for lots of different reasons: when I was franking letters using red ink and some ink spilt, Seth made a joke that the franking machine was having a period and it was just such a silly joke in bad taste, that I blushed because it was a bit shocking for me at the time and then I laughed. Seth literally had zero embarrassment about bodily functions: he was so open about everything and this was just refreshing after being surrounded by sensible, restrained and religious people who spoke very formally about such matters, if they were spoken about at all. Growing up in my faith, so much was out of bounds, i.e, same-sex relationships, masturbation; certain types of sex – oral, etc, so sex and anything to do with a sexual body, felt limited, private and with – if I'm honest - an element of shame attached, thus to spend time with someone who was completely the opposite was initially very shocking and then ultimately liberating, for me! I guess it was a wake-up call regarding how a person could be about life, love, sex and their bodies!

Seth broke all the rules of what a typical boss should be like. When I was queuing up in our local supermarket one afternoon, I felt someone rubbing up against the back of me and I turned around angrily to give whoever was grinding their body into mine, a mouthful, but my face froze as who I expected to be a 'dirty old man' turned out to be Seth playing a prank and he was shaking with laughter! How could I not see the funny side? Now in our current era of 'cancel culture/political correctness/me too' etc, these gestures would be seen as fundamentally abusive but I wager it's far more complex than that. Seth's behaviour wasn't abusive to me. It was actually welcome and I know that maybe to younger generations my outlook may seem controversial but I am simply being honest. I was so in love with him, we were both over the age of consent and were so physically and mentally attracted to each other, that he just made me laugh with his cheeky outrageousness. I lapped up his audacity because he knew how to judge what I needed and the way he was with me, gave me a sexual confidence that I'd never had before, along with the ability to be relaxed about life and my body. Seth taught me a lot – both good and bad.

Another memorable time was when I tripped over on my ankle and was unable to walk on that foot because I thought I'd broken it and my incredibly handsome boss hoisted me up tenderly and lifted one of my arms around his muscular shoulders whilst he put his arm around my waist and rested his hand against my ribs, helping me on my other leg to limp to his car whilst I leaned into him and he drove me to the local medical centre and waited patiently whilst I had it checked over. For the next couple of days, he ran errands for me, made me coffees and so on to help me with what turned out to be a badly sprained ankle. He was tender and kind.

Another night, when I was using the on-site laundry facilities at 10:30pm, as I emerged from the room into the dark night outside, Seth jumped out at me, yelling: 'surprise!' and I screamed my head off before collapsing into giggles! I was completely hooked on him. I'd literally never met anyone like him. He just made life so much fun!

***

Months' earlier at the Christmas party

At the Christmas party (which to my grandparents, I had pretended was something else), I saw Seth looking at me in a particular way as I was dancing and I *just knew*. It had been so exciting beforehand, because I'd taken myself off to the nearest city and treated myself to a new silver dress and it felt *so good* to get glammed up! But I was conflicted: just to be at this festive bash had involved a level of subterfuge that went against my conscience. I felt guilty that I'd spun lies saying that I was staying with a Christian friend from another church nearby and my grandparents had readily accepted this, not checking up on me. This meant that I could start drinking from 5pm with everyone else, knowing that I was going to be crashing out in one of the empty estate apartments. At one point that night, Seth had draped his arm around me and then started 'drawing' with his finger on my bare back.

Rose (the girlfriend of the guy who owned the hotel where our party was taking place), observed it all and told Amelia how much Seth was flirting with me. Rose asked Amelia if Seth's actions were reciprocated by me? I knew I was treading on slightly risky territory but when I saw Seth looking at me in *that* way when I was dancing, despite my naivety, I knew what it meant and morally, whilst I should have been horrified, secretly I was thrilled.

Later we went back to the estate and continued our party there. Susie had gone home early as she was expecting her third baby and she felt she should relieve the babysitter. Once she'd left, Seth made a beeline for me in front of all the many resident guests and staff who were dancing, drunk, chatting or combining all three. The lights were dark, the atmosphere was buzzing and Seth blurted out: "I have to say you do look very lovely tonight Lydia" and he just stared at me really intensely with his ebony eyes boring into me to the point where I felt awkward because it was as if he could see right into my soul, could read my mind and knew all my vulnerabilities. The next moment, I felt myself blushing as he took his flamboyant self onto the dance floor.

Amelia looked at me and told me that she thought Seth had a thing for me but I couldn't really accept it because he was so charismatic and so gorgeous that I couldn't believe he would be interested in me, but Amelia insisted: "No, he definitely likes you". But then she added: "just be careful with him, won't you?" and I remember nodding coyly whilst inwardly feeling both a little nefarious and proud that someone else had registered that Seth was interested in me, because it meant that it wasn't just my imagination conjuring up that such an incomprehensible attraction was actually there. I must be worth something for this incredible man to be interested in me.

Seth's attention was giving me some confidence in myself, it was beginning to take me out of my shell. A few days' later, Ian, my dance class teacher, sent me a bouquet of red roses to work, along with a card asking me out to dinner. Seth saw the bouquet even before I did and wasn't impressed but instead was jealous. There wasn't any spark between Ian and myself although I went out for a drink with him and then dodged his dance class because I felt awkward, but it was still an ego-boost to suddenly have this male interest and to see Seth's reaction. It sounds bad but I really enjoyed it because I'd led such a sheltered life and suddenly I felt I was waking up to what all the fuss was about!

When I'd worked in a tedious data-inputting job just after leaving school for a small business owned by 5 brothers, I'd been really mousey, quiet, totally unfashionable, a bit overweight and spotty and the brothers barely noticed me. However now, I'd had a bit of a glow-up with my highlighted hair, a body more exercise-honed and a spring in my step, so when I snuck out clubbing and I bumped into my former bosses, they suddenly noticed me too and gave me their numbers. The oldest: a really handsome guy called Mark, put his arm around me one night and told me to give him a call because: "we'd get on well". I couldn't believe it! I didn't act on any of this, I was too shy still, but all of this definitely gave me a boost! Just to have some attention and to be found sexy…!!

Tim had moved far away at this point, close to Brighton and I'd been really upset when he told me that this was impending after we finally got talking to each other one night in a club. I posted a goodbye present and a card through the letterbox of his estate agents a few days' before he left and then that was that. (A few years' later, we bumped into each other in a nightclub again and although I was pregnant at the time and married, he told me then how much he'd liked me those years previously, but by then it was too late).

***

With Tim out of the way and no legit Christian love interest on the horizon, my feelings for my married boss were continuing to grow, but for all the risqué fun, when you've been raised with strict religious principles and you actually grow to like the wife involved, life starts to become very conflicted. It didn't help that incidents like the following occurred: "Who's going to come and keep me company tonight?" Susie called out to me and Amelia as she strode into reception a few months' later. "Seth's flying up to Edinburgh and I'm all by myself…well, lacking in adult company".

Amelia had quickly piped up: "I can't, Rich has invited one of his colleagues around for dinner with his girlfriend", and so I awkwardly felt obliged to go to Suzie's after explaining that I had to attend my church meeting first. My faith had gone on the back-burner a bit but it still felt pretty integral at that point and I felt I needed it more than ever to try to keep me on the straight and narrow.

I remember Susie chuckling and saying: "you're so devout" (and I'd thought 'if only you knew what's really going on in my head right now'!!) and then she added: "it's a good thing Lydia, I'm not knocking it. I admire you. We'll watch a film and have munchies." Amelia said she wished she was coming too, because she knew that she would ease the atmosphere because she was aware that I was trying to keep Seth's wife at arm's length, knowing as I did, that some kind of unstoppable organic alchemy was happening between Seth and me.

I didn't know where 'it' was going, if it was going anywhere? But I felt static in it. I couldn't really talk to anyone about it either as Amelia was friends with both Susie and I, so her loyalties were divided. Furthermore, my religious girlfriends would never approve. Somehow I felt that I could cope with the situation if I was disingenuous and simply didn't acknowledge anything was actually happening, because otherwise I had to properly consider Seth's marriage and the fact that – even worse! - Susie was pregnant too!

Even just thinking about this aspect too, stopped me dead in my tracks and almost rendered me breathless because wasn't it just the lowest of the low to have feelings for a man whose wife was expecting a baby? It was totally disgusting and morally wrong and I was mortified by myself. So okay, that night I went to Susie and Seth's house to keep her company because I thought that actually the reality of the situation might shock my conscience into cutting off my feelings for Seth, for no matter how he behaved towards me, *nothing* was ever going to happen!! Also I wasn't *that* kind of person!! I didn't like *that* kind of behaviour and anyway he probably wasn't really interested in me that much really: he was just flirting, being a player – and I'd already been told that this was exactly what he was like!

***

Once Susie had delivered baby Caspar shortly afterwards, it became apparent that she was besotted with her twin girls and her baby son, but Susie complained to me that she didn't think Seth was as interested in the baby as she'd hoped, because he'd already had two sons with his second wife Rosa. There had always been suspicion amongst the estate staff, that Seth's relationship with Susie had come about as the result of an affair when he was previously married.

I remembered my gran's friend saying to me: "You can have anything you want at a price, but you must be prepared to pay that price". Also the saying, "be careful what you wish for", used to pop up into my head and I wondered whether Susie felt insecure because although finally she had her gorgeous husband and three beautiful children - if she'd tempted Seth out from under the nose of his previous wife - might Susie feel that she too was now at risk and that his attention could wane? - because as that horrible old saying goes: 'when you marry your mistress, you create a job vacancy.' I used to wonder if Susie truly felt at peace and I vowed that I would never put myself in *that* position with such a man but then of course I hadn't anticipated just how strong the pull of love and desire are.

***

DRINKS OUT TO CELEBRATE 'WETTING THE BABY'S HEAD'

Towards the end of the afternoon before baby Caspar's 'head-wetting' celebration, Seth called me again on the office phone: "you *are* coming out to the Crown and Thistle tonight, aren't you love?" (The Crown and Thistle was a local pub/ nightclub known for lock-ins and decent nights!)

"Yes, I'm just about to leave", I said feeling ecstatic that Seth had called me a second time, but then that wasn't untypical. I wasn't going to overthink it and I would firmly compartmentalise him. When I went into a moral mindset sometimes, I used to actually think about moving away as I didn't want this headfuck that I seemed to find myself in. I wanted to do the right thing: Seth and Susie had just had this third child. I wanted to take control of my emotions and remove myself from the situation. But that night, as the celebratory drinks' flowed and we all ended up on the dimly-lit dance floor, the strobe lights picking up the white of my sleeveless top, Seth moved up close to me, pushing his huge, muscular body against me and there was a massive electric charge between us. He leaned over to me and whispered in my ear: "you make my cock hard".

I gasped. I was shocked. Stunned, naïve until now. Nobody had ever, ever said anything like this to me before. Later that same night, Seth started playing footsie with me under the table, gazing into my eyes as he was doing it. I knew I was playing with fire but with the alcohol and the music, etc, it was so exciting. Another female colleague came up to me that night and jokingly made a reference to the fact that Seth was flirting with me and I laughed it off but I knew that my steely resolve was being undermined and that's the problem with ongoing sexual attention. No matter how settled you are in your life (and in your relationship – if you're in one), if you find the person who is paying that attention to you, sexually attractive back, it's so powerful and addictive and it plays endlessly in your head. You have to be really strong to resist it. I thought I was strong enough to ignore it but ultimately it was intoxicating.

That night I was meant to stay in a small empty apartment on site and so when we returned to the estate, that's where I headed, but then Seth knocked on my door. I let him in and we chatted. He was a tired drunk and he crashed out on my sofa and because I was worried that something between us might happen if he woke up and because I was also nervous about how it would look to Susie and the site staff if he was seen coming out of my apartment in the morning, I crept out of the apartment whilst he was asleep and went and slept in my car.

A few hours' later at about 4am, he knocked on the glass window of my car. He'd woken up, tracked me down and now he was going to stumble home. He was inebriated and incredulous at the lengths I'd gone to, to stay virtuous.

The following day in the office, Seth demonstrated that he was clearly affronted that I had slept in my car. He was defensive: "I wouldn't have done anything to you", he remarked curtly. He also tried to say that I'd been the one who'd come onto him. I talked to Amelia about it and she said it wasn't my fault: Seth had been giving me the eye from the minute I walked in the door at the pub. However, a few days later and his indignation had subsided and out-of-the-blue, Seth suggested that as I'd been looking to move out of my family home because I was finding it difficult with my grandparents' house-rules, I could stay in that same empty apartment on site for free until the estate owners decided to renovate it and let it as one of the holiday apartments, but for now, it was mine. I was delighted!!

***

At this point I was 19 and still hadn't had sex and Seth knew that. He had been curious and amazed when he had discovered this fact at our Christmas party previously when, in the early hours following it, we'd all been sitting around, drunk, revealing our secrets. When I was put on the spot and asked if I was a virgin, my embarrassed non-reply had made it plainly obvious that I was and Seth's face had lit up. He questioned me about this in front of the others, until seeing that I clearly felt awkward, he'd stopped quickly. But then he added that this was "admirable". I didn't really know where to look.

The only other time a man had been so blatantly sexual to me in the way Seth had been at Caspar's head-wetting party, was once at secondary school in the first year, when an older boy put his hand up my skirt and had a good grope in a crowded tussle in a doorway but no one had followed suit in such an explicit way until Seth that night. Even now, Seth telling me that I made his cock hard, still remains etched so prominently in my memory because of his sheer sexual audacity.

***

But back then, once that evening was over and as time progressed, Seth's comments seemed like a distant memory and sometimes I found it hard to believe that he had actually said anything. I waited for something more to happen but often days flew past with us just working together normally albeit with a spark in the air between us. I'd moved into my apartment and loved it. My grandparents (for all their reservations), helped me to move in and I thrived! I was more than ready for this next step and I was pretty busy with a full life: I was still going to church, swimming everyday in the on-site pool plus I started running and I upped my fitness classes. Because I lived for free in the apartment, I had to help out quite a lot with functions on site, but I didn't mind that as it meant I was never lonely and often Seth would be around so it gave us extra time to see each other.

In addition, I started hanging-out with a new girlfriend in my church, Claire, who'd moved to the area and she was a lot of fun! She was a single mum of two boys and had her own dad living with her too. Claire and I started going out for drinks quite a lot and we'd go clothes' shopping too. I also had a few girlfriends who lived away who I would go and visit, including Sophie and I had another friend locally, who was going through a lot of personal turmoil, so there was much to keep me occupied, aside from Seth and my job! All in all, I was generally pretty busy and when I wasn't working, at church, seeing friends, swimming or taking part in some other exercise class, I was simply grateful for a night's peace and quiet watching a film.

I tried to keep myself as distant as I could from Susie, but quite often, she would pop up to our office to deposit their children for Seth to mind for an hour whilst she dashed to the local shops, hands-free for once. I partly struggled with this because my heart was too involved with Seth but equally, I also admired Susie's assertiveness in landing the kids on their dad in the middle of his working day! Good for her! I wondered if subconsciously or consciously she wanted to get their father involved, as the more integrated he was with them, the less likely he was to leave them.

I sometimes felt I could read Susie's mind.

However, when Susie did drop off the children with her husband, Seth generally relegated the care of them to me and Amelia but we didn't actually mind as they were funny in their own way! In addition, because they were Seth's children, I found that I would always go the extra mile with them, even though at the time, I wasn't particularly good with babies and toddlers as I hadn't grown up with any younger siblings or cousins so although I was curious, I was a bit awkward with them. If I held a baby, I was all fingers and thumbs and they normally started to cry within a few seconds of landing in my arms.

At this point in my life (before I had my own family later), I knew that I definitely wanted children some day but I observed how they *could* tie women down, limit their choices and sometimes they turned sexy females into submissive, mumsy types, who whilst being so immersed in desperately trying to keep up with other 'perfect mums', channelled all their energies into creating immaculately turned-out tots and/or decorating nurseries beautifully, going through the boring horrors of potty training and pureeing veg. This seemed an alien world to the one I wanted then. I heard one of Susie's friends talk about going into 'mummy mode' and I just thought that wasn't what I wanted. It sounded a bit dull and unsexy.

In later life and after having children, I found a subtly-accurate passage in Monique Roffey's fantastic memoir ('With the Kisses of his Mouth') about the changes she observed in her female friends who had babies. It really stayed in my head. Even before I was 20, I observed all that Monique talked of, thus life without babies seemed much more interesting because at the estate, we often hosted Corporate 'team bonding' weekends for those in the private finance sector so there were always parties of interesting new people rocking up and that included handsome guys! However during these weekends, I observed men who were staying away from their wives and children, turn into sexual animals on the prowl. It made me feel that I didn't ever want to be the gullible, overly-trusting wife at home, saddled with babies whilst my husband played around. I witnessed these guys reaching out to both me and the other girls waitressing.

At one event, one male corporate guest manhandled me up onto his shoulders and started running around the bar with me draped half-way over his back. Another stroked my hand saying: "you have gorgeous soft skin", before adding: "so soft, I can imagine you running those gentle fingers and hands along my back." Whilst another guy had leaned in too closely against me and then patted my bottom causing Seth to come over to assert his presence. My Boss also intervened when he felt one Senior banker was trying to corner me. At that point, I felt lovingly protected by Seth. It wasn't that these men were unscrupulous or that they didn't love their wives or families. They were just away from work and home pressures, and this combined with drink and male camaraderie, led to a fervent desire to let off steam and have some crazy fun. It was a wake-up call about the male psyche, testosterone and 'lads-on-tour' behaviour… I needed to know this stuff, namely how guys could be when they were let loose…

I knew that whilst Seth loved playing the lively dad role, he also quickly tired of it and passed on the baton of childcare to his staff or left it to Susie. Long after the catastrophic metaphorical amputation that occurred between us, I found photos of day-trips I'd taken Seth's kids on because Seth had been too busy working when Susie had asked him to mind them for her. At the time I was happy to help because it made me feel close to Seth and I had fallen for him in such a big way.

My relationship with Seth developed and then it went horribly wrong because you can never predict how these situations will go. From this I learnt that you can never try to corral a man or a relationship. You have to go with it, however it unfolds. The best way for me to explain what happened next and how it became a complete headfuck (despite the fact that I tried to have other relationships to forget Seth), is simply to quote from my diary, which is what I've done below. I've virtually omitted all the other details from each entry other than those relating to Seth, so whilst lots of other things happened in each cited day, I've just included the details pertinent to my relationship with my boss.

SOME OF THE MANY DIARY EXTRACTS CHARTING OUR RELATIONSHIP

Early Summer: Seth got cross with me today over a few things I'd not quite done correctly at work, not as he wanted and I responded likewise. He said he would put me over his knee! Hmmm sounds like fun!

Late Summer: Seth gave me ice to put on my ankle and a Twix bar. To help me walk to the doctors, he hoisted me up, and put his arm around my waist and ribs and I put my arm around his shoulders as I couldn't fully walk on my ankle. I stayed up until 2am in the bar, for quiz night, drinking and we hung out together.

Autumn: Susie invited me down to hers after work and we chatted. Seth guzzled a bottle of red wine with Rich as they watched a boxing match, and Seth joked that he'd have to get rid of Susie and have his wicked way with me (I know this because Rich told Amelia who told me). Later Seth told me that I should watch '100 Sex positions' or 'Black Emmanuelle' (porn films). I said: "What's the point, I'd have to practice on my pillow". He laughed. We were just messing around but there's a current.

Autumn: Amelia asked me if Seth and I were having an affair because of the way we look at each other. She didn't believe me when I said we weren't. I'm having to switch off my feelings about him. I don't think he'd do anything. He loves Susie too much and I don't want to be *that* kind of person! I'm not *that* kind of person!

Autumn: After working in the office, I helped out waitressing in the estate bar and Seth jokingly asked me if I'd like to be in a pair of handcuffs?! Hmmm… sounds great. I must stop this!

Autumn: Worked all day, then waitressed for a function. All went well. I took 3 x different parties of guys back to The Dukes Hotel as there wasn't enough space on site for them to stay. Frank [one of the bankers] bought me a drink and was lovely.

BUT (I think?) Seth slept with Freya (she's the on-off girlfriend of one of the estate management team from Edinburgh; she was just down for the weekend), or at least they went up to the apartment next to mine. I could hear them laughing on the landing. He's gone right down in my estimations. Seth is just a user. I certainly don't mean anything to him. He just wants a leg-over. Earlier Seth and I danced but it obviously means nothing. One of the corporate guys, Geoff, said he liked my accent and my nails. Said he thought I'd committed some damage in my time. He gave me a cuddle as I dropped him off at The Dukes and then said I was "soft" and had "nice feminine hands". He was really good-looking but I'm pretty sure he has a wife and kids somewhere.

Autumn: Seth said he'd been offered a job in London. I could tell he was mentioning this to gauge my reaction at the possibility of him leaving. I was chatted up again by Geoff and then also by Frazer and another dishy bloke I don't know and by Frank. Is this what guys are like away from their partners? I found out that Amelia caught Seth coming out of the apartment next to mine, with Freya. Both Freya and Seth are absolute tarts. We had another corporate dinner tonight and I snuck out early and went to the beach and had a walk to clear my head. I just thought why am I wasting my time? He's literally not worth it. He's got no loyalty, no scruples, he's just led by his groin.

Autumn: Went out for dins after working all day. Seth and I spoke about him taking the London job. He said: "Don't you want me to go?" I said I didn't. But I just feel upset after the Freya incident. I looked up to him so much. He's disappointed me and fallen off the pedestal I put him on. Why is he behaving like this? He just can't be trusted.

He said to me that Amelia found him and Freya in the toilets – it was as though he was trying to create a new, tamer version of events and somehow justify whatever happened. I said that I had heard the front door to the apartment next to mine open at 2am and he quickly said: "It wasn't me, it was Frank" but I could see him squirming. He knows I don't respect him any more or believe him but stupidly I still love him. He just throws all my worst fears in my face.

Autumn: Went to work, asked Seth about staying with Freya. He said this time that he stayed in the apartment next to mine but that he didn't sleep with her because he wouldn't take advantage of her and I said I know that. He said no one believed him though. Then he added: "You believe me, don't you Lydia?" I said I thought I did. He said he couldn't have done anything anyway because he was too drunk. Then he said about me being young and attractive and that he was an older attractive man and that things can happen… aaagh talk about headfuck.

Autumn: I wasn't working as Seth's PA or in reception today, but I helped waitress for Julie & Tom's wedding reception. Amelia and Seth fell out badly. Went to bed at 4am. Seth knows I like him and I've got to stop now. He said to Amelia that I was cold because he was looking at my top and could just tell from my nipples! That man!

Autumn: Seth told me all about his first wife and his background today: it was really interesting and we had a good laugh. He has a friend who's a very devout vicar and who jokingly calls Seth a heathen who corrupts everyone. Seth said he needed looking after because his jaw was hurting so much. I'm trying desperately not to feel the way I do. Went to dance class to distract myself.

Autumn: Seth prodded me at work, asked me if I'd missed him when he was back in Scotland. Talked about his future plans and how we both like people who are cuddly. He said that he likes women with a bit of meat on them. Took myself off to the city in the afternoon to go shopping and then dance class in the eve with Claire.

Autumn: Seth dropped his trousers to show me his inflamed leg. He grinned and took the opportunity to show me his cool boxer shorts! Is anything going to happen? Am I imagining all of this? Is he just flirting? Went for a big swim at lunch to distract myself!

Autumn: Working in Seth's office. He told me that he and Susie aren't getting on very well at the moment. Said they hadn't spent any time together and he struggles with all the expectations upon him. He knew where I'd been to on Saturday night… (I sneaked out clubbing), I don't know how he knew…

Autumn: Ian [my dance teacher] called me to ask me where I was tonight as I didn't go to his class. He's booked me in for next week. He said he wants to take Claire and I out for the day.

Autumn: In work. Amelia said Seth had asked her if I was jealous about him and Freya? Amelia said I needed to wake up to what the real world is like. I know! I don't need to be patronised! But she doesn't understand what this situation is like? Seth told me that Freya had called him on his phone. He knows I like him and he's just flirting with me, trying to make me jealous. I can't handle it. I love him and I can't! I'm not even going to think about him. Went back to my grandparents for dinner and saw Rafe and Solly [Lydia's brothers; 'Solly's an abbreviation of Soloman].

Autumn: At work today, Seth and I were chatting and he asked if I thought he had a: (a) young face, and (b) a big bum?! We laughed… I said it was squidgy – his bum, not his face!

Autumn: Seth told me he had bad news, i.e., he'd be leaving soon within the next few months providing the London job offer is good enough. We talked about it and I said that if he goes, I'll leave here too – I don't want to work for his replacement. It would never be the same. He said I could go up to London and work for him there. I wanted to test the waters so I said he could always ask Freya or any others, but he said he didn't want them – he just wanted me. Part of me wonders if this is a ploy of his (and not actually a real plan at all), to see how I'll react. I don't doubt for one minute that he regularly has job offers away as he has such good contacts, but I'm scared of going through all the turmoil I went through when Tim moved away, so I'm trying not to think about Seth leaving too. I don't know if he really is serious about me going to work for him? - but I'd definitely try it. I just don't really know what he's thinking as he's so guarded. I don't know what will happen long-term, but he's such a lovely guy. I feel so at home with him as well as in love with him. He gave me his coat to wear because it was cold in the office this afternoon. I can't help how I feel about him. I also know that Seth probably did sleep with Freya and I just have to accept it.

Autumn: After work, I went to dance class and Ian ran his finger down the small of my back and it felt quite erotic. I actually got goosebumps and although he looks nice when he's serious, it's not happening for me because my heart is with Seth who's away in Scotland right now.

Autumn: Manic day. Went to church then worked in reception: Amelia was crying as her dog had to be put down. So sad! Saw my friend Erica. Swam, had jacuzzi, sorted out my washing. Went out for a drink with Claire. Seth must no longer be a part of my life, or in my dreams as it's just wrong on every level; it's a massive conflict. It has to stop.

Autumn: Work and later I watched the Princess Di interview. I missed it the first time around. She is so brave!

Autumn: Seth coming back tomorrow and he rang me at work saying: "I'm sure you've missed me", I said I had… I want him to know I have. However good or bad that is. I want him to fall in love with me.

Autumn: Again Seth rang and asked if I was missing him.

Autumn: Seth and Susie are back (she's been away with him as they were visiting their family). He made a big thing of asking me in front of everyone, if I was okay? Ahhh. Also Tim (estate agent) wrote to Rosemary. How sweet is that?! Felt a twinge towards him too!

Autumn: I'm going to invest some money through Seth in a building project he's involved in, in Edinburgh. He'll underwrite it for me. He is so lovely! Nothing is any effort now between us. But it's all forbidden. I can't let myself think this way about him: he's married and already spoken for and as much as I'm really, really fond of him, I know I can't think along those lines. Half the time, I'm never really sure whether he means anything by what he says or if he's just pulling my leg! But I love him and am utterly fond of him. Saw him in the bar tonight and he winked at me. He is so gorgeous but I mustn't. He said I could go to the Xmas party theme night as the Virgin Mary! His sarky humour. Hilarious!

Winter: Susie said that Seth would have to be careful that what he says to me over the phone isn't viewed as sexual harassment! We are cheeky to each other though... he rubbed up against me in the shop tonight... I was going to give the offender a mouthful and then I turned around and realised it was Seth and he virtually wet himself laughing... I couldn't help but laugh too. I love him and I love how he makes me laugh.

Winter: Seth said to Amelia that I was only allowed to bring myself to the Xmas party (no guest!)... he said: "it's not that I want Lydia for the whole evening, but..."

Winter: Working all day. Seth and Susie went shopping and I gave him my cheque for £2000 for him to invest. I trust him. I picked up their twins from school and gave them supper and then Seth picked them up from mine and made a risqué comment about the damage that could be done on my fluffy rug! Went out clubbing later... good to let my hair down and forget everything!

Winter: Seth and Susie both told me at different times today that Seth sleeps in the twins' bedroom on a fold-up bed as the baby is in with Susie in their bedroom. Why are they telling me all of this?! It's not helping me!!

Winter: I told Seth that my dance teacher Ian, was coming over to see me tonight at my apartment and Seth's mood instantly switched: he got really cross, saying: "I don't want any blokes up here, I told you about that!" He was most definitely jealous.

Winter: Seth asked me how it went with Ian last night (nothing happened – we only talked because I don't have any feelings for him). Then Seth said I looked rough. He was clearly peeved and trying to punish me.

Winter: Ian rang me at work to take me out to dinner and I think Seth overheard as he got really mad and shouted out in the background for me to hurry up. I'm desperate for my hols in January with Sophie to get away from it all...

Winter: Amelia gave me a good talking to, about Seth. I just want to get away. I can't love him. It's just wrong.

Winter: Seth rang me from the Mayor's Dinner in London. He was sitting on the loo. He wanted to go through the wages with me so I could process them but he also wanted to have a chat. We laughed. I love him.

Winter: Xmas party. Claire came as my guest (had a guest after all!) and we both wore silver. Lucy (the Chef) asked me if I liked Seth as he was flirting with me so much. It's not me! He pressed me up against the fruit machine and we danced together in the dark.

Winter: Seth and Amelia called me into the office. Ian had sent me red roses with a card. He wants to take me out for dinner on Saturday. Everyone was talking about it but I'm going to decline because I don't like him in that way.

Winter: Seth was asking me all about Ian today at work. Seth said he seemed very serious and Seth was concerned.

Winter: Went out after work and despite my nasty cold, I partied hard. Dean (my former Boss – a few jobs back), put his arm around me and gave me his number. Cheeky. He's pretty nice though! Very manly!

Winter: Ruth (another cleaner at the Resort) told Amelia that I couldn't take my eyes off Seth last night as he was out too. It's not like that though! I went out clubbing tonight after work again and had such a good night as I was given lots of Xmas kisses. Adam was groping my bottom! Rich put his hands on my hips and I was told I was beautiful... it's so lovely to hear this as normally in church, everything is so serious and sensible and I never receive any compliments along these lines as that's just inappropriate/forbidden but I do feel as though I'm living a bit of a double-life.

Winter: Seth is picking up his children from his second marriage today. He was asking me more questions about Ian. I do miss Seth so much when I don't see him but I'm trying to put him out of my head because I like both him and Susie. I switch all the time from one minute, enjoying the massive buzz from the connection between Seth and I and then just feeling so bad/torn because of Susie, my beliefs etc... I should leave and move away, but then I can't bear not to see Seth. He's like a drug to me and I need to keep seeing him...

Winter: Went to Church and then worked. Later went out clubbing, followed by popping into the bar when I got back to the estate. Seth gave me a kiss on my lips and said I was the best PA ever! That was my first kiss from him !!!!! Also one of the business executives (who's a friend of Seth's and visiting) told me he wanted to sleep with me and tried to kiss me... ick... he can keep his tongue! In bed by 3.30am!

Winter: Seth was rushed to hospital today as he collapsed three times in a short period. I worked in reception all day but it was so hard to concentrate as I just wanted to know how he was. I locked up early to take his family to the city hospital to visit him (they had dashed down from Scotland to be with him). I just wanted to give him a hug but I couldn't because Susie was by his side with the baby. Susie loves him and it's no use. Seth's been scanned for lots of things and thankfully they haven't found anything sinister, so now his consultants think his collapses were just caused by stress. They're keeping him in for a few days to monitor him and I really hope he'll be okay!! God, it's been such a nightmare. I can't imagine him not being in my life.

Winter: Seth's back from the hospital and I only saw him briefly but I'm so relieved. I love him so much. I'll just settle for whatever I get from him. I fly abroad tomorrow with Sophs on holiday... but at least now I feel I don't need to worry about Seth.

Winter: Abroad with Sophie ... it was our last night and I got off with a guy called

Alex who's staying at my resort with his family. It meant nothing. We all went out clubbing. I just needed to distract myself from Seth.

Winter: Back from my hols. Amelia told me that Susie finally knows about Freya and she discovered this because she overhead Seth ringing Freya up over Xmas. I'm knackered generally and tired of this too; felt like a low blow. Hurt to hear it. Went to see my grandparents earlier and I'm going out later to see Ian.

Winter: Worked 10-2pm, saw Rupert (groundsman at the estate) and Seth together and they were shocked that I'd sunbathed topless. After work, I did 100 lengths of the pool, then went shopping and saw Jackie. Missing Sophie and wish Craig would call me. Why am I at home? I don't want to be back in this mess - I'm so unsettled.

Winter: Seth took me into town to post a letter. He said: "let me give you a ride in my Audi." Lush. But I've fallen out of love with him (due to Freya etc!) I've just accepted he's not mine and never will be but I'm fond of him. I told him he had a great squidgy bum after it came up as a question of his, and he grinned. I did 70 lengths of the pool and went on the sunbed to remind me of my hols.

Winter: Seth and Susie have problems. He lost his temper with her and threw an ornament at her, which hit her. Maybe I'm blinded as to how he really is. Went to the gym after lunch. This is all completely doing my head in.

Spring: Went to work and Seth was back in the office. It was so lovely to see him. We had lots of laughs and he looked gorgeous. We just stare at each other a lot. His dark eyes bore into me. It's mesmerising. I've missed him so much.

Spring: Seth rang to ask what man was calling me on the phone tonight: Seth was helping out in the bar tonight with Ruth (bar tender) and Ruth put Martin (from my church) through to me when he rang, but I didn't tell Seth who Martin is. Seth was clearly unhappy about a man contacting me. I'm completely head over heels with Seth. It just can't happen.

Spring: I took Claire to the Indian staff meal at work tonight with me and of course Seth came and made a beeline to say hello to her and to talk to me.

Spring: Amelia had serious words with me about Seth. She said it was embarrassing to watch us laughing together last night. She tried to say it in a tactful way but she said that Susie is suspicious of me because Seth's step-mum had told Susie that Seth had rung me up to ask me which guy was calling me (when it was Martin), and that now everyone is a bit suspicious that there is something going on between Seth and me, but this is just stupid because I haven't done anything wrong. I can't help it that Seth and I get on so well. Seth told me he saw my dad today! I talked to Claire about it all tonight.

Spring: I saw Seth and Susie messing around by the freezer in the restaurant kitchen today and felt embarrassed. I can't handle it. They all I know that I haven't had sex and it's as though they're trying to imply that they're at it all the time. Plus one moment Seth is watching my every move like a cross between my father and a jealous lover and then the next, he's all over his wife. AAAGH! I went out with

Claire and kissed one of my brother's friends, Ben, to get Seth out of my head! It worked temporarily!

Spring: Waitressed with Susie. It was actually nice. I like her. God knows how I have got myself into this mess?

Spring: Susie had an op in hospital today. Seth went with her. This whole situation pulls me in so many different directions. I wish I could switch my mind off to it or I should just quit but I can't leave here, I couldn't bear not to see him... I don't know what to do as I feel so torn.

Spring: After work Seth had gone to the gym and I took all the work letters to the post office, when he drove past me, beeped and shouted out for me as I walked back to my car. We chatted. I'm not going to let these feelings develop. I feel pretty spiritual right now and I'm not going to let this get in the way. If only I knew exactly what goes on in his head though. I often wonder if it's at all on my wavelength?

Spring: Saw Seth in the evening in the bar and I'm sure he's ringing Freya. Why should I care? He's not mine. I thought of Tim tonight as he told me he was leaving a year ago and he's still ever present in my mind! I wonder how he's getting on.

Spring: I worked all day with Seth. He was really lovely and I enjoy being with him so much. He's given me his ticket for Royal Ascot. He winked at me and then later wrote a note about Freya on a post-it note, to wind me up. The problem is I'm really falling for him. If he asked me to sleep with him, I don't know what I'd do.

Spring: Arrived back at my flat and Seth rang me. He said that I can use Susie's car [I'd crashed mine a few days' ago by going into the back of someone]. Seth asked where I'd been? I really want to be in love with someone and have a lot of sex: to get it out of my system! I'm burning up with the need!

Spring: I booked my VIP slot at Royal Ascot today.

Spring: Seth was good fun today. I do love him and it's silly. It'll never go anywhere. It's just everything about him, his sense of fun, his looks, his dark eyes, his voice and accent, his physical presence and tall muscular body, his aftershave, his clothes – I love it all but maybe he doesn't feel the same?

Spring: I took Todd and Katie out for the day [Seth's children from his second marriage]. Seth left me a signed cheque to pay for everything. I'm so knackered but it was a good day. We went on a rollercoaster and log flume etc, and they bought whoopee cushions. They're lovely kids!

Spring: I went to a big Christian festival today; it was the second day as actually we went up yesterday morning and stayed overnight there. Met up with my grandparents and others. When I got back to my apartment, everyone from work was going out for drinks and they dragged me along too. We ended up going on a pub crawl and then Seth, his step-mum, his dad and I went for an Indian meal. Seth paid. A lot happened. We walked home across the fields, and then ... I'm in bed now and I can't sleep. It's 5.10am. Ohhhhh!

[What happened: It was a really sunny evening. Susie had taken all of the kids to her parents in Scotland for a week and Seth's step-mum and father were helping on site. Lots of the staff decided to go out on the spur of the moment and I was cajoled into going too. We all piled into a few cars and drove to a pub where there was always a good vibe. We parked up and the atmosphere was exciting to begin with! We all drank initially outside in the beer garden which was lit up with fairy lights and then as the sky darkened, we ventured indoors. Some of the guys played pool and I chatted to Amelia, Lucy etc. I didn't really have anything to do with Seth in the pub, it was only later that I saw him, but every so often I could hear him laughing.

As the evening progressed and last orders were called, numbers dwindled as different ones said goodbye and headed home. Before I knew it, I'd agreed to go to a lively Indian restaurant with Seth, his step-mum and dad in the nearby town. It was about 11pm when we sat down to eat and the chat flowed easily: Seth and I were sitting next to each other and opposite was Seth's step-mum and dad.

I can't remember at what point I felt Seth's fingers discreetly stroke the inside of my upper arm, unnoticed by his relatives, for they were pretty tipsy by then. We were all deep in conversation and Seth positioned his arm next to mine. I couldn't believe what he was doing. There was such a feeling of electricity in trying to carry on talking and looking normal when Seth's touch was setting off all these incredible reactions in my body... when he placed his hand on my thigh, I almost gasped out loud! He was my Boss for fuck's sake and I had dreamt of this moment if I was truly honest, from the first time I saw him and now it was finally happening...

When our meal was over, in the moonlight we stumbled over the network of footpaths to trek home. The path was bramble-strewn and sometimes we all tripped and laughed but as we got closer to the estate and when Seth's parents were out of earshot, Seth whispered to me: "pretend to go home and then come back to mine."

Immediately it took me right back to the night when he'd told me that I made his cock hard. The sheer audacity of that sentence and the blatant sexuality of it, still had the power to stop me in my tracks and this night, with this daring, naughty invitation, I was once again jolted out of my slightly inebriated state into a shocked trance. It was a proposition that could completely change everything.... .

Seth reached his house at the estate first and bid us all goodnight, then I parted ways with his step-mum and dad, before climbing the steps to my apartment. Once inside, I remember standing still, my heart pounding wildly... what was I going to do? Do the right thing or walk right back down to Seth?

Then he rang me: "Are you coming down?" I didn't say yes or no then... I was thinking... But then suddenly, standing in my bedroom, I knew immediately what call I was going to make......

I thought of what my grandmother would say (if she knew): "it'll all end in tears". Also I thought of another female colleague, Erin's, comment to me when she'd twigged that something was going on with Seth: "he'll chew you up and spit you out", but despite this, my mind was made up. I'd never done anything daring in my life ever, and for once, I was going to. I reasoned that he and Susie weren't right for each other because if they were, then none of this would be happening. They couldn't be happy because they slept in separate beds, separate rooms and therefore, this was okay somehow!

Seth was shocked when I ran down to his house in the darkness, but he was so pleased. He put some music on and we sat on one of his sofas, talked, drank and then he asked me to give him a massage. I ended up straddling him on the floor and then we got back on the sofa together and started kissing. For all my worldly ignorance, I just sensed that we were both desperate for this to happen and we couldn't get enough of each other. We quickly stripped to our underwear. I wanted him so so badly and I literally couldn't think of anything else. Hands, fingers, tongues went everywhere. I remember running my hands through his glossy dark hair and how good it felt. My mind just completely ignored everything else because doing this seemed absolutely right! Perfect in fact. We totally clicked sexually, physically, emotionally etc; basically we clicked in every way. It was all my longings coming to fruition after what seemed like forever.

About 3 hours' later, we kissed each other a breathy goodbye and I staggered back to my flat… what had I just done? He was my Boss! … Also I was going to see his wife in a couple of days… how was it going to be with both of them? How was he going to be with me in the office the next day? Was this the start of something more? What would happen next?]

Spring: Worked all day today. Swam and trained after work. I wanted him to ring so much tonight as Susie is still away but he didn't. He came into the office but was business-like today. There was no mention of what happened yesterday on either side. Maybe I shocked him because I went down to his house and he thought I wouldn't. One thing's for sure: he'll never leave his family, so it must end. I do love him though so much and I know it's wrong. He's married and it's all so complicated. How on earth did I get into this mess?… But I can't stop it… it'll take whatever course it needs to take… but last night stroking his face – I felt I was in heaven!… and running my fingers through his hair… I've wanted to do that for ages. When he was touching me, it felt so good and when I sat astride his back and massaged it… it was incredible! Yet today it's as though it never happened but I just want a repeat…

Spring: I went to see Claire tonight and when I got back to my flat, as I was getting out of my car, he tapped me on my shoulder to say hello and he's just rung me now. I must get him out of my mind. I'm sure it was a one-off and yet I want him to be so in love with me that he can't get me out of his head, that he thinks and wants me all the time; that he misses me when I'm not there but I don't know, does he? I just want to sleep with him now.

Spring: We had two large parties arriving today: a corporate team bonding group and a separate rugby party. I worked all day and had a few laughs with Seth in the morning; it's so lovely to catch his eyes. He even smells great all the time.

Stop it! He got cross with me though because after work, I was in the swimming pool and a load of the rugby guys came in and Seth saw me talking to them in the pool, when he looked in through the window… Seth banged on the glass and later when I came out of the leisure centre, he tracked me down and took me to task about not being overly friendly with them. I know his game though! He's just jealous – which I quite like!

Spring: Worked all day as Seth's PA and then went out for Amelia's hen night – we were all wearing our Pjs. I ended up getting off with one of the rugby guys called John who was out too in Jessies [a nightclub] because I just need to get Seth out of my head! Now everyone thinks I'm bad because I'm meant to be so religious! What's wrong with me?

Spring: Worked all day in reception and signed-out the Rugby party. John (the rugby guy I got off with last night in the club) came into reception and said goodbye to me, giving me a kiss and all the rugby lot cheered us from their bus! He was cute. I stayed working in reception until 4pm but first thing, I received a massive telling-off from Seth! He made me feel like a slut. He said: "I'm not very happy about it! I'm disappointed in you.. You're supposed to have high values… " it went on and on"; then later he rang me up in reception to ask tersely if my "lover" had said goodbye and at the precise point, that's what John was doing! Amelia rang me up and she was laughing. It was bad though. But at the end of the day, Seth is married to Susie and also had a one-night stand (at least! I dread to think if it's more than that?!) with Freya too, yet he expects me to wait around like a nun for him whilst he calls all the shots. I really love him but I'm trying my hardest not to – because I can't! He's not free! Yet I'm supposedly not allowed to do anything but wait for him to click his fingers … it's all a bit messed up…

Spring: Seth quibbled about some admin issue today and then looked directly at me and said: "up there for thinking, down there for… other things"… typical !

Spring: I worked and Seth was in and out of the office today. He smells so good. I must snap out of this. Last night he kept looking at me. He just gets me going and it's a total waste of time because it can't come to anything ever… I'm not going to let myself carry on falling in love with him. It's crazy, he's probably having amazing sex right now.

Spring: I had a note from a secret admirer left on my car… Seth was trying to suss out who it was from. Is a bit spooky, although nice to be appreciated but I just don't know who it's from.

Spring: Seth was so lovely today and funny! In front of Chris (maintenance guy), Seth said "you have to keep on top of this girl… well not literally" - I pretended to be shocked and said "Seth!"… we just have such a laugh – he doesn't mean anything by any of this though? Or does he?… but I care for him. I keep wondering if anything more is going to happen though?!?!

Spring: Seth jumped around the door today at work and made me jump. Then that made me spill my coffee on his shirt sleeves – it went everywhere and we had such a giggle… he's so much fun!

Spring: Think I caught Seth looking at my boobs today.

Spring: Seth called from Ireland today: he went over there yesterday to catch up with his Irish mates. They were all still drunk from last night and his friend Connor said to me over the phone: "Keep in touch with yourself"... typical men! Dread to think what Seth's told them. Seth didn't stay at Susie's brother's house over there last night as he was supposed to. I do wonder what he gets up to but I try to blank it all from my mind and just be busy!

Spring: Worked all day and Seth was so cheeky, he kept winking at me... I actually love him & I can't. He's away at the weekend – he'll be drunk and see loads of girls and forget all about me so that puts it all in perspective...

Summer: Went to Royal Ascot today: Seth had bought a ticket a while back, but he couldn't go, so he gave his ticket to me. It was just amazing!

Summer: Returned to the estate and saw Seth and Susie in the bar; it was Susie's birthday and he put his arm around her and I thought: why am I doing this to myself? It won't go anywhere...

Summer: Worked all day. Went to the gym. Finished at 5.15pm. Amelia mentioned the pressie which I brought from Royal Ascot as a thank you to Seth for letting me have his VIP ticket to attend. Amelia said that Susie had laughed about it. I mentioned it to Seth, he said Susie laughing over my present, was just her jealousy. He was standing up for me against his wife. I know he has feelings for me. But with regards to anyone laughing, I just thought 'fuck all of you' – I'm not going to look like an idiot. Went out clubbing and on my way back to my flat, I popped into the bar and Harvey (one of the corporate bankers) lifted me up and Seth immediately rushed over to my rescue. Then later... Seth and I got together in the bar ... ..just like we did at his house in April! We had to draw the curtains. He fell asleep in the bar after saying that nobody touches him like I do. He said I was a: "sexual rollercoaster!"

Summer: Amelia told me that she and Susie had a heart-to-heart. Susie confided in Amelia that she and Seth rarely go to bed together, she doesn't want to any more. I wish I could take him to bed!

Summer: Seth asked me if I shaved under my arms and my legs?!

Summer: Work, gave Seth the cold shoulder today. I've just come to the conclusion that he's a bit of a bastard. I'm sick of him flirting with me, encouraging me to reciprocate and then blabbing about it to Susie, implying that it's all me just because his conscience is bothering him. I don't want this. He asked what was wrong? He can have a taste of his own medicine. I've had enough. Susie's ex-boyfriend, Ned is staying nearby soon and she's dying to see him. She must be unhappy in her marriage if she's tracking down her ex-boyfriend and trying to work out how she can see him again. This is all a headfuck... she's confiding in me; Seth confides in me; Amelia tells me things that they've both confided to her... and I'm caught in the middle of it all... I never intended to be in this position: how have I got to this point?

Summer: Went out clubbing after work at the Heaven Lounge, then Seth asked me if I wanted to drive his Audi... and I did. We didn't quite sleep together...

but literally… almost everything else… when are we going to? It's driving me insane… I'm at his mercy…

Summer: Walked early to the Heaven Lounge as the sun was rising (it's such a cheesy name but guess it's fitting right now?!) to get my car, needed to clear my head, just don't know what to think, say or do. Worked all day, was so tired as hardly had any sleep last night. Swam at lunch. Found out about emergency pill. Had to. What do you say to that person the next day? We both said it would have to stop… or it would ruin everything. We both admitted we were to blame. I think I'll have to move away in Sept, he doesn't want me to, but I can't take this. Went to gran's in the eve and obviously I can't tell her what's happening with Seth…

Summer: (Writing this in the early hours of Tues morning); Seth and Susie away. Worked all day. He rang quite a few times. I took the emergency pill. Did my washing etc. Went to see Claire and went to my gym class. Claire said just to stop and think. I'm dreading tomorrow as we'll be working together again. What will he be like? Will he pretend nothing happened? Will he be all over Susie? Will he blame me? I never ever thought I'd be in a situation like this. He wants to call it quits for good and he's right. I'm still in shock from Friday. I guess he'll have blanked it from his mind and vowed for it never to happen again. I'm really trying to think the same. We will both have to work together though. He will never leave Susie and will never be mine. It's a lost cause.

Summer: Worked all day. Felt quite awkward around Seth. We talked about Friday. That it mustn't ever happen again – he would have to leave and it would ruin everything but we managed to have a laugh. Somehow we always do. He said he'd blanked Friday night from his mind. I wish I could so easily. Went to the gym at lunch…

Summer: Seth said his trousers made his crotch itch and then as he went out of the office door, I was whistling and he said "do that again… I've never heard you whistle before" and I said "I can't" and he said "I won't look" . We both smiled. I love him so much. I can't help it. Claire's mum told someone at my church that I'd been to a pyjama party and now they think I'm a bad influence on Claire.

Summer: Worked all day and then got ready to go out in my shorts. Seth saw me and said "where are you going dressed like that?" I said I was going for a meal but then he gave me the third degree as to who I was going with. (My church ministers have heard rumours and are suspicious of my behaviour apparently… this makes me nervous).

Summer: Worked all day, swam at lunch, went to the bar and had a drink with everyone including Seth, my head was spinning. I want to sleep with him so badly. When we're in the office together, we smile, our eyes meet and when we look at each other… I try not to think about him, but I'm desperate for him… I must get him out of my system but how?!?! I'm so locked into this. It's impossible…

Summer: Seth made me laugh so much today. He makes me so happy. I love him – I guess he doesn't feel the same as he loves Susie, but he makes me feel alive. I just want to sleep with him.

Summer: Had a long day at work and then a load of us went for drinks in the bar. Amelia mentioned the way Seth looked at me when we're in his office together and that he couldn't take his eyes off me but I don't notice it... it's just how we are with each other.

Summer: He jumped out at me when I came out of the laundry room tonight into the dark. I screamed! My heart stopped and then we laughed so much. I'm addicted to him.

Summer: Amelia said Seth is a big flirt leading me on when he doesn't mean anything. She's right.

Summer: Babysat for Susie so she could meet her ex-boyfriend whilst Seth was away.

Summer: Rafe dropped me off late in the eve and Seth came storming out of the bar to see who I was with and I said: "It's my brother!"

Summer: Susie gave me some pressies today to thank me for babysitting for her on Friday night when Seth was away when she sneaked off to drive to see her Ex. This is all so messed-up. How could I accept them after what Seth and I have done behind her back? I felt so awkward and guilty and I wondered whether she could read any of that on my face? How on earth have I got myself into this position? I have no idea where it will end? I wish Susie and her Ex would get together again and rekindle their original relationship … .and then I could be with Seth... but then Susie and Seth have kids! Aaagh. This is the biggest headfuck

Summer: Seth and I were working together and then he popped out and came back with a doughnut for me, saying: "I do think of you" and was singing a dirty song. Does he *properly* think of me? Amelia said he and Susie are sleeping together again now... that's absolutely the last thing I want to hear!

Summer: Seth winked at me whilst I was in the middle of sorting out some difficult guests: I looked up at him and he was already gazing at me and then he winked and smiled and he just looked so gorgeous and I was hooked...

Summer: A while ago, Susie borrowed a mag from me and in it there was a questionnaire: 'how normal are you?' One of the questions was: "what do you do after sex?" and I'd written beside it as a joke, 'how would I know?' but Seth saw it and he and Susie laughed about it... they mentioned it today and we all laughed but now there's an undercurrent...

Summer: Seth said I should wear white knickers with white trousers.

Autumn: Seth wasn't in much today. He's so lovely. I'm fighting my thoughts all the time. He's not going to be thinking the same. I'm a diversion – he's got Susie... so what am I doing? Ate all the wrong things today, went to my fitness class...

Autumn: Had a church meeting this morning, then got food shopping, popped to see grandparents, got ready to go out in the evening and went clubbing and then at 1.45am my doorbell rang...

[What happened: I let him in and I think we both knew what was going to happen as we've both wanted it to happen for such a long, long time. I was wearing a silver skirt and an iridescent cropped top with a zip at the front, which he pulled down. He sat in my arm chair and I sat on top of him and it all began from there. We couldn't stop kissing, touching each other but I hesitated about doing anything more initially because of my religion and everything… and then it just got to the point of no return and he said: "Fuck your religion" and I did, because I just wanted him to fuck me!

He wanted me to give him a blow job to begin with, but I didn't as being so naïve, I had no idea how to, but I remember him lifting me onto my rug and then he went on top of me and he was gentle…

Later, we ended up in the shower together, kissing, covering each other in a well-known brand of body wash that has literally reminded me of that night ever since…

The sexual energy between us was huge, just so powerful, the way we exchanged looks, touched, kissed, laughed together. It was so electric! It felt everything it should be and that he was the right person to lose my virginity to.

Afterwards, yes of course, I did feel guilty, but I was so high on the experience. I was completely and utterly in love with him and felt as though I was walking on air and sex was incredible. I just wanted more of it! More of all of it: kissing, touching, hands-everywhere… I'd had this rite of passage and now I totally understood why everyone was so obsessed with sex because when it's amazing there isn't any other feeling that is quite as euphoric! I was on the verge of becoming obsessed with sex and more obsessed with him too].

Autumn: I only got 2 hours sleep last night and then went to church this morning. I sat there listening to the talk and a biblical verse was read out from James 1:15: 'After desire has conceived, it gives birth to sin, and sin when it is full-grown, gives birth to death'. My heart sank… Later, I went to my grandparents for a Sunday roast and my mind blanked out what had happened last night. I kept thinking my gran would be able to read the guilt all over my face.

Autumn: Overslept for work. Got in and Seth rang me (as he wasn't in the office today) and he said: "you naughty girl". But then he added that he didn't know I was so involved with the church and that he didn't think being "so religious" suited me and that I should have a relationship. Patronising! He's obviously feeling guilty and looking to blame me. He said we had to talk about Saturday. It was the elephant in the room. I had to get the emergency pill. The doctor I saw, said that he'd been at the estate when Seth had collapsed and how Susie had written him a lovely 'thank you' card afterwards. He was telling me all of this and I said how nice Susie was and simultaneously I just felt so guilty. All of us (me, Susie, this doctor), tending to the needs of this man! Later, Seth wanted to know why I'd gone to the doctors. I wouldn't tell him.

Autumn: I rang Seth up late tonight to go down to his whilst Susie is away and he said: "We can't love, it's not fair on her." I'm trying to ignore what my intuition is telling me.

Autumn. Worked all day, we're back to normal... I can't pretend it doesn't hurt. I feel used. I just feel that he wanted to be the first bloke to sleep with me and now he has and that's it. Susie's away and every night I've wanted him and he hasn't come up. The only way to deal with it is to blank it out of my head, hell knows what will happen. Maybe nothing ever will.

Autumn: Seth and Susie went shopping and bumped into Claire, she said he looked sheepishly at her.

[We had sex some more times in late September/early October and then that was it... He told me it had to stop because people were commenting to Susie about us and he couldn't risk breaking up another family and losing his job! There had been such a massive lead-up for a few years!! - and then the comedown was enormous because the chemistry was so strong and because we were still working together so nothing had really changed but of course, actually everything had completely changed! I had all of these churned-up emotions inside me – frustration, anger, longing, disappointment, grief, everything... but I was still seeing him every day and also seeing him with an oblivious Susie and other women he came into contact with; it was torturous].

Autumn: Went for an Indian meal with Amelia, Rich, Seth, Susie and Seth's Step-mum and dad. But it only served to remind me of when everything started with Seth but I can sense it's all changed now and Seth is stressing me out.

Autumn: Really horrible day. I'm staying away in a guest house. I just had to get away to somewhere random. I worked for Seth earlier and he said that Toby [Norton-Jones] had noticed the way we were with each other and asked if anything had happened between us? Seth denied it to him. Seth reiterated to me that nothing further would ever happen and it would be a: "recipe for disaster". I didn't cry. I couldn't show him I hurt. I just blanked him. He looked at me quite menacingly with those piercing dark eyes of his and said: "you're very quiet Lydia".

Later I went to see saw Sally [another friend] and told her everything and cried. After work, I packed a bag and just drove here. I had to escape. I just remember those horrible words muttered to me before, about how Seth would be, because they've haunted me as I knew they'd be true: "he'll chew you up and spit you out" but I didn't want to hear it before because I was determined that I would prove her wrong. That he actually felt something precious for me! That what we had was different. It was pure. Special!

I will always love him but it's totally over. Never, never again... He's killed it all. He's just used me. I want to quit my job and move to Nottingham where Maddie is [Maddie was a primary school friend]. I rang her tonight and I'm going to stay with her next Thursday. I just want to die. Everything is over.

Autumn: Worked today. I thought Seth was having an affair with someone else, so I froze him out. He said he couldn't handle how I was being with him and that I should take time off if I needed to. What does he expect though? But I ended up apologising later because this isn't just about him, it's my job too! Went to see Claire and then after lunch, things felt better with Seth at work in the office and it was okay. I did my shopping, cleaning etc afterwards and went for a swim but yes, I do feel down because I feel completely lost in this.

[Between Autumn and early Winter my grandparents discovered what was going on and then a Church disciplinary procedure began into my conduct. I wouldn't agree to leave my job and not see Seth any more, so my grandparents felt they couldn't have much to do with me whilst I was working/seeing Seth and they were generally horrified. I couldn't really see any of my friends from the church either anymore. I don't think my grandparents could believe that their quiet Christian grandaughter had become so involved with a well-known married businessman (with a 'lively' reputation) to the extent that I would abandon them and my childhood beliefs.

I went to their house to collect some things but they had friends over and for the first time ever, I didn't feel very welcome. I knew I couldn't stay long whilst over there, so I needed to gather my items in a hurry. It felt as though I was tainting the atmosphere because of the life I was living.

It was difficult at work too because Seth and I were in the office and on-site together with all of our colleagues around. I didn't know who knew what but I tried to stay composed].

Late Autumn: I wrote a letter to my gran to let her know that I think about them all the time and I love them.

Late Autumn: Seth is such a shit. He told Amelia he doesn't want me popping into work on my days off or for us to be seen in the bar together. Amelia thinks he's scared that he's going to get found out. The estate is being sold off by the owners too, so I need to move out of my apartment soon… everything is changing… it feels like the good times are over …

Winter: Amelia said she'd had enough of playing piggy in the middle with Seth and I. Seth can't handle me working with Amelia after what's happened between us. He's worried that I'm confiding in her and because she's close to Susie… that everything will come out. That's *his* problem. I'm so sick of him.

Winter: Amelia said Katie (Seth and Susie's new 18-year old babysitter) and Seth had been seen out at a bar together but that Katie's mum picked her up and gave Seth a lift home too. Amelia doesn't think Seth has slept with Katie but it doesn't stop me feeling jealous because Pete [the new Chef] was saying a load of things about Katie and Seth, to wind me up but the problem is that Seth has mentioned Katie to me quite a lot recently and I *just know* he finds her attractive and that she feels the same about him. She has the body of a gazelle and is stunning. I'm shorter and a few years' older so next to her I actually feel frumpy and fat! This is horrible. Is this how Susie feels? It just makes me feel so rubbish. It's such a belittling experience. [Two uncomfortable sayings were coming to my mind at this point, which I hated: 'what goes around, comes around' and 'be careful what you wish for'].

Winter: Seth was lovely to me today. This is all such a headfuck. I am way out of my depth here.

Winter: Seth told Rich that he was going to get Ned to take me out, to stop me thinking about him! God, he flatters himself so much! I haven't lost my sense of humour or dignity! He can fuck right off…

Winter: Seth and I are getting on better again.

Winter: Seth made a joke to me about virgins… so close to the bone. He has a nerve.

Winter: Waitressed for NYE. Katie wants Seth to sleep with her. I can just tell. And he flirts with her too. I dread it because I sense it'll happen. It'll be a repeat performance of what he did with me. Rob said Seth and I were making it so obvious tonight that something had happened between us. I was wearing my clingy coral Appletree dress that's too tight for underwear and Seth took one look at me and said: "it's shocking" followed by: "you're a sexy bitch". I just stared at him and grinned but then went out clubbing to get away because whatever he says, I sense he's not as invested… he's looking for the chase with Katie! I hate to admit it, I don't want to admit it, I want to fight against it but this is what I know is happening… I am trying everything I can to win him back… but I can't…

Winter: He is a total shit. A bastard. I hate him. He's married, I lost my virginity to him because I thought he was special and I was special to him but then he flirts in front of me with an 18-yr old. What a total bastard. I really hate him. Katie's all over him like a rash. I've had enough. I will hand in my notice tomorrow. I don't need this shit. Also he told one of his Irish friends to basically try it on with me to preoccupy me!!!! What kind of bloke even thinks up this perverse, demeaning behaviour?!? I hate to confront it all… but it's staring me in the face…

Winter: Seth was really lovely with me again today. God I still love him. I can't cope with this.

Winter: Babysat for Seth and Susie. I get so jealous over him although I hide it well. It's ridiculous. He's not even mine. It's not when he's with Susie that I feel envious, it's when there's any connection with Katie because he's so flirty with her and she's gagging for it. I feel angry. I've got to stop it. I can't bear the thought of him doing to her what he's done to me. I have to switch off. I hope deep down that he does actually have some feelings for me.

Winter: I get paranoid when he goes out, in case he's ringing Katie or sees her. This is no way to live. I just can't handle it and he's not even mine! I would like to reverse the roles for once and see how he likes it if I find someone else (I've had enough interest but he's the only one I want!) Why is he under my skin so much?! Aaagh! He will be the love of my life, but he was right, it would be a total disaster. I would infringe on his space and independence because I couldn't handle him going out and I'd be jealous and suspicious and I think he'd be the same. So it's better that this comes to an end!

Winter: We just look into each other's eyes all the time but something's definitely shifted.

Winter: Another school friend, Harriet, rang me and she's coming to stay. I'm grateful. Seth was in the office for a bit today and he asked me if I'd keep Susie company when he's away again. Honestly he doesn't have any sensitivity to how either of us might feel.

Winter: Claire and I went to the cinema tonight. Saw Katie too. Earlier noticed that Seth had bought Susie flowers with a card that read: "Best wishes for the New Year. Yours in thoughts. Seth x'. What a hypocrite. She may have him but he's unfaithful to her. I could tell her what he's like but what would be the point because I don't want us to stop being friends, which is what would happen. I can get by without him and I'll get back on my feet. No one will take the memory away of what's happened but I don't need his affection any more.

Winter: I'm plagued by guilt. How could I do this to Susie? She's a nice person. He's right. She doesn't deserve it.

Winter: Susie and I trained together in the gym at lunch. Seth was lovely and we were both cheeky with each other. But I can't do it to Susie though – it's not fair.

Winter: I had to go into work. What have I got myself into? Amelia gave me a lecture about keeping distant from Susie and I am trying. It's so impossible though as she likes me and wants us to spend time together but how can I when I've slept with her husband?! I feel awful about the muddle I've got myself into. He keeps looking at me. I go into our office, keep my head down and when I look up, he catches my eyes and he's smiling at me. I don't know where I am with him. God, I love him but I can't. It's not fair. I trained in the gym after work and sorted out my kitchen so that I'm ready to move out of the flat.. what have I done? What's happened between Seth and I just isn't straightforward and it's not going to go away but it's not going to develop further either I think. I'm so confused.

Winter: Swam at lunch. Xander from the stationary shop drove to see me after work (he left a message on my car yesterday), but I just don't find him attractive. Met up with Amelia and Rich for a drink. Seth rang me from London and we were on the phone for ten minutes just chatting. I love him so much but I can't do this any more. I have to be busy and switch off from him. I'm babysitting for Pete and Tessa tonight. I'm trying to do as many things as possible to distract myself and not think about him or be around him, so that when we're not working together, I can detach and I can cope with whatever happens next.

Winter: I popped into Susie's to collect my washing which she'd accidentally taken from the laundry room. Seth and I joked around together in front of her but I don't think Susie would ever imagine how Seth and I are with each other or have any reservations about our relationship. Sometimes I like it like this: when it feels harmless. If only it were. Seth and I are good friends again and we flirt and it feels safe. I think that what's happened might not ever come out.

Winter: I went to work and Seth came in but he was subdued and I asked him if he was okay? We might never sleep together again and he may be a 'Jack the lad', but at least we're friends and I'm glad of that. Later Susie rang me as she wanted to offload. Seth had gone out to football practice with his mates (it's a new thing), then the 'boys' all went to the bar here [at the estate] and Seth hasn't gone home yet. She said she's so fed up as she feels like she's bringing the children up by herself. I wouldn't stick it at all. We wouldn't last. I would leave him if he treated me as he treats her.

Winter: Babysat Caspar. He was so good. I'm able to detach him from his dad! Had lunch with Lynne and talked about Seth. It was so good to get it all off my chest. She's right, it's a no-go; I can't honestly see Seth and I ever being together, so why stick around? I love him and I always will but it doesn't change life as it really is. I need to build a relationship with my grandparents again too – as feel bad about things as they are.

Winter: Babysat Caspar again and pushed him over the footpath into town and back. Changed his nappy and saw yummy Lee (who I definitely do fancy!) We chatted together. He is hot! When I took Caspar back to Susie, she showed me a journal she'd bought to record all the times that Seth is out because she doesn't trust him. She told me about when they were going out and she found a love letter to him from his Doctor! It all swirled in my head along with Amelia telling me earlier that Seth had asked Katie if she'd like to drive his Audi (this must be his classic 'go to' pulling strategy)… I don't know what happened but when Susie told me that she thought Seth is sleeping with someone else, something just snapped inside of me and I couldn't hack it any longer and I felt sorry for Susie, being stuck at home with the children, whilst Seth makes an idiot of her, of all of us women and basically it all became too much and I just blurted out to her what had happened with Seth. I didn't intend to but I just snapped. I think the pressure of keeping all of their secrets and lies and mine too, just got to me. It's also been impossible to work with Seth after what's happened between us. Susie and I both ended up crying. She said I had broken her heart… It was so awful. Susie then spoke to my grandparents (which was a bizarre and embarrassing moment!) to check I was telling the truth and she spoke to Amelia and… I just don't know what will happen now… aaagh

Winter: I was asked to go down to Susie and Seth's house and explain myself. They were both very cold. In front of Susie, Seth said that what happened between us was only a shag: "just a sexual thing." Then I had to see Seth in the office at 1pm. I went to see gran first. I cried my eyes out as I have loved Seth so much and he is a total bastard. In the office, he was different: we talked properly and I cried a lot but he said that he was at the mercy of Susie. He said it's unlikely they'll move away because the twins are at school here but I have employment rights so he wouldn't sack me (well thanks!) I said I'd have to leave (why didn't I leave all that time ago when I handed in my notice but then he talked me out of it?!) I went over to see gran again later. She's letting me come over now because she knows that my situation's burnt out. Later, I had to go into Seth's office and clear out my stuff in a box. Susie was nearby watching. Seth drove up in his Audi and told me to come and see him on Monday because he wants to: "sort this out". He said: "I don't want it to be this way" but how can he possibly sort it out with Susie?

Winter: Moved out of my apartment to houseshare with Miles and his girlfriend Kat. I've got a bedroom and then the use of the kitchen etc… but it all feels sad and bleak, partly because I loved my apartment but also it's to do with my current mood and what's just happened at work. It's also just that it's winter and raining lots. I feel so down. It's obviously definitely over with Seth. I drove to the beach and cried. Seth rang Amelia to ask her how I am? She said he definitely does have feelings about me but then when she tried to talk to him deeply about this, he just shut it all down and said that he loves Susie and his kids and that he has to make this marriage work. Seth said he wasn't attracted to me (I know he's just saying that though because he's always told me how attracted he is to me). He also told Susie that he wanted me to stay but not as his PA, but as a receptionist instead. Also he said that we got too close. Susie said I can't stay because she thinks Seth really likes me although he's tried to say he doesn't. Amelia said that I need to just blank it from my mind and attempt to move on.

Winter: It feels like a weight has been lifted off my shoulders and in a way I'm glad that he is feeling hurt because I've been hurting for ages and he's rubbed it in but I do feel for him and Susie. However, he should think before he plays with people's emotions. I feel really sad that we won't be the same with each other again though. (at least I'm able to see my grandparents normally again now).

Winter: It does feel as though I've taken a stand and stopped being Little Miss Nice who puts up with any old treatment. Feels like I've been set free rather than in this weird prison.

Winter: First day back at work after having last week off. I was nervous. Seth and I were a bit awkward around each other. Susie completely ignores me. She and Seth are going to work it out. Amelia was fine. It all hurts but hopefully it'll be okay. I miss him and the way we were together though. I still love him but I mustn't and I can't think of him. I gave the maintenance guys' chocolates to say thanks for all their help last week when I moved out of the flat. What a nightmare week. Seth asked Amelia if I was alright and if I'd said anything about him but she didn't tell him anything. I met a gorgeous pilot just to talk to… nothing else.

God, I wish Seth loved me.

Winter: Bad day. Went to work. Checked-out a big media group who had been staying. Seth had told Amelia it wouldn't work with me staying there because Susie is putting pressure on him about me being nearby – she can't cope with us being around eachother – and yes I get that. I'd feel the same in her shoes. Somehow I was hoping we could manage something. When Amelia said this, mentally I fell to pieces and was a nervous wreck. Went to my grandparents. I need to make a fresh start. It's just letting go of the past. It's so hard. I cried my eyes out. I told gran I'd never been so unhappy.

Winter: Seth and I had a good chat at work. I told him I couldn't believe he'd offered Katie to drive his Audi but he denied this. Went for a swim at lunch. Seth told me not to leave and said that Susie would deal with it in time. I can't afford to leave but I have to work something out. I don't know what goes on in Seth's head because even I know that Susie won't accept me being there and working in close proximity to Seth now. What wife would allow this?!?! Susie asked me to go down to see her at their house. She hates me now. She can't hate him or blame him so she has to blame me. I did go and see her though and we had such an awkward discussion. She said I only cause problems and that one of their relatives had complained that her partner had been flirting with me because I give off flirty vibes that men respond to - but I had no idea about this. I don't do it deliberately. I have literally no idea that this is how men take it as I'm just being myself. She's angry though and I understand and I feel bad and awkward. I would feel exactly the same as she does.

Winter: I've had enough of what's being said and gossiped about now. I just want to be happy again and to move on with my life. There's no point moping over him. It can't ever be and I know that. With Seth, I just can't see it working. I need to put myself out of his way so that I can leave him behind. I can't bear to see someone doing my job. I want someone who loves me for me, someone I can trust. Seth is just too good-looking and he knows it. I said to him that I was sorry and he said he was sorry too, because he'd hurt Susie and confused me. We did talk it out.

Winter: We're still working together for now but not properly together and I didn't see him today. I miss him terribly. I miss our friendship and chats and I hate not knowing what to expect from one day to the next. On one level, it's a relief as it's off my conscience but I dread parting with him and ultimately going our separate ways. I love him so much but there's no happy ending here. I love you Seth and I am so sorry for the way things are.

Winter: Seth was in the office with me today but Susie literally sat in with us awkwardly all day long so that he and I wouldn't be alone together at any point. Her mum has come all the way down from Scotland to babysit the children so that Susie can chaperone her husband with me and she can make me feel hounded and uncomfortable.

Winter: Seth has arranged for me to spend some time at another affiliated estate in Dublin, with the idea that I can transfer to working here again at some point in the future so I'm in Dublin right now. An attractive couple called Fin and Ruth oversee the site. Fin gave me the lowdown which included a piece of advice regarding management not getting involved with staff. Obviously something's been said. I watched their team at work with the Lightning Seeds playing in the background. They want me to work 6 days a week, including weekends but I don't want to be marooned over here. I miss Seth so much. I feel I've lost him totally now. It feels like the sparkle's gone out of my life. What can I do to get him out of my system? I feel like there's a big gap in my life and he doesn't fill it any more. I've swum everyday and tried to distract myself from the mess that is my life right now.

Winter: I'm back home and today I worked from 10-2pm. Seth came in and we talked and agreed that I would leave on Friday. I nearly cried. He was being so lovely. I am sure that Susie will stay with him to the end. He said he felt bad about me going. Later Susie rang me, she wanted to see me again. She said there's no way I can stay as she'll make it "nasty" - I think her and Seth have been having difficult conversations at home and he's trying to find a solution for me so that I don't lose my job and he can keep me employed in whatever capacity possible but she wants to sever all the ties and I get that. She doesn't owe me anything and I've broken her trust. I have no choice but to leave. I told her I really cared about Seth and she said angrily: "that's my husband you're talking about" and then she said that I didn't have a heart. What could I say? She said in Dublin, they'd called me: 'shaghappy'?!? I think she was just being a bitch (understandably though), but I replied I hadn't done anything to give them that impression and that I wouldn't just sleep with anyone, that 'it' (Seth and me) had meant something to me (that probably didn't help her though!) I said I couldn't carry on being friendly with her because obviously it just couldn't be but I felt so bad and conflicted about the whole situation.

Talking to her was the deciding factor. I came back from Dublin willing to see if somehow we could make this situation work in some way, but after chatting to Susie, I know it's no good. I can't stay and it would be cruel to stay. Susie and Seth have a chance now to sort things out. It's all so bleak and depressing… I can't even think about my life right now. It's just a mess.

Later, I went out clubbing with Miles and Kat and we had fried egg sandwiches at the end. They took me under their wing tonight. But where do I go from here?

Winter: Went to the gym, showered there, passed Seth in his car on my way to work, he didn't smile but he waved. I waved too. We had a chat in work. He knew I wanted to stay on but he was deadly serious about me leaving and as he spoke to me, his dark eyes almost looked completely black. I said I had no choice. It was up to him what he decided to tell everyone back in Dublin. Later he softened. I said I didn't want to make his job awkward and difficult and that his job was more important than mine which anyone can do. [Obviously, years' later as a much stronger woman, I definitely wouldn't view his job or role as more important than mine and I wouldn't have been manipulated in this way but then hopefully I wouldn't be in this situation in the first place]. Seth said he didn't want to lay roles on the line. He calculated me a final wage and asked what it was like living at Miles'? We had a little bit of a laugh about the Job Centre employee who asked what Seth was like to work for? I told her that he was a good boss (why am I so loyal?!) Seth laughed. It was like old times. Susie told me there was a rumour going around that I'm pregnant. I said it wasn't true… but to be honest I couldn't give a toss what anyone says now.

Susie was in the office all afternoon with the kids. Seth wanted to talk to me but we never got a minute on our own together. I gave Seth a letter to say how much I'd enjoyed working at the resort and would miss it and that I wished him all the best for the future and thanked him for letting me stay in my flat. I signed off with fond regards.

I got hugs from some of the staff today and all the girls from the other estates rang to say goodbye too. I cried my eyes out a lot during the day. Everyone wished me good luck. Seth said he would ring me as he left reception with Susie and the kids by his side. I think we were both upset. However unfaithful, however bad he is, I still love him and always will. It's just so sad. I was so upset. I took all the letters to the post office for the last time and that was hard because I remembered a day when he'd stopped me outside in his Audi to chat to me when things were beginning to build between us…

Afterwards I went to see Claire and had a cuddle. She was lovely and fed me lasagne. Came home to do my paperwork and realised I'll always love him.

Winter: Just got in my car today and drove and drove. It was a grim winter's sky and the wind was howling and the rain lashed on my windscreen. I ended up by the coast and I got out and walked along the cliff path. Everything felt so bleak. I stood on the edge at one point and watched the raging sea below. It was like a tempest. I wanted to call it a day as life feels so empty now; so grey, dull and meaningless.

But I couldn't.

However hopeless I feel right now, I'm not ready to quit yet. I got soaked as I walked and allowed myself to feel miserable and melancholy and then eventually I got a coffee and set off on the long journey back home.

Winter: Today broke my heart. I've moved from Miles' to a new place, as I've got a much bigger room in a lighter house, sharing with an older lady named Yvonne and 2 x trainee doctors: Crispin and Max, who will potentially be like big brothers I guess. I babysat for Pete and pushed their youngest daughter Verity to the park and we fed the ducks. Saw Seth's friend Hugo driving along in his massive Merc as I was walking along on the pavement and we both waved but then as the car got closer, I suddenly realised that Seth was in the front seat of Hugo's Merc and I went to wave. Seth looked at me. I still went to wave but he didn't wave and then I couldn't either and it cut me up so badly. I went to gran's and cried. Are we just going to completely blank each other now?!?! I can't cope with that! I love him so much and he broke my heart. Has he no feelings? I'll never ever be with him now. God, I love him so desperately. As time goes on, I miss him more. My life is so empty without him.

I redid my CV at gran's. That was hard.

But I saw an elderly lady who said I had a "lovely pair of legs." Bless her! It's amazing how a kind compliment can really lift your spirits. Maddie sent me a present in the post too and that really helped! Somehow I'll get through this.

POSTSCRIPT

I never got my money back from Seth that he 'invested' for me, despite the fact that Susie wrote to me promising that I would get it back. However, in the same letter, in an intimidating manner, she said not to come into their family life again. I read this letter once, threw it into the back of a cupboard and refused to look at it again. It was too stressful to re-read. Sometimes Seth and I would pass each other in our cars and he would completely ignore me, which I found incredibly difficult. In order for me to mentally move on, I knew I needed to get away from the area.

Initially before I could think that far ahead though, I applied for, and was offered, a new temporary job as a medical secretary at the local hospital and although I struggled with all of the losses (not having Seth in my life, the camaraderie with all the resort staff, the socialising, the pool, my flat, etc), I gradually fell into a different way of being, created a new routine and made new friends primarily with all the females I worked with and a couple of guys too. I found a comforting new structure to my weeks. I met a fantastic junior doctor named Aurelia, who enabled me to move to Oxford six months' later and rent a room in her family's home, with her sister Liz. Seth heard I was moving to Oxford and wanted to know why I felt I had to move so far away.

I absolutely loved my time living in Oxford. I didn't go out with anyone because I was trying to get my head around what had happened with Seth and despite everything, I was still really in love with him. Instead I just had a year of getting my mind into a good place, socialising, sightseeing and working hard as a medical secretary. As well as really enjoying Oxford, I used to take the train to London and discovered Carnaby Street, Bond Street, Tottenham Court Road, Covent Garden, Sloane Square, Fortnums, Fenwicks, Selfridges, Smollenskys Jazz Club, Kew Gardens, the Tate, the British Museum, the Royal Academy, Green Park, the theatres, cinemas, nightclubs and bizarrely it was at a London theatre one night that I happened to bump into one of Seth's best friends (we said hello and he said he'd tell Seth he'd seen me… ohhh!! There's no escaping that man!)

I also became a redhead. I refused to look back. I had to keep focusing on the future – however sentimental and nostalgic I often felt…

When visiting friends back home during this time, I bumped into Seth occasionally and he would smile at me and we said hello to each other, but he was always out with Susie. The last time we collided with each other was in a supermarket of all places and I was married and 7 months' pregnant with my first child. I felt more at peace seeing him then as we both knew our lives had progressed. Later I returned to my home county and he and his family moved back to Scotland.

I will never forget how bleak the end of that affair was, though. I felt so suicidal because life really seemed devoid of all colour. Back then it all felt pointless. I lost my appetite and as I'd had anorexia when I was 14, I nearly tipped back into it, but friends, exercise and always having something to look forward to, helped me to constantly stay positive. With the benefit of hindsight, I can see that I absolutely fell head over heels in love with him and he's been a regular mental presence throughout my adult life, but ultimately that's okay because the thoughts aren't raw, just comforting, whereas had I been married to him, I'd have been deeply unhappy. So although the ending was horrendous, it felt almost like a mini Greek tragedy, it had to end in the way it did.

I was also often troubled at how I'd behaved regarding Susie and I felt guilty of my betrayal of her. That ate away at me quite a lot, especially when I was pregnant and became a mum too!

I remember years' later learning about Assia Wevill (the late Poet Laureate, Ted Hughes', mistress), and how she was reduced from being a strong woman to a shadow of herself because she pined for Ted's love when he couldn't commit to her. It ended tragically for her and their daughter Shura. It's always stayed with me that these are the lows we can be reduced to, by a deeply damaging and toxic love affair, so bearing this in mind has enabled me to make my peace over what happened with Seth, because I had the experience of intense lust but then got out of it before it completely destroyed me!

What have your experiences taught you?

I have to say in my own situation and even on reflection with times and attitudes as they are now, as a naïve 18-year-old, people might say I was groomed and taken advantage of in a situation where there was clearly a power imbalance (so it would be deemed now as an abusive relationship). However, I was an adult and I absolutely wanted Seth as much as he wanted me. I made the consensual decision to sleep with him. It was one of the most exciting times of my life although of course, morally it was reprehensible!

Also I learnt that even when you're young/unworldly, you can be really strong! Sometimes it will be just you (and you alone), against the world, but you can do it! You may feel broken at the time, but you can survive. Always hang in there. Even if sometimes you and your sanity are hanging on by your fingertips… keep hanging in there, you will find you'll get sent at least one or two guardian angels who'll help you rebuild your life.

However I also learnt that some things just happen! You can't stop your heart falling in love with someone. It is what it is! It's absolutely true! We don't choose who we fall for – especially when those feelings are monumental (those huge, raw, passionate, stomach-churning love affairs… rather than the getting-on-as-friends-and-then-falling-into-a-relationship kind of thing).

If you are trying to get over someone who you love so much, distract yourself/ move away/be brutal with the realisation of what you need to do. It's not about forgetting him/her/the situation, but it's just about protecting your sanity and allowing yourself to breathe and focus elsewhere for now. Obviously now that involves distancing yourself (or better still, blocking them) on social media too, if you can be that firm with yourself.

Remember why it couldn't work out and this may take you into some dark memories (I had to recall Seth sending his friend Ned up to my flat one night towards the end of our affair – to distract me maybe? Or as a stupid prank? - and Ned ringing my doorbell. I was excited as I thought it was Seth but of course it was a drunken Ned. I let Ned sleep on my sofa and grimly he got up in the middle of the night to go to the loo but in his inebriated state he walked to my bedroom cupboard door, thinking it was obviously the bathroom door, and he opened it and drunkenly pissed all over my clothes whilst basically sleepwalking and I lay in bed and watched it all in the darkness and I just felt humiliated and tired of the whole headfuck situation). Because if you keep tormenting yourself by seeing that person in the flesh, on social media etc, it eats away at you and keeps you rooted in a negative place. Instead, know your worth and look after yourself! You have to! No matter if you're 16, 60 or 116!

What advice would you give to other women in a similar situation?

If you fall for your older boss and they're married too, there's pretty much a triple inequality: an inequality of age and experience; an inequality because they're your boss and an inequality because they're married. That doesn't mean that, bizarrely, love formed in this way might not work out, but please be aware of what you are signing yourself up for, which will potentially be A LOT of pain for you and the other protagonists, including the wife and any children. Just remember with the exciting highs, will come very dark lows, but if you're already in too far,... take care of yourself; build a support network around you who you can genuinely and honestly discuss your situation with.

Keep yourself strong. View it as a learning curve if you can't get out of the situation right now.

I'm going to rattle off the preachy bit – only because this is honestly how I felt years' later when I had a baby... So ideally try not to get into this married affair situation: Think of how you might feel years down the line when perhaps you are pregnant and/or waiting at home with a tiny baby, maybe feeling a bit vulnerable and expecting your partner to come back and they're running late and you're beginning to wonder if it's the tube, traffic or perhaps, your partner is being tempted by their sexy secretary?! I know I used to think like this when I had times at home with young children and felt a bit dowdy. I expected karma to catch up with me.

Try to support your fellow women by dodging this bullet also because the guilt/pain is traumatic/ongoing and it makes you question yourself and what kind of person you are?! BUT if you're already totally immersed in this type of situation and are completely in love/lust with someone, nothing I can say will change your mind. However don't give everything of yourself to that one person; keep your friends, families and hobbies too... you'll need them later.

Faith can be hugely comforting and provide so much depth to one's life, but I no longer believe in religion which imposes shame and judgement upon people, especially women. I do understand the need to uphold standards within a faith and to ask those who are not following such standards, to change or leave, but I cannot see love and compassion in ostracism and creating embarrassment for a 'fallen' member.

WHERE ARE YOU NOW? WHAT ARE YOUR PLANS FOR THE FUTURE?

I am in a pretty good place now with a busy medical career.

After Seth and I parted, I later married a man who was the complete opposite of Seth and then I got myself a decent education (which I knew he'd be impressed by as he hadn't been to Uni but was in awe of those who had, especially if Oxbridge featured). I actually ended up getting married and divorced twice with two children and I'm now a qualified doctor. However, I haven't forgotten Seth because he was monumental in every way, both positive and negative. He gave me the biggest adrenalin rush!

I apologised to his wife a few years ago when our paths happened to cross by chance. She was very gracious. I think maybe that Seth and Susie aren't together any more? I have absolutely no ill feelings towards him and often wonder if we'll ever meet up to talk. I'd love to. I did, as mentioned at the outset of this chapter, (cheekily, as it feels so naughty!) google him over lockdown and although I don't get butterflies or huge feelings of love towards Seth any more (there is a sense of attraction but a sense of detachment too), when I see his picture, I do feel a fondness for him and I guess I probably always will, but I think this is quite healthy (but also to complicate matters, I also feel a fondness towards Susie too… all these years later, it is still such a headfucky situation).

What happened with Seth is one of the most colourful sections in the metaphorical patchwork quilt that is my life, so far, but I know I absolutely couldn't have coped with him and his need for constant female validation, long term, so how things worked out – although it was so stressful at the time – was absolutely the best outcome. Sometimes the universe takes control of a nightmare situation not necessarily in the way you want it to but ultimately in the way that will enable you to preserve your sanity. You can't fight the direction that the universe takes you in. You just have to go with it and create a new life.

LUCY'S STORY

When your dad keeps trying to commit suicide but then fate has other ideas... the guilt...

My dad lost himself in his fifties.

We moved from Buckinghamshire down to a big farmhouse in the South West when I was 6 and my sister, Fran, was 4. We felt we had more than we needed but we were actually on free school meals so money can't have been that plentiful. Dad was a stay-at-home parent and didn't go out to work as he was renovating the barns adjacent to our house. Mum was the main breadwinner and absorbed a lot of the stress: she worked full-time in a school but she also waitressed some nights and cleaned at weekends. She kept all of the pressure from this to herself but I think she was exhausted by it all.

Our childhood wasn't huggy or lovey-dovey. There wasn't a lot of affection, so no: "I love you's" and whilst Fran was close to both of our parents, I clashed with my dad. Like all families, there were odd times too and Fran and I used to talk about who we'd choose to live with, if our parents ever split up. I remember once my mum and dad having a massive argument as he thought that she was having an affair because he was insecure and dad said to us: "Who are you going to choose to live with?"

Fran and I didn't know that our parents had an unusual history: they had been married to each other long before we came along, then they got divorced before getting back together after a year apart and then having us (me and then my sister Fran). Mum had threatened to leave dad long before and she ultimately did: she divorced dad but then he threatened suicide and turned to drink. Prior to marrying our mum at their original wedding years' previously, dad had been married before and had two children with his first wife and he'd also used this same emotional blackmail on mum's predecessor.

When my parents reunited just before we were born, they didn't remarry but they pretended to us all along as we grew up that they were married. This was a big secret that the rest of the family knew about, but not us. Thinking that they were married made Fran and I feel secure so when we finally discovered that mum and dad weren't actually married although they pretended to us that they were, we felt lied to and wondered what else they might be hiding? My view of marriage was suddenly tarnished and shattered.

Our parents were quite liberal with us during our teenage years but they didn't really know what we were doing or some of the things that were happening to us. For example, I was getting bullied and cut myself and Fran was quite a wild child but we had friends over for sleepovers and we'd go out in our local town, so everything seemed okay on the surface.

I didn't think my parents were insecure in their marriage and I don't remember any particular rows. They co-existed and seemed normal. When I was in my early twenties and working, I moved out of the family home and into a flat with my boyfriend Jason whilst Fran lived in a barn adjacent to mum and dad's place, paying rent.

But then Dad turned 60, both of his parents died and he became down in the dumps. Then mum had breast cancer diagnosed and she was unable to work for a year. It was a tough time: they remortgaged and she was really poorly. I remember her vomiting and then having to shop for wigs when her hair fell out because of the treatment. Dad was quite supportive of her then, because I think he felt needed and validated. But as mum began to recover, her outlook changed. On the surface, life started to return to normal, however, their mortgage payments resumed and debts began to creep up… but everything seemed fine outwardly.

I became pregnant with my son, George, and saw my parents regularly but dad definitely seemed quite flat although it was hard to differentiate between dad being 'normal' and dad being seriously blue, because he was a 'glass half empty' person anyway. George was one of the babies used in the filming of a popular TV programme, so mum and I often used to dash off to the filming of that whilst she was still off work recovering from breast cancer. Dad doted on George and overall, he and mum seemed okay. Life progressed: Fran moved out of the barn, and into a separate place with her boyfriend Sean, and Jason and I swapped with Fran, moving into the barn where she'd been. It was a win-win for us all as we paid rent to mum and dad. However, spending more time next door to them, it soon became apparent that my parents weren't happy at all. Mum couldn't cope with the fact that dad was so depressed.

Dad had a daughter from his first marriage and she came down to visit us but dad stayed indoors and didn't join in at all with the fun, not even having drinks outside with everyone else. Mum was fed up with him, complaining: "that's what he's like". We all ended up saying: "dad's being dad" and his withdrawn behaviour was normalised but he'd even lost interest in doing things that he'd previously liked, such as cooking meals and baking. He'd been proactive before, but it all ground to a halt. Prior to having us, he'd even once worked for British Airways, but all of his previous oomph had evaporated. I think he felt that now the barns had been renovated and the garden was done, we were all moving on with our lives. Mum was now working full-time again and he was uncertain of his niche in life and suffering from empty nest syndrome.

But then things took a sudden turn for the worse: mum decided to leave dad in the October. There had been no sign that she was going to do this but she suddenly packed a few things and took off to Fran's. My parents plodded through Christmas and tried to present a unified front but dad cried during it, saying: "this is our last family Christmas" and yes, it was shit.

Afterwards, mum got her own place in a town about 25 minutes away but dad still thought that they would get back together again. [At the time of this interview, he still thought that they would]. Because he held onto this, dad didn't make any effort with any of his friends (some of his childhood friends had already passed away either through illness or suicide). He had no real hobbies although he'd previously been interested in antiques and chair reupholstery, but everything had stopped and dad had isolated himself.

DAD'S SUICIDE ATTEMPTS

Dad's first suicide attempt was about 6-7 years' ago. He left a note in his house on the dining table addressed 'to my girls'. Inside, it basically said that he was going to end things as he couldn't go on without mum but he loved us. There was no indication of where he was or where he had gone to. I had George with me, who by then was nearly 2 and I was going out of my head with worry. I rang the police, Fran and my stepsister.

The police found my dad at a local beach in his car, watching the sea. His plan had been to walk out into the waves and drown himself. He hadn't taken anything but was sitting with a newspaper. The police talked to him and mum was angry with dad for putting us – his children – through this stress. I was cross with him too because I thought he was being selfish. But he responded by coming across as not really being bothered about the whole scenario and he continued to be withdrawn.

Nothing really happened in the short-term following this incident and he refused counselling. However, it was a big turning point in terms of honesty, because I learnt that he'd made a previous suicide attempt when my mum divorced him before Fran and I were born and he'd ended up in hospital then. After this second 'cry-for-help' suicide attempt, dad turned to drink more and we tried to keep him occupied But dad continued to expect mum to return to him and she couldn't cope with him. She was also busy with her career now and had made a a good recovery from cancer.

Nearly two months' later, dad tried to commit suicide again and this time, it was much more severe:

Fran and her boyfriend, Chris, Jason, our son George and me were all in the barn next door to dad's place. Fran and I walked into dad's house as we'd been keeping an eye on him and we noticed immediately that his red dog lead was missing. I had been living with a constant intuitive feeling that dad wasn't stable and that he might 'do something' and as soon as Fran and I couldn't see the lead, we panicked. (Mum was aware of my anxieties about dad, but had stayed out of the picture because she didn't want to keep checking in on him as that gave him false hope that they would get back together).

We basically found dad hanging from the banisters of his barn. He was barely alive and yes, he'd used the lead to do it: it was tied to the top of his neck and around the banister. I just remember a lot of screaming and us desperately trying to work the lead loose. We had to make a split-second decision regarding what to do. Fran urgently rang the police and I had to leave her in the same room as our hanging dad, listening to her screaming whilst I raced next door to get Jason and Sean (and make sure that George didn't stumble in on his granddad!) I stood in the hallway of our house with my hands over George's ears, so he couldn't hear the screaming. I shouted at the guys to help us urgently. Fran's screams still haunt me as does the fact that I had to leave her with dad whilst I rushed to get assistance.

After Fran rang the police, she called mum who heard everything and was so wound up that she drove straight over. I rang a close girlfriend to come and look after George as I knew from dad's previous beach suicide episode, that we would all get interviewed. Dad didn't have to be resuscitated but he came around lying on the floor as the police arrived. Dad acted as though nothing had happened. The Police and paramedics wanted to take him off to the Mental Health Unit for an assessment but he refused. Mum arrived and when she realised that dad refused to consider professional support, she started smacking and punching him because she was so frustrated with him and she had coped with his behaviour for years. She was going crazy and the police intervened. The aftermath was a blur.

It wasn't that mum was angry immediately with dad but she was at her wits' end when she saw the state we were in and realised that dad was still unwilling to acknowledge what he had done and wouldn't consider obtaining professional support (even when we literally begged him to and when physically he was also in such a state: the police and paramedics were concerned about the damage to his neck). Dad had attended a Mental Health Unit after his earlier beach suicide attempt because he was in a public place when it happened but there wasn't really much of a follow-up. They couldn't make him go to the Mental Health Unit after this next suicide attempt as it took place in his own home but they did send professionals out to his house a few times.

I was plagued by the fact that George could have walked in on my dad's suicide attempt, but dad wouldn't take any responsibility for his actions. He had a Mental Health assessment but he was discharged, albeit with some home-visits planned. Fran and myself had counselling and that was a support. I continued with it for a quite a long time. I was angry with Jason because he wouldn't go for counselling and neither would Sean. This is something that I know Jason has regretted since, because he still suffers from nightmares 6 years' later after trying to cut down my dad, but at the time, Jason felt he could cope with it all.

Eight months' after dad's suicide attempt, he sold his house and for a time, dad stayed with us, Fran and his brother and sister too, sofa-hopping. He purchased another property but he never apologised for what he had tried to do and the whole situation really affected me. I felt resentful of him because of what he had put us through and the fact that he refused to seek help. I also continued to feel guilty because I had left Fran with him, trying to support him physically whilst he was still hanging as I rushed to get Jason and Sean to cut him down.

Right now, dad is still trying to make a new life for himself but he relies on us really heavily and I am just trying to get through this whole situation and lockdown [lockdown 1]. I am trying to be positive!

WHAT HAVE YOUR EXPERIENCES TAUGHT YOU?

Be honest with your children. Don't have dark secrets because the secret my parents kept of pretending they were married when they weren't and maintaining that charade, really affected me. Now I don't believe in marriage and it changed my relationship with my parents, although my mum and I have really healed our bond now.

Men must take control of their well-being, reach out for help (including counselling) and not rely on wives and family to provide all of their support. Many men mistakenly still feel that it is a weakness to seek emotional support in this way but that has massive repercussions for those around them. What happened with dad has definitely affected my husband. Men must feel able to include self-care in their lives and address their issues. Dad wouldn't address his mental health issues even after his almost-fatal suicide attempt and as mentioned before, he is still sending messages to me saying he's thinking of packing everything in. I had one recently from him where he wrote that he was: "in a dark place". These messages send me into a panic.

When a parent attempts suicide or goes through with a suicide, you feel a sense of abandonment and that as their children, you're not good enough for them to stay around for. Dad was so fixated on mum so it felt like an extra slap in the face that he didn't want to be there *for us* especially because he was the one that was at home with us when we were little; he was the one who read to us and taught us how to ride a bike for example.

If you're in a relationship and it ends, don't be fixated on your ex and internalise. Get support and build your own life, otherwise you make it really difficult for your children. For example when there have been Christmas and Birthday parties, we've wondered who to invite, because dad wants to use them as an opportunity to pressurise mum about getting back together with him. Mum has a new partner now and dad keeps asking us questions about him and that's awkward for us. When mum talks to dad as a friend, dad gets his hopes up and then when he realises nothing's going to happen with her, he gets shitty.

WHAT ADVICE WOULD YOU GIVE TO OTHER WOMEN IN A SIMILAR SITUATION?

Go for counselling if you experience something like this. I suffer with anxiety and depression now and I put off having a second baby for quite a while afterwards because I felt as though life was tarnished. My boss was empathetic but having an anonymous Counselling professional to talk everything through with, made such a positive difference. She said it was okay to be resentful and angry. Counselling also helps you to cope with the aftermath and ongoing difficulties, because sometimes with these situations, life doesn't just suddenly get better. (For example, in our case, dad continued to make things difficult: he bought a house that wasn't in the right location for him so he was more dependent on us than ever and would message us frequently with sentiments such as: "I don't want to be here. You don't love me. No one loves me" and also implying that Fran wasn't his child. He would also constantly text mum too and ultimately she had to block him).

WHERE ARE YOU NOW? WHAT ARE YOUR PLANS FOR THE FUTURE?

After I had my daughter Freya, I was diagnosed with postnatal depression and PTSD from dad's suicide attempt. I felt a numbness towards him for quite some time. I was sad too that because of what happened, the family home was sold but we've tried to make our peace though. Dad has George after school sometimes which is lovely. I want to say to dad: move on from mum; enjoy your life. Find new hobbies. I keep hoping he's about to turn a corner and will make new friends. I almost want to give him a kick up the backside. He's 73 years' old now and has 6 grandchildren and I want him to be a role model for them. I want him to get out there and live! To stop being so emotionally dependent on us because we've got so much of our own stuff to deal with. I want him to take responsibility for his mental and physical well-being.

My own life feels a bit of a mess right now and lockdown has made it worse, because I've had more time to think. Feeling depressed and being stuck at home with 2 little ones whilst furloughed and the world's turned upside down because of a pandemic, hasn't been easy. It's as though I'm looking for the perfect family. At one point, I even asked Jason to leave because I worry that I will end up like my mum with a grumpy old man who doesn't have any friends and/or is like another child or becomes like a pressure cooker because of stress, which they then take out on their families. Male friendships are so important to men, they must keep them going even when they settle down with their wives and have children. I keep telling Jason to go to football training and to go fishing. I have made it clear that he is not my everything. He must have a life of his own too, outside of me and vice versa. I'm having to emotionally hold-up my dad and I don't want to have to hold-up my husband in the future too.

However, I'm a young mum in my early thirties and I do feel that I will thrive soon with lots of bright possibilities ahead…

Lucy's postscript

Lucy's dad died suddenly in January 2021 of natural causes, not suicide. Lucy was devastated and I thought that she would pull out of the book project, but after I tentatively checked in with her, Lucy decided that she still wanted to take part. These are her unedited words (there is some repetition here but I felt that it was important to literally relay her stream of consciousness):

After Dad's death

I had a million thoughts going around in my head last night, so I thought that I would send them to you.

When someone attempts suicide, it makes you think why was I/our family, not enough to make that person want to live. You start doubting yourself: 'am I not good enough? Why am I not enough to make you want to live?' and it's been something that has been on my mind.

Dad wanted to die and didn't think about anyone else, not even his grandchildren. He didn't want to live for so many years. He was unhappy, alone, unsure of what he wanted in life, moving around from Cornwall to Spain, Scotland, etc, before buying a house. You begin to think: 'yes, he's finally happy and building a life himself' but then on another day, he would send a message saying: "I can't do this. I love you and the kids but I can't see you knowing that I'm not with your mother", and he would message my sister saying that she wasn't his. This behaviour would usually last a couple of days then he would turn up at my house as though nothing had happened. It wasn't until my daughter, his granddaughter, Freya, was older that dad decided he did have a reason to live.

Latterly, Freya became dad's everything and he would come around everyday. During lockdown, he rang her everyday. He started having a life and made friends with a bunch of lads, regularly heading to the pub with them and beginning to go to social events. He was finally finding happiness again although at the back of my head, I was always wondering, how long will this last?

He was then hit by news towards the end of 2020, that he would need to have part of his leg amputated but he joked around about it, telling the kids that afterwards, he would be like a pirate and the lads in the pub said they would wheel him around. Whilst all of this was going on, he was surrounded by loving family, friends and neighbours and he seemed happy even though he was in pain. The last thing he said before going into hospital is: "I have room now, so come over with the kids". It seemed like for once, dad wanted to live!

The day after the operation, he was in high spirits, the kids asked to see his leg and he was laughing during our video call; he was smiling and looked healthy. But all of that changed within hours and he was gone. A blood clot in his lung had taken him just at the point when he wanted to live and was excited, although still worried, about life.

His grandchildren idolised him but now he is no longer here. The numbness and pain are unreal.

And then my thoughts become overwhelming! I spent years wishing he could have his wish to be at peace, because that's what he wanted [not what Lucy wanted!] He wanted to die: no one was good enough for him to live, but now that he's gone, all I want is to have him back. I hate myself for previously wishing he could be at peace and I relive the thoughts and feelings of the past 7 years. Why was he not taken when he wanted to go? Why has he been taken when he wanted to live? Why now? The guilt of: did I cause this somehow? It's so hard to think those thoughts now, when I would do anything to have him back.

The heartache this has caused the family. Everyone's guilt of not being there enough; of, we could have done more; Why didn't we see him more? Why didn't we push him [more] to get help when he needed it? I should have gone over [to see him] more, invited him over more. The times I dreaded him turning up everyday and ringing everyday, when now that's all I want. I arrive home and hope to see his car there or my phone rings and I want that to be him.

Then there was telling George and Freya that they had lost someone else (they had already lost a nan and their other grandad within the year), so telling them that there was another new star in the sky, was heart breaking. George went quiet and doesn't like to talk about it, whereas Freya does talk about it but George tells her not to as it'll make us all cry, but she mentions her nan and grandads daily and asks to look at the stars.

I think of all the events dad will miss seeing: Freya starting school and growing up. Dad loved Freya and George both with all of his heart and it breaks me to think they don't have him any more, but then it will hit me again, the guilt of: 'you wanted him to be at peace at one point Lucy.'

Seeing how broken the family are without him: his sisters, brother and close friends too, that's tough. Also I dread the mountain ahead of dealing with all of dad's belongings: like, what do you do with someone's whole life? Where does that go? That's dad's life. Who has what? His clothes, treasures he's collected and so on?

Then more thoughts come in... would this have happened if mum hadn't left, would he still be here? If I had stepped up more, would he still be here? You go to bed at night laying there, crying for hours before you finally fall asleep to wake up and face another day. Telling yourself he's at peace now but knowing that for 7 years, he wanted to die because he was unhappy and felt alone and in pain and then just when it was all looking up for him, boom, he went.

How I feel now: I'm suffering from anxiety and depression and this stems from dad attempting suicide and having postnatal depression after Freya's birth. (I was put on 'happy pills' that numbed feelings for a bit, but they don't numb them now). I have a personal fight on, to get up in the mornings and face a day of overwhelming thoughts and hope that I don't just break down. I want to shut the world out and just stare at nothing, but I have to dig deep as I have my 2 kids to look after but the thought of entertaining them for another day in lockdown 3, fills me with dread, but I just have to. I am resuming counselling again next month to try and work through all of the thoughts in my head. I want to see a light at the end of the tunnel and get 'myself' back so that dad will be proud of me when he looks down, but meanwhile, the thoughts consume me.

Author's note

Lucy is taking all the necessary steps with professionals to work through her pain and she is currently getting support from her friends and family. She wanted to open-up regarding her experiences and feelings to help anyone else out there going through a similar time.

FERN'S STORY

Whilst undergoing a divorce, facing total ostracism from your former friendship group and at your wits' end with endless financial stresses, a car that constantly breaks down and impossible workload, you crack and are unintentionally supported by a forbidden person

PLEASE NOTE

This was a really tough process and I gave my interviews during lockdowns 1 and 2 primarily, because I couldn't psyche myself up to churn it all out in one massive go.

HERE'S MY STORY

The best way for me to describe how I felt about everything that happened, is by asking you to imagine shaking up a snow-globe and watching the snowflakes manically swirling around, because that's what all of this felt like in my head. Because I have my private emotions and then I have what has felt like my official emotions as I dealt with formality after formality: with a very stressful long divorce and another set of proceedings following an implosion when I was teaching at a school in the North of England. The latter was traumatic and so expensive too. I nearly moved away from our life in the North to get away from everything and have a totally fresh start elsewhere, but I decided not to, but to stick it out and to be around for me and my boys…

I cannot talk about why I had to leave my marriage, so I have to start my story mid-way through and apologies for this. I know it's hard to understand what happened when you only have half of the story, but one day, maybe I will be in a position where I can explain the full context and everything that happened next will make more sense, but for now this is what I can share. Also when referring to my divorce, I cannot go into any specifics of the process but all I will say is that it was a particularly difficult and drawn-out divorce. I will consistently use the words 'very difficult' when mentioning my divorce in this chapter, so that you will understand its nature but cannot particularly infer anything further.

***

Quite often back then (as alluded to with the snow globe analogy), my life felt like a masquerade: namely the expressions on my face and how I presented myself.

I felt like it was an act, because in my mind, sometimes I felt as though I was in the wilderness, a bit of a pariah and just completely overwhelmed by everything, but somehow I got through the challenges, one step at a time, because women are resilient. People who didn't know what I was going through then probably thought I'm always really sunny and positive and yes, that's my default but at times – like lots of you – I suffer from imposter-syndrome and I just put on a brave face because I fight against being a mood-hoover! I know I'm not alone in having these dual lives of looking like a metaphorical swan: calm and serene on the surface and keeping all my crazy shit together, but underneath the water, I'm paddling frantically! Looking back, what happened to my life was enormous as I was dealing with so many huge challenges simultaneously.

I know so many people feel the same way and they are dealing with massive issues too: we have our private and public personas and we don't want any turmoil which is occurring in our personal lives to cross over and derail our professional lives. Thus, inwardly in our personal lives, some major chaos has kicked off, but outwardly, that middle class respectability doesn't belie our inner turmoil, but my God, it's so there within us, tripping us up in our daily thoughts…

For me it used to be that hearing certain songs, expressions and so on, reminded me of those difficult events and the most seemingly-insignificant triggers would set this off. It could be something as simple as pulling a bright dress out of my wardrobe and suddenly being catapulted to the day I was marched out of school, which was the last time I wore it, or seeing a Netflix series which we used to talk about all the time in class.

***

So this Senior man in authority said to me back then: "and it goes without saying that you shouldn't discuss this with anyone", and at the time in my shell-shocked state, I blithely mumbled: "yes of course", but then later, I thought: 'Fuck, I have to talk about it to people I trust', because actually this whole experience was pretty massive and life-changing for me in so many ways and I never, ever intended this situation to happen as I literally was the least-likely person to find myself in this position. However, nobody talks about these things publicly but I AM speaking about it now that the years have passed, because I know I'm not the only person to experience something like this – all of it: a very difficult divorce, bitchy and isolating friendship ostracism, a long-standing financial nightmare, mental overwhelm, work overload and an implosive teaching derailment – and it's absolutely not intentional that I got myself into the latter situation! Everyone who knows me, completely understood that! It's the last thing I ever wanted to happen!!!

Basically all of my experiences have taught me that none of us ever know what life might throw at us and people who read this and think: 'this is shocking, shameful, disgusting… I'd never behave like that', just don't know how they might feel and act if they found themselves facing a vortex of challenges, simultaneously in a perfect storm, just like the ones I found myself confronting!

In terms of acting in ways that are completely out-of-character for us, I was talking to a friend recently who had a very intense, unexpected passionate heterosexual affair for a few years and both respective participants in the affair were married with children who were on the cusp of their teenage years. They were all framed within a wider circle of friends, living close to each other in an exclusive city area and enjoying their social camaraderie. This powerful liaison between them, reactivated everything that this woman thought had died within her. She thought that her latterly-sexless marriage was simply how it was going to be for the rest of her life and that she had come to terms with it but then along came this man and awoke her from that stupor and it just completely recharged her life in every possible way! When you fall madly for someone, it overrides everything and it doesn't matter if they're out-of-bounds/unsuitable etc, because it feels as if you're walking on air and that you only need two hours' sleep as you're so high on the endorphins that being in love and feeling desirable, gives you... You feel invincible!

...and that's how this woman felt and then...

...then his wife discovered the affair and the man severed all contact with my friend with breathtaking rapidity and coldness. It was like a brutal limb amputation. After constant promises of reaching old age together, suddenly: no contact at all. How do you recover from that? The rejection. The loss. A future built on hope and promises. Endless messages, affirmations, incredible sex and then... literally nothing. A silence. A blank. A void. A rejection. A big bleak nothing. Total ghosting. It made her question whether anything was really there in the first place... was it all in her mind? And it was the severity of the separation that was so difficult for her. So in order to process it all, she found – like me – that actually she needed to talk about her situation, because talking about it, helped with the healing.

So I couldn't go along with what the senior man said at the outset of this chapter because it was actually damaging to me not to talk about the stressful experiences I was going through back then. I understand that keeping schtum is the traditional way that English people have functioned for millennia, especially people of a certain age. However, that's the old-fashioned method of dealing with trauma: shut it down.

I remember my mum telling me about an elderly gentleman who I knew when I was little and he was kindly but a bit forgetful. He had suffered horribly in a WWII Japanese Prisoner of War camp and had witnessed brutal executions, flogging with bamboo canes and had drank polluted water which – his doctors felt – had caused him to develop a condition which later affected his memory. This man was never encouraged to have counselling or to talk about his experiences and so he used to have night terrors because he had never been able to process everything he had been through. Obviously my situation wasn't in any way comparable with that older chap's turbulent past, but it made me realise that it doesn't matter what stresses you go through, that actually you can't or shouldn't shut those experiences down: because that trauma, the questions afterwards, the wreckage of your life immediately following a set of monumental life-changes like the ones that happened to me, cannot simply be switched off from.

Sometimes I wished I could have just blocked these experiences from my mind, but I couldn't, because in relation to this precise episode, every time I heard something about teaching or "noble teachers" on the news, I felt such a deep pang.

I felt that it should've been me helping my students, but of course, after what happened, it couldn't be me.

All of the feelings, the scenarios I went through, had to be rationalised, understood, processed and discussed because if I had simply blanked them all out of my mind, I know I would have gone to pieces at some point later on in my life and I'm sorry, but as anyone who's gone through a really difficult situation[s] knows, trying to compartmentalise stressful, life-changing experiences away in your brain, is an impossibility because they find ways to leak into your subconscious and later these traumas only resurface and cause havoc elsewhere in your life! I had flashbacks in dreams. So in terms of shutting 'it' down. No, that was impossible, especially as I believe in openness and transparency. I always feel that it is much better to be upfront and then you have nothing to hide. Also if you are an open person and are willing to share the difficulties you've experienced, then that enables other people to offload to you because you have revealed your vulnerabilities and turbulence, so individuals feel that you're a safe space for them to share their stresses with.

**

During my teacher training course (the PGCE), the latter topic is completely ignored, along with the ramifications, so I AM talking about it and some of the pressures that led to it - so that others know not to get themselves into the crazy muddle I got into when they are having a really difficult time in life and lose their oversight! If you look at any public misconduct websites for various professions (i.e. for doctors, lawyers, police, accountants etc), you will see thousands of cases listed for some kind of upcoming hearing or tribunal and incidents with teachers are the same. There will be people all around you every day in different professions, who like me previously, have had some kind of judicial process looming over them and their lives, for perhaps a few years and it just becomes a part of their lives: they learn to live with it and to stop dreading every related email, phone conversation, meeting and postal letter related to it, but instead adapt to dealing with it all headlong, just as I had to, those years' ago.

Obviously some teachers will have committed grave acts deliberately but for others – like me – it was a case that their lives just went monumentally off-piste because of other overwhelming stresses. Just recently I heard a similar case to mine involving another teacher and an A-level student who had just left the school where the teacher taught and as far as I know the two met up to talk as they had become close, but nothing else happened. The teacher had to resign when this became known.

Thus these situations occur and there needs to be a nuanced dialogue, rather than just the assumption that adult teachers and A-level students do not make connections. It may be an unsettling taboo and one that UK society is fearful to even think of, but it happens and it needs to be discussed in an intelligent, intellectual manner. My hope is that by covering this issue in my chapter (along with my other stresses), that moving forward, all training courses for every profession where there are concrete boundaries will stop dodging these situations and talk trainees through what would actually happen if you form a strong bond with a person which would breach that boundary or if such a person puts themselves forward in your professional path on a regular basis until you take notice of them... What processes follow? Who should you be able to discuss such an issue with, without fear of putting your job/career trajectory in jeopardy or of causing the person concerned, to feel any kind of awkwardness?

In terms of life fuck-ups, lots of public figures have had second chances after either finding themselves in unexpected crazy situations or by making decisions that have poleaxed their lives, but they have talked publicly about what happened and have learnt from their experiences and thus their stories humanise them and they comforted me. I am completely aware of 'cancel culture' but everyone does insane stuff (even the most ardent proponents of cancel culture often have done/ or are doing, ridiculous things in their lives that if were revealed, would cancel them out too), so anyone calling for the nullifying of others, can't have any of their own skeletons-in-the-cupboard and cannot ever trip up themselves in the future...

We need to show empathy and try to understand the reasons why people find themselves in a situation they didn't intend when life-stresses become too much. Then we need to help them to move forward positively (and use social media for good, not for declaring death threats or vocalising endless maliciousness)! So yes I am bravely talking about a few really tough situations that happened to me because by sharing my story, I know it will ultimately help people being ostracised, teachers and those in similar positions with equivalent boundaries, and so on... (having given my interview to the author of this book, I want to say that if anyone reading this, feels they want to troll the author for including my story, then they should know that the author's lawyers will utilise the powers of new Online Safety laws, to publicly expose any such trolls and bring them to justice, because it is crucial in an educated society that we are able to talk openly about difficult life experiences, without the risk of trolling and attempts at silencing brave voices).

Over the years talking to people I can be myself with, has been a huge help in processing everything that happened to me and enabled me to move on to the next part of my life. Everyone has twists and turns in the road that they didn't expect and anyone can do crazy things sometimes when they're totally overwhelmed by stress but pretty much everyone should have a second chance. I realised that I have so much knowledge to pass on that I definitely couldn't slink away and I had no intention of slinking away as I knew that I wanted to use my tricky experiences in a positive way! As mentioned before, there are so many current public figures I can name who have also experienced huge personal failings but by the very force of their personalities, they have ignored and overcome any criticism levelled at them in their private lives and then soldiered on and I had to do the same!

I know people will either understand my story, try to understand my story or they will judge what happened in very black and white terms, but I had to own my narrative, I held my hands up and took all of the penalties involved and absolutely promised that yes, of course! - I would never, ever, ever let myself get in a situation like my teaching situation again! - because I wouldn't.

Some people might feel that I am trying to justify what happened. I'm not justifying what happened and trying to say that it was okay - because it certainly wasn't. I'm just saying that with the benefit of hindsight, I realise why my teaching situation happened and I'm explaining my life implosions honestly in the hope that this helps others to avoid some of the mess I got myself into! I also hope that by sharing my story – which I really hope all school leadership teams and governors will read – that schools will support teachers and staff going through really difficult personal situations if they're aware of them, because such a huge amount of pressure is placed upon those in the teaching profession and we're not robots: we're human beings who crash and burn too when everything gets too much. For me personally now, telling this means I can leave my past behind me and continue to focus on my scientific research.

I'm going to tell you what happened to me and then I'm going to detail some of the events that led up to it (notwithstanding that I can't talk about my divorce), and then I will explain the immediate and long-term aftermath.

**

So I'm relaying this to you whilst I found myself sitting on a rug on the worn terracotta tiles of my landing, surrounded by a heap of laundered washing which I'm trying to relegate into smaller piles belonging to the different members of my household (who stay with me and their dad). I've discovered that this is how life is for lots of kids of divorced/separated parents and that's fine: it kind of works! I never expected my life and their lives to be like this but it's much better for us to be in two separate, calmer households than to be as we were before I called time on our old lives). However, for now, my kids – who I love very much - are downstairs and they're busying themselves on phones, devices, watching the American version of The Office and doing other stuff. But I find myself reflecting on the way my teaching career ended abruptly...

Basically some years' ago when I was feeling isolated and really overwhelmed by a very difficult divorce, insane workload, intense money stress and I was also being ostracised from my former middle-class friendship group because they felt that leaving a marriage was unseemly, I accidentally became too close to an extremely bright A-level student just briefly, having previously had a professional rapport for a few years, but I tried to ignore how well we got on, because I couldn't really believe it was 'a thing.'

My self-esteem was at rock bottom at that time and I was barely keeping everything together so I never seriously considered that there was an actual bond developing between us until it was too late. Absolutely nothing physical ever happened between us. We never ever met up. We just exchanged some messages by text one evening. That's it. He had been really kind and supportive of me especially when he realised that my personal life was a car-crash and that I'd had to leave my family home one school holiday.

In one of the ensuing and brutal 'fire and brimstone', dehumanising processes that followed in the proceeding years (as these matters get dragged out over a long period of time). Things were taken out of context in order to fulfil a particular narrative. The 'findings' also minimised all of the horrendous external pressures I had been under at the time of my school implosion. Thus in this one process, I felt my voice was taken away from me and ignored. These lengthy procedures were horrendous and so stressful. Latterly I had to legally fight to clarify events and I had a fantastic team of legal minds who championed me, some for free because they could see the overall picture. Those people know exactly who they all are and I will always be grateful to them!

This episode made me realise that in some situations, society quickly flicks to 'witch-hunting' mode to suit the attitudes of the time and in doing so, society ignores the context. I had to fight back at a time when I didn't feel I had the capacity to, but it made me realise that the legal summaries, verdicts and records of any court case, can be cherry-picked and presented in specific ways that seek to further punish the person at the heart of a matter.

Going through any legal process like this is such a long, drawn-out, highly stressful scenario with endless twists and turns in the road and no one tells you how it's likely to play out, so it can feel such an isolating experience. I ended up having to offload to my friends about it and find a way to live normally whilst it was still going on in my life, or I would've cracked-up. Sometimes it felt as though it would be with me for the rest of my life as whenever I anticipated that there was an end in sight, there would be a new reason for it to rumble on and on. At times it felt as though I'd never be able to put it to rest but eventually it finally came to an end and I felt such a huge sense of relief. I'd been carrying such a massive load for ages.

I need to categorically state that I never ever intended to feel a personal connection with an A-level student (or definitely ANY students!) I had NEVER been in that position before and this is why I am writing honestly about my experience because I want all teachers (and those in professional roles where there are specific boundaries in place), to be aware that if you are in a vulnerable place in your life, emotions can get the better of you in your workplace, without any unprofessional intentions! It baffles me too because this came completely out of the blue. I certainly never looked for it and would never ever look for it in the future in a similar setting because I am not that kind of person.

My A-level student, who I will call Jack, and I, just naturally got on really well and in my overwhelm, I stopped seeing him as a student and saw him as a person who was always chatting to me, making his strong presence felt and trying to lift my spirits with his high energy. When we messaged, Jack felt someone I could confide in and I know to others that sounds totally inappropriate and of course, now I'm in a much better psychological place, I completely realise that.

Just before Jack and I exchanged messages, I had tried to contact other colleagues at the same school as me to discuss my work stresses but I hadn't heard back from them and because of my impending divorce, I was being ostracised by my former friendship group so I couldn't turn to any of my closest friends within that circle and then Jack replied to me during the holidays regarding a school email and I just flipped and offloaded to him…

***

A while after my school disciplinary and before a few standard-procedure hearings that I had to undergo, I talked to an erudite guy who's a great friend to rationalise the dynamics as I couldn't get my head around it all and he said: "it's something that happened, that you can't explain and that you didn't look for, but it was simply there"… and he summarised it completely. I know that this totally goes against the extremely demarcated, delineated, very black and white lines of society right now, but life is messy and complex and this was my real experience. I am sharing it to help others know to keep their emotions in check and to make sure they seek professional support if events in their lives make them feel overwhelmed.

I never ever for one moment, thought I would be in that situation: dealing with the repercussions of inadvertently becoming too close to one of my A-level students as I've always, always been so overly-conscientious in my teaching posts! But then again I never anticipated that I would have to instigate the process of going through a very difficult divorce after a long marriage which took a few arduous years to complete, move out of my beloved family home, start afresh in a rented pad as a single mum and that I would also be ostracised by the women I thought closest to me and who said I could turn to them when I was desperate...

At the time I had a friend try to ignore my 'school thing' and when she alluded to it occasionally, she'd make comments such as: "well that other business is in the past now" and I would think: 'actually, it's not. It's always present somewhere in my mind. I just don't mention it. I try to compartmentalise it, but how could I forget it all?' Because I can't. The person involved made me feel I could cope at a time when everything felt as though it was falling apart!

Later, I learnt to totally embrace life once again because that is the only way to be (certainly for me because my default is to be positive and look forward), but there's no doubt, the person involved will always be a fundamental and intrinsic part of my story, and it's a story of the very difficult ending of a long marriage, the ostracism and maliciousness of 'friends', financial turmoil, an unsustainable workload and then support from an unconventional and unexpected source that I didn't seek... but which resulted in an even greater fallout and me questioning everything about myself and life in general!

***

For the first time in my life after this implosion happened, I went to see a counsellor and as I scrolled through the list of registered professionals, in one of those moments of wry humour, 'Fleabag' sprang to mind. I'd been an advocate of counselling for ages but had never actually been before: there was never time (chatting about myself and my baggage for an hour every fortnight seemed a bit indulgent/unnecessary when I thought I could just stoically push through), and the waiting lists were too long via the GP and I couldn't afford to go privately.

Maybe if I was brutally honest too, I also subconsciously felt that going to see a counsellor was pinpointing the fact that I wasn't wholly 'sorted' and that's how I always wanted to be perceived. Nobody wants to present themselves as though their life's a bit of a car-crash! We all want to look 'put together'! We don't want to look like one of the dysfunctional harpies in Hogarth's Gin Lane. Anyway to hell with all of that, I thought: now is the time to seek support and I booked myself in to see a counsellor.

Lockdown was the time to get myself into a good physical, mental and emotional head-space, so I decided to embrace this process. From the very first session, I just thought 'this is really helping me; everyone in the UK should go to see a counsellor just like people see a therapist in the US'. It should be as normalised as walking the dog or going to the gym because I hadn't realised how many mental burdens I'd been carrying around, weighing me down throughout the years and I know that so many others will be feeling just like me.

This safe space (in the counselling room) and my kind, warm, experienced professional let me unspool the tangled threads in my mind and I wished I'd gone years' ago instead of feeling that I had to manage all of the big stuff by myself. It was so liberating to get everything off my chest. This counsellor was actually the second one I went to see, because she had experience of working with clients who'd been through similar situations to me and so she was totally able to help me (my first Counsellor wasn't practiced enough to benefit me and she actually imposed her own issues upon me, so even counsellors don't get it right sometimes – again they are human beings – I've learnt personally that with regards to counselling, you have to 'shop around' until you find the right one for you and your circumstances, so some will be more of a perfect fit for you than others).

Getting divorced cost a huge amount of money for me because of my divorce's very difficult nature and this second legal matter cost more, which obviously was devastating but money is energy: it comes and it goes so I simply couldn't let myself freak out about it all. When a life implosion or several life implosions happen at once, it's as though you're involved in a shipwreck and you almost lose consciousness through the process and then you have to gradually wake up, see which island you've been washed ashore upon and what is left from your old life with you and then how you can use what's left and the tools you have personally, mentally and physically, to rebuild your life.

I've always been anxious about finances but post-divorce and all of these implosions, I've gradually rebuilt a totally new life and so I couldn't endlessly fixate on this aspect of life, or I would have gone crazy. I had to let it all go knowing that as long as I could work in different capacities, pay my bills, continue to stay in my home, provide for my children as and when they needed me to and have lots of different life experiences, then I had to simply stop constantly stressing about it all because money anxiety had already absorbed far too much of my time in previous years.

Undertaking my scientific research as I started to, after my life implosions, and reading about female pioneers decades' ago, who had to exert themselves in a man's world, fortified me from beyond their graves, sometimes when I felt depleted. What a positive legacy they left! I realised that looking back over time shows us that throughout the centuries, there are the same or similar themes which endlessly repeat on a loop and that if we keep that context in mind, that we are one of millions of people undergoing these tricky experiences and thus that we're not on our own – then anything is survivable!

I want to explain the background of what happened to me and why I never expected to be in this position because I was always a committed wife, mum, loyal friend and conscientious teacher and then my life just imploded in so many ways with one impossible situation leading to another…

**

Initially the flashbacks which I sometimes got, were at times like a form of living insanity, but I just distracted myself endlessly with hobbies, my research and seeing friends as much as possible. I became a mistress at hiding my interior life and initially I told my closest girlfriends and then latterly all of my friends about my school implosion and in all honesty, most were very supportive.

One thing I noticed was that all of my male friends totally understood everything and weren't shocked or scathing at all. I did feel disapproval from a couple of female friends that I told. Interestingly though, what emerged was that such women seemed to be jealous that I had received some attention - albeit from a forbidden source – and I could tell this from the sarcastic, catty, scathing comments which they made. Even the first counsellor that I went to see (before I changed counsellors, because I realised their remarks were inappropriate and unhelpful), said sarcastically: "Oh well it must have felt wonderful to have attention from younger males. I would love some of that myself" and I just thought 'wtf?!?!?!' because it wasn't like that at all – I would never have chosen to put myself in that situation.

However, overall pretty much everyone else fully understood and they have been there for me ever since! Overall, I've found that it's so much better to be transparent as people are generally very kind and either just understand or try to understand and often they're then open about difficulties they've experienced or are going through. Anyone who's been very judgemental has just excluded themselves from my life or I've deliberately exited myself from theirs, but that's fine, because I know that they were just fairweather friends, not there for the grit!

My newer group of genuine friends have buoyed me up when I sometimes felt what was the point of carrying on, because back a while, everything just felt too massive! Even the brilliant policewomen who interviewed me told my duty solicitor that they could empathise with my situation, realised that I didn't pose any threat whatsoever and that they didn't want to damage my career and life. What occurred for me, felt at times so impossible to comprehend, but somehow, day in, day out, as all the daily ritual stuff was undertaken and I went for another hike with my dogs, I realised life just had to continue… Yet all of these experiences have been seared upon my mind.

But how did I get to that point where I got too close to someone I wasn't allowed to be close to in the first place anyway? Where did my series of life implosions begin?

***

All I can say about leaving my husband, is the following: For mothers, instinctively, we will try everything we possibly can to keep our families together and especially when our kids are little or they're hitting exam season. Therefore, if a woman, a mother, leaves her husband and the family home and it's not because she's running off with another guy, then it's because she has exhausted all other options to stay in her marriage and leaving is the only one left to save her sanity.

At this time, when students were lovely to me at school, sometimes I would feel tears start to form, because I wasn't expecting kindness. When you go into a profession, you are told that you have your private life and your professional life and you must keep both boundaried and separate, but in a situation like mine was, without professional help, with work overwhelm and feeling isolated from all of my former support structures, I found that my private life, was insidiously inveigling its way into my professional life.

When I reflect, the stress of it all became completely subsuming, especially when combined with a demanding teaching career and at that point, I confided in my Line Manager, a few colleagues who I was close to and to those within the Senior Leadership Team. I told them of my extraordinary external pressures and that I was looking to move out of the family home to support my mental health. One of the leadership team said: "my office door is always open" but it was a token comment and others said similar but there wasn't any follow-up from any of them.

My Line Manager sometimes asked how it was going, but then in the next breath, would say: "but I need that data in" (from marking assessments) and no practical suggestions were touted to support me, ease my workload or offer any time off for all the many solicitors' appointments that followed. Therefore, I felt I had to try to keep it all together because as a woman, I didn't want to be labelled as 'emotional'. At this point, my personal life was affecting every aspect of my life, including now the job I loved.

To cope, I started training for a Tough Mudder. I also started planning a scientific research proposal which would enable me to develop my career and earn more money in the future, as I knew that this would mentally distract me (studying has always been a form of solace for me). Sometimes on the way home from work, I'd take a detour to a salsa club to lose myself for a couple of hours of complete escapism before psyching myself up to go home. Those times kept me going. Again I know it could be argued that staying out more probably didn't help my home situation but home didn't feel like a place of sanctuary any more.

I used to drive past signs for 'Bed sits available to rent' and I started planning how I could move into one. I'd reached the stage where I didn't care if I could only afford to move into one room but then obviously I couldn't simply do that because I needed to find a property wherein there was room for my kids to stay too. However, emotionally, I had detached even further from my former husband. I think it's a coping mechanism that kicks in, when we just withdraw into ourselves and I was developing my own protective carapace.

Hitting the gym a lot massively helped me to feel stronger and mentally focused. It started to give me a little bit of confidence that had diminished as I really felt in a David v Goliath situation. I just had no idea how I could leave my marriage. I had no access to any money for a start and I didn't really feel that I could talk to any of those who were close to me at the time. I constantly questioned myself.

FEMALE OSTRACISM

I feel that I should set the context a little more regarding our friendship group: the core of it was formed by the women I got to know at my youngest children's baby/toddler playgroup, which was called 'The Milk and Honey Club'. Every Wednesday morning, whilst off on maternity leave and then beyond when I resumed my studies and simultaneously worked part-time, I would head to this lifesaving club for lattes, pastries and toast with butter, jam, marmalade and of course, honey! Mums could sit, breastfeeding their babies in comfort whilst catching up with friends over drinks and breakfast. Meanwhile, babies who were bottle-fed had their formula milk heated and toddlers were provided for too. If we felt zombified because we'd had little sleep, it didn't matter as it was such a relaxed atmosphere. These sessions were filled with such an eclectic mix of women and they kept us sane!

Sometimes afterwards a Milk and Honey session, a load of us would head off for another coffee either to each other's homes or a local cafe. We bonded so much during these times, trying to chat and grab something to eat and drink whilst our babies were being nursed at our breasts, crawled off us or as toddlers, started bawling… these sessions knitted what I thought were genuinely-tight friendships. We all organically became immersed in each other's lives and ultimately many of us became part (maybe unintentionally), as cited earlier, of a group of middle-class professional friends, whose careers included veterinary practitioners, medical experts, accountants etc.

These friendships and sessions really helped fill the void of a demanding professional adult working environment for me, because as much as I absolutely love my children 100%, I'd felt a disconnect from my old life whenever I'd had babies and a feeling of isolation could wash over me so I had to fight this by keeping my mind active whilst I was on maternity leave and dealing with young children. I'm definitely not the only mum to feel this but women think they can't say it because there are such taboos around discussing the realities of parenthood/ motherhood.

At the time of giving this interview, one British actress got a media-bashing for basically saying that sometimes motherhood just wasn't stimulating enough for her, because when you have a baby/toddler, quite often you can be spending longer periods of time away from people.

If your infant isn't a good sleeper, then day and night can merge into an exhausted blur and you're changing nappies, feeding, trying to manage on little sleep and you are spending much longer within your home instead of mixing with other people at work/uni or in another social environment. It can be quite a lonely/ challenging time in many ways, whilst in others, of course, you're so grateful to have your baby but it can make you question everything and you can feel really torn and guilty, wondering who you are as a person after this phenomenal life-change? It can be hard just to get one thing achieved in a day, let alone tick off all the many tasks which pre-baby, could be easily accomplished in minutes.

For example, every time your baby cries – if someone else is holding it – your baby is automatically passed back to you (as the mother generally; babies still don't tend to be automatically passed back to their dads) and people continue to eat their meals, carry on chatting, whilst your food goes cold, you can't participate in the conversation because your baby is crying or needs changing. As the mother of a baby, you can be on the peripheries of life, just tending to your baby's relentless needs (and simultaneously often, you're tending to the needs of toddlers too), for hours and hours. You try to have grown-up conversations over crying, vomiting, bowel explosions and so on and so as much as you absolutely love this beautiful little human being that you have made and carried in your womb, you can feel as a woman/mother, that your own personal life has dropped off the edge of a cliff and that no one sees you any more as you, as a woman, as a person, a sexual being, an attractive, intelligent individual in your own right.

It's even worse if you are struggling to lose pregnancy weight and are feeling less confident with your body because you regret all those times when you could have so easily gone to the gym or for a run but you didn't because there was always tomorrow. Whereas now it can feel impossible to organise the energy and the childcare to get to a fitness class and then it can become a self-defeating endeavour. This is because sometimes you think: 'getting my body into any fit shape now is going to be such a massive undertaking that it's just an impossible challenge' and you can talk yourself out of even kickstarting a new regime because you are simply too exhausted and are craving some hot buttered toast, something sugary and an espresso to keep you awake!

As a mother, you can very easily and completely morph into your family, into your husband, into your children. You become known as 'so and so's mum' – this happens a lot at school parents' evenings. It's all a pretty massive life-shift! You can hugely lose yourself and simultaneously everyone around you expects you to automatically adapt to this new role and to absolutely love it without question; no one automatically imagines that you might be struggling.

Basically, new motherhood can provoke a whole maelstrom of emotions, especially if you're not quite sure what will come next? It can be either a return to work post maternity leave; or a sudden happy transition to being a full-time parent; or to God knows' what?… and that can be the scary part! The redefinition of you. You are thinking: Who am I? What am I? What is my role now? How can I square this new role of mother with the person I truly am? Quite often as women, we lose ourselves at this point.

Conversely having a baby is also the most wonderful gift too and I've had so many special, precious times with my children doing all kinds of things, from simple activities such as colouring-in, baking, going for woody walks and to the cinema together to watching them perform in school plays and music concerts and feeling incredibly proud of them. I remember holding them when they were newly-born and being unable to comprehend that they had arrived as they looked so perfect and I felt such a massive rush of love for them. When they fall asleep on your tummy or in your arms as babies and when they're snoring toddlers or say gorgeous and earnest words to you expressing that they really love you, your heart fills up, so there are many, many beautiful moments involved in having children. However, there are also times when it's tough and yes, as women we can completely get lost as individuals when we become mothers.

With my new group of friends via Milk and Honey, we ultimately ended up doing all of the clichéd stuff in a cosy bubble before bubbles became a claustrophobic lockdown term. We held dinner parties, birthday parties, movie trips, weekends away and drinks' gatherings. A load of us even went to the theatre, cinema and on holidays together. New families moved in with higher earnings, more lavish holidays multiple times a year, bigger salaries, second homes abroad, tennis courts, swimming pools, fishing lakes, £40,000 tree houses, thoroughbred horses and so on and I watched from the sidelines at how money changed our dynamic. Lots of our group suddenly started to 'pimp themselves out' to emulate more luxurious lifestyles and to win free invites to the villa in Cannes owned by one family.

Some of the friends were now becoming so materialistic/superficial – not everyone – but many. It was as though they only looked for their self-validation via money and status. One family had a huge house with an indoor pool, a tennis court and the tree-house, so then others – who already had the huge house – wanted a pool too, then the tennis court and the tree-house! Same with the holiday ratio per year; public schools; horses; private land; extra tutoring for children from the age of 5 years; Oxbridge expectations and so on. It was industrial-scale materialism.

Of course, there wasn't anything wrong with all of those individual things whatsoever but collectively a trend had taken root and it represented a very prescriptive and particular way to live life. I observed how it led to many beginning to feel inadequate and discontent with their lives when previously they'd been satisfied but they did not have the financial means to keep up, whilst others balked in their perceived superiority. Our expanding group of buddies which had initially started out as a safe, warm and fun group of people to spend time with, now started to feel a bit toxic, fake and riven with jealousy, insecurity and one-upmanship.

A couple of the new wealthier families were massively into supporting the local countryside shoot scene. One of the other women in our group absolutely despised shooting and hunting and all it stood for, but because she wanted to ingratiate herself with this new wealthy family, she told me: "I totally hate the shoot and all the hunting, but if Benedict asks me if I want tickets to go to the shoot and hunt ball and be on his table, then of course, I'll go". All of her principles flew out of the window in a sycophantic instant because she wanted to be part of Benedict's monied inner circle. The disingenuous behaviour continued but simultaneously, many of these people had been my long-time friends and yes, I did enjoy all the parties and getting glammed up as there was always something to look forward to.

My intuition told me that something was going to blow up soon with this group but I couldn't figure out what but I just knew that things were simmering towards a massive blow-out of some kind: it was like the feeling you get when you know a physical storm is brewing: you see the sky darken, the clouds become dense and oppressive, everything feels a bit ominous and you wait and wait because you know a storm is going to kick off in a big way… and I had that same sense with our group… but I tried to ignore all of these thoughts and reason it out in my mind: So people in my friendship group liked the nice things in life? Didn't we all. I could live with it. They were just aspirational.

Initially even as the group was morphing, I remained close to Jen and Ava (my two closest allies within it) and we shared pretty much everything… but then of course, my marriage died and I soon discovered that separation, single-parenthood and even worse, divorce (let alone Universal Credit and renting a tiny pad), were not compatible with my female 'friends'. Such social dynamics were unseemly.

***

Once my marriage imploded, I felt totally abandoned by those I most relied upon. It was weird, as my so-called female 'friends' would only give support jointly to me and my husband as a couple, not to me as an individual, which is what I really needed. Basically we were gossiped about and then many of our close friends just 'went to ground' and I felt as though I was a leper because I was about to leave my husband and no one spoke about it but they all knew and I could sense the disapproval! My closest friends who knew of our difficulties, completely evaporated. Ava had told me previously that if I needed to, I could move in with them and bring the children. However, when I finally left, I heard literally nothing from her for a week when she sent me a generic text advising that we both received counselling and then she fell silent. I felt utterly isolated. However, in addition I felt as though the words they did manage to text, implied their judgement that they felt my marriage break-up happened because I was working too much (but as a teacher, you don't choose to work all those extra hours, it's just unavoidable. I had to hold onto the truth of my situation). I also received ambivalent messages from Jen: "not sure how to help" followed by: "I care for you both" and: "I can't comment." Other messages Jen sent me were all about my husband, Saul, and supporting him.

I didn't know then that Jen had tried to get Saul to kiss her, behind my back, a few years' prior at a party. Thankfully he'd pushed her away (she wasn't seeking a peck on the cheek!) An hour earlier at that same party, she'd had a photo taken of her arms around me whilst telling me what a wonderful friend I was! She obviously had never 'had my back.' When I found out about this, her lack of support completely made sense and I thought back to all the times when she was overly-tactile with my husband and once again, my intuition had given me a prod but I'd tried to rationalise it then that she was just touch-feely. However, I now knew that basically, if my husband been 'up for an affair' with her, any thoughts of her friendship with me, would have completely dissipated: it just would've happened. I remembered a photo which I had on my phone of a beach trip where amidst the big gang of us in the picture, Jen had deliberately positioned herself next to my husband and draped her arm around him with a huge smile on her face… she wasn't next to her own husband. My ex hadn't done anything wrong in this regard, but I felt totally betrayed by Jen. I also felt that I was an idiot for not knowing at the time what she had been trying to do but absolutely no more! They could all fuck off now! I was done with the whole charade!

SONYA (ANOTHER PREDATORY NEW 'FRIEND')

And it hadn't just been Jen who had been making a play for my husband. A new bored housewife, Sonya, had moved nearby and I'd introduced her into our friendship group as she had children the same age and hadn't met other women locally: she said she was feeling marooned in the countryside. Sonya had a manic career as a newly-qualified vet and was married to a senior vet, Simon, and they had young children but she was restless and insecure. She needed lots of attention and her husband was completely absorbed in his work. Upon meeting Sonya, I'd immediately felt that for whatever reason, I needed to be cautious with her, but I wanted to be friendly and she seemed fun, which she was, but she had another side to her. Sonya basically made an unreciprocated play for my husband from not long after they were first introduced and often in front of me. I don't think this was because she was actually really interested in him 'in that way' though, but rather it was an alpha-female gesture I think, to boost her own ego. To know that if she wanted to, she could.

My husband and Sonya had had a disagreement not long before I left our family home but then she couldn't help excitedly gushing to me at the next opportunity that my husband had been "so sweet" in his apology to her: it was all about her and 'my' husband. I cringed. I found myself feeling that after being nice all the time on the surface, sometimes I just wanted to say how I truly felt. Back then I nearly told her where to go, but I gritted my teeth. Once before, Sonya had uttered earnestly, in my face at a children's play-date: "I love your husband so much, we have a thing" and I had just stood there incredulously listening to what she was saying about my husband whilst smiling as we do with that ridiculous English politeness. Why did I just stand there taking it? To be fair to him, I knew that he wasn't doing anything to encourage her and that he wasn't flirtatious with her but she was just like a heat-seeking missile and was bizarrely seeming to get a huge kick out of trying to rub my nose in her endeavours.

It was such a difficult situation because we were all interwoven within the same group of friends and if I spoke to Sonya of my concerns about her behaviour, I thought everything would 'blow up' and then news of it would travel around our big group of 'friends', so I bit my lip and stayed quiet.

SONYA - EARLIER THAT YEAR

In a text previously sent to me from Sonya earlier that year one evening, when she was drunk, she'd written: "your husband makes me laugh so much". I didn't really know how to react to Sonya's focus on my husband. It was true that our marriage was massively hitting the buffers but her making a play for him, right in my face, when we lived nearby each other and were all in the same friendship group, was making me feel awkward and unnerved. I couldn't really believe she was behaving like this as it was an anathema to me. Sonya even went out of her way to track down a rare music CD that my husband had told her he really wanted, and then she presented it to him as a private gift.

Sonya and my husband regularly came into contact with each other and so I had to trust them both, but now I felt uneasy. I confided in Jen and Ava at the time because they were my closest friends. They also revealed their own concerns at how Sonya was with their husbands too although not quite to the same level she was with mine, but Sonya's overly-flirtatious behaviour and comments about their respective husbands were unnerving them also. Jen and Ava didn't just complain about Sonya's behaviour but they used to complain individually to me about each other and I used to think if they're saying this to me, behind each other's backs, they must also be bitching about me to them... I knew it was all becoming unhealthy and I didn't want to be in it, but I felt trapped.

Sonya organised a huge Valentine's Ball at a big country estate and as the DJ started his set, she pulled my husband up onto the dance floor to provocatively grind-up against him. I was told he looked uncomfortable about this and I guessed that this was to get a reaction out of us both and everyone else. Sonya wanted me to witness this because afterwards she'd apparently rushed up to mutual friends and asked if I'd seen it all, but at that point, I wasn't even in close proximity. When I heard this, I felt a mix of emotions because by then, although I knew my marriage was over, it was still such a toxic situation to be in. I felt that Sonya was making herself look a bit desperate not just for my husband's attention but anyone's. I felt sorry for her husband too, because he must have felt that she emasculated him sometimes. Furthermore I felt completely disrespected as a fellow woman. Looking back, it was all a bit surreal as at that same party, another married husband from our group, made a pass at me when his wife had taken their children home. I brushed him off and then he tried to say it was all a big joke but it was all a bit of a hot mess when combined with me approaching the end of my marriage.

SONYA, JEN AND AVA

Towards the end of the year, it became very clear that Jen and Ava had completely withdrawn their friendship towards me. I got the odd text but despite them living just a few miles away, they didn't suggest meeting up. I literally felt ghosted. My husband had to go away to deal with some family business and I'd been managing everything by myself whilst he was away.

Our eldest came back from Uni for a few days in his absence and I rushed him to/from the train station; one of our younger children had a birthday and I was dashing around for that and then I was back at school teaching, driving here and there and organising impromptu childcare, whilst simultaneously working out how to leave my marriage. Whilst my husband was away, one of our cats became very poorly and I had to rush him into the emergency vet one evening which cost hundreds of pounds which I had to borrow from my parents and then in my stressed state, I reversed into a wall and broke a back car light and had to get that fixed... my angst mounted.

My 'friend' Jen then sent me a text saying how 'uncomfortable' she felt hearing anything I had to say about my marriage coming to an end, whilst Ava simply retreated. I thought it was both bizarre and weird because they were my two closest friends and God knew that I was fully in the loop about lots of dysfunction in their own marriages because they offloaded to me regularly and included the most intimate of stuff. I felt abandoned and hurt because this was when I absolutely needed them the most, but my gut feelings told me that something wasn't okay with them, so I stopped honestly confiding in them and instead turned to a couple of long-term friends outside of that intense friendship group. Ironically, it was Sonya, who I happened to bump into in a local shop (but who I had pulled back from), who told me that Jen and Ava were annoyed that I was no longer confiding in them. Basically, they were missing the gossip.

I didn't know it then but life was about to turn very nasty in a manner that only scorned women could conjure up.

***

Not long after my husband returned to our family home from being away, our kids had returned to their usual routines and I was teaching again at school and under pressure with the marking, lesson prep and so on, but in addition, I was now also quietly trying to plan my escape. It had become clear for several large reasons that our marriage was definitely over and that I needed to move out as soon as possible. Yet doing this was tricky because I had so little time to make enquiries, start looking for rental properties and everything else involved when I was up against constant teaching deadlines and trying to run my home, look after the kids and pretend that everything was normal (looking back, I honestly don't know how I kept it all together at that time! It's no wonder I crashed and burnt later!) All of this felt like such a mammoth task and I'd never been responsible for my own place before as I'd always house-shared before getting married, so I felt a bit out of my depth but nonetheless, I couldn't even think about it as I just had to do it.

A few weeks' before the Easter holiday, I discovered that Jen had drunkenly blurted out to my husband that I was going to leave him. She hadn't been able to help herself after they stumbled across each other outside a pub one evening as she was on her way home from a dinner party and he'd popped out to get a few basics. Jen had thrown her arms around his shoulders and in an inebriated mess, had impulsively gabbled out to my husband: "I probably shouldn't tell you this but you know she's leaving you". So before I'd even found anywhere to rent or picked the right moment to properly tell my husband and our boys what I was going to do, my so-called best friend had whipped the rug out from under my feet and deliberately revealed my plans to my husband. After it happened, I thought a lot about her motive for doing this and settled on it probably being her warped attempt to create intimacy and the sense of a shared-secret between the two of them.

Horrible scenes ensued that weekend because I was now forced to have really stressful conversations with all of my family and rush the moving-out process. My eldest son was aware of the situation: he had recently asked me the rhetorical question, during a car journey, of: "you're going to leave dad aren't you?" and I'd had to be honest with him, but our younger children were still shocked. It really helped at that moment that I had already been able to get free legal advice regarding the children so I knew my rights as that topic immediately came up.

It was such a difficult time and I couldn't believe that something so personal and private which I'd shared with Jen in absolute confidence a few months' before, i.e. that I was actually going to move out of the family home and leave my husband, had now been used by her deliberately to pole-axe everything. We were going to have a very tense Easter as at that point we were all living under the same roof knowing that after the holiday, our family was splitting up! I'd been hoping to tell everyone in the summer once exam-season was over and I was planning to move out then, to get the Easter hols out of the way first and also so that I could try to get some more money together as a safety net, because financially, everything felt scary and precarious.

Furthermore, I also needed the extra time to find a place to rent which was impossible when I was teaching all week and marking/lesson-prepping in the evenings and over the weekends. It felt like such a huge deal to survive all of this. Meanwhile my Line Manager was putting pressure on me at work regarding marking nearly 70 Mock Exam papers over the school holidays saying: "I need the data the first day back after the holidays". Sometimes internally I felt as though my brain was about to explode!

***

I was later told that I should've ploughed through all of the exam papers during the end of term but because the school term was always so manic and as teachers, we were constantly 'chasing our tails' with lesson-planning, meetings, admin and the day-to-day workload when in school, the only time to catch up with the enormous marking-load, was in the holidays. Other teachers had to do the same and complained about this too as it depleted their family time during the school vacations because they had to shut themselves away for hours/days to mark endless exam papers and unnecessary assessments. It wasn't just me in this situation with the relentless workload.

On that Easter Sunday with us all together as a family and with my impending exit looming, water started to drip through the ceiling of our family home onto the kitchen table in the middle of our dinner. It felt like an ominous sign. Miraculously in the space of a weekend, I managed to find a little place to rent and get everything organised. I would be moving out of my family home just before I returned to school for the summer term. I had such mixed feelings about this. It was absolutely the necessary thing to do but it's so massive to finally part with your husband of a few decades and your family house and I knew that our children would be split between two homes now.

Half-way through that strained Easter break, my husband and I went to another mutual friend, Isobel's, party. This woman was another member of our friendship group and her gathering was being held in a beautiful medieval coaching inn. As I walked in, it felt like entering a saloon in an American Western film where everyone turns around from the bar, stares you out and then turns their backs on you. This is what happened to me: the women (my closest former friends in the friendship group including Jen and Ava and others), all huddled together, completely ignoring me. They were making a very powerful but silent statement that I had been judged unworthy by them and that I was now being frozen-out. It literally felt like being the most unpopular teenage girl at school. I was floored. I'd been trying to steel myself to move out of the family home and I needed support, but instead I was getting publicly ostracised. In fact, much worse was to come from these women.

Thus as I was being openly ghosted at that party: the women continued to giggle together, looking disdainfully over their shoulders at me. It felt as though they were part of a malevolent witch's coven. A couple of the husbands came over to me to make small talk, obviously sensing the nasty atmosphere. I felt so awkward, humiliated and embarrassed. I had no idea where my husband had gone to and I could no longer rely on him for moral support anyway. Suddenly I felt incredibly alone: there wasn't anyone there to prop me up.

However, then Sonya suddenly stormed over to me whilst I was sat at a table with one of the few women who were still talking to me and whilst the latter got up to order drinks, Sonya seized her moment. Clearly angry, she stood over me, wagging her finger in my face as she spewed out: "I hear you've been calling me a slut". It was a rhetorical question. My heart was pounding. She hadn't finished and was off on a poisonous torrent: "You've been saying that I'm after your husband. That I have a thing for friends' husbands!!" (I thought back to the day when I first met her and red flags had waved in my head saying: 'you need to beware of this woman!' but I had overrode that initial gut reaction because I thought I was being overly cautious).

I remained weirdly calm as she ranted at me. I told her that Isobel's party wasn't the time or place for this, but she was incensed and I was cornered. Her voice was raised, everyone had deserted us. She was firing off accusations and the metaphorical gloves were now off, so I retorted:

"I told Jen and Ava in total confidence about your messages regarding Saul because they made me feel uncomfortable and I didn't know how to handle it. I never called you a slut. I didn't expect them to tell anyone else."

Sonya had shouted back: "why didn't you speak to ME?"

"Because you're so volatile" I replied.

She continued firing off but I shut it down saying: "it's not what you do to your girlfriends but I'm not discussing it here" and I walked off, trembling and feeling so stressed because I hate confrontation and especially in front of other people.

Sonya was clearly extremely angry. A couple of other female friends in my group then stepped forward to check that I was okay (a few years' later, out of that whole circle of 'friends' of about 14 couples, I remain good friends with just one of those women only – I virtually lost everything through the end of my marriage and school implosions. However what followed eventually was a complete rebuilding of me, in a sense; the beginning of my whole new life).

I left that party with my stomach churning. A realisation dawned: I knew that everything had irrevocably changed and there would be no going back in terms of my former 'friendships' and social life: everything that I knew and that was familiar and comfortable, was well and truly over. I would be pretty much alone. I remember walking home crying and my kids all giving me a hug and one of them threatening to confront Sonya.

I didn't know then that Sonya would attempt to wreak further revenge with a malicious rumour… or that Ava had gone out of her way to whisper in my husband's ear that night: "don't make things easy for her" [I.e, the 'her' being me, regarding our impending separation]. Goodness, I had expected maybe some awkwardness from my 'girlfriends' but not such a targeted assassination. Three days later, I underwent the stressful process of moving out of the family home which was a huge tug on my heartstrings but I had to be strong.

***

I later heard that a few months' after I'd moved out of my family home, at the wedding of a more distant member of my former friendship group (which I couldn't go to because it would've caused issues), that Sonya's drunken husband, Simon, tried to hit my ex-husband along with several other people, late in the evening. Things took a more sinister turn, because as the row progressed and escalated into a walled courtyard, an equally-drunken Sonya fell onto the ground, proferring her hand up to her husband, Simon, asking him to help get her back onto her feet. However, in Simon's inebriated and exasperated state, he accidentally ended-up dragging his wife across the rough, stony ground for several yards until his cognitive powers kicked in and he realised that his wife and onlookers were screaming at him to STOP because her back was raw!… Someone was about to call the police…

Afterwards as Sonya was helped, she mumbled vitriol about me, my husband, the friendship group, and then said that it was her fault that her husband had hurt her in this way because she didn't spend enough time with him. It was all pretty messed-up and I was glad I was out of it… although I knew the friend- comedown was going to be really tough as I'd loved all the social stuff we used to do.

THE FALL-OUT OF OSTRACISM

Being ostracised from my former friendship group was really difficult in lots of ways: when I went to collect my younger children from primary school, my former girlfriends would congregate in a large gaggle and ignore me and they did the same that summer at the local park. I'd have to walk past them all sitting in a group together and I would get stared out. It was just like my experience at the birthday party where Sonya had stormed over to me. I couldn't invite most of my youngest children's schoolfriends over, because I couldn't contact their parents now. They made it apparent they didn't want to hear from me. If my youngest children were in the car with me, these former friends would wave at my children, whereas if I was driving by myself in my car, I would be ignored. It was a horrible situation and later I stopped looking for any recognition or friendliness from them as I grew mentally stronger. However, I was going through all of this 'friend' ostracism during my school implosion.

This adult ostracism has been one of the most bizarre aspects of the last few years. Almost a desire to publicly shame and humiliate but now I rarely give it a minute's thought. I've only reflected again for the purposes of this interview. I realise I would have outgrown them all because they lack emotional intelligence. I definitely don't want to hang-out with bigoted, superficial people; instead I like warm, genuine, fun, non-judgemental, bohemian types and I have now finally found them… my life implosions have led me to my tribe and it's absolutely the best thing (although I should just add that a couple of the husbands of my former 'friendship' group do talk to me when they're by themselves and they always try to be completely kind and sincere. I'm grateful to them for this).

After I left my marriage, rumours continued to circulate about our family. On one occasion when I had to see my husband, he said that one of my former friend's husbands had relayed to him: 'They say they don't know how to treat her [me] since she left you.' I was a bit dumbfounded when I heard this. I also started to get snubbed by some of the husbands (obviously not those mentioned in the previous paragraph). I heard about parties that I wasn't invited to any more and I dreaded going to school plays, concerts and other local events, where I knew they would all be too and would blank me or just be weird with me. Combined with my ongoing very difficult divorce, it was a truly, truly horrible time but I tried to power through it. One of the husbands had a dig at me in a passive-aggressive way one night when we both went to collect our respective daughters from an after-school ballet class, saying that he wouldn't ever let his wife talk to me again otherwise I might: "put flighty ideas in her head" (this couple don't talk to me any more – they sided with my husband). Normally this husband and I used to have a laugh, but I could see he was a bit nervous with me now because I was an unknown quantity. Previously they knew I'd been unhappy in my marriage but they never thought I'd do anything about it and I was viewed as the easiest-going of all of the wives, thus the shocking fact that I had left my husband, meant that anyone could take this action and therefore all relationships needed fresh scrutiny. All relationships were vulnerable.

This isolating backlash was so hard for me to cope with, that in order to attempt to understand it, I googled what I was experiencing and I learnt about the fear of 'divorce contagion': where the fact that you've made a break from an unhappy relationship, makes the couples around you jittery, as it highlights the flaws, cracks and insecurities in their own relationships. Married/partnered-friends who are nervous of divorce contagion, pull back because you've become incendiary: they're worried you could spread the desire to call time on toxic marriages and relationships. I did cry a lot in private as I struggled to comprehend what my life had become (I felt I'd suddenly become an island, cast adrift from everything I knew), and I couldn't obviously talk to my kids about it because I didn't want them to feel more conflicted than they already felt.

LEAVING MY FAMILY HOME

Incredibly, literally after praying in desperation and just before I had to move out of my family home, I received a completely unexpected small inheritance which gave me enough money for a deposit and a few months' rental payments, so in-between teaching, I immediately set about finding a pad! This money came exactly when I needed it! In my head at this point, I had basically already left my marriage and my family home – I had had to detach.

The small place I found to rent was perfect! In order for the 2 bedrooms to be shared by my kids, I ended up sleeping in the attic and had to pull down a rickety ladder to reach it but I just felt lucky to have obtained it! This pad had such a happy atmosphere, was tastefully decorated with lots of quirky features and it had a cute fenced garden. Furthermore my landlord kindly agreed to let me have my two dogs, Ross and Rosa there, so it was wonderful! My parents said they would act as my guarantors. I just had to get all of the practicalities organised.

This was a mammoth mission as I hadn't been responsible for a property ever fully on my own before. Previously I'd lived with my parents, then in a rented flat as part of a community, then in house-shares and latterly with my Ex and our children. In my new rental property, I had my landlord but otherwise I was responsible for sorting everything out!

Over that Easter holiday, I was organising removals' men, wifi, services, buying things I desperately needed, applying online for the benefits I now needed to rely on (hopefully temporarily), trying to navigate a difficult atmosphere in our old family home as obviously I was about to move out, plus I was trying to mark so many GCSE mock exam papers and a couple hundred other school assessments… I don't really know how I did it, but somehow I did, all on adrenalin, and I built some of my own furniture too, which I'm still very proud of!

As cited before, it was a huge emotional wrench to leave my beloved family home with its gorgeous old quirks, my shepherd's hut and also, as I was only taking my two dogs, I had to say goodbye to the other one, Myrtle and our cats as I couldn't take them. Although our place was a bit ramshackle when we'd moved in a long time before, it was the kind of place I'd always dreamt of living in. It had a gorgeous garden with a big pond and a Greek goddess fountain and we had lots of wild flowers growing too. I used to wander around it in floaty dresses, picking flowers to put in jugs and trying to track down where the chickens had laid their eggs as they liked to sabotage our expectations of actually nesting in their hen-house but once again I had to mentally detach myself from it all as I could not let myself look back! This was not the time to be sentimental. (Later, it was the little details that I really missed sometimes such as the clucking sounds which the chickens made, but I wouldn't allow myself to reflect very much then because I had to keep focusing on survival and on the future).

I'd received a lot of judgement from our friendship group for leaving my marriage but if only they knew how hard this decision was for me! Again as said previously, anyone who thinks it's an easy choice to walk away from your lovely home and to leave all that you know, your sanctuary, your pets and so on… is completely ignorant. You absolutely never choose to take this course of action unless you have to and have tried every other method first to try to work things out. One of my girlfriends who'd been through the same process before me, said: "just remember it's only bricks and mortar" and that helped because if a relationship has completely broken down and is irretrievable, then the love's gone out of that home too, the soul of the home has already left. However, it was still very traumatic, but I just had to grit my teeth because there wasn't any other choice.! I absolutely had to keep looking forward.

My wonderful parents came up to help me move everything out and then that evening, like other evenings over that school holiday, I was having to mark Mock Exam papers (and the next few days and evenings too), because I was about to return to school. I still find it a bit upsetting that even though my Line Manager knew that I was moving out of my family home over the school holidays because of my divorce, there was no offer to help with the huge pile of exam papers I had to mark, but just a flippant and insensitive: "have a nice holiday" as if having to leave my husband/home and simultaneously do marking/lesson prep was going to be nice! (This is when I think a lot of schools completely lose the human touch. They pay lip service to you as a member of staff – you are a cog in the wheel - and then when you're having a really horrendous time, they don't reach out at all pastorally; they don't value you enough to follow anything up).

I think many schools are like this because they are basically businesses and are so intent on positive data and upward trajectories that they forget that support staff, teachers and pupils are all individuals… people! We are NOT just conduits for superior results on league tables. They ignore the fact that these life events – i.e. having to leave your husband after a long, long marriage, having to share your youngest children, walking away from your lovely family home and leaving some of your pets behind, during a school holiday, are absolutely MASSIVE - they warrant more than just a robotic grin and: 'I'm sorry about what you're going through but you know I need all the exam papers marked for the first day back after the holidays' - that's just morally inept and deeply insensitive! If I come face-to-face with my former Line Manager and Leadership Team in the future, there is so much that I will be articulating to them. Expecting a person to mark hundreds of assessments and mock exams over a 2-week holiday whilst they are experiencing the turbulent ending of their marriage and are having to move out of their family home AND are then moving lock, stock and barrel into a new house and trying to set everything up and have some kind of rest (I didn't!) with traumatised children in tow, all in the space of 14 days, is HUGE! It was extremely stressful and felt an impossible nightmare. The whole situation completely overwhelmed me!)

Teachers are not just throwaway pawns in the system of quantifiable performance and what constitutes 'performance' is subjective anyway. It's no wonder that so many teachers quit the profession and escape after just a few years' because their life becomes completely consumed by teaching and the despair at not being able to get a handle on the impossible workload, or they just get bitter and burnt out. The whole nature of teaching/teachers' workloads in England, must be reassessed and recalibrated urgently if the government want to retain incredible educators for more than an average of 5 years' post training.

***

Post-separation

The following year was one of huge adjustments:

For a start my friendship group had pretty much completely gone. During the month that followed, setting up my new home whilst being back at work teaching, was pretty challenging: not just with the bigger things but all the little things too such as tracking down my meters, unblocking drains, getting aerials to work when they wouldn't, calling out engineers and trying to suss out when I could possibly be at home to sync their visits and so on, but I just kept telling myself, I can fucking do this! I was determined to succeed, however low and tired I sometimes felt. I would not be beaten!

Also it was so weird when occasionally I returned to my old former home to drop off post for my husband that had been mistakenly directed to my new address, because I found myself darting to its letterbox pushing the misdirected letters through whilst feeling like a trespasser and I wanted to leave as soon as I could. It was bizarre, because it was as though I had never actually lived there. You're now an interloper but once upon a time, (for many years in my case), it had been my home.

Having my own sanctuary though, did gradually help me to reconfigure my life but it was still tough! I was having to dig really deep and I didn't really think of it then but I was actually about to experience a period of personal growth in having to move on with my life in huge ways without any of my former security structures: my home, marriage, friends, family structure etc, because all of this had completely gone... and yes, I really struggled and this led to my school implosion...

Highs and lows of that year

The highs included some fun stuff: I took part in a large, exciting charity event in a UK city, also I budgeted like mad to go to a music festival and I attended a prestigious Science Conference and I participated in a hardcore military-style weekend boot-camp to challenge myself, again for charity. The latter involved crawling through filthy tunnels, wading through stagnant pools and slithering along the ground under netting and I loved it! All of these situations which put me out of my comfort zone, simultaneously gave me such a lift during what was an intensely difficult period.

In addition, during that summer school holiday, I managed to take a few weeks' off from school prep to try to blitz all of my stuff in my lovely rented home that I'd hastily shoved literally anywhere and everywhere when I'd moved in so quickly early in the New Year. I took a couple of days out to walk cliff paths with my dogs, visit exhibitions in a couple of different cities and catch up with friends and my parents whilst my ex took the children on holiday.

Throughout this year too when I was teaching at school, my brilliant students sussed that I was having a difficult time and were so warm and appreciative of my lessons (I obviously didn't ever reveal what was really going on but there were a few brief moments where they sensed I was facing challenges). I tried to be a bubbly energetic teacher with them and they responded well. Their happy upbeat energy enabled us to have dynamic lessons. I organised quite a few charity and science events at school and my students got behind all of these 100%! They were really enthusiastic in their endeavours to help and I was hugely buoyed up by their energetic support. Ultimately my students then, were giving the support that I wasn't getting in any other areas of my life (my parents had obviously supported me, but I didn't want to lean on them too heavily as they were semi-retired and I didn't want to worry them).

I had some continued lows and these were mainly related to the ongoing divorce. In addition, for me, money was a constant source of stress because it was so expensive to run a house by myself. I was on Universal Credit before it became a lockdown thing because my teaching wages were so low and having teens in the house, ongoing car problems and a difficult divorce - all equated to lots of expense. My amazing family solicitor let me pay small monthly instalments until my divorce completed, because there was no way I could pay all of his bills at the time. I was simultaneously trying to apply for child maintenance. However, even applying for child maintenance takes time and that was time when I was meant to be marking, preparing lessons, working… aaagh!!! Inwardly, I was permanently stressed during that year, so much, even if I hid it well.

Also the process of getting divorced [this was before the 'no-fault divorce' was introduced in the UK], is a huge time-consuming slog in itself! It involves (or it did back then), finding lots of documents, having meetings, writing down accounts of what's happened plus there are lots of emails and telephone calls and forms to fill in… divorce is a massive task in itself. It took a great amount of effort and I used to dread receiving any emails relating to it, even though I had a fantastic lawyer acting for me… but everything people say about divorce is true: it is incredibly stressful!

I thought I was holding it all together with the distractions of endless work, gym sessions and rushing around. All of this mayhem stopped me thinking about the trauma of my marriage break-up, uprooting from my family home, having some time apart each week from my boys and the subsequent loss of my decade-long social group.

WHEN THINGS START TO SNOWBALL…

But then things got worse: my finances were getting stretched even further because my bank called in my student overdraft which was over £1000; my car - which had amassed over 100,000 miles - started to break-down unpredictably with increasing frequency which was a nightmare as I had a lengthy commute to school every teaching day and I couldn't move closer to my job as my boys were so settled at their local schools and they had to be in close proximity to both myself and my Ex to be able to stay at both of our respective homes each week. Then my Utilities company said that they had underestimated my gas and electric bills so I owed them an additional £800... aaagh! The stress kept ramping up!! Things were so desperate, that one kindly female teaching colleague left money for me in the Science office so that I always had the financial means to fall back on to buy petrol to get home if I was totally skint. I really appreciated that utterly practical, kind gesture. It is a good deed that really stands out from that difficult time and as a side-note, I can tell you that I remember the names of each and every person who really put themselves forward to support me over that difficult time and at some point I will repay the favour by doing something to help them too! Conversely it is impossible to forget (not in a bitter way – but just in a learning-curve manner), those who completely dropped-me and/or treated me appallingly at that point.

That following winter felt a bit pitiful and not just for the big reasons but for other seemingly insignificant reasons too, which combined with everything else, made me feel completely overwhelmed! For example, I didn't have a tumble-drier and couldn't afford to buy one (I'd had to leave my former one in the family home), so drying towels when there was constant rain was difficult. I put them on radiators but they would start to smell before they were properly dry and I was trying not to have the heating on for too long because I worried about the bills, so that necessitated a very depressing trip to the launderette at weekends. First I would have to go into shops so I could get the right coins to operate the dryers and then whilst sat in front of the machines finally watching my towels get blitzed, I couldn't even read a book or a magazine to make it more bearable as I would be balanced on the flimsy benches hunched over, ploughing through a seemingly-ever bigger pile of school marking!! What had my life come to?

Counting out coppers to buy milk and bread happened sometimes too... I asked my employers at the school via email, to check that I was on the right teaching pay band as I was certain that they hadn't moved me up to the correct one, but I didn't hear anything back. I emailed a few times and tried to speak to the Finance Director but no responses from anyone. I was teaching virtually a 0.7 fte on £16k per annum. It entailed 6 days a week of working (including all the marking and prep at home) for so little pay. £400 of my monthly wage went on petrol to get to school. I kept telling myself that at some point the divorce would be over and financially things would ease. I was trying to hold it all together, to keep going...

Christmas was approaching: money was really tight as the divorce was biting; my car was getting worse and worse: in the space of 6 weeks, I'd had to call out a car breakdown service 7x to fix it because it overheated, then the clutch and gearbox went and then it kept losing power at totally random times when I was driving it and it would just grind to a halt, always midway between home and a destination. Literally every time I went to drive it, I said a prayer that I would get to my destination because frequently breaking down, especially in the dark in country lanes or on the motorway, at night-time, was really stressful. Once, when it overheated during these weeks, it was in the middle of a massive traffic jam on a motorway and 4 x warning lights were simultaneously flashing bright red on my dashboard but I was in the middle lane, boxed-in by traffic on either side of me and I couldn't get to the hard shoulder. I turned off the engine every time the traffic jam paused to try to cool the engine, my heart pounding - because I thought my car was going to catch fire! I was so frazzled!!! That night, after calling out the breakdown service yet again!! - I got home at 9pm and had to start marking/lesson planning then…

I didn't want to have to ask my parents to borrow any more money for repairs and I had no idea how much longer my divorce was going to continue for. They'd already lent me money to get a new clutch and gearbox and other basics and I couldn't face asking for more. I felt embarrassed because I felt as though I was at an age where I should be treating them to the finer things in life and taking them out for meals etc, whereas instead, the reality was that I was desperately having to ask them to lend me money and I felt ashamed at this.

I reached a new low one December evening that Christmas when I found myself marking year 7 assessments under strip-lights, standing up in a petrol station kitchen (they had no chairs), as I waited nearly 2 hours from 6.30-8.30pm for a car engineer to come and fix my broken-down car which I'd managed to somehow get to 'crawl' in the wind and the rain at about 5 mph to a garage forecourt as my car's engine kept cutting out, again on my way back home from school. By the time I finally got through my front door, it was 10pm but before I'd finally got my car back on the road, the car-repair engineer told me it might play up again, so not knowing if my wheels were going to give out after he'd waved me goodbye until I got back to my place during that wild windy night, simply added to my stress. I felt totally at my wits' end and I just cried in my car. I'd had enough!

I only had pennies in my account until payday and had to pawn jewellery that I couldn't affort to buy back, to survive. I'd also taken on extra private science tutoring to help me financially but then this required that I did additional prep work on top of all my normal teaching work because a separate exam board was involved as opposed to the exam board that we used at my school (we taught a different syllabus)…

I was absolutely shattered and felt a bit defeated: wondering when anything was going to get better?! When I told my Line Manager about my financial situation and having to take on extra tutoring too, that person glibly said, insensitively: "well just think of all the extra money you'll get". Despite the fact that they had a family too so one would hope there would be empathy there, that person was so caught up in their own ambitious career trajectory, that as long as I produced the data on time and turned up every day to teach, my personal difficulties were an irrelevance. Conversely, the lady who asked me to tutor her daughter was so considerate however, paying me upfront for 10 x lessons in order that I had a lump sum of money to afford to service my car (things were that desperate!) I couldn't even sell my car to get something more reliable as it was owned via a lease agreement through my Ex's employers so it wasn't even my car to sell… aaagh!

I was getting to a point where I wondered just how much more I could take but I was also touched that there were people out there who didn't really know me very well yet were still incredibly kind such as the female teacher who left the petrol money for me in the Science office and the mum whose daughter I was tutoring! I was very grateful for these gestures! As stated before, such kind acts – even the smallest ones - always stay with you.

Work overload, constant stress and my school
implosion

During the early months of the following year, I was marking early mock exam papers and when my eldest son was visiting briefly from Uni, I had to tell him that I had to shut myself away for a bit to get more marking done otherwise I'd simply never get them all completed. I felt really guilty for doing this but I just had so many papers to get through: there was zero flexibility to this. I also had 90 x Year 8 assessments and 60 x Year 7 assessments to mark plus lessons to prepare and also now, private tutoring lessons. I felt snowed. Totally, totally overwhelmed and demoralised by everything…

Also I went into my Bank to ask if my overdraft could temporarily be increased until my divorce went through (I could provide proof of the latter plus my potential settlement etc). I had a long 2-hour session with a female Customer Services Assistant and I ended up crying because all they would do was pause the interest on the overdraft on my current account which would only save me a few pounds per month – nothing more. (I obviously didn't have any savings because all of my inheritance money had been used to move out of the family home and set up my rental property in the first place and just survive).

During this 2-hour bank appointment, I'd had to list all of my outgoings and income and the Bank Assistant made various phone calls, telling me her personal life stories in between but everything was seemingly okay for her so I felt myself getting internally stressed because I could've been using that precious Bank appointment time that I was effectively wasting, to undertake more marking, but it felt as though I was squandering it in an institution that was too corporate to care. It was humiliating as it was a bit of a dehumanising and patronising experience (I was picking up a kind of: "why can't you manage your money?" vibe).

I received a similar reception when I called my Utilities' company re: my gas/electric bills. I was talking to a young guy on their switchboard who literally had no idea about electricity and gas-use when you're running a household with teenagers during a bitterly-cold winter in part of the country where the weather is often harsh! When you're well-educated and clearly having hard times economically which are outside-of-your-control, but you're still treated like a dumb idiot, it's so demeaning and insulting!… I was now having to dig really deep to keep any kind of spirits up. However, I tried! I got involved in a charity trampoline event, which was fun and for a good cause and I thought to myself, I can keep going… somehow!!! I'm not quitting yet… But it was two of my sons' birthdays and I didn't really have anything to give them much as my car needed a new engine.

I felt myself sink into a pit of despair.

Thus it was at the end of this time following a short school holiday and a few days before I was due to return to school that my school 'episode' happened. I was at my wits' end after marking every single day over the holidays. I was feeling completely overwhelmed with the whole build-up of ongoing divorce stress, serious money angst, worrying about my car, the relentless work burden, friend ostracism and I was mentally and physically exhausted….

and I just cracked!

I felt that Jack would understand the teaching pressure I was under from the other side of the spectrum as there was huge pressure on us both. I had tried to get hold of my colleagues but none were available and I just needed to offload and I needed someone to listen.

Obviously I should NOT have offloaded to Jack via text - this is just simply a no! However erudite an A-level student is (and Jack was very erudite), teachers have to keep separate perimeters from their students. At the time, I felt completely defeated by everything and I had lost sight of important boundaries: I was about to return to school after this 'holiday' but I hadn't been able to have any rest. I was so incredibly tired of battling everything by myself but was simultaneously trying to psyche myself up for another exhausting round of teaching, my ongoing difficult divorce and all my other very-real worries and I just didn't think through the consequences of my actions for all parties involved and that was absolutely flawed!!

Once we were back at school having messaged each other a few days before, Jack and I were suddenly, understandably both a bit awkward with each other in class initially but then we had a chat to clear the air. We said that we would try to continue as normally as we possibly could at school but I would hand in my notice very soon to start a Science research project as it was clear that I couldn't stay in school any longer but I needed a job to go to first with a wage, in order that I could pay my rent to keep a roof over my children's heads whilst my divorce continued.

Feeling mentally 'shot to pieces' I certainly didn't want any kind of teaching/ school job: I just felt numb and needed headspace from everything so I applied for basic admin jobs and was going through interviews for these outside of my school role, when the whole school situation with Jack blew up! Had it not blown up and had I left school beforehand to start an admin post and my academic research, then I am 100% convinced that I still would've officially declared what had happened with Jack otherwise I would have had such a guilty conscience. I know I would have wanted to do the right thing. Anyway as it happened, although Jack and I managed to get our equilibrium back a few weeks' later and continue working together professionally at school before I was going to leave anyway, matters were totally taken out of my hands...

Before I describe how my school situation imploded, I want to add that this situation – on top of the divorce - did completely upend my life at the time - but it wasn't sought by me... it just arose and since then, I have taken steps to manage my work and stress levels to make sure that I don't ever cross any inappropriate boundaries again. As said previously, I realise that I ended up perceiving Jack as an equal person to me, as opposed to seeing him as one of my students, which I know with hindsight, was completely wrong.

When you're going through a horrible time and someone makes you feel valued every time you see them because you get on really well with each other, it's a massive lift but obviously in my situation as a teacher, that's just not allowed and I have always fully accepted responsibility for this. I hold my hands up. I unintentionally crossed a red line and it's totally right that I've had to go through the official procedures afterwards to explain my actions and take the rap. However, I have to add that the procedures are made to be as stressful and brutalising as they possibly can be and that puts huge pressure on the mental health of those going through the process. You are very much left on your own to deal with it all – you cannot go to your legal team with your constant anxieties over it – because of the escalating fees. This is why I turned to my new friends who were so supportive. This is also why I had to write about it all in this book and express my view that these situations/ramifications should be discussed in a pragmatic, intelligent and realistic manner, as part of the formal training process in any professional role where boundaries might at any given point, become unintentionally and unexpectedly blurred.

I will always view Jack as an incredible person who will have a very successful future. Somehow in my head, I have been able to separate him and the brilliant experience of teaching him and all of the fantastic, supportive students there - from the stressful aftermath - which I am really relieved about, because I didn't want my whole time at that school or my teaching prior to being there, to feel tainted after I had to leave under a cloud on top of my other life implosions.

***

Our message-exchange came out soon after because a third-party found out about them and anonymously informed the Leadership team (I saw copies of all documentation later on so I knew exactly who had done/said/typed/written anything regarding me). Jack stayed quiet about it until he was officially confronted at school. That weekend, I'd had a day away on a sailing course which I'd been given as a gift. Again, I should have been marking, but it was a welcome escape from all the recent stress! I didn't think I'd be any good at sailing but with lots of encouragement on the day and some determination, I thoroughly enjoyed it! Little did I know how much I would have to channel that same determination during the coming weeks, months and years to survive the fall-out after my school situation.

The day before I was dismissed, Jack came to find me to warn me and to think of excuses to protect me but I knew I would have to accept the consequences and that this would result in the end of my teaching career and my time at that school. I immediately thought how much I would miss my amazing students, as they were/are incredible people! It was a mess. How had I got myself into this situation?

My intuition had told me that this would end badly and as usual, my intuition proved to be accurate. That evening, in a state of stress, I met up with a girlfriend and talked everything through. I didn't want to go into school the following day but trying to call in sick didn't feel an option either because teaching is one of the few professions where calling in sick necessitates a whole lot more work than if you just turn up (because you still have to prep and send in all your lessons from home), plus I knew I had to face the music. Despite everything, bizarrely in this situation, I still felt really conscientious about not leaving anyone in the lurch if I failed to go in (I think I was burying my head in the sand and pretending that the metaphorical tsunami heading my way, was only in my imagination), so I turned up as usual, but of course, my stomach was in huge knots as I sensed what was coming.

BEING PUBLICLY MARCHED-OUT

The following afternoon during the middle of a lesson, two teachers, one wearing a high-viz top, walked in to my class and told me to pack everything up. One took over my lesson whilst some of my students clocked that something weird was going on and they suddenly asked what was happening? I tried to pacify them and said that I had to go to a meeting and that one of these teachers would continue their lesson. I quickly gathered up all of my stuff, carrying it with me as I was marched out of my classroom and then publicly marched across the whole school site to the Head's Office. It felt like a medieval shaming.

I was read a formal notice by the Headmaster, who was accompanied by an Assistant Head and the Safeguarding lead. I just felt numb, on auto-pilot. I almost couldn't believe that this was happening to me. It felt like an atomic bomb was going off in my life. In a fear-instilling way, the Head strongly urged me to speak to my Teaching Union Rep as soon as possible to get legal help, but I'd not even been able to afford to join a Teaching Union and as of that moment, I didn't even have a laptop any more as 'my' laptop belonged to the school and was immediately seized. I couldn't really take everything in… things felt as bad as they could possibly get but of course they were going to get a lot worse…

Next the Assistant-Head walked me to my car. Everything I said to that person in the minutes they accompanied me were memorised by them and later included in the formal disciplinary processes. On the way home, my emotions were a complete roller-coaster: lots of tears, maybe some relief for all kinds of reasons because I'd been carrying such a lot of baggage for a long time. Driving home, everything that I'd been going through: dealing with a stressful divorce, pressurised workload, money angst, being a new single mum, having been ostracised from my former long-term friendship group, the scary unknown ramifications of having Jack's support - all came out in big sobs. My life was now a complete disaster… Would my car even get me home okay? (However, for once it complied. Thank God it did, because if my car had broken down on that day, I literally don't know what I would've done as it would've been the 'straw that broke the camel's back.')

…and I had no idea what would happen next…

AFTERMATH

When I got home I piled my dogs into my car and took them for a long walk in the countryside. The sky was overcast as a storm was brewing and we all walked silently, even my pups were quiet for once, perhaps because they sensed my mood? I couldn't even think. My brain felt shot-to-pieces with everything.

My ex found out very quickly that I'd been despatched home. Initially I told him that I was off work due to stress, but the news had travelled to his workplace via the grapevine. At first he suggested that my actions implied that I wasn't able to think clearly by myself and therefore I should get back together with him, but however fragmented my life felt at that point, I had left him for fundamental reasons and as it had been so difficult and expensive to leave, there was no way I was going to reverse that decision. Whatever had happened in my secular life, my marriage was still completely over and I had to hold my nerve even though I felt vulnerable and in need of support. I knew that no matter what further turmoil lay ahead, it would definitely not be right for me to return to my failed marriage. So I said 'No' and this decision created more difficulties within our divorce.

After being marched out of school on the Tuesday, I stumbled through the rest of that week, job-hunting and dealing with the official emails that began firing- up as the ramifications of messaging Jack began. As I no longer had my school laptop, this admin necessitated long days at the nearest library using their free computers but doing this made me feel purposeful and gave those early days a sense of structure. I tried to distract myself by practically preparing for an immediate research trip that I was due to go on and that I had planned for some time, but my mind was in a daze. I was just 'functioning' because I felt numb and couldn't really comprehend what had happened. I had to tell my older children about my school situation too and they understandably struggled to comprehend it, so life was tense.

The following Saturday, I went to visit my parents and siblings and they were all incredibly supportive and said that whatever the outcome, they would always be there for me. Knowing this was a massive comfort! Mum and I went for a walk by the sea and grabbed a coffee and chocolate. No matter what difficulties lay ahead, just seeing the waves and the wide expanse of the ocean, helped me to put everything into perspective.

THE POLICE EXPERIENCE

Shortly after I'd been suspended from school, there was a knock on my front door on a weekday at around 10am and I was in my gym clothes during the 'school investigation time'. I was about to head off for a training session because I knew I needed to stay physically and mentally strong by creating a new routine in my day whilst my life felt so out of control. In recent years, the gym had become an essential ritual in my life. As I'd been a teacher for a while by this point, I felt pretty institutionalised and although I'd previously struggled with the fact that my week days were mapped out to the eighth degree, I now realised that to prevent myself sinking into a depressive void, I needed to carve out a new weekly structure to keep my mind together.

I thought the two ladies dressed in smart casual clothes standing on my doorstep were Jehovah's Witnesses but they quietly showed me their I.D. "We're from the police", one said. 'Oh my God', I thought in horror and led them into my front room where they arrested me and read out my rights as my dogs continually barked at them. They just wouldn't stop and it all felt so surreal.

As they drove me to the city Police Station, the policewomen tried to normalise everything. I was so out-of-my-depth though. When we arrived, I was put in a holding cell before later being led to a cell upstairs and I remember sitting on the firm blue-coated mattress on the 'bed': a raised oblong block of plastic underneath the window. My back was leaning on a plastic pillow positioned against the wall and I just thought: 'wtf?' because I couldn't believe what had happened to my life!

A dark-haired, tattooed policeman brought me a blanket, water and offered me a hot drink; even asking if I took sugar? He gave me a knowing smile as if to say 'you are well and truly out of your comfort-zone here, aren't you?' I had no idea how long I would wait in the custody cell for, before seeing the duty solicitor and being questioned in a taped interview by the two detectives who had brought me to the city police station. 'Line of Duty' sprang to mind but that was based on dodgy coppers being investigated internally. All I could think of was the arrest 'speech' and always those taped, filmed interviews!

The female officers had told me to bring a book along to pass the time and I brought 'The Salt Path' by Raynor Winn as I'd read it before and it's such an uplifting, comforting true story about how a couple coped when their whole life was thrown into turmoil by a Court case, bankruptcy and illness, by walking the South West Coast Path and camping along the way, surviving on very little money (if you are feeling at your wits' end, I highly recommend reading this book!) Whilst the officers were waiting for me to choose my book, I'd felt I should bring something wholesome to absorb because my brain had gone into overdrive considering what was risqué/safe to take. On my kitchen table was a historic novel: 'The Honest Courtesan' which I'd loved reading ages' ago and had been about to revisit. One of the policewomen said she'd thoroughly enjoyed it too, but I panicked that if I took a story about high-class Venetian prostitutes to the police station, judgements would be made about me: there were just so many unanticipated layers to this scenario.

Whilst sitting and waiting in the cell, my brain both wanted to reflect and try to process everything that had happened but then I also felt it needed to shut-down because I'd been under so much stress for a long time. I'd been living on adrenalin for months, years really and I was exhausted. I just needed rest and some mental peace but that wasn't going to be happening anytime soon. All that was familiar had now completely ruptured and I had no idea how the school situation/ my divorce/career plans etc, would all play out....

I thought about my arrest and the car journey to the police station in an unmarked car. The two female detectives had asked me if I had a second phone (a burner phone), but I hadn't joined the realms of hardcore criminality: I'd never been in that world and I could barely afford the monthly cost of my mobile as it was! Rather, I'd just had a few moments where I'd lost sight of everything. However, these female coppers showed me genuine warmth, asking about my dogs, my childcare arrangements, reminiscing about great novels they'd read after observing what I had on my bookshelves and offering their personal opinions regarding which ones they'd enjoyed the most. They tried to make small talk on the hour-long drive to the station, enquiring as to whether the local shops stayed open during the winter and so on. But I couldn't respond normally to them because there wasn't anything normal about this situation for me.

They told me that what would happen at the station that day could go in: "one of two ways" but they planned to have me back at home that evening as they too had children to collect from school. I was touched by the way they tried to mitigate my anxieties. Even when one officer accompanied me upstairs as I changed out of my gym clothes and into a dress, she sensitively looked away so as not to embarrass me.

Back in the cell, I tried not to think but to sit and read my book. However the thoughts swirled around in an overwhelming way and I had no choice but to confront them: I'd always been a really professional, conscientious teacher and I never ever looked at my students in that way: I just didn't. Because that would feel so wrong and it literally never even entered my head! I loved teaching them and felt humbled and honoured to do so and loved their lively, enthusiastic banter so much! I learned from all of my brilliant students as much (hopefully) as they learned from me but then something had just happened: all of the stresses I had been under meant that somehow, the way that Jack and I naturally interacted, had completely unintentionally intensified to the point that I almost felt that Jack was a safe 'go to' person for me. I had never ever meant for things to become like this!! I just wanted to be back in my classroom teaching normally and not to have got myself into this situation because I hadn't been thinking clearly and had allowed myself to treat a student like a confidante.

***

I looked around my police cell. Aside from the bed, a camera was fixed at an angle on the wall and in addition, there was an adjoining door-less room with a loo inside and a roll of tissue paper. The camera could watch me perch on the toilet but I just didn't care any more by that point.

When I first arrived at the station, I'd been put into a smaller open cell with bars (it was like a cage and was one of 2 cells literally opposite the reception desk), whilst the detectives waited for a slot to officially register me. Once my admin was processed, the kindly male Custody Officer bagged up most of the items I'd brought with me, disclosed to me my custody terms, asked if I understood everything, if I needed menstrual products (Standard-issue pads!) Also he asked if I wanted to see a professional to verbally offload to. Then the Custody Officer explained the various procedures and asked me to sign a print-out of the terms. Next, I was led upstairs to my cell by another friendly officer.

I thought of prisoners who had the prospect of 15 years in such a cell or even worse, a shared cell (God knows what it must be like to share your cell with a psycho you hated and/or who hated you?! how was that permissible?!) or who had life imprisonment. It would be a huge punishment in itself to hear and know that the world was going on outside of your cell walls but not be able to participate: the ultimate fear of missing out: because when you're in a cell, you're in the world but you're not present in the world. You're in an intense sterile bubble whilst a much bigger life goes on beyond it. You're missing out and you're fully aware of that!

I also started thinking of the experience of having to go back into the world after prison? I couldn't stop thinking of what this must be like… How hard must it be to rehabilitate yourself after the stigma of prison? I suddenly saw these issues through a completely different frame of reference having entered a world I'd never ventured into previously or intended to be in! This situation was making me explore and challenge all of my preconceptions. It was teaching me so much about life. How could I use what I was discovering?

The Custody Officer was allowed to make two phone calls on my behalf, so he rang the solicitor I'd been recommended and then my mum. I knew that my ex had told my mother about my predicament. Later this became another issue in our divorce but again for the sake of my sanity, I literally had to zone out of it, because I knew the truth of the whole situation and I didn't have the capacity to cope with the stress of thinking through everything in minute detail.

After I'd been sitting in the murky gloom of my cell for what felt like an infinite period of time, the hatch in the door slid back and another friendly male officer peered in and beamed warmly at me, offering me a cup of sugary coffee in a plastic cup. His smile really lifted my spirits: it was a gesture that made all the difference. Later a new female officer drew back the hatch again and pushed through police-issue sanitary towels and a disposable paper bag.

Hours passed. My life was out of my control and I had no option but to relinquish my grasp of it and just succumb to my thoughts, read my book, drink my coffee... just simple things. My weekly routines were normally so time-pressured and regulated by bells: I couldn't ever be late to the start of the school day, lessons, meetings, rushing home for this and that, giving my children lifts, manically tearing around, getting up at 5am to squeeze in an hour of marking before another chaotic day began... and now at this moment in time, all of the mania had ceased. It was so bizarre. The natural light came through the square, brick frosted-glass panes: it was a grey day outside and the light in my cell was dim but The Salt Path eased my internal disquietude. Reading about another woman's eviscerating life experiences but her desire to push through and survive, really comforted me at that time.

After maybe 2 hours, I heard keys turning in the lock on my cell door and I was led downstairs to see the Duty Solicitor. The police had kindly arranged for it to be a woman, Liz Reynolds, who I'd been recommended to by Meg, my new employment lawyer. (Even this fact wasn't lost on me: I'd never had my own personal solicitor before but now it felt as though I had a whole legal team: a Criminal lawyer (Liz), Employment lawyer (Meg) and my Divorce lawyer (Rory) too. Meg was fully supportive and capable. Rory was so warm, professional and lovely. Liz was someone I also knew from years' back when we'd happened to cross paths. Now she was a fully-qualified, experienced solicitor and mum, oozing empathy and humanity. In a text to me later, she described how she'd always viewed me as being: "a breath of fresh air". Positive affirmations like this were so powerful and kept me going at that time because my mind was running riot! I mentally banked that message. Liz and I talked in a small interview cubicle for probably half an hour initially and then we were taken into a meeting room for the taped police interview and Liz told me quietly that she hoped I'd be given a Caution as opposed to anything else.

The tape was switched on. There was a laptop which contained the downloaded messages between Jack and myself. The two policewomen went through each and every one with me. I cried a lot during that session as I honestly divulged all of the mitigating circumstances which had led me to message Jack, who'd made me feel supported, appreciated, happy and distracted whilst I was going through such a fraught divorce and tackling numerous other challenges. This interview was the first time I'd stopped to think and talk about everything completely openly with anyone else for years, after living on such an adrenaline rush. Everything came pouring out. It was like therapy! Every so often Liz would say something to help and the two officers, although firm, were very compassionate.

***

After the interview, I was returned to my custody cell to await the detectives' decision and I wasn't deemed to pose any risks to anyone (as I don't!) A blokey, gym-honed officer with intriguing bicep tattoos said: "come with me mate" and smiled as he took me into a side-room where he scanned my fingers and thumbs. Next he took a mug-shot of me. This made me think of the infamous pictures of Hugh Grant after he was arrested when caught with Divine Brown in LA and I was suddenly aware of how crazy, unpredictable things can happen to anyone. As the saying goes: 'One day, you're cock of the walk, the next you're a feather duster.' Finally, the insides of my facial cheeks were swabbed and I was done.

A different male officer signed me out, chatting away cheerily as he went through the formal paperwork with me. It was only months' later when I was out-of-time to appeal, that I realised that some of the notes from that experience and which would be used later in my disciplinaries, were incorrect but as I was so unfamiliar and out-of-my-depth in that situation, I hadn't thought/known that I could challenge this at the time. I was also so desperate to get home and I was still in shock about the whole situation. Now with the benefit of hindsight and this tough experience which I never want to repeat, I know differently – so to anyone else in this situation – if any information on anything official is inaccurate, don't feel that you can't say anything! Try to get yourself out of your foggy, overwhelmed headspace and read everything thoroughly and if something isn't quite right, you can speak up! Don't worry about it getting you into further trouble but rather be strong and be assertive. Defend yourself.

As this officer reacquainted me with my belongings, he muttered: "I used to be a teacher too – a PE teacher" and he smiled as he said he felt that sports' teachers are never viewed as 'proper' teachers and then we both exchanged anecdotes about the stresses of teaching! I told him that I'd just applied for a temporary admin job at an animal charity as obviously I wasn't going to be teaching now but I still needed an income: "Well that's fine" he said kindly, "no hazards there", and when I asked him whether he knew if there would be any negative implications for me going into the science research that I was planning to do, after this saga, he reassured me in this regard too: it would all be okay! It was such a relief to be treated with warmth and dignity! In a state of overwhelm, I had messed-up, but it was totally unintentional!

If some of you are reading this and feeling that the policeman's empathy was inappropriate and that in mentioning it, I'm making a mockery of everything that happened – I'm not! I'm including this as it's a genuine part of my story and shows how different people react to certain situations and that when you're going through difficult times, it helps so much, to have support and to be treated with compassion because often you feel completely rubbish about yourself at that time anyway and the last thing you need is people bringing you down even further.

Finally just before I left the police station, I had to collect my phone from another jolly female officer, who wished me a nice evening. As I walked out of the station, now a free woman again, I felt relieved, still shocked and overwhelmed, but with a sense of the enduring gift of humanity. In particular, I reflected upon the parting words of the two policewomen to me: feisty dark-haired Bea had said: "you'll go through some shit (her actual words) but then life is going to get so much better for you", and the gentle blonde lady (whose name I can't remember) had added: "you'll be like a phoenix, rising again from the ashes." My faith in the sisterhood/humankind had been restored!

Next in what then felt like such an ironic gesture, I walked to a nearby deluxe deli to get a latte with the five-pound note I had kept on me. The physical juxtaposition of bustling, twee foodie-types -v- potential criminals sitting in cells in such close proximity, certainly wasn't lost on me as I called my friend Abi and explained that I was so sorry to ask her, but please could she possibly come and collect me later? In the meantime, back in the real world, I suddenly remembered that I had a nail appointment at 5.30pm in a beauticians that I'd booked ages ago with a Christmas present-voucher and I hadn't been able to cancel it, so I raced there. As the nail technician started my treatment, she asked me if I'd "had a good day?"!?! How could I respond to this?!?! At that point, my life seemed even more bizarre than ever. I just felt in a complete daze. Abi later collected me and drove me home, listening to my ordeal without judgement. This felt another defining example of true sisterhood. In the following year, our friendship elapsed a little because she moved to the other side of the world and she had to navigate her own challenges but we're still in touch occasionally.

FURTHER AFTERMATH

The disciplinary formalities then began in earnest: After my police interview, the school undertook their own internal investigation and held a formal meeting to which I had to submit a detailed response. This in itself involved a huge amount of work, time and expense as I had to instruct my employment lawyer to help me prepare all the documentation. I resigned from the school as I knew I'd have to leave. Following the school's investigation, I had to face a few other official bodies with their own individual investigations too.

It was all pretty massive and it soon became apparent that no matter how I tried to explain the situation, these official bodies had a specific narrative which as cited before, they were determined to run with and they weren't really interested in my mitigating circumstances, although one very erudite member of the judiciary completely understood the situation and was really supportive and I am truly grateful for that person's insight. However, overall these processes are incredibly brutal and intimidating in the extreme. Those are the only words to describe them.

Every time a letter came through the post or an email notification arrived, my heart sank heavily… was it going to be more stressful, intimidating communications from the School, one of the other official bodies, or was it another nightmare divorce email as simultaneously I had regular emails about my very difficult divorce flying into my inbox. Sometimes I would receive emails literally from all of these sources in the same day and I just had to get out of the house otherwise my brain would've exploded!

I used to dread receiving all of these communications and would go off for a run or a walk before I could face looking at them. I tried to limit opening them to just one per day if say, three emails pertaining to any of these life stresses arrived all at once. I had to pace myself otherwise it was all far too much for me to cope with. I hated even turning on my laptop or seeing notifications on my phone. Had I unintentionally completely derailed my career plans for good? Blackened my name? After having a very sound professional reputation, my teaching disaster loomed large over all of this… it was so stressful !!

I absolutely never meant to - but in the absence of other ways to meet people, working all the time and feeling broken because of additional money stresses and an ongoing bitter divorce - I simply got too close to Jack without realising it. If he popped up in my head back then, I tried to brush it all aside because I was a really conscientious teacher and just felt 'it wasn't like that' and by thinking there was an issue, I felt that I was creating an issue that simply wasn't there as there was no way I would allow it to be there. I wouldn't acknowledge it.

Additionally because of the discomfort we have in Western Society of discussing any potential dynamics along these lines, I couldn't talk to anyone about this at the time, which is why I wanted to speak about it when I heard about this book project via social media. We just shut any dialogue about this kind of thing down because we – especially in the UK - are so frightened of having these conversations. We avoid any difficult discussions in this country such as deep and detailed chats about death, religion, graphic side-effects of sickness, sex, any taboos… but we need to recognise that life is not black and white. We need to have these uncomfortable discussions.

When I had to leave school, I had the most amazing support from students, some parents, other teachers, my own parents, girlfriends, male friends and complete strangers too. Although I had made an inappropriate decision, I wasn't a bad person and I was so grateful that many people were able to see the nuances of the situation rather than just take a black/white view.

The whole experience made me re-evaluate everything in life and think about my judgements and boundaries. Bizarrely, I think it really enabled me to develop far greater insight. I decided that I had to incorporate this situation into my life in appropriate ways and not try to run from it, however difficult that might be, at times. I would no longer feel intimidated by anyone. I was not given a criminal conviction by the Police but I decided to tell my research colleagues about my situation as I wanted to be transparent and I received nothing but support and understanding from them.

A few months after my police interview, I was rushing to catch a plane to undertake some science research abroad and I was so grateful to leave the chaos of my life behind. It was the first time I'd properly travelled by myself outside of the UK for decades and although I felt completely at-sea with everything, I absolutely needed to have a complete change of scene. I finally arrived in Talinn late on a Friday afternoon and spent 4 days there and then 5 days in Prague, meeting academics, and going to labs. That trip was healing. People were so kind and they lifted my spirits!

Whilst there, I was flirted with and mentally scooped-up. During those days away, my mind was occupied by the practicalities of looking at previous experiments and case studies and finding the offices and homes of Professors I was meeting. In the evenings, however, when free, all the turmoil back at home would cloud my mind and I could feel my thoughts sinking into a void, so I sat and wrote everything down as I ate out. Back in the UK, shortly after my police interview, I had developed a newish friendship with a woman named Grace, a psychologist and she was a Godsend too, messaging me every single night to check-in with me and so along with physically getting away from my messy life back there, Grace's support as a friend, also helped to save my sanity.

Over the coming months my lawyers and I were fighting on, what felt like many fronts, regarding the divorce, maintenance and my school fall-out. When I returned from Prague, I managed to find a job working 20 hours each week in a popular high street fashion chain store. It was perfect for that moment in time and I'd previously spent lots of time browsing in there. As fate would have it, they happened to advertise for staff, just as I needed a job!

I have to be honest though. Sometimes I did have private 'omg' moments because my life had just gone boom! Having been relatively autonomous in my classroom, whizzing through powerpoints and going off into deep scientific tangents... suddenly I was putting clothes on hangers, getting hassled for taking 5 mins too long for my lunch break and making small talk with customers. It was all a bit of an unexpected transition and I was a fish out of water initially. However, I tried to view it as a levelling experience that would present me with a new perspective on life and give me time to think about my future, alongside practically helping me to pay my bills. It would shake everything up and push me off along a new path. I actually had to be totally grateful for this job!

The staff who – whilst being of all ages – were predominantly younger, welcomed me with open arms – but internally I felt raw and was trying to process everything that had happened, without initially feeling able to be transparent about it with my new colleagues. I felt I was hiding such a momentous secret. I confided in one of the guys, Stan, who had also trained to be a teacher and his friendship and understanding really helped. Sometimes I struggled to adapt to my new life as I was grieving for my old one, its respectability and the feeling of being worthy and doing something really worthwhile vocationally but I knew I had to work through these feelings and my new job and give everything time. Financially, Universal Credits topped up my newly-lowered income and God, I was grateful for that too!

But I felt pretty traumatised for quite a while afterwards. I missed all of my students so much as they were always so upbeat, positive and lovely! They provided so much positive energy and dynamism when I was teaching them with their enthusiasm for all the charity fundraisers and other ideas I had. I'd have dreams where I'd panic because I hadn't prepared my lessons for them and then I'd wake up and the stark reality would hit me that I'd been suspended and I felt grief-stricken at the loss of my sense of purpose, my normal life, not having the amazing sparky buzz from my students and not teaching the subject I loved.

TEACHING

When I had to leave the school, I was told that I had to completely lie low in terms of contact with other teachers for a short while. A few did message me and I sent brief replies back and two are still good friends. One sent a lovely card which arrived just after I returned from Prague and she shared an experience of a difficult time in her life too. I'll always be so grateful to her for sharing this with me as it gave me such a boost at exactly the time I really needed it, as initially I felt I would be so judged and after being so sensible and conscientious, that I was now the 'black sheep' amongst the teachers. (Other teachers from previous schools that I'd worked with, got in touch to offer support and empathy).

I literally didn't hear a thing from my Line Manager after working intensely together for quite some time and when the communication embargo against me was lifted a few months' later, that silence continued. Part of me does understand this because I know that my Line Manager has approached my situation from a completely detached perspective but another part of me feels that many people in these roles, become completely robotic, inhumane and unrelatable. Again they cut ties because they are fearful about how any contact with me could possibly affect their teaching careers but it wouldn't now. Sometimes I passed former teaching colleagues from the school where my teaching implosion happened, in the streets of the nearby town and they would pretend that they hadn't seen me. With one of them especially, that was tough as that person had previously said lovely things about me and they had previously written a really important academic reference for me.

I think this episode has made me think so much about humans and 'fear' – how we go into 'fearful mode' in so many situations and that stops us reaching out to people who need our help; how it stops us fully living our lives; how fear prevents some from making important decisions – such as changing careers, friendships or ending relationships and how it stops us talking about the deep issues in life that causes us crippling anxiety. Fear causes us to live half-lives. It's so much better if we can face our fears, process them, rationalise them, consider the worst possible outcomes of any situation and then know that we can deal with these and survive but also know that our worst fears may not come true.

In any workplace (but especially in one such as teaching, where you are giving of yourself all the time, it's manic and you're often hearing of/dealing with, stressful experiences too), I think there is, at the very least, a small duty of care to look after your staff. This is especially so when they have confided that they are going through a really traumatic experience. Time-off should be proposed for legal appointments, for example, as these are not regular events. It's not easy to share our personal tribulations in the first place and when we do, it's because we need some temporary flexibility, understanding and support – especially with our workload.

However often in many schools, children, teachers and support workers become mere cogs in the wheels of data-gathering and performance targets. I absolutely love education and from a personal perspective, academic research is something I've taken refuge in, to save my sanity at many difficult times in my life. I believe that school education should be about helping children thrive and become happy, well-adjusted individuals who are able to work towards their full potential and are excited about stretching their brains and about life itself. Additionally those who work in education should be assisted also in continuing to develop personally in their careers if they wish - but often all of these elements are lost in the targets, data-drives and league tables, which suck the marrow out of teachers.

For teachers at all state schools, there are endless trajectory charts of where every child is; endless projected grades. You have to pick out 3 weak kids from every class – what are you going to do to make them get better grades in your subject? How do your subject results compare to other subject results? Which department is top of the leader-board? Which department is failing? Often departments are pitched against each other. Sometimes individual teachers are verbally taken to task for their personal failure at enabling students to achieve their predicted grades. When you step outside of this unhealthy dynamic, you realise it's pretty depressing because actually where are the kids in this discussion? No one is thinking that, for example, Student A didn't obtain her projected grades because her dad took an attempted overdose, her boyfriend dumped her and then she developed anorexia which is why she didn't do so well in her exam for that subject; instead, the focus has shifted to good teachers v crap teachers / good students v crap students.

To give an example of the workload involved for secondary school teachers: they'll often teach right across the year groups: year 7 up to year 13, and in just one of those year groups – year 7 for instance, they may teach 3 x different classes of approximately 34 students in each, so that's 102 assessments to mark every few weeks plus all their other classes' (across the year groups') assessments to mark every few weeks and lessons to plan, reports to write, parents' evenings, department meetings, school duty rotas, school meetings, team meetings, preparing resources, emails to reply to, writing new schemes of work, planning lessons, photocopying, etc, etc... and that's all on top of the actual classroom teaching that they do between around 8.30am-3.30pm! All of this work is pretty much outside of the school day, so if you think teachers have it easy because they get all of those holidays and 'finish' their working day at 3.30pm well that's ABSOLUTELY NOT SO!! - because for a big proportion of those holidays, teachers will continue to work and all teachers work into the evenings, over the weekends and often get into school early in the mornings too. It's only really in the summer holiday, that teachers have a proper rest but even then it's not the whole 6 weeks as there's lots of pre-term prep to do, all for your kids, so actually when you weigh up the amount of holiday teachers actually get, compared with the hours they work and the pay they receive, it's a no-brainer as to why anyone would choose to be a teacher right now in the UK, because the relentless workload is completely off-putting and that's just for starters.

What is the actual point of school if we forget about the children, teachers and support staff at its heart? When we overlook the students with anorexia because 'that's not our problem', or students who self-harm, because 'they're just attention seeking' etc... all of these sentiments I've heard expressed in different schools. If you're in education, and especially in you're in education leadership, and you stop seeing students and teachers as individual multi-faceted human beings but rather as cogs amidst graphs of projected targets, you should quit!

***

I had a lot of mixed feelings in the months that followed that year. At one point, I tried to email the school as I had to sync an app that was linked to my former email address there but of course my account was deleted and so my email bounced back to me. This immediately made me feel pariah-like and I had to give myself a talking-to regarding getting into a positive headspace and retaining my dignity, which I did.

Working in the shop one day just before the third lockdown, a former teaching colleague came in and she was surprised to see me but was lovely. Another teaching assistant came in with her daughters (one of whom I had previously taught at A-level) and they were all so warm and friendly.

But then the director of my PGCE course came into the shop. During my teacher training course, this director had liked me and I think that they may have heard what had happened to me. In our covid facemasks, that person was served by my colleague and I pretended I hadn't seen them as I thought that they would be so disappointed that all their hard work in teaching me the PGCE had been upended! But that same evening walking back to my car, I bumped into one of the guys in the year above Jack at my former school. He was so pleased to see me and we had such a lovely chat. Those impromptu chats that happened when I bumped into random former students or friendly colleagues, helped so much! They reinforced that I was okay and that many of the students understood what had happened. (Another student saw me in my car just yesterday and came over to say hello! He's off to uni in September and will be a huge success!)

After my teaching implosion, I found that hobbies, fitness - especially dance, seeing friends, seeing my parents, looking after myself, being busy with my kids, having counselling, getting 'stuck into' my research project and receiving lovely messages of support from former students and teaching colleagues who I'd known for years, all massively helped. Also I found that it was better for me to try to keep my (simultaneous) very difficult divorce compartmentalised in my head as much as possible. I simply would not allow either my divorce nor my teaching implosion to take over my mind or my life and I made a conscious decision about this.

Additionally constantly having things to look forward to, was a really positive game-changer; it's such a simple thing to do but it hugely helps as it means you always have to try to look ahead in a positive way because at least one awesome thing is coming up!

I had an injury later that year too which necessitated a period of rest and I did have another 'wtf' moment, worrying how I'd cope at not being able to get out of the house and drive/run/walk, especially as all of these were lifelines. However, I was determined to get back to normality asap. An acquaintance regaled a 'prophet of doom' tale to me about how someone she knew had the same injury and was impaired for years… and I just thought to myself: "Sod that! That won't be me!" so I did everything I possibly could, to speed up the healing process. A few months' later, I was back to normal and driving, walking and going to the gym etc again… it felt amazing and I appreciated my body so much! All the tough times I had been going through had definitely made me far more resilient and determined to succeed!

When you go through the things I have been through over the past few years, you do feel that the stuffing has been knocked out of you but then something stronger emerges as you develop new ways of finding strength. It is like that sense of a phoenix rising up out of a fire… Occasionally something will happen where I feel a bit vulnerable again but I now know how to self-soothe by doing everything I've cited in the paragraphs above.

Since coming to the decision to get divorced, I have often felt completely overwhelmed by events, but I have known (to use an earthy metaphor), that it's a bit like childbirth: once the process starts, it just has to take its natural course until it reaches its conclusion. I've learnt with all of this that I've had no choice but to keep going and simply believe that life will get better, which it has done and whatever I face in the future, I will continue to push through!

When it comes to my former friendship group and the ones who hung me out to dry when I most needed them… well what I was actually looking for - rather than all the bitchiness and ostracism - was a big hug and just to be allowed to offload. I didn't want them to criticise my husband, but rather I just needed to talk. However, I've learnt the hard way that sometimes those you trust the most, refuse to accept how things actually are and instead impose their own narrative on events because it provokes too many uncomfortable feelings within them to do otherwise, but that is their issue! It's also sometimes because additionally they have their own agendas, like Jen and Sonya had.

With the school situation, I sometimes felt totally out-of-my-depth with the mire I found myself wading in afterwards, but I totally acknowledge that I sleepwalked myself into it. I let my emotions get the better of me at a time when I was vulnerable, but I have and always will, own my narrative. All the paperwork, emails, conferences meetings, telephone calls, texts etc, that this episode has entailed took up such a huge, huge part of my life. Financially, it cost more than my expensive divorce but again I learnt to accept it all and make my peace with it. I will never be bitter about anything. None of this is a journey I ever expected to go on but I learnt to incorporate it into my life, take it step-by-step and I've met some of the most wonderful, kind and erudite people along the way.

I've learnt so much and feel even more compassion and love for humankind than I had before. Even people from long ago in my past have stepped forward to support me! I am undertaking crucial research currently which will impact positively on the lives of others. I know I will be judged by some but I have to talk about these issues because they do happen. I refuse to look back at my teaching career in a negative way, because that is not the person I am and because we learn and grow from every experience and I was very lucky to teach the amazing and inspiring people I did (including Jack), and who I will never forget.

As a society, we are nervous of discussing any kind of taboo but nuanced dialogues are essential in civilised and educated nations. It's naïve and ignorant to just assume that people over the age of consent in various settings don't form organic connections in all walks of life, regardless of status, gender, religion… sometimes people just click and rather than pretend they don't, we need to be able to talk about this.

My divorce finally completed some time after I'd got a free half-hour's legal advice about the process and moved out of the family home and started proceedings. I'm sure not all divorces become as difficult but if you're about to embark on one, gird yourself mentally and be strong, because although it can be a bumpy ride, you CAN do it!

Now, I've got a wonderful new set of friends and I've stopped feeling anxious about the future because as stated earlier, it's pointless to live in a headspace of fear. I just accept that the human experience is complicated and nuanced and that we need to learn from everything we go through and speak openly to help others to avoid those minefields too. Just to be alive and healthy is the most incredible gift and I'm totally excited about the next stage of my life!!

What have your experiences taught you?

Anyone going through any ongoing legal situation needs a huge amount of support because they are so overwhelming at times and consume vast quantities of time and money that most people do not have. They are nightmarish situations which can feel totally out of our control but don't let them take over your life – because there is definitely a normal life to be had outside of this! You cannot let any process like this take over your entire life. You must be determined to retain a large part of your normal life throughout to stay sane and you must realise that this judicial process is not the be-all and end-all, rather it is a fragment of your life and you will get through it, so hang on in there! Also if you are going through a legal process and something that the judiciary have undertaken, concluded etc, is not right and does not reflect the true facts, then you still have a voice! You may feel that you should just 'take' whatever rap you have to take because you got yourself into a mess but that penalty must be accurate/justified; Thus if something is not right in a judicial process – fight your corner!! You absolutely can and must!

Sometimes unexpected situations can happen in an instant/a short space of time, which change your life forever. Thus, you can find yourself grieving for a person, your able body, your health, a career, a friendship, a relationship, a way of life, etc… having been plunged into that desperate state without forewarning. You will crave for your life to go back to normal the way it previously was and you will be low, pining for how things used to be… but you will gradually, gradually build a new life, I promise. Allow yourself to feel as down and desperate as you need to (it's okay to wallow briefly), but be aware that in time, you will have another wonderful life again – it will be a different life – but you CAN create a new wonderful life too.

Talking of feeling low, I have had a few times where I've felt completely overwhelmed and down, I wrote down one episode. This is how I felt on that particular day and I wanted to share it because I think it's important to say that as much as we always try to be strong, that sometimes as women/people, we just need to be open too that there will be days when life feels really tough and impossible and we should express this also.

"To be honest, I've had my moments where everything has got on top of me and my endless attempts at trying to stay positive, have run out of steam at one point. Not long ago, on one bitterly-cold, dull winter's afternoon, I just found myself feeling really, really overwhelmed by a whole series of events, both big and small and I broke down whilst out on a walk to clear my head whilst facing imminent research deadlines, the ending of a quick fling I'd had (which I'd just needed to catapult me back into life!), some big unexpected bills and the ongoing school ramifications), and I just felt that I no longer had the energy or inclination to keep going. I felt that I was too tired and worn-out for this struggle and that life squeezes you dry. On that day, life felt an ongoing, exhausting fight and I was sick of it. I felt that I'd tried to be upbeat for ages and tackle each new challenge head-on, one trauma at a time, but not knowing how everything would pan out had been making me anxious for so long and now I'd reached a stage where I really couldn't tackle any new challenges any more. I had just completely run out of steam. It was all too much.

In that moment, I found myself googling guaranteed ways to commit suicide and for a few hours' that afternoon, I genuinely imagined doing it and ending all the stress I'd been under, for years. I thought of what a relief it would be to fall asleep never having to face all of these endless pressures again. But then I thought of my parents, my children, my closest friends and the legacy that a suicide would leave behind... it was only that thought on that particular day that stopped me. It was the combination of managing everything by myself that had overwhelmed me. I thought 'what's the point? It's too hard, all the time. It never gets any easier. It's a constant fight and I'm so tired of it and I'm tired of people thinking I'm really strong all the time when I'm not; I'm just a human being.'

I found a small sparse tree high up in Yorkshire and whilst the wind blew and the sky was bleak, I sat under it and had a cry, listening to Radiohead's 'High and Dry' and thinking about famous people from the past who had committed suicide and how I could totally understand them giving up on life and just needing to end their lives to find peace. This little episode of allowing myself to wallow and feel fully miserable, enabled me to let off a lot of pressure and afterwards I felt loads better. It's okay to have days where you are immersed in the gloom as long as you pull yourself out of it.

Exercise is an absolute lifesaver! I now (pretty much) do something that gets my heart-rate up daily and it always makes me feel mentally strong! Once you get into the rhythm, you can't stop! I can't advocate enough, the power of exercise to radically transform your life in the most positive way. Even if you feel completely alone in the world, all it takes is a pair of trainers and going for a mini jog, to start feeling so much happier and in control again. Just the structure of a daily run in your life can be positively transformative!! Also if you're bored of one form of exercise – i.e., running/the gym – try something different – I've recently joined a hockey team and I absolutely love it!

If you are a very open person, then be mindful of this if you go into a career where you are teaching teenagers, so that you can try to put some distance in place between yourself and your students. Or indeed remember this if you go into any career where there are very strict boundaries in place regarding interactions with others.

On the subject of being marched out: Why do institutions/companies feel the need to use this medieval form of humiliation which is akin to putting people in the stocks or worse. A female teaching friend said she felt I was publicly marched-out of my lesson, mid-flow in full view of all of my students and made to walk across the site, to send an extremely visible and almost-symbolic message of punishment and to make an example out of me, as a woman who had transgressed. She thought that a male teacher would not have been dealt with in such a way but rather that their dignity would be respected and I have to say that I agree. The leadership at my school could have sent me a discreet email instead for me to attend the Head's office, rather than drag me across the whole school concourse half-way through my lesson, inciting gossip, news of which travelled to pupils in other schools, their parents and my ex, very quickly, which precipitated further stress. If I had felt suicidal then, this additional unnecessary shaming ritual could easily have tipped me over the edge. I feel very strongly that such deliberate public humiliations are always unjustifiable and belong to times' past.

I've reflected on this a lot since, as I remembered a lawyer I used to work with called Richard, and he must've committed some kind of misdemeanour and was made to pack up all of his stuff in a cardboard box and marched-out of the law-firm we both worked at, back at this time, one weekday morning. Whilst Richard was being made to gather all of his stuff in record-time, the company's Chief Executive, Alex, stood over and heckled Richard, making Richard feel harassed and at the time I thought that Alex – who I had previously liked - was an absolute bully for doing this. I didn't know what Richard had done or what he was accused of, but the treatment of him reflected badly on Alex not on Richard, because there is a much more dignified and respectful way to treat people. Richard was a man, a colleague, a husband, a father and had been an employee. Whatever had happened, Richard still deserved some decorum and kindness for God's sake.

I hope all institutions, corporations and employers stop trying to publicly shame people by marching-them out of their workplace mid-flow, making them frantically clear their desks and carry all their stuff out! It adds trauma to often already-traumatic situations and those practising such behaviour should be ashamed of themselves for implementing this method in 2021 onwards!

Please don't ever march someone out of a job or publicly humiliate them visually/verbally in front of lots of people! There's no need. Remember people never forget how you treat them and you may be on the receiving end one day yourself. Treat people with dignity and respect, no matter what. If a member of your staff is having a nightmare time, be kind, do not be smug and insincere with them. Offer genuine and practical help. If it's a teacher who is in a similar situation to the horrendous one I found myself in, with my impossible workload, very difficult divorce and financial and friendship implosion, then a pragmatic way to really assist them would be to: (a) check they are getting paid the correct salary; (b) ease their workload, and (c) offer time off for legal meetings with their divorce lawyer for example, also to (d) regularly check in with that member of staff and see how they are and ask them how they can be further supported? I can promise you that if you take this course of action, you are likely to have a teacher who absolutely wants to continue putting their heart and soul into your school and won't fall into the messy void that I crashed into.

What advice would you give to other women in a similar situation?

You should never stay in a marriage or relationship to please other people, that includes your friends, parents and even your children! To gain the strength to leave, empower yourself, i.e. you could train for a sports' event to get yourself in a strong mental position and gain confidence, thus enabling you to make the break.

Ditch friends who are: 'glitter deep', to use a brilliant term coined by Boy George. I realised on reflection, that I didn't want to hang out with disingenuous, superficial people who ran a mile when life got raw. Unknowingly, I'd wasted enough time with these types.

For people reading this who've never had to struggle with money, I just want to say a few things! The following can be the experience of not just women in low-income families but of women in high-income families too if they aren't allowed to have a say in their family's income but are expected to pay for groceries, bills, etc and any attempts to discuss finances as a couple are 'shot down in flames' and/or become a source of anger from the other party. If you live in a supposedly-wealthy family but this is your reality, often friends and onlookers have no idea of the genuine state and real financial stresses that you as an individual are experiencing. Thus this all becomes another dark, shameful secret.

When you have very little – I.e. literally every pound and penny is so essential and you become familiar with pawn shops, cash converter shops, auctioneers, payday-cheque shops and so on, you become totally 'stuck'. You lose autonomy and you don't have choices: for example, you can't get your car/printer/phone/ washing machine/laptop fixed; a lack of money holds you back in so many frustrating ways. You can't afford to do lots of things; go out; meet friends out etc, so you feel embarrassed, isolated and ashamed. It takes up so much of your time because you're constantly totting up what's coming in and going out as there's so little wriggle-room. You waste hours every week thinking what can you afford to pay and what direct debits/standing orders will bounce? Will your card be declined in public? Do you have to go into a bank to withdraw the only £2.03 that is in your account? Does your bank branch even open any more because if it doesn't, then you can't even withdraw that. What can you ebay?/Sell at a charity event? You end-up selling your bike, camera, metal detector, anything of any value and it all gets pretty shitty and pathetic and makes you feel rubbish. You are robbing Peter to pay Paul. There's no end to it: it's depleting and utterly depressing...

On the flipside: having money – whilst not bringing total happiness – certainly does give you opportunity and experiences. It buys you time, space, choice, stability, security, confidence, self respect, the respect of others and the ability to travel and have all kinds of adventures. Basically having money (to a debatable degree), IS a positive game-changer. It's obviously about balance, but anyone who says: "money doesn't you bring happiness" can't ever have been in a position where they've been so financially desperate, because without a certain amount of money, you're completely trapped in misery in so many depressing ways.

With regards to teaching, if you find yourself getting too close to a brilliant, kind A-level student, don't bury your head in the sand and pretend it's not there because 'how could it possibly be like that?' Instead, just acknowledge it and pull your dynamic right back to a professional space. Talk to a trusted colleague if you can and think about leaving your school if you need to. Learn from the fallout I've had and just think of the official ramifications if you don't remove yourself from that situation and that those ramifications would be really stressful for both of you.

Accept that in the UK, it's really difficult to find a work/life balance when you're a teacher because the workload is relentless, but try as much as you possibly can to carve out time for yourself and your family, otherwise you'll drown in it. Teaching can chew you up and spit you out, so self-care is essential !

When you have to deal with a stressful situation, don't look at the big picture because it's too overwhelming, like standing at the foot of Mt. Eiger. Instead, just get through the process one step at a time. You can do it! Also go for counselling: it's amazing if you find the right counsellor. You will be surprised at how many burdens you've been carrying on your shoulders for years. Release them and feel free. Also plan lots of treats/fun times to keep you going along the way!

If you're struggling in a relationship, do open up and talk about it. You may feel you're betraying the sacredness of your intimate family space but if you're not transparent and talk about your experiences, it's hard to have a sense of perspective about your situation.

When you have an implosion, do whatever you need to do, to survive! Initially after the school incident, when I felt sure that the police would be in touch and I was so stressed, I found some diazepam leftover from a stressful time in my life previously and I combined taking some of those with wine and cigarettes to calm me down for a couple of days and then I eased back on everything!

Meditation, talking to people and letting everything go, massively helps. Use whatever you need: a few harmless cheap tools include candles, oils, calming podcasts and losing yourself in books that cover similar life experiences. Opening your mind up to new adventures is another fantastic way to start looking ahead to the next exciting stage of your life: maybe plan some epic travels and allow yourself to think outside of the box. Explore every side of your life and find who you truly are. It's such a liberating process. View it as a time for recalibration.

WHERE ARE YOU NOW? WHAT ARE YOUR PLANS FOR THE FUTURE?

I do feel really excited generally about my future. All the official ramifications of my teaching implosion are over and I've put them behind me now, whilst mentally retaining what I learnt from that episode, especially with regards to boundaries. One of my French girlfriends said that my episode reminded her of the Macrons and yes, I could totally understand their situation.

With regards to my work, I'm involved in paid scientific research studying a particular medical condition and I have wonderful support from the London University which it's affiliated with. I'm building the career I've always wanted. I still feel a pang that my teaching career ended the way it did and that's mainly because all of my students at my last school and some at my previous schools, were an utter joy to teach and did such a lot to lift my spirits. I think they know that I was and am, so proud of them all and that it was an utter privilege to teach them. They will all have incredibly bright futures. They inspired and energised me a lot!

I'm now back to feeling really positive, optimistic and excited about the future. I heard that years' after my former toxic 'friendship' group ostracised me, that another key member of that group (who had joined in, in excluding me), had herself been ostracised from that group later, for some reason. When I learnt of this, I didn't feel any schadenfreude, instead I just felt sorry for her because I remembered how horrible that experience was personally but I am really grateful that I am no longer part of that unhealthy circle of individuals and my life has gone off in a completely different and wonderful tangent.

I've had incredible support from friends and family and I have thrown myself into my hobbies and fitness as it keeps me in a really good headspace. Aside from my role as a mum, I'm really enjoying my career, social, cultural and fitness life. Although I had lots of messages and approaches from guys between the ages of

20-50s after my divorce, I wasn't in that headspace for a long time (when some guys in their twenties discovered I used to teach, they said that they wished I'd been their teacher! - and this has been difficult to hear for obvious reasons!) I'm 'kind of' seeing someone at the moment but also consider myself quite free, going with the flow of life…

I hope that in sharing my story, I will help some of you who have/are having, similar stressful experiences. I want to say do the right thing, take care and be strong: even if you have moments when you are completely at the end of your tether and thinking about suicide, please don't. Keep going, even if it's just getting through one hour at a time, one day at a time, but just know that lots of others are suffering like you are, right now and so you're not alone. Also having gone through so many difficulties myself, I am rooting for you to get through your difficulties too…so keep fighting! Don't forget the phoenix analogy: you'll rise above the embers and you'll soar! All of this, will be the making of a brand new, amazing you!

GILL'S STORY

When your beloved husband is diagnosed with a very aggressive brain tumour…

Matt and I were a dynamic duo for a long time: we were such a tight team! We were together for 22 years and married for 12 of those. Matt was 10 years older than me and we met through our careers as engineers. Initially, we both had to work away a lot due to the demands of our jobs but there was a huge spark between us and we were soon going out on dates and taking holidays before we moved in together. We then followed a traditional trajectory of getting married and having two children.

Like all couples, we had our ups and downs: I had to leave a very well paid job when we had the kids as we didn't have any childcare or family support nearby and so money became very tight! But then that changed when my husband received an inheritance and all of a sudden, life started looking up: we paid off some debts and our bank account actually looked rosy!

Before everything started to go horribly wrong in August 2019, we had just taken a lovely yurt holiday in Devon. Before that break, Matt had experienced wrist problems and he'd had to take 6 weeks' off work for this because it required an operation, but towards September 2019, Matt's wrist was on the mend and he was in the midst of a barn-renovation project: this was our new home.

One day in August 2019, Matt came home from work with a horrendous headache and it just got worse. He couldn't walk down the stairs and he had issues with the right side of his body. Matt then had a bad fall in the bedroom and I had to call an ambulance out. He was a huge 6 ft rugby-playing guy and I didn't have the strength to lift him up. On 31 August 2019, he was whizzed off to our nearest city hospital. I thought maybe that he'd had a stroke caused by a blood clot following his wrist operation.

It never crossed my mind that it might be a brain tumour because overall Matt was generally healthy! He was 55 years' old and although he had high blood pressure, otherwise he was sound. I couldn't go with Matt to A&E in the ambulance because I couldn't leave the children but once at the hospital, Matt was given a CT scan and they found a mass on his brain. I obviously needed to be with him and so a friend looked after the kids so that I could dash to see him.

The hospital didn't know if the mass was cancer and Matt needed an MRI scan to provide a clearer picture. By this point, he was struggling to walk. Doctors gave him steroids to reduce the tumour's swelling, ease the effects and enable him to be more

mobile. Matt was transferred to a ward and the following day, he was given the MRI scan and we were told that it was a cancerous brain tumour. The Consultant said it was disappointing news and he became part of a multi-disciplinary team that were going to have a meeting and discuss the best options for Matt.

After receiving this initial shock, we both became stubborn in our attitude towards the cancer. I was devastated by the diagnosis and Matt was too; we were both so worried. I cried and just remember saying: "don't die!" and he said: "if I do, you'll cope", followed by: "don't talk like that". But then we were told about the treatments which the hospital were able to offer Matt and we both became positive then that an operation combined with treatment, would deal successfully with the tumour. We would tackle it together and then we could go back to normal.

So we were sent home with a walking frame and a commode for Matt. This was all a massive learning curve: I now had to help my husband wash, dress, walk, get outside and so on… I couldn't get him into the bathroom because of the steps. I just dealt with one thing at a time in stages. So the next stage was to adapt to life at home with Matt's needs and for us to see the children and try to regain some normality. Then the next stage would be Matt's operation, chemotherapy, radiation and just getting through it, and so on.

On 16 September 2019, we had a clinic appointment at the city hospital and the Registrar told us more devastating news: Matt had a: "very nasty" tumour. It was a Grade 4 Glioblastoma, however Matt was just so determined that he would beat it and in his words, give it a: "good kicking". He underwent preliminary tests for an operation to remove the tumour, which would take place in a matter of days. Matt said: "I'm going to make five years". Our daughter had just started senior school and our son was 2 years behind. Matt was determined to see both of the children undertake their GCSEs as they were studying at his former school. Although Matt was optimistic and positive, he was also a realist.

We were given lots of support by friends in our village who popped around all the time for a brew and who offered to help look after the kids and to check that I was okay. Sometimes I needed practical help such as to move furniture. I would send a message around and lots of people reached out to support me. It was wonderful. Also my own girlfriends, aunty and brother helped a lot too. However, I was really upset that some people close to Matt, both men and women, didn't really bother. They stayed away. Matt had supported them in the past but now when he needed them, they turned away. Conversely, one of my female friends drove from Manchester to see me and it was so lovely as I could completely relax with her and it just gave me a sense of normality.

When Matt had his operation and he was going through radiotherapy, his engineering apprentice said he would come and watch the rugby with him and he did, bringing breakfast too. They watched all the rugby matches together and this kind man offered to help and would talk to Matt about different issues. We found that the people you least expect, deliver the most, whereas those you think will be there for you, just fail to support you in your hour of need. For example a few friends turned up once and then simply stayed away. Matt asked one of his friends if he could cut our garden hedge and this guy just didn't turn up. It hurt Matt that friends he'd known for fifty years, couldn't be bothered to help when Matt was so impaired.

On the flip side, one of my friends from a baby group arrived at ours, one day with her partner. They knew I had been trying to decorate my daughter's bedroom and they did it for me over two weeks, boarding up her room and putting electric in and so on, whilst also running their business. They were amazing! Once it was finished, we said how grateful we were and they just said: "the fact that you and Issy are made up about it, is all the thanks we need." The guy was a mechanic but he was so lovely, he gave Matt a big hug and talked to him. He was also in tears and wasn't afraid to show his feelings. They were so kind and helpful and again they were people we didn't expect to get that support from.

***

The operation to remove Matt's brain tumour was at 7am. Two friends came to keep me company during the op. So before the procedure, Matt basically had three women sitting with him and we were making him laugh by telling jokes about his hospital gown. Whilst Matt had his op, the girls and I went to the hospital cafe and got lattes and cake. They stayed with me all day and another friend, who's a Critical Care Sister in another hospital, joined us for lunch. Eventually we went to the HDU (High Dependency Unit) waiting room and didn't really get back to the ward until 7pm. Matt's operation had taken 3 hours and the Theatre had been in chaos with bookings that day. He was brought back to the ward and the Sister said it was okay for me to see him. Matt looked really well and he was talking to me. I had expected him to be hooked up to machines and although monitors were being fitted to him, he was happy. My girlfriends brought me home that night as Matt needed rest. I felt so positive and really happy!

The surgeons had given Matt something called a 'pink drink'. Its actual term is: '5-ALA' and it's taken as a drink prior to surgery. It causes tumour cells to glow bright pink under UV light. This allows the surgeon to tell tumour cells apart from healthy cells and helps surgeons cause less damage to healthy tissue as they remove more of the tumour. This was quite new at the time Matt had it, and we were lucky because the late MP, Dame Tessa Jowell, championed it when she had a brain tumour and the hospital Matt was in, happened to offer it.

The next day, Matt was sitting up eating fish and chips and again he was in really good spirits! He was moved from the HDU to a normal ward. He looked fit and well and he was very talkative. He was in a better condition that he had been before his operation. Mentally he seemed a bit sharper. We were both looking forward to the next stage of his treatment as we just felt it would be an upward trajectory. On Monday, when I got to the ward, he was walking on his frame with two physios and he was doing really well. Then the Bed Manager appeared and I was told that Matt needed to go home. It was a bit tricky as they expected me to simply take him home but I asked for hospital transport. The physio said that Matt would now need handles to get up and down the stairs and she told me to order rails from Amazon.

I rushed on ahead home to organise everything. My brother had looked after the kids and had been running them to their various activities. All of them had bought in Matt's favourite foods and gave me time to spend with him. My brother helped put up the handrails as Matt hadn't liked me using his drill in the past (although now I use it like a pro!)

We had to wait two weeks before the Community Occupational Therapist ('Com') turned up. Matt was still using the commode at home. The Com helped us acquire some gadgets to help Matt use the toilet. Also a stool, so that Matt could sit at the sink and wash himself. Furthermore, she arranged physio at home for him. Initially we arranged for Matt to have his oncology appointments via his work-related BUPA healthcare at a private hospital but that was the wrong decision because lots of the appointments were in the evenings which made it difficult with the kids.

There were lots of daily challenges. Matt had to have a mask fitted for radiotherapy but as engineers, we found the process of making it fascinating. Matt had a neck issue as he had broken it previously but he coped. The guys that made it for him, were so supportive. But Matt at this point, was struggling to get about and he needed a wheelchair. I asked if we could have one and a nurse told us we needed to buy one. A different nurse gave us amazing alternative advice though and told us that the Cancer Charity, Macmillan would assist us. With that, I felt a bit more optimistic, and popped to Macmillan. They really helped and got us a blue badge, a wheelchair and an appointment with a Benefits assistant.

In mid-October 2019, Matt started his 30 x sessions of radiotherapy at Hospital X whilst his chemotherapy would be given by the staff at Hospital Y and then he would have blood tests to check that everything was okay. The hospitals were close together but it was difficult juggling getting him in and out of the car, up ramps, and in and out of the wheelchair. Parking was a bit of a nightmare at the hospital as there were only 3 disabled spaces in front of the hospital. I ended up thinking: "I've got a blue badge, I'll park where I like!" and felt like a stroppy madwoman screaming, but it was an added trial !

We still felt quite upbeat, juggling chemo and radiotherapy. Matt posted on Facebook: 'I'm toxic now. I'm kicking this thing'. We got into a new routine and fitted it around the kids. It became our new normal. However, as the treatment progressed, Matt got more and more tired and he didn't want to go to hospital. Once a week, we had coffee and cakes in hospital as a treat. Our poor son even had to come and watch his dad in hospital on his birthday. At first it wasn't too bad, but then Matt had one week of chemo and tests showed that his platelet levels had dropped in his blood and because they didn't go back up to an acceptable level, the chemotherapy was cancelled. This was a bit of a blow.

More difficulties were to follow though in November. The week before the end of Matt's radiotherapy, we went straight home afterwards and Matt had his first seizure. The plan had been that he would have a month off radiotherapy over December and Christmas, then he would resume chemotherapy again but no radiotherapy. I panicked when Matt had his first seizure because it had never happened before and I was at home with him. I called his Oncology Nurse and she said: "no problem, it's quite normal sometimes. We'll put Matt on anti-seizure drugs". But then Matt had 3 small seizures and actually dropped a plate but he had no idea what had happened.

December 2019 came and Matt finished radiotherapy and we celebrated. But he was just so, so exhausted and he said that to me. He couldn't get out of bed much. We had to go to the hospital to see the Oncologist, who said: "Matt, you look so tired." They put us in touch with a local Hospice who could send someone out to see us. At this point we were still positive and focusing on the chemotherapy drugs. We just thought Matt's fatigue was very normal.

Sometimes Matt was too tired to even make it onto the commode and he would have to wee into a bottle. One of the hardest things I had to do was to wipe his bum. I'd always said that I would never do that but after having 2 kids and our life together, you just end up doing these things: you have to but Matt was really upset about it and he said: "you didn't sign up for this." I joked to him that I was the worst nurse ever and he said: "no, you're the best!"

At Christmas time we went out for a meal. I had experienced a bad night as Matt was struggling and I was trying to get my daughter's bedroom finished. One of Matt's friends came over and Matt started being difficult as this clashed with going out for a meal. I noticed that his attitude and behaviour had changed. It had become: 'I don't really care'. For example, he didn't want to change the shirt he'd slept in and so on. It was just as though he'd given up. He simply said: "I'm so tired Gill".

When we got home from the meal, trying to get Matt indoors was really tough. He asked me if I could move the car closer to our front door as he was too exhausted to walk to it, saying: "I don't think I can make it" but I had to try to cajole Matt. I encouraged him to attempt a bit of a shuffle with the tough- love words that I knew he liked: "you have to, unless you want to stay in the car all night". Somehow I had to try to mentally-push and assist this big man indoors and eventually we made it: he sat in a chair and didn't move all night. Matt was so tired that he couldn't make the steps upstairs and he was too hefty for me to help further but at least he was out of the car and out of the cold night air.

The next day, somehow I managed to get Matt upstairs to bed for a rest. My brother came over before Christmas itself and he chatted to Matt, who spent most of the day in bed. Over that festive period, another person arranged to come over who didn't understand the logistics of getting Matt upstairs and so they didn't really help. There was a Parents' Evening at the new school my daughter was going to, and my son was coming home from school in-between so I asked this person if they could possibly babysit my son whilst I went to my daughter's Parents' Evening, but that person said no, because they had a hairdressers' appointment and it couldn't be changed. So I came home to watch a very ill Matt trying to supervise his son cook a pizza. It was at moments like this that I realised that some people exasercbate an already-difficult situation by hanging-around but being quite 'precious', so they become almost an additional source of stress because then you are having to run around after them too (please - if you visit with the intention of helping – do offer some practical help; this goes such a long way!)

But then things suddenly deteriorated a lot: Matt had 3 massive seizures and lost his bladder and bowel control. He was completely wiped out afterwards and he couldn't talk. Matt did come around later and he was horrified because it was all so embarrassing for him. He was devastated and very tired.

There are brain tumour support groups but I didn't want to get involved in any of these as it made me feel sad and negative and I needed to find positive people because I was the first person out of my friendship group to go through anything like this. When you realise that you're going to lose your husband (my rock, best friend and confidante), then it's such a huge, huge upcoming trauma that you have to find a way to cope that works for you as an individual.

Just before Monday morning, 30 December 2019, Matt had been quite well and my brother said he was really chatty, however Matt got up in the night and sat in his chair but then started having seizures. I panicked as I thought he was dying. I rang a friend and said: "I need you to come over" and I explained what was happening. This friend came over immediately and took the kids off. I then called the hospice and they organised palliative care support. Paramedics arrived too and they told me that what Matt was experiencing is what happens with a brain tumour. I cleaned him up and another friend turned up with a pile of disposable sheets and calmed Matt down and then we settled him in bed. Rachel, the Palliative Care nurse was so reassuring and practical: she brought a load of pads for Matt to wear, to tide us over the New Year period, and she offered to help us access further support.

The hospice were going to send carers to help with Matt, once a day. A man from the local government department called and said: "I understand you want some help for your husband?" but he was so unhelpful, rubbish in fact, because all he said was: "well I don't know how it's going to be paid for!"

New Year's Eve 2019/2020 was quiet. We watched TV. Matt nodded off. It all felt subdued and it wasn't positive but the kids were okay though. A new carer came in on 2 January 2020 and it was the first time I'd had someone coming into the house who was going to help me with Matt on a regular basis. She said: "point me to the bathroom so that I can get Matt washed. You sit yourself down and I'll do it all." She was so lovely and recommended a few things to assist me. We had a chat together and again that massively helped.

Friday was a very emotional day. Everyone turned up to help, especially a lovely physio named Elysia and she also managed to get hold of Matt's chemo nurse too but I was told: "Gill, there is no way Matt is going to chemo. He's not going to make it", but they couldn't commit to telling me anything further.

The local healthcare manager from the Hospice, Bryan, arrived too and he had a big chat with me about what Matt needed and what was going on. The physio ordered a special hospital bed for Matt to replace the one he had. At this point, Matt would sit in a chair and simply be too exhausted to do anything. So there followed an epic bed-moving mission and I asked 6 of my friends to help and they all did; the house was turned upside down. One fantastic friend Jen, said that she'd make me lunch and put the kettle on and sort out my son Sam, getting him ready for his sleepover. Jen took over all the little things that my brain couldn't process because of dealing with Matt's needs and Jen wouldn't leave me until I'd eaten my lunch.

That was the night Matt woke me up at 4am to use the commode. He couldn't understand me telling him to use the rotunda, which would spin him around to position him on the commode. Matt then pulled his pad out of his pants and threw it on the bed: he had soiled himself and then the bed too! I had to clear everything up. It happened twice! I had an implosion moment at that point! He was unable to process why I was so upset. He could see me crying but didn't know how to reach out. Previously he would've put his arms around me to comfort me but this time he looked bemused/confused. It really upset me as I knew everything had changed so much and there was no going back.

Matt's breathing was off too. I called the District Nurse but someone answered the phone and said: "what do you expect the District Nurse to do?" I then called the Hospice but they didn't pick up my call either. However, second time around, I got through and they said: "he's rapidly gone downhill. We'll sort something out for you and send assistance". Carers came through the door at 10am. I was so relieved that I almost kissed them. They said: "Give us everything: sheets, a bowl, everything! You have a cup of tea and sit down". I overheard them talking to Matt and they were so nice and kind.

Then someone Matt knew, turned up unannounced, declaring: "we've just decided to come and see you", then they said: "he needs a hot water bottle" and they snatched the already-made bottle out of my hand and gave it to Matt as though they'd filled it up. A doctor turned up and gave Matt antibiotics and I went to give Matt his dose, but this person Matt knew, took these off me so that they could give the antibiotics to him. Next they tried to force-feed him toast and he was struggling with it all. That just increased my stress!

The District Nurse turned up in the afternoon with the Occupational Therapist. They were trying to get a hoist for Matt. The carers then said that I needed more than one visit a day from them. Things started to be put into place with nursing staff arriving and checking on Matt and then trying to find a solution for us both in terms of care. I felt a bit better then because we were having support but Matt was a little distressed. He had an air-filled mattress underneath him and it kept making a noise which he didn't like. On the Sunday, I took my son to rugby and my daughter let Matt's carers in. A friend came over too. People were beginning to realise how ill Matt was and wanted to see him before it was too late but it could be shocking: one particular friend was devastated by the change she saw in Matt.

On another morning, I had the district nurse, a friend and a physio arrive simultaneously and they got me laughing, which massively helped. It was stressful as the District Nurse had to put a catheter into Matt and apparently this is much more stressful for men and Matt got really upset about it but then he was also really depressed about wetting the bed which he did sometimes now. The nurse also bought him liquid morphine, tranquillisers and other drugs that could be given to him, to ease his symptoms. Every hour, Matt was crying in discomfort from the catheter and I was constantly running from the kids to Matt to soothe him. Eventually because Matt was metaphorically hitting the ceiling with the pain, the

District Nurse took out his catheter and gave him tranquillisers. They worked for a couple of hours.

I was told that we would have carers four times a day and this would be free. This team got to know where everything was and this was a huge help! They gave advice on everything such as special sheets for the bed, etc. The District Nurse and Hospice Manager turned up with a big box of medicine. The Physio turned up again and we sat and had a chat after the District Nurse had gone. She told me about a device called a 'syringe driver' which would automatically pump pain relief into Matt.

I asked her how long she felt Matt had. Her opinion was devastating: she basically said: "a matter of weeks", but at least, I had a timescale. Our G.P. popped over that afternoon. He was very shocked at how Matt was as the last time he'd seen him, Matt had been in a wheelchair in the surgery and was quite chatty but now he was starting to get confused. Matt would chat to the carers about our local area and whilst talking to them, he would kind of recognise that our kids were coming and going, but he found it difficult to distinguish between day and night.

Matt had his meals fed to him but he wasn't really eating. He was having soft food such as jelly and custard and although he looked forward to this, he couldn't really eat much. At this point, I felt that I'd lost him, that the Matt I knew had completely gone already. I tried to explain that he wouldn't be going to chemotherapy as he didn't have long to go. Our son, Sam, started to withdraw from wanting to see his dad. He would call out: "Hi Daddy" but wouldn't voluntarily go in and see him. Our daughter though, would just go and talk to Matt, she didn't care if he responded or not.

On the following Tuesday, a Palliative Care nurse, Rachel, turned up. Matt had stopped responding on Facebook to friends so I put up a message to say he'd stopped using social media as he really wasn't very well. We got all the usual: "keep on fighting Matt" messages. Also we received comments such as: "we're praying for you". These sentiments didn't sit easily with me because I'm an atheist and so was Matt, but I knew they were well-intentioned. Finally, his friends who got in touch, wanting to see him, came over and this was poignant as we all knew that it might be the last time they saw him.

Rachel from the Hospice, brought a 'Respect Form' for me to look at and we discussed Matt's care and his entry into the Hospice. In that week, his deterioration was so rapid. I was absolutely devastated. His prognosis had gone from 1-2 years left, to 6-12 weeks left and now it was only 1⅓ to 1 week left but I was grateful that Rachel was honest. I remember making a joke of it to help me cope, saying wouldn't it be typical if he died on my birthday.

One of our friends who had come to see him, had to stop on the way home in the midst of driving as he was so affected by it. Our carers were so lovely with the kids, me and of course, Matt. He hated being hoisted up when he needed to be, as he felt vulnerable, hovering over the bed pan.

On the Wednesday, we lost our local carers to a Derby-based company and I found that hard as I'd got so used to the local women that came in. I was worried too as to whether the new care would be any good, but with this change in provision that I was being offered, I would have an overnight carer for Matt every other night. A Care Manager came to see me and was reassuring. Also the hospice said that they'd try to find overnight care for Matt on the in-between nights. I felt everything would be okay.

I discussed with my girlfriends when best to tell the kids about Matt's dire prognosis. One of my friends had lost her mum in her teens and her dad had been honest with her. She said it massively helped as otherwise it would have been too much of a shock. So two of my friends, Jen and Katy, who know my children really well, came over to help me tell the kids that their dad was dying. I found the best way was to be direct, so there was no ambiguity. It was the hardest thing I have ever done. I literally said: "he's going to die." We all sat there crying in a huddle. It hugely helped having friends there for this. Afterwards we made a drink and my son said: "I want to go upstairs" and he did. Meanwhile Jen and Katy talked to my daughter and said: "if you can't talk to mum, you can talk to us." Jen told Issy about her mum dying when she was a similar age to my daughter.

One of the school mums told me that Sam had messaged a friend saying that his dad was dying and that we were going to be a family of three, and this friend didn't know how to take it. But then they chatted and it all opened up. My friends made me dinner and put the washing on. I had spoken to Issy's form teacher at her secondary school about Matt's operation back in September and the kids wanted to go to school the next day following my discussion with them, so I emailed Issy's teacher again. She was brilliant and spoke to all of Issy's other teachers and they said they'd been unaware that this was going on for me at home. Sam's primary school were more involved because of his age, but both schools were fantastic. Issy's way to cope with it though, was that she didn't want all of her teachers to know about it. Her teachers told her not to worry about homework and that if she wanted to sit in a library or leave a class at any point, she could.

The days leading up to Matt's death (although we didn't know how soon he was going to pass), were hectic and maybe people outside of these situations don't realise how busy life can be at these times, in terms of how much organising families have to do. Therefore, on Thursday, I had arranged to have a chat with the oncology team and two friends Sarah and Alice were going to come with me so that I wasn't on my own. Brian from the Hospice, came over to 'man the house'. Another friend told me that I had to sort out the Will and I asked Katy to be a witness. We had brand new carers in and out of the house. I had Katy with me at home to sign the Will and I was brewing up for everyone. Jim came and helped Matt sign the Will too whilst Brian sat with Matt and his mother. It was actually all-go!

I walked out of the house to go to see the Oncology team at the Hospital and it was a relief to leave. I parked in the same space I used to go in with Matt and that felt really poignant. I asked John, the Oncology Nurse, lots of questions such as: "why did this happen?" and he replied: "It just can". Also: "why did the radiotherapy work and then stop working?" John assumed the tumour had just grown and then Matt had become too ill to continue it. After hearing all of this, one of my girlfriends said: "do you want to go for a brew and cake?" and it was such a lovely gesture as life had been so intense and we went to a little teashop. It was the first time I'd done something normal for ages

When I got home Brian said that he would come and see me next week. One person turned up who was special to Matt but that person just sat in a chair. My friend Katy meanwhile emptied the dishwasher, put a wash-load on and helped out practically and she said to the other person: "whilst you're sat there, you could do some ironing" but that person didn't help at all. They simply sat down relying on everyone else to run around after them. It was bizarre and I couldn't understand it because that person had cared for one of their own family members for years but they couldn't help Matt when he and I needed them the most.

We had a new carer and Matt had rolled out of bed with his face down. I overheard the carer say: "I told you to stay in bed" and I went in to speak to her and said: "he doesn't understand". The carer couldn't use the special support that we had, so I called 111 and they said they'd send someone out to help. The carer said: "I'll sit up with him until the paramedics arrive, you go back to bed." The paramedics said to Matt: "Can you get up?" and he said he couldn't. They called me, it was 3am. They saw the 'Respect form' regarding Matt staying at home. They put Matt in a hoist to get him off the floor but then he had a seizure. So they put Matt on the bed and couldn't do anything more for him and then they left. I got up at 6am so that the carer could go home. I'd hardly had any sleep and was really disappointed with her.

I asked for side-sections to Matt's bed to stop him falling out and then I ordered a bariatric bed for him which would go into the living room. I organised the moving of the bed for the following Monday. The plan was that Matt would be in the living room with the woodburner going to keep him warm. Matt seemed quite happy with having the side pieces to his bed as he felt safe that he wouldn't topple out. He didn't have any visitors on the Friday afternoon and it was so nice to sit and have my lunch with him.

On the Saturday, lots of friends came over who wanted to see Matt. So many people were supportive at this stage. Another friend, Sarah, turned up to take the kids for a sleepover. Matt had messed his bed so myself and a nurse went to clean him up and then Matt said: "I don't feel very well" and started going into a fit. I swapped sides with the nurse but Matt didn't come out of the seizure. It just didn't seem to be stopping and all I could do was hold his hand. Eventually the seizure did stop and then he involuntarily gasped… and then he stopped gasping…

…and he had died.

The nurse went to get her stethoscope and I gave him a hug and a kiss and closed his eyes. Matt looked so peaceful. The nurse confirmed he wasn't breathing and then she left the room so that I had some time with him and I could tidy him up. Then she rang 111 and arranged for the doctor to come over. I rang his mum who said that this was the phone call she'd been dreading. Next, I had to call the funeral director. Meanwhile one person in our wider family was already being difficult regarding his funeral care.

A couple of friends came over and I was calm. I didn't feel really upset: it was weird! Almost like a numb party atmosphere after all the continued stress and unpredictability of Matt's condition for a long time…

On the kitchen table was all the Christmas chocolate and biscuits and my German friend, Inez, who is pretty direct and lovely, just said: "I'm going to have to have one of those chocolates" and she dived in and then everyone else started eating them too and it broke the ice. Inez cracked on with lunch, making a beautiful salad and a frittata and she rearranged the fridge and the cutlery drawer. The kids were still on their sleepover. They thought - well we all thought - that Matt would be with us for nearly 2 weeks, but in fact, he'd died 4 days into that 2 week prognosis, so it all ended much more quickly than we expected. I decided to let the kids have their sleepover and try to process it all and then tell them the following day. I remember drinking lots of tea and eating chocolate.

Matt had been dead for less than 3 hours when someone had posted on Facebook that he'd passed away and I was stressed as even the kids didn't know about it then. I just thought: 'Can you people not stop for 2 minutes and think of the impact of what you're doing?' My children didn't have Facebook but I was worried that somehow the news would get to them via their phones, so I notified my friend, Sarah who they were staying with. There were some insensitive comments too.

As time progressed, the funeral firm came and collected Matt's body and the nurses came too. Sarah, her kids and another friend, Alice and her daughter, all came to support me and my children. One of the girls said: "you know I fell out of bed once" and it just stopped the seriousness of the mood. My son Sam wanted to go and play on his X-box. The kids were shocked when I told them that their dad had died, but they dealt with it. I had been nervous about them coming home as all the sheets had gone etc, but they just wanted to play on the bed and get back to normal. They played with the hoist before that too went back the following day and then my daughter made me a cheese sandwich!

The following week, the kids decided they wanted to go back to school and a member of Matt's distant family rang, trying to organise Matt's funeral and asking lots of difficult pressuring questions in a very matter-of-fact manner. In the end I had to put the phone down as Matt hadn't been dead for 48 hours and I hadn't even had time to process it all without feeling more stressed.

Jim went with me as a friend (he's not so emotional) to register Matt's death and then he came to see Frank – the Funeral Director - with me. We plumped for what Matt would have wanted, which was a cremation and a non-religious service. Jim said Matt would want us all to go to the pub after the funeral. I knew the Manager of a pub called 'The Green Man' in Ashbourne because he was involved in local rugby and was known as 'Big Pete' so I went to see Pete. He gave me a massive bear hug and was full of ideas for the funeral buffet, which really helped as I was still a bit numb. We sketched out an idea of what we wanted and agreed on a cash bar with any profits being donated to charity. We set Thursday 13 February 2020 as the date for the wake. I felt quite positive. The order of the funeral was basically going to be a celebrant, which Frank was organising, the cremation and then the wake at The Green Man. But there was pressure from a member of Matt's family regarding burying Matt in a church graveyard but as Matt was an atheist, I stood my ground.

We decided that we would ask for any donations to be split between two charities: one was 'Helen's Trust' as they had really tried to provide lots of help for us and the other was our local Hospice, who had assisted us in enabling Matt to be cared for at home in his final days.

My birthday was looming and I was told by one person: "I don't expect you'll be celebrating your birthday?" and I said: "Yes I am. The kids are so excited". And we did. We needed to! We had to have some semblance of normality. My Aunt and Uncle loved our village pub and they took me out for lunch. My brother came over too. That evening I had a phone call from one of Matt's friends, Johnny, who lives in Canada, to say – bizarrely - he wanted to make a donation to the local swimming pool in Matt's name. Matt hadn't actually used the pool much when they were younger but hey, people want to give in different ways!

On my actual birthday (a week after Matt's death), my brother got me my breakfast and my kids threw balloons, pressies and cards at me. I went to meet my friends, Sarah, Alice and Nicola at a reservoir and they all made a fuss of me. Other friends, Tracey and Katie came over to my house and made me a cake! In the evening, I celebrated with a Chinese takeaway and gin with my brother! It was lovely to celebrate life again!

As time progressed, I needed to go through the paperwork and put all the bills, etc, in my name as most of it was in Matt's name. I explained to different companies that Matt had died and was offered help via a service that can do it all for you, but I decided I wanted to do it myself. Matt's former Boss came to see me and he brought all of Matt's personal belongings from work. I received Matt's 'Death in Service' pay and Matt had also taken out 'Critical Illness' insurance, so Matt's Boss sorted that out for me too. Various benefits started coming through and so financially the pressure was taken off me.

It was tough though as every evening at 6.15pm, I would expect Matt to walk through the door but he didn't. I had been used to Matt being away sometimes as part of his job involved travelling to Germany, so in my head I just imagined he was back in Germany and that was my way of dealing with him not returning from work. I was surprised at how manageable I was finding it and that talking about him, helped me cope. I decided to put together a slideshow about him and our life together for the funeral and I went through photos of us backpacking and travelling together. I remembered really incredible times we'd spent together.

The funeral came. My Aunt and Uncle brought my grandparents over for this and my Cousin and her husband came too. I didn't want to be fussed over. My friend Helen (the nurse) came to my house and my Cousin's husband was there entertaining the kids – which is what he is really good at! One person turned up at the funeral and they were very aloof and causing stress. The funeral cars arrived early and I overheard that person say about me: "Well, is SHE coming?! They're blocking the road". None of my neighbours were stressing about this though, it was just that one person, trying to dominate the situation. I remember telling my brother not to let that person upset the kids.

During that day, this person kept talking endlessly and I just wanted to say: "will you please give it a rest?" but of course I couldn't. When we pulled up for the funeral, I looked around to see whose cars I recognised and there were people everywhere. It was rammed. I just didn't know what to do! Loads of people came. It was so comforting to see all these supportive friends. The Funeral Director, Frank, helped guide everyone to the car park spaces. The chapel held 100 people but there were people piling outside because Matt had been so popular.

Sally gave a speech that we had written together as I wanted to say something myself. Good tip: practice in front of the kids. As soon as I started talking, my mother-in-law was in tears, the kids were in tears and I tried to focus on someone in the room that wasn't crying. I said that I was going to cite a pulled pork recipe in memory of Matt and his infamous BBQ skills. As I talked about him, I could see people smiling. It was so nice to see that! Two of Matt's friends talked about his party years and they struggled but they got through it and said funny things too and then the slide show worked really well and again, people smiled. Matt's body exited to Fleetwood Mac's Formula One music. The song we originally liked was called 'Brain damage' by Pink Floyd. I liked it and so did Frank but we didn't think everyone would approve.

The Celebrant had suggested that we didn't shut the curtains around the coffin as the kids might not like that. Some of Matt's ex-work colleagues came and they didn't wear black. I had asked if quite a few could wear rugby shirts as Matt had loved rugby so much. One person attending, started being rude and difficult at this point. We went to the pub for the Wake and I mingled and had a few drinks. People from our village came too. The kids chatted as there were other kids there and they were all having sweets. I started speaking to a work colleague of Matt's that we both knew and then I spoke to a local Councillor named Simon but I started getting a few glares and stares for this from a few members of the funeral party. Some walked out without even talking to me. However, their departure lightened the mood. I realised that even at funerals, family dynamics can be tempestuous!

The next day, the kids went to school. Issy was taken out of lessons with a friend for the morning but she and Sam had wanted to go in: it was their choice. The kids had half term in February and I arranged for them to go to Wales with my brother.

Before Matt died, I had made the decision to sell our house so that we could find somewhere easier for Matt's wheelchair and for me to get a job. The house also needed further work doing to it. After his death, I still wanted to sell it as there were too many reminders of Matt and it's half-way up a hill so it's difficult when we get heavy snow/ice. Just before our holiday to South Wales. I fell in love with a new house and signed up to buy it. After our Wales' trip, 3 x estate agents valued our house and the range of valuations differed by £200,000 (one valuation was completely insulting). I couldn't raise enough money to buy the new house and had to pull out of that, which upset me but I went with an estate agent who I felt I could trust and put the house on the market and then we went straight into lockdown 1.

I suddenly was forced to take on all of these roles that previously Matt would have managed: so the TV broke and I had to sort one out; I started fitted carpet tiles; then I got a new sofa and decorated the living room; I painted the window frames and bought shelves. I bought the kids' flat-pack desks and put them together. I treated myself to a treadmill because I wasn't going outdoors' running. The freezer packed up and I had to sort that out... and then things calmed down a bit... but there came a realisation of being able to do things by myself as a woman. For example, I used a circular saw for the first time to put a new worktop on and I virtually finished renovating our kitchen. It all gave me a sense of practical self-confidence. Previously I had made a hash of using a drill to put my daughter's curtain rail up and I cried when it went wrong, but after Matt's death and because of lockdown, I just thought: 'there's no one else to do it so I've got to do it myself' and I had lots of uplifting comments like: "wow Gill!"

As it was the spring, I decided to spruce up our outdoor area too, so I got new patio furniture, a pizza oven and I learnt to BBQ – which had been Matt's domain – I created a lovely space! Issy's birthday was coming up and it was meant to be at Center Parcs but that had been cancelled because of Covid. I found an old tea set and we decided to hold a party for Issy at ours with loads of bunting. I bought pom-poms to hang up around the house and we made beautiful cakes and had martini glasses. It was genteel and twee but she adored it. I cooked a pizza in the new oven and friends dropped off presents for her on the doorstep – it was just the three of us but Issy loved it!

As lockdown continued, we had games' nights, quiz nights, film nights and we'd have a box of chocolates on the go. Homeschooling was fine. Sam's really into science and so I ordered a science kit and he started learning guitar. At Easter, I laid a trail around the garden and again we had fun.

I started therapy over the phone. It was a support group provided by a Bereavement Charity and run by a guy named Rob. He suggested that when someone dies, it's as though you have a circle and all the memories are in that circle. As time goes on, you build new memories around the circle. That really helped. He also suggested that I tried mindfulness: so just to have 10 minutes on my own every day to sit by myself, relax, do what I wanted, be in the moment. Prior to Matt being ill, I'd really gotten into running and it had been my hobby but now I couldn't go out running for long as I didn't want to leave the kids by themselves but I did start jogging around the village. I found that sewing became therapeutic for me too and I could sit outside and do it. I also signed up online with a Personal Trainer and he gave me activities I could do each week.

I signed the kids up online for Tai Kwondo lessons and having these online sessions gave our weeks some structure. I would sit with friends also and have zoom catch-ups over coffee. The kids' teachers rang too, to check in with us and ask how we were all coping. That was so lovely. Sam has a particularly lovely primary school teacher and she said that if we needed any help or support, for us to ring her. Furthermore, she sent flowers for me and book tokens for the children. That teacher showed such compassion and the kids missed their little chats with her. She confided that her partner had been injured in battle and so she could understand and empathise with some of what we were going through. Because of her actions, I felt that I couldn't move Sam from his school as he was so happy.

Lockdown 1 gave the kids a break from all the dashing around and it pressed the pause-button for us.

I have had sad times though when I remember Matt. He always had a twinkle in his eye and this comes back to me often, so whenever I felt down and unhappy, I lose myself in a book or an activity like crafting. During the first lockdown, we were given more time to spend together and gather ideas. Having more time with each other has enabled us to bond properly as we work our way through the next stage of our lives together.

WHAT HAVE YOUR EXPERIENCES TAUGHT YOU?

I am a lot stronger than I thought.

Be appreciative of what you have. I had over two decades of amazing times with Matt and that's comforting.

A lady said to me recently that by the time she gets to her 40s/50s, she wants to have life: "sorted" and I said: "Really?" because I want to go through life crashing, blundering, laughing hysterically… I don't want my life mapped out in one neat tranche.

I don't feel guilty about being given money. It's released me financially from additional stress during lockdown. I would much rather have my husband walk through my door though.

I will eventually chuck some of Matt's stuff away and get organised. He'd be horrified at the state of our garage, there are tools everywhere. But I think 'haha I've made it messy!' I am free to behave as I please.

Love: I feel so lucky to have had Matt. We met at 22 years' old and irritated each other a lot. He made me laugh, cry, feel angry and everything else. He may have died too soon but we had a good life together. I wouldn't have done half the stuff I did, without him. Our chats were often so bizarre and odd and I love the memories of that. I would rather have had those 2+ decades with him and lost him than not have had him in my life altogether. We travelled to South Africa, Australia, the Caribbean together and did such a lot!

There are lots of aspects that I struggle with: I miss his beard trimmings in the bathroom, his boots by the door, his slippers by the fire, his coat hanging up. I feel he's still kind of with me. I made a duvet out of his rugby shirts and made a teddy bear with his stuff and I had Matt's photo printed onto fabric so the bear has Matt's face on it and I can cuddle him!

I also had jewellery made using Matt's ashes. I have a ring and the kids both have necklaces so it feels as though he is still with us. When we can go on holidays again and we visit places that Matt wanted to go to, basically having Matt in our jewellery, will make us feel as though he's coming too.

At the end of July/August 2020, I fell down some steps in our barn conversion and thought it was a sprain, but it ended up being a break… so I'm in a cast and on crutches… but I really want to get running again… watch this space! (Running helps me with everything).

Handling Matt's illness and death with our kids

I didn't say too much to them initially. I didn't tell them it was cancer in case they researched it online and freaked out. I simply said dad was ill as I didn't want to give them false information. Later, involving friends and the people we did (who we felt comfortable with), helped, as did preparing the kids for the fact that Matt was dying. I talk about Matt in front of the kids now and sometimes I cry in front of them too and we'll all have a group hug. We also have a laugh about him too. We're just very open about it all.

What advice would you give to other women in a similar situation?

Don't be afraid to ask for help. People will help you! Someone made a load of food for my freezer. Another lady set up a rota before Matt died, to give the kids' lifts to their activities. Another woman even put the bins out for us when Matt was sick… all these kindnesses made a big difference and I was so grateful!

Find a hobby that works for you to help you cope: I enjoy quilting and I'm going to make another quilt using Matt's clothes.

After your loved one's death, don't be too hard on yourself. Do whatever works for you. There's not one set way that's right. Ignore any suggestion as to how you should be feeling.

Don't be afraid of creating new memories or of being happy again. Don't feel guilty about that person dying because you can't change it and you're here to live your life.

I'm not even thinking of meeting anyone else but some people have said that if I met someone, I wouldn't be able to bring them back to this house because it was Matt's house, but you do have to put other people's opinions aside. I now feel it's me and the kids -v- the World!

Where are you now? What are your plans for the future?

When Matt was diagnosed, I was referred to see a Counsellor/Psychologist and in the summer [2020], I had some online sessions (I could have seen a Counsellor in the hospital but I didn't want to go back there as it would bring back the memories). However I found myself telling my Counsellor that I felt: "I've got this sorted" and I was discharged.

I've had lots of time over lockdown to process what happened with Matt and to deal with it all. Before Matt was ill, I'd get frustrated and cross much more easily but now I just give things a go and I feel that I have grown and developed in confidence. I know I can do stuff! Living by myself with the kids has taught me to become more resilient and resourceful and I am a lot more relaxed about everything now. I don't feel guilty about being upset over it all too. If I'm not in the right mood, then no worries – I'll have a cuppa and get sewing!

I think you have to give yourself permission to go with the flow of how you feel and that's changeable.

The kids are much calmer too and I think they've taken the lead from me. The cancer was so visceral and so now we just roll with life.

I'm planning to put the house on the market and if it hasn't sold after a while, no worries. Career-wise, I was thinking of going back to engineering but it's so stressful. I think maybe a sociable job perhaps as say, a part-time receptionist, would work really well for me as I'd enjoy the communication aspect and I'd be able to work it around the kids' school hours.

Financially, the house and car are paid off so I'm in a good position in this respect and can enjoy life and sewing without putting pressure on myself to rush into anything. I've been thinking of making things I can sell on Etsy such as weavings, wall hangings, bunting and I love the idea of making dresses with embroidery, sequins, beads... I've even been thinking about going back to Uni and studying textiles. When Matt was ill and I thought I'd have to go back to work, he said: "you can do whatever you want". It was great to have that affirmation of choice.

I treated myself to a car online over lockdown 1 too: a Discovery Sport automatic. I picked up the ashes from the funeral and put them in the passenger seat and talked aloud to Matt, saying: "Look no crunching gears" :)

Life will be wonderful again. I know this but we will ALWAYS love Matt!!

JOY'S STORY

Not fitting in, a family secret that makes you doubt your heritage, sexual harassment, a huge culture clash with your husband and his homeland... later your husband is shot and your mother dies

My implosion has not been one main disaster but rather, two significant crises but *somehow* I've got through them both... Let me begin with my childhood implosion:

I grew up in a designated New Town north west of London. It was divided into five areas each with its own shopping arcade, local pub, doctor and dental surgeries, a health centre, recreational grounds and a primary and secondary school. There was an old town centre and then a new one too with cinemas, lots of high street stores, restaurants and a weekend open market. There was an entertainment and events' hall and a large open air pool plus a big public library. A light industrial zone connected to the M1, provided the lion's share of jobs. Public transport was plentiful and the housing was good, modern and well built. In fact it was a surprisingly clean and healthy environment to grow up in. There wasn't any class system plus little to no unemployment and excellent schooling. No smog just green belt countryside which was conveniently connected to London in twenty minutes by train and conversely a relatively wealthy lifestyle on the edge of the Chilterns. It was a brave new world in real terms.

The problem for me I soon realised, was that the monotony of this quasi perfect little world of mine was not to my liking. When I laid down in the long grass obscured from my friends playing hide and seek, I was fascinated by the aircraft high in the sky above, which increased in number every year. To me they represented freedom and the lure of the world beyond. We lived near three major London airports and it was the age of continental package holidays and intercontinental flights and it fascinated me. My father told me I had a bad case of 'wanderlust' and he was right. I never quite felt comfortable in my little suburban world and the desire to leave it every year grew until eventually I did leave it. I never felt like I fitted in where I was growing up. The French have a word for this feeling of not belonging and feeling weirdly uprooted and placed in a different environment and this translates to the English: 'deracination'. That feeling stayed with me for many years of my life.

Admittedly my maternal grandmother told me tales of her time in Malta (where my mother was born), India, Sri Lanka, Egypt, Gibraltar and Hong Kong as my grandfather had been in the army and posted abroad with his family. There were exotic tales similar to Kipling about the animals, the jungle, long railway journeys and travel by ship. My favourite was the one about a massive earthquake in the Himalayas in India (now Afghanistan). I was later to experience one for myself in Europe and I realised that nothing she had told me had been exaggerated. My grandmother loved travelling. She loved the luxury of it all. In fact when I visited her, we always had our lunch or afternoon tea in a nice hotel with silver service. She only took me though, which was great as my mother was never one for that sort of indulgence. I know it all sounds rather Edwardian, but it spoilt me and since then I have never liked slumming it in the local greasy spoon if I can help it. Aged nine I was able to navigate the uses for all sorts of cutlery at the dinner table.

Life was not easy for army families though. Disease was rife. My grandfather contracted malaria and my grandmother had all sorts of stomach issues. They also lost two children under the age of two: one of whom is buried in Malta, the other here in the UK and both died of meningitis. Infant mortality in the British Army before the 1950s was abysmal. My grandparents brought back with them to England a Mynah bird and he swore in Hindi and in English and terrorised the neighbourhood when he escaped a couple of times. He was truly a rascal and I rather liked his total lack of decorum. That personal trait has remained with me too and was a stark contradiction of what I realised was the repressed psyche of the British in general in those days. I learned from an early age that if used shrewdly, being outspoken was a powerful weapon and a brilliant deterrent. Being frank is not exactly the English way but I have always preferred it as it is tedious having to second guess what people actually want to say.

My perfect little world imploded when I was ten years old. It would be fair to say that before then there were happy memories where summers were full of blue skies and hazy, lazy days spent at the swimming pool or rowing out on the nearby fish ponds with my brother and father or playing cricket in the nearby field on light sunny evenings. That all stopped immediately when my mother discovered my father was having an affair...

My father was a keen angler so fishing trips had been his convenient excuse for escaping at weekends. My brother had knocked dad's jacket off the banister at the bottom of the stairs one day and a letter from dad's mistress had fallen out. Mother, ever the tidy one, picked it up and the rest is, as they say, history. My life changed irrevocably that day.

My father left the family home for three months and did not visit us during that time and my mother became a shell of herself. She had a nervous breakdown and was fuelled by prescription tranquillisers which incapacitated her to the point that I found myself having to do basic chores, cooking and the shopping. She became the child and I became the adult. Suffice to say that I vowed two things to myself after that experience: be self-sufficient and never rely on a man and secondly, I would never, ever allow myself to be affected that way by anyone. Needless to say, it put me off mind-altering drugs for life as well. The worst part for me was losing a father whom I adored, admired and most of all respected. I was always closer to him than my mother and I felt betrayed and abandoned. It felt like a death. My respect for the man diminished. Respect for men in general disappeared. That experience has stayed with me all my life and has had an effect on all close relationships since. I suppressed emotions to avoid ever feeling that way again. Father returned but things were never the same after that.

My parents stayed together until he died first. It was not a happy marriage. I loved the man dearly but I realised I never really knew the extent of his actions nor his deception until my brother let it slip fairly recently that this 'other' woman had in fact been the wife of our father's best friend. My mother never ever knew this. I am happy she didn't discover it as this woman was a close friend of the family, so much so that she was like an 'auntie' to us. This adopted 'auntie' was privy to secrets I felt I could discuss with her and not my mother.

Words cannot convey the disgust I felt when I was told this. It was like a punch to the stomach. My brother looked at my face when he dropped that bombshell and was horrified as he realised I did not know. The woman had confessed it to him on her death bed. My brother had worked with her and my father for twenty years but had no idea. As they say, secrets and lies. A horrible life-destroying reality. The whole deception was frankly hard to absorb: this woman had been my father's secretary for over twenty years when he went into business by himself and before that she had been a co-worker at the company where he worked as an aviation engineer. Yet he purported to be best friends with her husband. In my mind, nothing on this earth can adequately justify how those two people could have done what they did.

When I was 22 years' old, I went to Morocco. I had a job working in a holiday club on the Mediterranean coast. I remember having a lump in my throat as I said goodbye to my parents at the airport. That soon passed though. I'd excelled at languages at a grammar school where I had achieved A levels in three languages so I had a chance to use them working abroad. At that time foreign languages were a rare attribute for a Briton but they came naturally to me. This fact alone made me question my origins.

I looked at my mother and I was so like her physically that there could be no doubt that I was biologically hers. I looked at my father and his family and wondered if my father was really my father? It also worried me that my mother favoured my brother who was a year younger than me exactly as we shared the same birthday. I was good at languages whilst my father was a scientist, good at maths and engineering: his affair made me question whether I was actually related to him or whether everything was a lie? I harboured these feelings until I was twenty-six years old when I discovered that my father and I had the same blood group, a rare one and so this allayed some of those insecurities.

A little part of me is reluctant to look at my DNA even now. My brother has. I really do not want to, as a part of me would be devastated if we did not share the same paternal DNA. I often asked myself why I was a good linguist though and it was only later on when my maternal grandfather died that we found out that his mother was Spanish from Galicia and his father was German serving on merchant vessels. Both died when he was a baby and he was illegitimate. He was brought up by a couple who ran a pub in Plymouth. Not even his daughter, my mother, was aware of this fact as illegitimacy was a social stigma in those days.

Realising that I needed to put my parents' dysfunctional marriage aside and carve out my own life, I knew early on that education was imperative to achieve my independence. 'Have language will travel', fast became my mantra. My intention was to see the world in comfort by working and actually experiencing living in the country I was based in at any one time. I decided that I did not want to go to university at this stage of my life as I felt institutionalised, so before going abroad I undertook a couple of jobs in London offices before I made a break for freedom. Britain was grey and miserable in the seventies. There were strikes. Women were still second class citizens. Examples of this were entrenched in society: no equal pay, not being able to get a mortgage without a male guarantor, separate bars for men in some pubs and clubs and on a double passport a husband could travel without a wife but not the reverse. Furthermore a child born anywhere in the world whose father had a British passport and was born in the UK or its territories was automatically granted British citizenship. The same rights were not extended to children born of British mothers. They had to pay to register them as British citizens until 1983 when that law changed.

The thought of working nine until five doing the same thing every day then getting married, having children and getting a mortgage were not at all in my game plan. These things terrified me. Rather, I wanted a life in technicolour. I had ambition and a desire to travel. I wanted a chance to spread my wings and to make my own decisions before considering settling down. I achieved that goal for ten years of my life and I have never regretted that.

So I went to work in Morocco, then switched to Portugal and later Italy where I eventually met my husband. At the end of this book in the Appendix is a sub-section detailing some of the nuanced experiences I had on placements in these countries. After some of the many places I travelled through across the globe, Italy was a real treat. People were very attractive and mannerly. The men were very handsome and impeccably dressed. I undertook four months of city tours around Venice, Florence and Rome and loved all three cities, my favourite being Venice. I had a boyfriend there who was from a family of glassmakers in Murano. He did not have a Ferrari as cars were not allowed there (there weren't any roads), but he had his own very speedy motorboat and my schedule meant I was in Venice once a fortnight for four nights. So when there was no fog or floods, we went out to places where the average tourist never ventures.

However, I did have some strange incidents with Italian men at which the modern-day #MeToo movement would be horrified and these were hard to comprehend. The first event wasn't sexual but it was abusive and it happened at my first hotel in Cattolica, when I was verbally savaged by the male owner for the sin of eating my breakfast in the bar opposite. I thought the man was deranged as his language was absolutely foul. He said I was forbidden to do this along with a couple of other unreasonable requests and he threatened to have me removed. I told him that I had my own free will, that his requests were unreasonable and that along with his foul mouth, he could do what he wanted but that I was leaving there and then. My boss, a Swiss Italian, moved me to a better hotel which certainly had nicer management, further up the coast in Rimini. What a difference! It was beautiful! However, another unsavoury incident occurred as next, I was offered the equivalent of two thousand pounds for a sexual encounter with an Arab businessman attired in Armani who propositioned me by a newspaper stand where I was reading the headlines. At first I was shocked into silence as he spoke to me in very good Italian, then he tried German then English.

I shook my head in despair as I told him in English, very assertively, that I was not for sale and to stop insulting women who were trying to read a newspaper. He looked at me, smiled and downgraded the offer to dinner. I just ignored the man but was sorely tempted to slap his arrogant face very hard. Who does this I thought? It was a life lesson. I was offended but I tried to see the funny side of it. I mean it was so ridiculous!

One of the scariest moments happened at Rome Ciampino airport in a totally empty ladies' toilets on the basement level. The flight had been delayed but it had landed. It was after midnight so I ran off to go to the loo before the passengers came through. As I was about to do my business, I heard heavy footsteps which stopped outside my cubicle. The feet were that of a man in combat boots. There was a gap under the door and when I looked underneath I saw combat trousers and the butt of a rifle leaning against the door. I heard a zip being undone and the sounds of a man masturbating. I was nervous but instantly thought 'I've started to pee so I will finish that' because to be frank that need was greater than my fear. By that time the man had also finished his business and exited, after I found the courage to shout at him to get out.

When I told my Italian colleague, she was so outraged that she found a random officer and gave him a piece of her mind. As I had not seen a face at all, there was no way of identifying the man in a normal manner. However, despite this fact, the random officer had a unit of ten soldiers all dressed identically and all armed with rifles, line up in front of us and he made them say one by one what the offender had repeated again and again in the toilets. The officer made each soldier repeat the words. It was surreal. Nevertheless, I pointed out a suspect who, it turned out, had a partially unzipped fly so he was frogmarched away for interrogation. He admitted it and was punished accordingly. I received a very humble written apology which arrived in the hand of a senior officer again at the hotel reception. Future trips to the toilets at night were done in pairs, for obvious reasons.

Another unwanted sexual encounter happened in Lake Como: in April the following year I found myself in Lake Como for the Summer Season. Como was a beautiful little city at the head of the lake of the same name. The villages were all nestled on the shores of the lake. The lakeside road wound its way all the way to Lugano in Switzerland. As the lake is situated in the Prealpine region of Italy, the roads twisted around rocks with waterfalls from the snow melt higher up. The scenery was spectacular as were the beautiful villas and gardens. The hotels were all built in the same Italianate style. I spent a happy summer here and I made the acquaintance of the local police chief with whom I had a very passionate liaison but I was faced with a disproportionate number of men who exposed themselves to me or who were peeping toms. On my second day there before any tourists arrived, I took the lake ferry to do a bit of reconnaissance. As it was a warm, sunny day I sat on the open top deck in wonderful peace and solitude. I was reading a book when a man decided to use his penis as my book marker. I did not look at him but I slammed my book shut. That was enough to send him running.

Behind our hotel was a winding little road with a small field in which there were two well-looked after tethered ponies. We used to walk up this road to get to the little local pizzeria up the hill. We had been hearing complaints of a peeping tom. In fact it turned out to be a flasher lurking in with the ponies obviously multitasking as he leered at the rooms at the side of the hotel. I shouted some choice abuse and he ran, tripping over his trousers as he went. Then on another occasion we were driving to Como, all females, and a Fiat sped past and stopped in a lay-by and the driver got out and flashed at us as we drove by. He did it four times so he clearly knew the road. Unfortunately for him we took his registration and I passed it on. All of these instances didn't cause a life implosion for me but they taught me to always have my wits about me as a female traveller in **any** country. I know from speaking to other women that such behaviour happened in various countries at these times, but I hope today women are not subjected to the same unwanted and intimidating episodes, or that if women do experience these, that they call them out!

My second big life implosion occurred after I met my husband abroad and 3 children later, the horrid realisation dawned that I was marooned in a foreign country, feeling trapped and that we had far too much of a culture clash to have a future together…

The following summer after Lake Como, I met my husband in Sorrento and by the following Autumn I'd left my job and moved to live with him in a small village between Pompeii and Naples. I was also expecting my first child with him so my life changed very quickly. To be fair he was the only man I had a real emotional attachment with. I stuck out like a sore thumb where I lived. I was tall and fair whilst the locals were short, dark haired and had olive skin. So here I was again with feelings of deracination. I often thought I would have made a simple task for a hitman. That was the first thing that struck me. The second thing was the language. They spoke local dialect whilst I spoke standard Italian and for that fact alone they thought I was posh and gave me the nickname 'la Marchese' (the marquess). To be fair as nicknames went, I thought it was classy.

My husband's family were blue-eyed, fair skinned and quite tall. They owned property and agricultural land on which they grew hazelnuts and walnuts. My brother-in-law was quite frankly rude and ignorant for someone who was supposedly educated and a maths teacher. Xenophobia did not even begin to describe his attitude. I was pleased to hear that he had his car damaged on many occasions primarily due to his second job as a car insurance assessor. He deserved it to be honest because he was rude and unfeeling. I had two sisters-in-law: one was married with a son and a daughter and she lived in a nearby village with her husband. The other one was unmarried with mental health issues and lived at home. I had little to do with either. We were surrounded by lots of extended family and everyone knew everyone else's business.

I spoke standard Italian fluently but initially my husband and I spoke English. He had been in Chicago for seven years and had married an Italian immigrant like he was, when he was eighteen. They were divorced five years later. Then he went to work in New York for two years before he returned to Italy. There were no children. When we met, I was 25 and he was 38. I got pregnant despite being on the pill but I knew I wanted to keep the baby when I started bleeding in Venice. I saw a gynaecologist who managed to stop the bleeding. I did not want to leave it to fate so I committed to the pregnancy irrespective if the father did or not. As it happened, he wanted the child too. So I resigned half way through my coach tour contract and my lover picked me up in Rome.

We travelled to his home village where he rented an apartment. We weren't hitched but that didn't bother me in the slightest. However, thirteen days before my son was born, we did get married at the local town hall mainly because life was harder for an illegitimate child in Italy. I did not want a church wedding and nor did he. At first everything was fine. I was nesting so I had a lot of things to occupy myself with. Then my first child was born: a son!

Until then I had never even held a baby. My son was big with blonde hair and blue eyes and he had such a happy demeanour. He was healthy, ate well and was literally the light of my life. I had never felt so much love for another human being as I did for him. Italians always want a son to inherit the family name so he was spoilt rotten by the extended family. He became the 'golden child' - the first son of the first son. Given that he was the only boy born in that family amongst the cousins who all had daughters, there was a lot of underlying resentment directed towards me.

However, when my son was six months' old, Southern Italy was hit by a major earthquake. I remember it being early evening and we were visiting my in-laws. They lived in an old building opposite the church in the village square. It started with a sound like an articulated vehicle right outside the door, rattling and vibrating. I picked up my son and went outside in the square. At that moment I heard a whooshing sound and watched as the street lights started to sway and the ground moved. It felt like being aboard the deck of a ship on a very rough sea. What I witnessed was the displacement of air as the plate moved due south in Calabria. It lasted only 56 seconds but felt much longer. Then the power cut out and that continued for three days. Freak snow and abnormally strong winds followed and we had to resort to using candles and extra blankets. Luckily we had an open fireplace or we would have been in dire straits as our windows and the buildings there, were not designed for Arctic weather. Our stove was gas too, so we kept warm. Normally there is never frost or snow unless you go higher up into the mountains. Thankfully for us, our building sustained zero damage but some were destroyed or severely damaged. Phone lines came down too. The aftershocks seemed worse than the initial event and they continued for about a month on and off. It was traumatic.

My daughter was born the following year. By then we had moved to a bigger apartment in a market town nearby. It was modern with large balconies, a huge lounge, kitchen, two bathrooms and two large bedrooms. The strange thing is with unfurnished apartments in Italy, there is no fitted kitchen and no light fittings: you are expected to provide them. I preferred this environment though and set to work making our home comfortable. There were parks and shops nearby but it was a difficult pregnancy and my daughter was born two weeks' late. It did not help that I had to endure one of the hottest summers on record.

My daughter weighed 10.5lbs. She was enormous! Very pretty with strawberry blonde hair and light brown eyes with green flecks and she had cream-coloured skin. But she soon displayed a bit of a wilful nature and she cried a lot at night. So I had a fifteen-month-old son who was like a Duracell bunny during the day and a newborn who slept during the day whilst at night, it was the reverse. The first two months were very hard and it didn't help that I contracted a terrible cold virus as well. A lack of sleep and being ill is not a good combination but I endured the hard times and refused to give in. Things got better and peace resumed. My daughter was a good eater and her sleeping pattern stabilised by three months but it was all incredibly hard. My third child, another son, was born 21 months after his sister. He weighed just over 11lbs but he was a placid child and by then, we were adept at handling babies and toddlers.

A year later I got pregnant again but I had a miscarriage and I think that was the beginning of the end for me. I was having a quiet internal implosion realising that everything was coming to a head for me and that my situation really wasn't working for me at all any more but how on earth to get out of it?! I'd become bored at home with the monotony of my life. I was on my own with my children a lot because my husband was away on business so much because he ran his own company. He often had to travel abroad to the US and Eastern Europe and he was very set in his ways. The longer I remained in Italy back then, I realised there were few choices there for me. I grew homesick and wanted to return to Britain or live in the US or Canada even but there was no way my husband would consider that.

I was questioning everything about my life. Everything felt quite bleak. Then my father-in-law died of a heart attack and as I watched the earth filling his grave, I silently asked myself if I wanted to be buried in that black, volcanic soil? The answer was no. I thought I am not a Catholic and I am not going to be buried in a Catholic cemetery. I kept that realisation to myself. I was not even thirty years old. I was not going to think about death but those ideas remained nevertheless. It occurred to me that my husband was completely oblivious and unsympathetic towards my worries, despite having had many a conversation about the concerns I had for our future and that of our children. It occurred to me that he was fine. He had not lost nor sacrificed anything in our relationship. He had gained a wife and three children which I didn't think he appreciated enough. Furthermore my husband was selfish, becoming overbearing and he expected me to put up, shut up and simply be grateful. A huge gulf had grown between us over our different cultures, lives, future expectations and possibilities.

Matters came to a head and I had to make a life-defining decision: stay and hope for the best or leave and restart a life in the UK? I wanted to go to university in the UK where I could get a grant to do so. No such thing existed in Italy for me. Plus I wanted a future for my children based on meritocracy not nepotism. The decision was based on me hedging my bets to take an opportunity. So I had to channel my inner steel core and I took off! I flew to Britain taking the children with me on the premise of visiting my parents and we remained here especially as the eldest was five and I wanted him to start school in England.

I had had the wherewithal to have the children put onto my passport because had they had Italian documents instead, this would have necessitated that I provide a notarised permission letter from their father agreeing for them to travel without him. I then sued for divorce in the UK as I had registered the Italian marriage at the British Consulate. My husband formally contested this so we ended up in the High Court in London. I had to have the children made 'Wards of Court' as I started to be harassed by people sent by my husband and there was a real threat that they could be taken back to Italy without my consent. In fact, on one occasion I found myself being constantly followed over two days by a car. I gave its registration to the Police and they told me it was a private detective hired by my husband. Typical I thought as when I did not respond to his apologies or attempts at empathy, he followed through with coercion. I knew that had I returned to Italy, I would have been on curfew: even my limited freedoms would be over and the resentment at the action I had taken and the impact on my husband's pride, would be severe. I could not risk those repercussions. Thus I had to be stoical and my pragmatism overrode any emotions I felt. I simply did not allow myself to feel sentimental. However his attempts to intimidate me and this time in my life, was incredibly stressful.

I was granted the divorce and my husband was granted visitation rights accompanied by a designated social services employee. He made one visit only and then he got on with his life, never providing any child maintenance. Effectively I returned to the UK with four suitcases and I had to start all over again from scratch. There were no reciprocal agreements between our nations to force him to pay and he honestly believed that because we were not living with him, he had the right to relinquish all financial responsibility for his children. But I couldn't feel battered by life for long! I just had to find the strength to push on and seek a better life for myself and for my family.

Even without receiving any divorce or maintenance money from my husband and having to start completely afresh, I felt optimistic! I had the support of my family and we rented a house nearby. I got second-hand furniture, a grant for new beds and my parents bought new carpets for me and had them fitted. My father provided me with a car as he had motor businesses and he became a father-figure for my children. They loved him dearly. I regret that they grew up without their own father but I do not regret returning to the UK. It was very hard initially but we had family stability and life got better after I started work.

I turned my attention to my career at long-last and decided that I would go to university and undertake a Degree in French and Italian, followed by a PGCE so that I could teach. I was playing the long game. The pension potential was good so I wouldn't be living in penury when I was in my dotage nor be beholden on the state or my children. I was determined to remain independent. The job would fit in well with childcare too.

The children had experienced a lot of upheaval. They had to learn English fluently and incredibly they did within three months of arriving in the UK. I did not want to add to any feelings of insecurity that they already had, so my aim was to give them consistency and security as well as the love and affection they deserved. I am not perfect. I hide my feelings well but I had to be both parents, so it was really challenging at times but I supported them as best as I could in all respects. I just had to be resilient and focused and think forwards all the time!

Back then, teaching was one of the few professions where it was not a man's world. The salary rose every year one was in service and there was opportunity for career progression. My children were all of school age so I began my Degree in London which I completed. As I had to do an entry test for French, I was nervous but I passed with 100% and I spoke, wrote and read Italian fluently too, so I was accepted in that department after a short interview in Italian. Effectively I undertook a joint doubles award. I was apprehensive at first but I soon made friends and not everyone on my double honours' Degree was eighteen or nineteen years old. It involved a large workload and included a course on Modern European History and Linguistics, but I enjoyed it all!

I found it amusing that some of the younger students were complaining that the study workload was too much for them, given that I had to cater for three children and my commute too. But I worked in the evenings when the children were in bed and I read on the train. I rediscovered my love of learning and specialised in literature. Later as part of my Degree, I had to spend a year abroad in France and Italy with six months in each and I took two of the children with me. I organised my own accommodation and the children went to school out there too. My eldest remained with his grandparents and we returned for holidays. So yes it was challenging but it was not insurmountable. My youngest spoke French better than I did and played a mean game of French Bowls and marbles.

Time progressed and my parents purchased a large house in Devon and we moved down there with them and I completed my PGCE at Exeter University. I received study grants for fees, maintenance and travel which enabled me to do all of this, for which I am eternally thankful. My parents helped with childcare. I was also given a bonus at the end of my PGCE as teachers of my subject then were highly sought after. I was grateful for that as I ended those five years of education without debt and I had a job to go to in September when my PGCE concluded. The most difficult part, ironically, was getting a student bank account as if you didn't fit into the 18-25 bracket then the computer literally did say no but fortunately one bank came to my rescue.

Thus I became a teacher and latterly a Head Of Modern Languages, a Head of House and for a while, an Assistant Deputy Head (pastoral). Teenagers didn't frighten me. I never had problems with poor behaviour and we had a mutual respect for each other. Furthermore I loved what I taught so I think that helped a lot. With me, there is no grey line and children respected that. Furthermore I finally felt grounded and part of a group of people with shared goals. I was able to organise many school trips abroad without the services of a designated schools' travel company and my trips were always oversubscribed. It was cheaper and the hotels were of a better quality plus we flew there rather than spent days on a sweaty coach. I am grateful that so many children had those experiences and I'm proud that I was able to arrange them.

But I had another really emotionally-challenging year to deal with: it was the year that both my mother died and also my Italian ex-husband, when my youngest child was eight years old. My husband was shot by his business partner who then went on to shoot himself. It was ruled homicide/suicide. The shooting took place over a weekend in a factory which they both ran, so they were found on the Monday by a member of staff. It was a pretty tragic ending to be honest and shocking too. However badly things had ended between us previously, it was still so final, dramatic and upsetting especially as he was the father of my children and I had to tell them what had happened to their dad.

It took twenty years to sort out the property division and part of that is still ongoing. I dread to think what would have happened to us had we been living in Italy as a family when this happened as there was no friendly family left locally and zero government support. I attended the funeral in Italy and returned the next day, after visiting the Police station and claiming my husband's personal effects which were no longer required by forensics. I still have the blood-stained bank notes he had in his pocket and his blood-stained gold chain and watch. It was a sad ending despite our history. Telling the children required a certain stoicism as they had lost their beloved grandfather six months previously too. I now had my mother to look after too, although she coped very well but she died soon after of a cerebral aneurysm. That was indeed a sad and really difficult year. Sometimes you get these times of just one major shock after another… and somehow you have to get through.

I still love Italy but I am settled now in the UK. I never remarried. I was far too busy bringing up my children and furthering my career. I had no need of a partner. I was self sufficient and in a secure profession. I am retired now but I am full of life and grateful for all of the incredible experiences I have had which have made me the person I am today, and yes, that does include my life implosions too!

WHAT HAVE YOUR EXPERIENCES TAUGHT YOU?

Basically with determination and resilience, anything is possible.

All three of my children went to excellent universities in the UK and got Degrees. I was the first woman in my family to attend university and get a Degree. My children were the first of their generation to have achieved the same. My two sons work in the City in prestigious jobs. My daughter has her own e-business and is a fluent Italian speaker. They are all married with children. Not one of them turned out to be a natural born linguist though, like me. My daughter had to work hard at learning Italian, so I think this ability may jump a generation or two. All three children own their own property. In fact both sons own multiple properties. They have never been on benefits and have always worked even when they were at university.

After listening to the poor expectations in the media and their negative stereotypes of children in one-parent families, I am proud to dispel that stereotype. I got fed up with being judged by this negative stereotype with all the poor expectations and aspirations that came with it. I certainly did not fit the stereotype of how a single parent is often portrayed and I resented how easily we pigeon-hole people in this country. Sometimes it is better to live in a stable one-parent family than in an unhappy two-parent one. What matters is instilling goals and ambitions and the self-belief required to thrive, in one's children, and to set an example ourselves.

Finally, I think I bucked the trend when it came to aspirations for my generation of women. In my mind I was equal to any man and sometimes much better in most of the employment I held in my lifetime. I did discover, rather amusingly though, that being assertive and outspoken does not win many friends and scares insecure males. I have a gift for scaring them unintentionally so I have been told. I learned quickly when to use that weapon. Ironically I much prefer working with strong males than females as fellow females tend to be more treacherous towards their own gender than the male of the species who is more pragmatic generally speaking and less emotionally prone to criticism or insult. As they say, the female of the species is the deadliest. Shame they do not always support their fellow sisters though as they are potentially the instruments of their own demise in a world still dominated by men.

WHAT ADVICE WOULD YOU GIVE TO OTHER WOMEN IN A
SIMILAR SITUATION?

For me it has to be to do what is best for your mental health and well-being. It is very hard to remove oneself from difficult family situations but you have to accept them as they are when you realise that there isn't a positive change in sight. Otherwise to stay is ultimately much harder and most of the time, breeds contempt and unhappiness. These days there is help to leave an unhappy relationship and start afresh and there are so many happier possibilities to embrace.

WHERE ARE YOU NOW? WHAT ARE YOUR PLANS FOR THE
FUTURE?

So the circle goes back to the beginning. I knew very early on that I wanted to be independent and that I should not rely on anyone else to achieve my ambitions and sadly I was proven correct. I achieved that goal eventually. I can honestly say that my mental well-being and the future of my children mattered more than my relationship with my husband. I started to feel myself descending into a dark state of hopelessness before I left Italy with my three children and our suitcases. I had to make a very difficult decision. I had a good life before I married and I led a secure life after I divorced. Now that I have retired, I have my freedom and a comfortable lifestyle.

Despite everything, I feel happy that I achieved what I planned all those years ago hiding in the long grass watching those aeroplanes above me. Ironically I no longer have that same need to travel any more, preferring the simpler things in life like my pets, my garden and spending time with my grandchildren and watching them grow, content in the knowledge that when I depart this mortal coil a little part of me will still be walking the Earth. Quite happily I imagine.

I am currently enjoying a fulfilling retirement. After years of sixty-hour weeks and bringing up my children alone, I can now sit back and enjoy the fruits of my labour, leading a stress-free life. I am enjoying every minute of this part of my existence too.

CHANTAL'S STORY

When at 41, life seems relatively normal one minute and then the next, you've got a permanent life-changing diagnosis…

The first thing I knew about the beginnings of my brain tumour journey was seeing paramedics in our bedroom during the night of Sunday 31st May 2020, when I had a full tonic-clonic seizure in front of my terrified husband and children. My husband Andrew (Andy) thought I was choking because of the sounds I was making and he couldn't wake me. He called the ambulance and managed to move our dog safely out of the way. When the paramedics arrived, I remember hearing my name and being jolted to. It felt like a dream as I awoke to four paramedics in my bedroom and I was unable to communicate so I just kept looking at Andy.

The paramedics were asking me questions and I knew the answers but my words wouldn't come out. Andy said that they didn't know how they were going to get me down the stairs and they called for back-up. But somehow I ended up walking down them and out to the waiting ambulance. I then had another seizure in the ambulance and a further two in A&E but I remember nothing of these. I was very much out of it as I was in and out of sleep. Due to the Covid lockdown, the resultant hospital stay, tests, appointments and diagnosis had to be dealt with by myself. I wasn't allowed Andy or my children by my side.

I remember a doctor coming to see me and saying that they were going to take me for an MRI scan. I'm not sure how they got me in the machine as I had obviously gone to sleep. I woke up in the machine and started to reach for the head guard, not knowing what it was. A kind voice came over the tannoy and asked me to keep still. Then I must have gone back off to sleep.

That doctor turned out to be my Neurosurgeon, Mr Iyer, who later told me that they had found a brain tumour. Whilst he was telling me this devastating news, I remember looking at him and thinking he had such a kind face. I was so out of it that I didn't really take it in. However, my brain tumour was in the left frontal part of my brain: the area controlling speech, coordination and memory. Mr Iyer telephoned Andy with the news that would change our lives forever.

I was discharged on the Tuesday evening and Andy was waiting for me. I cried all the way home. I was more devastated for Andrew having to receive the news via a phone call and also about the fact that my poor girls had had to witness their mum having an unexpected seizure.

Once home, we had a video call on the Friday from Mr Iyer. My nan drove from Bedford so that she could be with me for the call. My mind was so frazzled that again, I couldn't take it all in. It was such a surreal time. I was told that they thought it was benign and I would need an 'Awake craniotomy' because of where the tumour was sited. This was surgery which would remove the tumour under local anaesthetic rather than general anaesthetic in order to avoid brain damage.

It was actually a relief once I was diagnosed as I realised that I wasn't lazy or going mad and there was a genuine reason for everything, it just wasn't the reason

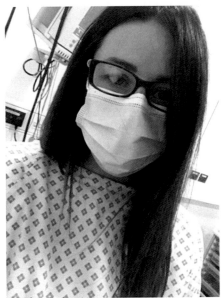
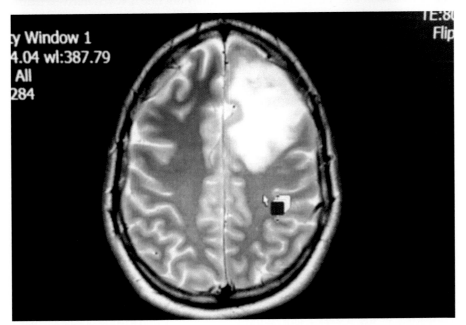

I was expecting or wanted. My symptoms were real. I was constantly tired and once I had cooked for my girls, I would climb back into bed. Andrew would often return home from work and find me in bed before we realised what was wrong with me, yet never once did he moan at me. He is amazing.

The thought of an Awake Craniotomy was terrifying but they put so much in place that I didn't really have time to think about it. It involved two months of tests and video calls with a lovely speech therapist called Helen. I had to undertake tests with her that were so simple, for example, she would show me a picture of a spoon and several other items and I would have to match it. She would pick a letter and I would have to say as many things as I could that were beginning with that letter. These would be the tests that she would do in the surgery.

Once the date was fixed for my operation, I had a week of self-isolation and a Covid test, before finally on 10 August 2020, this procedure went ahead. I remember coming around when it was time to start removing the tumour and Helen was going through the tests and a couple of times my words were stuttering so she would notify Mr Iyer and he would then move to another area of the tumour. I remember being so tired and just thinking, 'please let me sleep'. Helen said that I was awake for quite a bit of it but it's more than I can remember. The operation required 2 neurosurgeons, 2 anaesthetists, several nurses and Helen as it was a full day in surgery and I was their only patient that day. It took 7.5 hours and then I needed an additional 3 hours to recover. Whilst in recovery, Mr Iyer told me that they had managed to remove 90% of it but that it would likely grow back.

Just three days after my brain surgery, I made a really good recovery and was allowed home. Then, 2 weeks' later, I received the results about my tumour via another video call. The biopsy showed that it was an Oligodendroglioma, Grade 2. I was told that this was a slow-growing tumour but one that was likely to return and could also change grades. As a result, I would need to be under the care of the Neurology department forever so that any growth or change could be dealt with immediately. Mr Iyer said that he couldn't tell me how long I had had the tumour for but looking back my symptoms started around 10 years' ago but then they were so generic, so it wouldn't have been easily diagnosable.

My symptoms included the following: I'd struggled to sleep for years and used to wake up having night sweats but I just assumed I was going through an early menopause. I had been to the doctors numerous times as I really didn't feel right, but I couldn't articulate why. Each time I had a blood test, the results were that I had a Vitamin D deficiency and that I was low in magnesium. In the past I was offered anti-depressants, which I didn't take as I knew I wasn't depressed or not in the sense that the doctor thought I was. I assumed that I was exhausted because of working in a stressful job combined with looking after a family. I just thought it was the norm of being a working mum and I needed to get on with it.

I remember times when I lost the strength on my left-hand side, and I'd wake up with a fuzzy head as though I'd been drinking. But again I pushed this all to one side as I just assumed it was a lack of sleep as I was only managing on a few hours' each night. Three weeks prior to the seizure, I lost my balance in the garden and tripped over 'nothing', I hurt both of my feet and could hardly walk. Also on the day of the seizure I said things that were just nonsensical: I knew what I wanted to say but the words wouldn't come out properly.

***

I've had moments where I've cried and been so scared and that's only normal as it's human nature but I've had to stay positive for myself to get through the treatment and also for my family. I've had to go to all of my hospital appointments by myself. Andrew has only been in two of my oncologist appointments and the first was following my surgery, when I was told that I would need 6x weeks of 30 radiotherapy sessions from Monday-Friday. I never expected it to be that many and I just sat and cried. The second appointment which Andy attended, was when we discussed my new chemo.

The radiotherapy involved lots of travelling every weekday and the loss of my hair. This was tough! I actually found the hair loss to be the most traumatic aspect from all the treatment. I loved my hair and I didn't realise the amount of hair I would lose. It really came as a shock. They tell you at the beginning that there will be hair loss and they kind of give you a rough idea and I assumed I would be able to hide it, how wrong was I?!

I cut my hair into a short bob, just to have some kind of control. I went down to washing my hair once a week and towel-drying it only. During the first week of radiotherapy my head felt as though ants were constantly running across my scalp. It was such a horrible sensation and was obviously related to the impact of the treatment upon my hair follicles. My hair started to fall out around the 3-week mark, exactly as I had been told it would. It didn't stop falling out until the following January.

I remember just sitting and crying the first time a clump of hair came out. I was losing hair rapidly and not once did I pull my hair, I just had to touch it and it would be in my hands. At the time, I took and have kept, photographs of this as a record of the rapid hair loss but also to show the positive side of how much it grew back in a short space of time.

When my radiotherapy finished at the end of November, I had a break in my treatment over Christmas to relax and give my body a rest before the start of PCV chemotherapy. My chemo involved six cycles with each cycle lasting six weeks, so it was a lengthy process up until September 2021. I started PCV Chemo at the end of January 2021 and just to explain, 'PCV' stands for Procarbazine, Lomustine and Vincristine and I've been told that this is the best chemo to treat gliomas at present. Vincristine goes into your bloodstream intravenously, whilst Lomustine and Procarbazine are taken as capsules.

The chemo cycles went like this:

Cycle 1: I coped really well and only had mild side effects. I actually thought to myself: 'this isn't so bad', but again, how wrong was I?

Because my veins are really hard to find, my Oncologist decided that I would drop the Vincristine;

Cycle 2: My blood tests came back showing that my healthy liver levels were low, so I had to wait for them to come up. This took a week and then the nausea and dizziness started pretty much straight away;

Cycle 3: Again my blood results weren't great and as before I had to wait a week before they were at a level at which it was safe for me to carry on with my treatment. After a couple of days, I started to be sick and had diarrhoea. This lasted for 4 days and I said to my husband that he needed to call the out-of-hours' team for me. It was on a Sunday afternoon and I could feel that I was becoming weaker. I was asked to attend the hospital where a blood test quickly showed that I was dehydrated. After a couple of bags of fluid and a change of sickness tablets, I was allowed home. I was asked to stop the rest of my tablets;

Cycle 4: This cycle was going well until day 7 when all of a sudden, I came out in hives. The pain was horrendous. I popped back to the hospital and was prescribed a tube of steroid cream. I honestly thought that they would stop my chemo at this point but no, they wanted me to carry on. (Before I started chemo, I was told that most people only make it to cycle 4);

Cycle 5: The nausea and dizziness felt constant and I slept quite a lot for the 10 days of the treatment;

Cycle 6: This was pretty much like Cycle 5, I could hardly lift my head off my pillow as the room would spin. It was such a horrible feeling and all I could do was keep my head flat.

From the start to finish, the chemo lasted 9 months. It was amazing to finish it and also to finish all 6 cycles. When you're in the middle of the treatment, you really can't see the end. You just have to take each day slowly: rest when your body needs you too and boy, your body will let you know when it needs to stop!

During chemo, I trained for the Bristol 10k run. I'm not a runner but I wanted to raise money for Brain Tumour Support. I got a team together and we ran the Bristol 10k. To train, I used to start my chemo tablets and run for the first day and then I was so sick, that I would rest for the next 8 days. Looking back, I don't know how I did it but it just shows what you can do when you put your mind to it. Each year, I will do something to raise money for brain tumour charities (there are many different types of brain tumour). The Bristol 10k was an amazing experience and one I'll never forget. The relief at the finish line was unbelievable. I couldn't believe that I had just ran the 10k whilst on chemo!!

The after-effects from the chemotherapy are still with me: my short-term memory isn't great but I've improved without realising. When you're in that moment, you can't imagine 6 months down the line, but here I am living my best life! Since the chemo finished, I've had 2 stable scans and I've now been able to move to 6-monthly scans. When my Oncologist told me, I cried with relief. Waiting for scans is horrendous. SCANXIETY is very real and you don't realise how scared you are until you get the results, which can be anything from 3-9 weeks!

The day-to-day reality of living with a brain tumour includes the acceptance that fundamental aspects of your life have changed. From my very first seizure, I had to surrender my driving licence. I lost my independence straight away and have had to rely on Andy to drive me everywhere since. I'm on seizure tablets twice a day, which I'll probably be on for the rest of my life.

As much as I look well and healthy, I find conversations can be draining and I get fatigued quite a lot. My concentration levels and energy can be very low, just normal family life with our daughters can be exhausting. I sometimes struggle to find the right word and need time to find it myself. I feel like I need a badge to let people know that I do struggle to process information and it's not me being 'thick'.

There are some days where I'm able to multitask and these are good days, but other days, if I manage one thing then I'm proud of that. I'm still not sleeping brilliantly and there's a fine line of over stimulation and under stimulation, which

I'm still trying to manage. I'm only six months post-surgery so hopefully all of the above will get easier, but it can be incredibly frustrating. It really is a hidden illness. I look fine but I'm not really.

However I have to get on, my girls depend on me and this last year has taught me not to waste time and to challenge myself more as you never know what's around the corner. Life is blooming precious!

What have your experiences taught you?

Live your life to the fullest! Take yourself out of your comfort zone. Life is truly for living and I don't think I really appreciated everything around me before. Take yourself out for lunch on your own. Enjoy spending time with yourself.

What would you advise other women in your situation?

Stay as positive as you can. I believe that's what got me through. Yes, you can cry and have really shitty days but don't spend too long there. As hard as it is, you've got to keep going. Small steps! Benign isn't fine and you're never the same after hearing the words 'Brain tumour' You're just a new you and that's okay!

Where are you now? What are your plans for the future?

This whole experience has been completely life-changing. I'm just a new me now! I'm very much enjoying living. Just to wake up every morning is a real blessing, which sounds really cheesy but that's how I feel. We have bought a static van last year by the sea and eventually we will move to the coast. The sea air is good for the soul and walking on the beach with my family and our dog is the best feeling. I have also got a new job and enjoy working again.

I am also now determined to raise awareness of brain tumours and encourage people to look out for symptoms. Furthermore, I want to highlight the impact that a brain tumour and the resulting treatment can have, so that those who receive a diagnosis feel more prepared and supported.

Post-script

I've just been diagnosed with the menopause. Chemo: the gift that keeps on giving. My symptoms are nightsweats, hot flushes, low (non-existant libido), dry vagina, brain fog, sore joints/bones, low moods and I haven't had a period for a whole year.

My doctor is writing to my Oncologist to check if HRT would be suitable or if it will encourage my tumour to grow? My GP has put me on Citalopram for now to help with the nightsweats and hot flushes. However, as before, getting a diagnosis (this time the menopause), has been a relief. It proves once again that I'm not going crazy. Fortunately I have a very understanding husband and he has been there with me all the way through my treatment. This is just another thing we will get through together. I know my own body and I just want to feel well again.

I would also like to add: you know your own body better than anyone If something doesn't feel right, then please keep going back to the doctors. If you're not happy with what they have said, then see another doctor. Doctors are human beings too and they don't always know everything.

AUTHOR'S NOTE

Although she is terrified of heights, Chantal has, incredibly, actually booked to take part in her first-ever charity sky dive this September to raise money for Brain Tumour research! HUGE Good Luck wishes to her!

ROSIE'S STORY

When you've fractured your ankle and en route to the hospital, your angry husband says: "I'm just going to leave you by the side of the road" and you just know you can't go on coping with this behaviour which makes you feel as though you're living with a human pressure cooker…

Years after I left my marriage, my ex-husband Joe, an Orthopaedic Surgeon, would still contact my parents to berate me to them. On one occasion he rang my mum and berated me to her for an hour. Joe refused to acknowledge that there could be any behaviour on his part that contributed to our marriage failing and thus he was overwhelmingly angry that I had left him. His rant to her on this occasion went along the lines of: "your daughter did this, your daughter did that!" Obviously my mum didn't want to hear him talking about me in this way but she was trying to maintain a relationship with Joe as she had viewed him 'like a son' until recently. Also because he is the father of our children/her grandchildren, it felt in everyone's interests to keep things as amicable as they could possibly be, but ultimately she had to hold the phone back from her ears as his tirade went on and on…

My story is about how to recognise damaging behaviour within a long marriage and feel able to leave even when you know it's going to be an uphill struggle. I wanted to describe how unreasonable behaviour can insidiously creep into a marriage and destroy it but that it can take ages to recognise what's truly going on and to feel justified in being able to walk away from it. I found coping with my former husband's behaviour before, throughout and after our divorce, incredibly stressful as he went out of his way to make it increasingly acrimonious: for example, by completely cutting off my child maintenance without even giving me any notice. To this day, he continues to be difficult but I have tried my hardest to ignore it and have instead focused on building myself a brilliant new life.

I wanted to tell my story to say to other women that if you're experiencing similar behaviour, you don't have to put up with it indefinitely, thinking that it's better to have someone in your life and maintain your marriage as opposed to being on your own and/or breaking up your family and starting afresh. Actually it's so much better for everyone in a family to call time on a dysfunctional, unhealthy, toxic relationship as opposed to allowing it to fester out of a sense of misplaced loyalty or martyrdom.

My marriage had been deteriorating over the last decade of a nearly 22-year-period. This was particularly so after the arrival of our twin sons (who are now 13), when there was a noticeable tenseness during the time Joe and I were in hospital together with one of the twins when he was critically ill as a toddler, with sepsis. Rather than pulling together at that crisis point, I 'withdrew into my shell' in our hospital room because Joe got unnecessarily cross/snappy with me a few times when I needed him to support me because I was so stressed that this son was going to die (for example, Joe angrily berated me for telling one of our consultants that a nurse had let me hold our child for a cuddle - when he was attached to his drips). I felt embarrassed especially because this was also the hospital where I worked as a nurse (Joe worked at a different hospital, equidistant from our Scottish home).

After this experience and in the following (but also preceding years), I found myself getting emotionally close to a couple of guys: work colleagues in my hospital. Nothing physical happened with these men, but we just connected emotionally and they filled the void that I obviously felt in my marriage.

It feels a very delicate task to peel back the lid of my broken marriage but I am going to quote from examples listed in my Divorce Petition on the grounds of 'Unreasonable Behaviour.' When I left my husband who I am calling Joe in this piece, he was so bitter and angry that he tried to throw everything at me via my solicitor. He tried to say that I was an exercise-addict, an anorexic, a neglectful parent and an alcoholic; anything he could think of and twist basically. It was horrible to think that someone I had once loved and who I thought had loved me, could attempt to destroy me in this manner.

I had to have some time off nursing because I was accused of accidentally giving a patient the wrong medication dosage whilst I was so stressed because of my marriage issues. I was suspended and this was investigated officially but then Joe inflated this to try to make it somehow seem more than it was. Joe ranted about the fact that the Divorce Petition was coincidentally served on him on his birthday, angrily uttering: "how could I?" I had a whole irate email about this because he still refused to believe that I had left and wasn't coming back but I had no idea when the divorce petition would be served and I hadn't thought about it as I just needed to get it underway.

I knew that Joe and I weren't in a good place together and everything had been deteriorating for years but although I tried to fix things and stay buoyant and upbeat about my relationship, I knew it was sinking and my husband refused to countenance this. Our marital decay gained momentum a few years' ago when one Sunday morning I was running through a dark forest and then I tripped up and I knew I'd injured myself...

***

That summer had been a stressful time because my marriage was seriously breaking-down and we'd had a horrible holiday abroad in the Mediterranean where the atmosphere between us all as a family and especially between my husband and I, was particularly dire. I knew then that my relationship with him was completely over. It was so ironic too, that we were in this picturesque setting but the chemistry between us was just so wrong and not only wrong, but it felt toxic. I've talked to other women since and heard lots of similar stories of being away in picturesque holiday destinations but those being overshadowed by the ominous behaviour of spouses and partners.

Just days before that holiday, through an answerphone message from a high-end estate agency, I'd found out that my husband was secretly trying to buy another property in a hamlet which I'll call 'Oakford' that we could never afford, when we hadn't even been able to pay for the building work which we were then having done at the same time, on our more modest home. This bigger property at Oakford, also needed a massive amount of renovating, which would have increased the costs further by hundreds of thousands of pounds. When I asked Joe what was going on, he'd got irate with me for having the audacity to question his right to fulfil his dreams, even though had we gone ahead with the purchase of the Oakford property, it would have bankrupted us, but he refused to acknowledge this, trying to wave off my concern with a condescending sweep of his hands in the air as though my worries were completely irrelevant.

Joe had already promised our kids that they could hold huge parties at this large Oakford property when they were older so me saying that realistically it just wasn't financially viable, didn't make me popular. Joe portrayed me as the bad parent and a selfish wife, spoiling his lifelong dreams. My husband attempted to manipulate my children to take sides with him, against me, so the atmosphere on that holiday was very tense and I felt that I was being ganged-up against. It felt as though it was 'divide and rule' and pitching one parent against the other in the popularity stakes. It was weird as we were meant to be working together but I just felt undermined and humiliated as he made jokes aimed at me, to denigrate me. It was a strange situation to have my husband competing against me whilst we were all living together.

This wasn't the first time my husband had been privately making plans to buy other properties for us to move to, miles away from our home. In fact, he was always viewing houses with a view to buying/relocating, behind my back and it was stressful because I'd ring his mobile at work and he wouldn't be either in the hospital itself or in surgery because I'd find out he'd taken the day off to go and see a place he wanted to buy and for us all to move to and these properties would be in a different county to the one we lived in, at least 70 or 80 miles away. It would often be a biggish pile with land, outbuildings and in need of renovating – basically a massive undertaking that we could simply neither afford nor had the time for (and as anyone who's ever been hands-on with a building project knows, they always cost more than you assume, they take more time than they're meant to and they are generally stressful – they're certainly not a romantic venture. When I recently watched 'The Nest' on Netflix with Jude Law, I have to say that there were so many similarities with his behaviour and Joe's behaviour, that I actually found it hard to watch how his wife kept trying to accommodate his delusional ideas just as I had done, until I cracked up).

Joe never considered how any potential house-moves would affect me or the children's lives (potentially having to change our jobs/schools/completely start afresh with friends, etc, in a new area), because he was completely autonomous and felt in charge and in control. Joe simply felt that he would get a new position wherever and we'd all just go with it. Thus I felt permanently unsettled and as though my left hand didn't know what my right hand was doing because Joe wouldn't consult me about any of this: he just went 'off on a jolly' of his own.

After finding out about this huge building project at Oakford that Joe had his eye on, the tension before we left for our holiday, was palpable. I nearly didn't go away with them all because I felt very stressed and I couldn't face being with him, but after a manic year at work and having to take on overtime and night-shifts, I was really looking forward to some time with my children, so I didn't feel I could stay at home for two weeks whilst they were away.

I desperately knew that because my husband would never leave our marriage or the family home, but that also after nearly 22 years together, Joe would never change and our financial issues were rapidly intensifying and our debts escalating, that somehow I needed to leave him for my own sanity. However, I had absolutely no money and no idea how on earth I could make the break that I knew had to be made. The reason I didn't have any spare money was because my nursing wage was very low as I hadn't been nursing for that long and what I did earn was used to pay my car insurance, phone, gym, get the family food shopping and pay other bills. I had nothing left to save. Joe refused to give me any financial help even though he earned such a mammoth amount by comparison. I hated it in the last couple of weeks before my payday when I'd have to ask him for money to buy the family food shopping because my wages had run dry.

In order to survive mentally, I knew I needed to leave because his irascibility was increasing. We had separated once before in the past, for a period of weeks but I reconciled with him because our eldest child was very young at the time, so I felt I had an obligation and duty to really try to make my marriage work. Also back then, he too really wanted 'us' to work and he seriously tried to meet me half way and so we both were invested in having a second attempt!

Furthermore, I was raised in a religion where marriage is virtually for life and also within those beliefs is the notion of 'headship', namely that a man is the Head of the House and everyone else in the household, including a wife, must defer to her husband's authority. Therefore although I know it sounds completely archaic now, I'd been conditioned to think that even in the 21st century, I shouldn't ultimately question Joe's authority.

My parents' marriage was also based on the principle of male headship, so that made it hard for me to explain everything to them. They have been married for decades, so it was ingrained in me that one must try everything to make a marriage work, in good times and bad. Thus it was very difficult to actually leave, even mentally coming to the conclusion that this is what I had to do as divorce – even separation – felt like such alien and forbidden concepts to me. Additionally I found it went against my nature to tell myself that I didn't need to try to justify the behaviour I was experiencing from Joe, especially when he used to constantly twist things around via 'gaslighting' to make me question my own sanity/behaviour all the time, to think that all of our issues were actually just my issues. I think this is why although I miss my faith now, I struggle with lots of different faiths, because they still have this fundamental belief that women should be submissive to men.

***

However, on that one particular September day, my attention faltered, and I suddenly went over on my ankle and knew immediately that I was in trouble. An hour later and my narky husband, was driving me to the nearest city hospital for an x-ray. Our older daughter stayed behind to look after the boys but now it had got to the point where I didn't want to be on my own with Joe as it was too difficult and stressful.

On the journey to the hospital, Joe's mood felt menacing and I'd made the mistake of mentioning something to him about a business he had bought on the side but he was meant to be in the process of winding-up because it had become a huge cash liability. Joe didn't like the fact I mentioned this and just had an angry outburst, saying: "I'm just going to leave you by the side of the road!" and he threatened to perform an emergency stop. I immediately retreated into silence as I regularly found myself doing. It was the only way to survive how things were between us. All of it: the regular, everyday occurrences that were perceived as slights by Saul: the main ones being teenage untidiness and their flighty moods and my hospital shifts. However, often because he was just generally stressed but wouldn't tackle it, anything seemed to trigger the metaphorical pressure cooker set deep within him.

I reflected about what had changed so dramatically and when? Because once upon a time, we had been incredibly happy: I remembered one evening 8 months into our relationship, pre-children when we were living together and were engaged. On that particular day, before I was working as a nurse, I'd taken time off from the medical centre where I was a receptionist and had spent ages cooking Joe a special chilli with all the extras. I'd timed my prep for his arrival home at around 7pm, but he didn't turn up and didn't have a mobile phone on him that I could ring. By 10pm, I was getting pretty anxious because I was young, in love and a worrier. But then he casually strolled in the front door, having had a last minute crisis at the hospital which he'd had to stay late for and I just felt a big wave of love for him when I knew he was safe. Back at that time, he had incited a lot of feelings within me but now I had mentally zoned-out from him a long time ago because I just couldn't cope with him and our relationship.

How many times over the years had I felt that I could not continue with this? Acknowledged that there was no real love there any more as it had all been shouted away. Admitted that this loveless 'marriage' left me feeling completely empty? Felt a pang of missing out when I was visiting a pair of our friends, a married couple: Jason and Claire who had been together for ages and had young children and I observed them romantically pull a wishbone apart from their roast chicken, make a silent plea each to the universe and then giggle about it. I'd been having a cup of tea with them on that Sunday afternoon after dropping back their daughter from a children's birthday party which I'd also taken the twins to, but seeing Jason and Claire's intimacy together even when displayed publicly in their kitchen, made me feel as though I was intruding on them as a couple: I felt like an interloper. It emphasised all that was lacking (and if I was truly honest, had been lacking for years), in my own relationship. It just made me really sad.

I also had a flashback to when the twins were babies and I'd gone into the city Careers' Advice Centre whilst they were asleep in their pram so that I could make a plan for my future. Next to me were a very tactile couple of students: a guy and a girl. They'd pulled two chairs up, right next to each other in front of a computer. From the corner of my eye, I'd caught the students' hands meeting and saw them stroke each other's legs. Then they leaned in together and kissed, and in the quiet of the waiting room, I could even hear their lips meeting. Within a few minutes the girl was sitting astride her boyfriend's lap and they were kissing passionately. I'd carried on reading intently from a careers' manual, not daring to look to my right side as the students' hands were going everywhere… I couldn't focus on the book as I suddenly felt nostalgic for young, visceral love.

What did it feel like to love like that again? It seemed so long ago since I had experienced those emotions because life: namely children, jobs, mortgages, stress, domesticity, tedious routines etc, had just got in the way. I'd ached to feel the way these students obviously did. They likely had days where they simply bunked off college or uni and stayed in bed all day… I felt jealous of what they had: would I ever know that intensity again? I loved my family but hadn't had any hugely spontaneous intimacy like that for years… I craved it, missed it. Was this it? I needed more than the domestics especially as this side of our marriage sometimes dropped off a cliff. For example, when I applied to undertake my nursing degree, Joe was so incensed at me asserting my agency that he threatened to divorce me, and then when I pushed ahead with Uni, regardless, he stopped sleeping with me. At the time though I thought his reluctance to go near me wasn't because he resented me but because he must be having an affair until one night, feeling bewildered and rejected, I confronted him and he said he said how annoyed he'd felt with me.

Two members of staff had walked past the kissing couple before one, a matriarch in a shapeless shift who gave off the vibe that she'd never felt sexy, turned around and ambled up to them demanding: "Right, who's not using the computers?" her eyes were averted from the couple but it was obvious that her words were intended for them but they simply ignored her and continued kissing. She'd moved closer towards them and said: "do you need to be in this space?" before pausing, then continuing, obviously annoyed: "there's another person who would like to use the facility", although there clearly wasn't anyone else waiting. The loved-up students finally pulled apart. The woman responded: "well you can continue *talking* in the main section of the waiting room or outside."

I'd smiled inwardly at the matriarch's choice of the word: '*talking*', … the couple definitely weren't talking and I'd wondered then why it was often so awkward for people to observe affection and I concluded that maybe it's when they're not having any in their own lives, that they feel jealous and thus take affront at the display of physical intimacy between others.

But it was about **all** of it though: I had come to realise the importance of simple everyday kindnesses that couples who **really** love each other display, and that these aren't to be overlooked. For these are just as essential as the grand demonstrations, but in my relationship and in lots of other long-term relationships where complacency has set in and a spouse feels that their partner would never be able to afford to leave them and doesn't have the confidence to go it alone, those little moments of feeling loved, are missing. For me back then, there was just a huge void.

Furthermore, it had got to the point that often I longed to escape or in the last few stressful years of our marriage, hoped that Joe wouldn't come home from work when he returned in an unhappy, stressed and confrontational mood. But after every working day, Joe walked through the front door at some point after his surgery was done and I continued to perform my wifely/motherly role. I just accepted that this was it for the rest of my life, as the old saying goes: 'I had made my bed... '

Deep down I'm an optimist and outside of my marriage, I was generally always happy and bubbly and people mentioned this, but I used to think, if only you knew. When it came to my relationship with Joe, in the latter years I kept thinking: 'I won't let you crush me' and I kept telling myself to bide my time. I'd tried for ages to be loving but when it's not reciprocated over a long period of time, love just withers away and dies. Ultimately you end up with two individuals living in the same house and co-parenting but without any real feelings for each other any more. It's sad because it's a complete waste of two people's lives.

This process of completely falling out of love, care even, didn't happen because of one main event, but was triggered incrementally by instalments of meanness, sneery and sarcastic comments, unkindness, being ignored, antagonism, flare-ups, a constant desire to pick a battle and an unwillingness to talk about anything...

I knew I needed to make the break after just over two decades of marriage from when I was in my very early twenties, but the words of my daughter - when we were on our last family holiday - stuck in my head: "if you try to leave dad, he will wipe the floor with you." That holiday was awful because as mentioned before, Joe attempted to manipulate our family to take sides against me because I had said that we could not afford the huge Oakford property which he had put a secret offer on. We stayed on the mainland on the first night of that holiday before we caught a boat to our island the next morning and he shouted in my face loudly in the taxi ride to the hotel. It was humiliating as he was belittling me in front of our children and the taxi driver. On our second night away, because of Joe's money-mismanagement, there was no money to pay for food and he had to ring up his mum and get her to lend him some money. This was what it was like. There was financial instability all the time and if I raised this, I felt as though I was walking on eggshells, daring to question him.

But I didn't feel strong enough for the battle which I knew would lie ahead and financially I had no access to any money to enable me to leave. So I just kept going. My own nursing career kept me really busy and I tried to forget how unhappy I was. As a mum also, you often live for other people and you try to push aside how you really feel and how you need to be. You bury the real you.

The unreasonableness of the situation I was dealing with, included these incidents which were typical over the course of the last few years of our marriage: When I smelt gas outside our back door the day before one Christmas Eve and said we should call the Gas Board to get this checked, Joe got irate and shouted at me saying I was imagining it. But I did call the Gas Company and there was a leak caused by the builders, which the Gas Company fixed.

When our gas boiler was flashing and refused to work so we couldn't turn the heating on or get any hot water, he became irrational again and said we couldn't afford to have it serviced. When the bath flooded the floor each and every time someone used it and I asked to call a plumber to have what was an obvious leak repaired because I didn't have access to money to get it fixed myself, Joe got mad again, saying our finances wouldn't stretch to that and actually: "no one needs to have a bath anyway." The leaking bath situation continued for over a year! Looking back it was pitiful but I felt too trapped to do otherwise.

Living with erratic moods, a simmering temper and unreasonableness, whilst not being allowed any say in our defective family finances and earning very little money myself, made me emotionally withdraw. I was stuck with someone who felt like an-impossible-to-please-domineering-father, as opposed to an equal partner. The dynamics of our relationship had completely changed. We were trying to raise children, run a home, undertake our professional careers too, but he didn't consider me to be on a level footing with him. Joe always wanted to be in charge and he would say that as an extremely busy and important surgeon, I simply couldn't comprehend the level of pressure that he was under, whilst I was "just a nurse". There was no way our marriage could possibly work like this.

Without available funds to have essential repairs undertaken, but then apparently enough money for Joe to book expensive holidays to boast about to his medical colleagues, I just felt more disempowered. When you're dealing with someone like this, lots of everyday situations become difficult because of the unreasonable behaviour. Also not having the financial means to fix things, results in lots of relatively minor issues becoming much bigger problems until they become overwhelming. For example, with the leaking bath, each time one of our children or I had a bath, I had to use three x king-size towels to mop up the flood of dirty water that immediately gushed out from underneath it every time the plug was let out, because Joe said he couldn't afford to call a plumber out and yet simultaneously he'd ordered himself a brand new deluxe car on credit that cost nearly £400 every month!

When I tried to talk to him about money, he'd patronisingly say: "you don't need to worry about that" and wave his hand in the air at me, but I'd reply that I did need to worry about it because it affected all of us. However, Joe would either get angry and shout at me or walk out of the room, and then if I tried to continue the conversation by following him into another room, he would say: "stop harassing me; you're being abusive". It was completely impossible to have any kind of adult conversation with him.

Joe had been sent away by his parents when he was very young and thus he had become used to being completely autonomous from an early age. When we started our relationship and I knew about his childhood, I used to make endless excuses for how he could act, because I felt sorry for him being packed off from his family home when he was little, but then a friend said to me: "you can't keep on making excuses for a grown man who won't help himself." However, because he'd been used to being in charge from such a young age, Joe couldn't countenance the need to tell or really involve me in any important decision-making.

However, not having any available cash for the urgent basic needs in life was a common and stressful theme in terms of lots of aspects of the house, the business he bought and even our cars. For example, we couldn't even afford new brake pads and so he would get cross when I said my car brakes were grinding, and because there wasn't any money available to fix this yet I'd still need to drive my car to work, this would ultimately result in the brake discs getting ruined and then that would be even more expensive and cause him additional annoyance. There was no rhyme or reason to it. Yet his new car had been ordered. It was all insane and I wasn't allowed any say. I put up with all of the inconveniences, all of the unnecessary extra grind because I didn't know how I could leave. I felt I had to accept that this was my life and I was boxed-into it. He knew that too. Also occasionally things were actually okay and so I metaphorically 'trod water'.

But then confrontational, unreasonable and difficult episodes started to become more interwoven into the fabric of our daily lives so much so, that I dreaded going home if he was there. I felt the same about family holidays because he wanted to call the shots about what we did every day. I found myself making excuses to go off alone for a coffee to recalibrate, just so that I could cope with it all. Also to have the head-space to deal with the petulant strops which were triggered for example, if no one wanted to eat at the time when he wanted to eat, or if a family member suggested we try a different restaurant/café to the one he desired. The outcome was always the same: beautiful settings spoilt by a tense and stressful atmosphere. On our last family holiday for example, he was angry because the kids didn't want to have a meal at 5pm and so in the middle of looking around the town as a family, he just walked off in a petulant strop for over an hour and a half and I couldn't get hold of him. The rest of us as a family ended up waiting in a central park for him so that he could find us, as my mobile wasn't working at the time and he had our hotel room key. When Joe finally came back to the park (and by this time the kids were all bored and restless), his mood had flipped – he had treated himself to some pastries – and he was happy. He behaved as though nothing had happened and that him just walking off, without saying where he was going, and then returning much later without uttering any apology, was absolutely fine. During the hours afterwards, there was just a horrible atmosphere between us all.

On a previous holiday, if I wanted to swim at a different beach or in a different pool to the one he'd chosen, or go for a bike ride without him, he would get cross and refuse to do what I wanted to do or he'd come along and then kick-off or he would say tersely when it was just the two of us in a room: "you don't want to be with me; you're deliberately trying to avoid me!!" This was his method of generally always getting his own way. His presence began to set my nerves on edge. All the shouting, angry combative moods, egg-shell-treading, etc, was filed away as, 'dad's being dad' but as time rumbled on, the pressure of coping with it all and feeling really unloved and isolated in my marriage was beginning to seriously affect me.

I couldn't cope with living with a man who was aggravated by the slightest little thing and who got annoyed and shouted at me a lot. If this was how it was going to be for the rest of my life, then I needed to get out fast because I knew I was wasting time. The penny had finally dropped that nothing would ever change. The pressure of trying to keep a lid on a very stressful home life when we were running out of money all the time because Joe was trying to live a life we couldn't afford, combined with a busy career, was taking its toll on me.

I'd suggested to my husband that we should go to Relate for marriage counselling for a number of years because of how bad things were, but his retort was always a very blunt and cross: "I'm not doing that. I don't need counselling!" When his stress levels were high, I'd booked him GP appointments so that he could go and talk to the doctor and towards the end of our marriage, he was put on anti-anxiety tablets but he wouldn't seek counselling or any other ways to manage the pressures he felt, so the impossible behaviour continued. When I said to him that

I thought he was stressed, he would gaslight me, menacingly shouting: "It's not me! You're the one who's stressed because I don't think you can cope with nursing; you couldn't do anything without me; you'd never have become a nurse in the first place if I hadn't helped you with your exams!" His words were beginning to have a hurtful, corrosive, drip-drip effect on my confidence levels.

For the last few years of our marriage, I realised that we desperately needed time apart to work out if there was any way we could save the marriage and I suggested this to him a number of times but he just wouldn't accept it and wouldn't listen. He didn't think I would ever follow through with potentially leaving. He would shake it off, even telling the children: "your mother's not leaving me", he simply refused to even contemplate this possibility as he thought I was completely dependent on him and that I wouldn't have the guts to do it. The last time I said to him that I couldn't continue as we were after our final disasterous family holiday, his reply was: "You keep saying you'll leave but you never do. I'm not going anywhere because this is MY house, so if you want to leave, you leave but you won't be able to afford to because you're *just* a nurse."… and I walked off, feeling mocked because of my lack of financial autonomy, racking my brains, thinking how on earth could I get the money together to leave? But I was quietly manifesting a little bit of fighting spirit and beginning to think, 'whatever it takes, I **will** leave you because you are making me feel worthless'.

That same summer, we had gone to a talent show at our younger child's school where we met up with our group of friends whose children also attended the same school and Joe was mocking me under his breath, in front of our group. I knew that night, that everything was ramping up in terms of his lack of respect for me and his attempts to undermine me.

I started confiding in my parents properly about how things really were. Initially they wanted me to try to continue with my marriage if at all possible, but as I began to break down in tears to them on the phone more and more in desperation, they began to realise the severity of the situation I was in. They didn't offer to lend me the money to leave at that point because I think that like a lot of parents, they didn't want to be seen to be assisting in what amounted to the unravelling of their daughter's family, which would also impact on their grandchildren. But later they helped me financially by lending me some money and I am so grateful that they did.

***

But then with my fall in the silent mossy wood, everything began to unravel faster than I had ever contemplated. In the car on our way to A&E that day when Joe was bellowing at me, I asked him quietly: "why are you shouting at me?" and he simply replied tersely: "because I'm frustrated!!"

In A&E on that September Sunday when I was there with my possibly-broken foot, I watched as a frail, elderly Scottish woman who looked like she was in her late-eighties, whimpered to her daughter in a constantly-revolving, pitiful loop for two hours: "let's go hooome", elongating the last word so much that it became a painful wail. On and on it went: "I want to go hooome. I'm freezing Anne. What have I done to be put here? It's taking hours. Why are you punishing me with this? I have such a sore throat". The old lady's face looked so miserable and wan, all the colour had drained out of it. The woman's daughter tried to keep her own sanity by undertaking a crossword whilst sitting next to her mother but every so often, the daughter would roll her eyes and sigh exasperatedly.

Although I didn't mean to be, I was transfixed by them. The daughter sometimes whispered in her mother's ear and then alternately would write a message to the weary older woman on a mini whiteboard requesting that she was quiet because she was disturbing others. I caught the younger woman nodding in my direction as I sat with my book open in my lap and my pained ankle stretched out. Mother and daughter were in a frustrating bind that was obviously 'doing [both of] their heads' in', and it made me think of how much people put up with before they get to breaking point. And I thought of my breaking point and I realised that it was much easier to stay in an unhappy marriage than to leave, but I kept remembering a quote of writer, Anais Nin. The words of her powerful quote were basically along the lines that: life gets bigger or smaller depending on how brave one is. I knew that I needed to get psychologically strong and be brave enough to leave my marriage.

I reflected upon all the holidays, family days out, expensive meals, camping trips and so on, over recent years since my husband's stress levels had risen, when his tension had been taken out on us in verbal outbursts or moods: these times should have been pretty idyllic but they were laced with tension: i.e., the accommodation not quite as expected in Paris, so he embarrassingly lost-it with the Reception staff and I disappeared out of earshot because I didn't want to be associated with it; kids arguing on the way to a beach day-trip and so a burst of shouting later and nobody talked full-stop. Restaurant meals tarnished because the waiter arrived with the wrong starter and Joe took him to task causing a scene which made other diners stop eating and tune into what was happening and I wished a sinkhole would open up and swallow me because I didn't want to be connected to him. We were often in such beautiful places but those times were marred by stressful atmospheres.

There was a camping trip with friends where, civil amongst company, the air inside our tent became toxic because driving down separately to Joe because of my work shift, I'd stopped at a supermarket en route to get supplies, but then that meant I 'made' Joe too late to go to the local bistro before its closing time, so he railed and ranted at me inside our tent in whispered anger because he'd missed a dining-out opportunity. Everyone else in the group had happily thrown something together, on their camping stoves but no, unbeknownst to me, my husband had set his heart on going out for a meal to one of the beachside cafes and I'd 'ruined' his plans because I'd arrived too late. Even though I quickly rustled up some stuffed pasta, his expectations hadn't been met. Latterly, he seemed permanently ready for a verbal confrontation and I found it exhausting and far too stressful. I felt on edge all the time.

Towards the end of our marriage, even family walks became a source of bitter recrimination because again he thought I was "deliberately choosing to ignore" him when I was hiking with one of our children rather than being at his side. But it wasn't this way at all: family walks were just walks, you naturally tend to alternate who you walk alongside and talk to – there wasn't a game-plan to spend more time with one family member rather than another. Furthermore, at the time, I'd have no idea that this was his perception, it was only later in a quiet but intimidating verbal volley, that I'd learn of this view.

A third party told me that at work, Joe was meticulous, dedicated, laughed a lot and everyone thought he was "jolly". Hearing this was so hard and hurtful because in private, I had the flip side of the coin. To me, he was a Jekyll and Hyde character. With our friends, he was known to be a 'little bit tricky' but he was the sarcastically witty one and they all loved coming over to ours for dinner parties. Like a lot of men now, Joe discovered he was a naturally gifted chef and so we often had friends over but at such dinner parties, Joe would dictate to me that he was going to make the starter and mains and I was only 'allowed' to create the desert because he wanted to receive adulation for his food and he said I would "get too stressed" if I had to create a whole meal (this of course wasn't true as I was more than capable, but he just dominated these evenings).

Due to Joe's hard childhood, the maternal pity of my girlfriends was there for him in abundance but I got the annoyed, confrontational, disgruntled side. This was the part of our marriage that I could no longer cope with, the part that incentivised me to work diligently in my career, to manically take-up swimming, max my heart rate out at the gym, have days out with the kids one-to-one and evening drinks with girlfriends… anything but be at home because I found it too stressful. To survive the atmospheres, I had to disconnect, be passive when he was worked-up over something trivial. Towards the end, I remember telling him so many times, that I would only talk to him once he had calmed down and that the way he was with me, was: "making me feel like a cowering whipped dog" and I remember him saying in reply: "well I'm sorry I make you feel like that" and that was it.

***

And I knew I had to leave, but I couldn't see how as I only had my small nursing wage. No access to any savings. How could I possibly afford a deposit to rent a place and to pay the bills? Even if I could somehow get enough money together for a deposit and the first month's rent, I didn't have enough of a financial float to cover me for the unknowable bills to follow. A very real worry I had was, what if I moved out, but then couldn't afford to stay in my rented place? There was no way I could face leaving and then not be able to sustain that. I couldn't possibly leave Joe and then have to ask to move back because I would never hear the end of it – my life would be completely ruined. Thus I had to be able to move out and stay out.

Joe had financial control of his income which was 11x greater than mine and he would book holidays that we couldn't afford because he said he needed to escape and he was entitled to do so. He felt deserving of a two-week break and although I totally understood this because it's better to have a decent length of time to unwind, we couldn't even afford a week away as we were so heavily mortgaged up. So when I'd say: "should we just go for one week instead as it won't be so expensive", his cross reply would be: "No! I'm having two weeks. I'm entitled to it." But then these holidays gobbled up all our household funds so my broken car key couldn't be replaced (for years, it was sellotaped and I constantly stressed it would get stuck in the ignition as it wouldn't fit together properly); unpaid bills stacked up and we'd be chased on our home telephone endlessly several times a day; builders who were due to finish work on our house renovations, refused to return because their invoices weren't settled so they left their mess lying around and their work in limbo, for weeks and months at a time. I had to ring the building company owner to try to keep him on-side. I just basically had to put up with it all.

I wasn't allowed a say in any of the spending, instead during that fraught taxi ride at the start of our (final) family holiday (as cited previously), when Joe shouted at me in front of the taxi driver and our children, that after over two decades of marriage: "I will never trust you with my money! You'd waste it all", I knew it was over. Later I sat on the boat en route to the tiny island which was to be our base for the next fortnight, with tears rolling down my face. It was then I realised that enough was enough and nothing would ever get better or change. This episode followed my discovery just days earlier, that as mentioned earlier, behind my back, he'd been planning to buy the Oakford property, to renovate. But because we'd already struggled to pay the builders who'd only just finished extending our current property, I knew that attempting a much bigger project with lots of land/outbuildings too, would have completely bankrupted us.

***

On our first wedding anniversary, money had been a nightmare and we couldn't afford to do anything and in the years that followed, sometimes money was a little easier if my husband got lots of private medical work or remortgaged and then it would be tight again, but throughout all this time, I had always, always remained optimistic; I'd used to think that things would improve, get better in every way: our relationship would get better; Joe would be less stressed and be loving/demonstrative, our finances would improve... but I finally, finally realised on that last family holiday, that it was over. I simply couldn't do it any more.

In previous years, my parents would help me out practically by paying for my new car tyres and so on, but I hated asking them as they'd scrimped and saved all their lives, so it felt wrong that I should have to approach them in the first place. I continued to manage on my small salary. I paid my own bills: phone, gym, car insurance, got the kids' the items they needed as much as I could, put household essentials and clothes on store cards for them and me because how else could I afford it and I couldn't ask Joe to pay. He never questioned how I paid for anything, he just assumed I'd find the money. In the ten years before I left him, I had to find all kinds of ways to bring in extra money (not prostitution!) but I had to get resourceful, even selling my Ipod for £40 and Christmas presents so that I could buy food shopping! (Joe laughed with his friends about me selling the Christmas presents, making a joke that I didn't appreciate what he had bought me and I found it so humiliating! How could he not appreciate the stress he was putting me through and then to additionally embarrass me like that publicly by turning it into a sarky comedy moment!) Back then, I did whatever it took to manifest cash to get basic groceries to live because I ran out of money and couldn't buy food or pay my car insurance but he got cross if I asked him for any money in the last decade of our marriage.

I remember having to wedge our broken double bed mattress for 2 years with books because springs stuck out of it and would dig into our backs, but there was no money to replace it... but I put up with it... Looking back, it was all pretty insane when fundamentally a lot of money was coming into our household. It was humiliating!

Once I started nursing, I was paying for our food shopping every week and when I ran out of money, I had to (cringely) ask Joe to put petrol in my car as I had no access to any money to pay for it myself. As Joe didn't trust me with "his money", he would physically take my car and fill it up himself. But sometimes when I was low on petrol and needed to fill up my tank in the evening to get to the hospital early the next morning, he would be irascible and say: "no I'm not going out now – I'm too tired" but as I'd have to leave very early the next day to drive the hour-long commute to the hospital and Joe hated getting up even slightly early in the morning, if he wouldn't get me petrol at night, then there was no way, he'd get it in the morning and then I would panic about how I was going to get to work. But again, at other times he would be fine. I never knew how it was going to be. I hated having him to ask to fill up my own car as being at this stage in my life, it felt so utterly pathetic, demeaning to be living like this at this age.

Occasionally, I would be given some money from him if we remortgaged but there would be such an outstanding backlog to pay for as my credit cards would be high having supplemented my low income for ages and also I'd have to budget the money out for months of future food shopping, so there wasn't any spare cash.

I just felt so boxed-in/trapped! I'd listen to my girlfriends talking about going away to stay with girlfriends or family abroad or in the UK without their partners and I wanted to do the same taking my kids too, but I could never do this because: (a) I had no money to be able to and also because: (b) Joe would say incredulously: 'why would you choose to go without me?' and: 'if you do that, then when you're working, I'm going to take them off to the Caribbean' or some other beautiful location that he knew I'd never be able to afford to take them to, in order to compete.

My husband told our children that if I left him, I would be back within a year, because I would run out of money. Later when I had to apply for child maintenance from him, he was difficult and patronising, saying that if I wanted more money, I "should train to be a surgeon and not just a nurse!" Years went by like this and I should've left sooner but then I wasn't quite ready to because I felt I had to try everything to make my marriage work. But ultimately, there is only so much unreasonable behaviour that anyone can put up with. There is always the final straw that breaks the camel's back.

One Spring, an incident occurred where Joe swore and ranted at me publicly in front of a group of our friends, reducing me to tears. I was mortified and its nature led to Claire (who was an anaesthetist), saying that she didn't think I could/should stay with him. It was awful because it was so humiliating and degrading. One of our children called my parents up mid-flow and they heard his anger too. Then I knew I absolutely had to leave because I felt like a victim and it's the most horrible, belittling feeling ever, because I don't think any normal person wants to be pitied. However, I was also a little relieved because I felt that others would now see how things were (but most chose to completely ignore it). That night the physical and emotional distance between us was palpable. I just decided that whatever it took, I was going to leave imminently.

The next day was a Bank Holiday and what had happened the day before was everyone else's fault, according to Joe: it was my fault, it was our friends' fault etc, but I caught a glimpse of him outside in the garden when he was unaware and he was sitting at our patio table with his head in his hands at one point and for a few seconds my heart reached out to him. I hoped that if he got support for his stress levels and realised that this was a turning point, maybe there might just be the slightest chance we could save our marriage? However, he ultimately wasn't interested at all. A friend of his popped in and Joe explained his actions but still placed the blame on others, including me. A few days' later, this friend of his vanished into the ether, panicked by the heightened emotions. The rest of that day was spent with a moody Joe: cross one minute, down the next. I just took a huge deep breath because the kids were around and told myself to *Stay calm.*

Another male friend of Joe's, kindly messaged him to ask him if he'd like to go for a beer which was really appreciated, when others just shrank away. Joe managed to take some emergency leave from work and he went away for a few weeks. I was so relieved because I needed thinking space. I had to quickly organise additional childcare for my youngest for the days when I'd be working nights at the hospital and my colleagues used to remind me about these to help me because everything felt up in the air and on my day off the wards, I was helping on a mentoring programme for trainee nurses to earn extra money, whilst trying to hold everything else together. Looking back, life was insane…

Driving to the hospital early one morning for work, not long before the events which finally made me leave, occurred, the song 'Lady hear me tonight' by Modjo was playing and I found myself welling-up because I was so unhappy in my marriage. It was really starting to affect my mental health.

Whilst Joe was away recuperating after his verbal meltdown at me, he rang home a few times but I found it too stressful to talk to him as he kept saying that ***I had made him react the way he did.*** That week I managed to take a few days off work and I booked an appointment with my local Citizen's Advice Bureau to get advice regarding how I could leave and what financial support I'd be entitled to. The advisor, (Lucy), was just incredible. She gave me tissues as I cried and she listened and was so helpful. Lucy calculated exactly what I could claim to help me pay my bills and then she wrote exactly what steps I needed to take, in which order, and who to contact (i.e. the local council and so on), to get particular help/discounts. She reassured me that what I was dealing with was abusive behaviour and that I didn't need to put up with it. Lucy also told me that she was experiencing a lot of similar cases but that *I could leave* and she would talk me through the process.

My decision to leave Joe was cemented when he angrily complained about me keeping some of my university resources in our home, saying that they cluttered it and that he was going to set fire to them all. This was after he'd promised that when we undertook the building work to our home, that there would be room for a study for me to store all of my nursing resources in (because I wanted to develop my career), but later he backtracked, got angry and said there wasn't enough money left for that, but he still didn't want my resources around. It was stressful because I worried then that one day because of how much he'd irrationally flare up, that in the heat of a moment, he might just get rid of all of my essential nursing uni paperwork. I was constantly living on my nerves and continuing to dread coming home each day. Joe had said that if I ever came into any money that I needed to give it to him so he could pay for more work to be undertaken on our home but mentally I was fixated on leaving him and thought absolutely 'no way' as it would be 'throwing good money after bad'.

When I moved out of my much-loved family home, I was only 'allowed' by my Ex to take items which I had physically purchased. It was incredibly stressful. The removals' men came to help me take my boxes and a few pieces of furniture I had from the family home and my former husband was very hostile to them.

When you leave a long marriage and have felt disempowered for so long, there is a period of time when there are crossed wires between the parties but when children are involved, there's a desire to keep things civil. However, it's important to get real and accept that however much you try, sometimes this isn't always possible. So about 5 weeks after I moved out, Joe and I tried to go for a walk together to see if we could be amicable with each other, but my former husband arrogantly just assumed I would be coming back to him and said matter-of-factly: "what I'm dreading is when you come back with all of your junk as I don't know where we'll put it and I don't want it cluttering my house", I was a bit incredulous that he just assumed my moving out was a temporary blip and that I would return when things turned pear-shaped for me as he believed they would. He did not think me capable of running my own life and household without him.

In addition, when I popped in briefly to my old family home shortly after leaving, to collect a painting which I had bought and paid for years' before, he 'caught' me taking it and angrily shouted: "what are you stealing from me now!" physically trying to manhandle it off me until one of our children intervened and told him to stop.

However, I still wanted to try to make peace with Joe because he is the father of my children. A few months' later, I invited him over to a Sunday roast I was making when my parents were coming up and our children were going to be there too. I thought that having my parents with me would neutralise any potential atmospheres. But Joe kept on making snide comments about my rented home – such as when he prodded my 'thatch-effect' back porch roof – which is actually reproduction, not real thatch at all - and then said sneerily: "is everything in your house fake?" It was one of several similar digs he said to make me feel worthless, such as when he discovered I'd had to apply for some state benefits and he said, sniggering: "What's happened to your life?!" When he made the "fake" comment about my home, it just triggered me as I felt it was simply disrespectful after I'd invited him over for lunch. So I quietly asked him to stop and then he got in a huff and stormed off, creating a scene in front of my parents declaring loudly: "I can see you actually don't want me to be here" and other words along the lines that he was trying to be the bigger person in this situation. These were all comments to twist what had just happened and then cause tension, which obviously it did for a while before the rest of us carried on with lunch! We were determined not to let him spoil our time together.

There were no boundaries with him: for example when I was doing a shift in hospital, he got hold of a spare key to my rented cottage through one of our children and he let himself in without my permission and helped himself to a pair of spare curtains that he took back to our old family home because he said he was short of some and he was overseeing a potential house-purchase viewing (at this point, he'd put the house on the market to sell). I found out about this and asked for the curtains back and he said: nonchalantly: "have them. I don't like them anyway". Sometimes he would turn up on my doorstep of an evening when I'd been nursing all day and he would start getting verbally aggressive and put his foot inside the door and I had to tell him to leave or I would call the police.

In these types of situation, there are headfuck moments, when an ex shows you kindness and so for a moment, you start to question if you're 'reading everything correctly?' So for example, Joe saved me back some Christmas lunch that he had prepared, on the first Christmas Day after we had separated and I went over later to his home (our former family home), on that day to see the children (who were there), but when I arrived, the atmosphere was so uncomfortable and I didn't feel welcome, so I just couldn't wait to leave. I had to accept that trying to reconvene like this, simply couldn't work any more.

I knew all along that I had absolutely made the correct decision to go, but these relationships and behaviours are never easy to process and particularly as mothers, we often feel incredibly torn, so until we completely process the truth of our situation, we can oscillate between a sense of undeserved loyalty where we try endlessly to rationalise totally unacceptable behaviour AND then also a desperate need to get the hell out before we crack up.

Going through the financial side of the divorce was tough. Sometimes, I only had £10 in my account until payday and was depopping stuff right, left and centre to survive but my Ex, despite his six-figure salary per year, had even demanded I provide statements showing what income I was generating from depop, which was only between £0-£40 a month: hardly a fortune.

Over the coming months. Joe tried to use my nursing incident to 'punish' me for leaving him. He said that I "self-sabotaged everything." Initially, he attempted to seize upon it as a blackmailing tool, threatening to tell various official bodies to try to get me to accept a lower financial settlement in our divorce, but there wasn't any merit in his threats as I didn't have an obligation to declare anything because the police and hospital investigations had not deemed it was warranted. I have always been open about it. The investigation proved that I did not deliberately intend to administer the wrong dosage to my patient. Joe said that he and our children wanted me to change my surname as they didn't want to be associated with me with regards to my nursing incident in case anything went in the press. He told me I should move far away or go and live with my parents.

After everything else, it was horrible to continue to get these bullying communications from someone who was still trying to control me and who deep down, was still bitter that I had left him. If anything, his behaviour just made me more determined to push through with the divorce and although I knew I had made the right decision to leave him originally, his conduct over my nursing incident reinforced this. The amount of phone calls, texts, emails, letters, meetings that revolved around all of this was huge, but some wonderful new girlfriends and hobbies kept me sane. Ultimately I came through.

My divorce finally went through and the children adapted well and continue to be a big part in my life. I have created a new version of myself and I am far stronger now. I am certainly not cynical or jaded about love and marriage and but

I am less naïve and more pragmatic too. I met a new partner a year ago and am currently very happy but taking it really slow as I learnt to be self sufficient as a single woman before we got to know each other and I don't ever want to become too reliant on anyone else again. I have a wonderful new life now, after rising through the nursing ranks. I continue to enjoy practising nursing, managing nurses and teaching trainee nurses at University. I've taken up pottery in my spare time and when I'm not dashing around seeing the kids, friends, other members of my family, then I love nothing better than to curl up with a good book. I am content, happy and enjoying life so much more than when I was desperately unhappy in my latterly-miserable marriage. Anais Nin was absolutely right: life has definitely expanded in a perfect way!

What have your experiences taught you?

This loss of equality and power in a marriage/relationship, can happen very subtly over time, without even any intention of it happening initially, and we need to be aware of this. Ultimately if you become trapped in a domestic situation that has become toxic and you don't have any money to leave, it's an ongoing nightmare as you feel trapped and disempowered.

Equally for everyone in a relationship, it's worth remembering that if you treat someone without love and kindness, at some point, you're likely to lose them. Don't think they will put up with poor behaviour (and you know when you're behaving badly – we all do!) until you both pop your clogs because you think they will never leave you because they haven't got the balls and/or they can't afford to, because when people get desperate, they find the means and the willpower to make those big leaps. Believe me there is nothing more incentivising than someone laying down the gauntlet, telling you that you can't do something, for example, that you can't afford to leave them. So don't be complacent. Be kind. If you truly have any love for your partner, treat them well.

When a relationship is damaging, you need to be able to open up and talk about it. It's vital as toxicity breeds in privacy. Once you tell others you trust about what's going on, it helps you to process your next steps and to become strong in your resolve to tackle the situation.

What would you advise other women in your situation?

You don't have to stay in a relationship that is damaging you. If it's not going to change, you are wasting time and you are wasting your life. Furthermore, if you have children and you stay, you're instilling in them that it's okay to resign yourself to put up with questionable behaviour and an unhappy relationship for the rest of your life.

Instead you'll wish you'd broken free years' ago because your life will open up. If you don't have any savings to enable you to leave, then your first step should be to make an appointment with your local Citizen's Advice Bureau. They will talk you through each part of the process and help you work out what you might be entitled to if you are on a low income. Know your worth as a woman. Make a plan. Do it! I promise you, that you won't regret it. (There may be other funds available to help you too but you need to make enquiries to discover this; for example, my local County Council have a special fund to help people in situations such as the one I found myself in).

WHERE ARE YOU NOW? WHAT ARE YOUR PLANS FOR THE FUTURE?

I've had to set firm boundaries regarding my former husband, for example, he texted me to ask me to get him dog food for his dogs as he didn't have a car at the time (I did it once but said it was a one-off and I received an aggressive response). A few weeks' later, I received another text from him, virtually ordering me to transfer 50p into his bank account so he could pay for a house valuation for a loan. I said no because we had cut all financial ties by that point, to which I received angry text replies from him. I stood up for myself and said that if his messages continued, I would block him. I did end up blocking him when he sent further aggressive texts because I refused to sign something he wanted me to. It's regrettable especially for our children, that it's been like this, but it is, what it is and it is important that others realise that sometimes in these situations, you just don't have harmony (even from a distance).

Furthermore, he has sent me patronising emails speaking of his "concern" about me but it really helps that I have physical and emotional distance from him now and I simply copy all of his emails and my replies into a third professional party to protect myself – whenever I need to. I have finally learnt to be strong and stop being a people-pleaser. I have learnt to accept the situation. I try not to be drawn into further complications regarding our children, but I know that I may need to engage legal assistance again in the future.

I realise that it is really important to have a partner who you can properly talk to (this includes talking about matters they find uncomfortable), otherwise without deep communication over a period of time, your interactions and understanding of each other, becomes superficial, hostile and full of resentment. Also financial security and parity are absolutely crucial in a relationship and I wouldn't even consider having children with a future partner/husband if I didn't have this, because otherwise it's a recipe to feel demeaned and completely disempowered. It's vital to really respect each other and keep being kind to each other/make an effort with each other! That's definitely essential.

Regarding my future as mentioned earlier, I am now flourishing in my career and looking forward to the next decades of my life with an extremely positive outlook!

APPENDIX

JOY'S EXPERIENCES WORKING ABROAD (WHICH SHE WANTED TO SHARE)

Morocco was indeed an experience. It was a cultural shock. People in the north spoke French, Arabic, Spanish and English. The younger generation were well educated following the French school system and many had left to go to university in France. Tourism was of the cultural sort mainly and modern hotels were springing up along the coast, east of the city of Tangier. Many small rural fishing villages had suddenly found themselves surrounded by the odd tourist village. The best thing was that builders were not allowed to erect anything over two storeys high and they had to be in keeping with the local architecture: in this case, white-washed, Star Wars-type, block buildings with large open quads.

These holiday clubs were isolated though and whilst popular, as they catered for all their guests' needs, they were not in the sort of places you could just walk out of and explore as there were simply no large villages with shops. Just small isolated hamlets. The roads were good but given the manic driving style, the lack of street lighting and pavements and the frequent intrusion by the odd goat or donkey, it would be fair to say that one took one's life in one's own hands venturing upon them. Added to which there was no law against smoking 'kif' whilst driving, so while there were drink drive laws clearly aimed at foreigners (as very few locals indulged in alcohol at all), there was no differentiation whatsoever between smoking tobacco or smoking the Moroccan equivalent of cannabis whilst driving. There was, however, strict laws against smuggling it. My first coach transfer to the airport was quite an eye opener. Weaving along the coastal road with its bends was an education as I had a driver who drove with his foot on the steering wheel as he merrily smoked a joint. Suffice it to say, he only did that once. I do not think the man had ever witnessed such a vocal and irate foreign woman able to insult him in French as I did that day, more out of fear than anger.

Life was very good here as we only worked eight hours a day and had to do one coach airport transfer every Saturday morning. All food and drink was provided and there was an air conditioned nightclub open until 4am. Needless to say it attracted some local residents but only those dressed like Westerners with enough cash in their wallets were allowed entry. Some were nicer than others. Some were sexual predators and I quickly learnt to tell the difference. I did go out with a few on the odd date but there was nothing serious at all. I made a concerted effort never to get emotionally attached to anyone.

Despite the maelstrom of emotions that I felt after my parents' marriage meltdown when I was younger, I still managed to have some memorable times with them when I was older. One of these was when my parents popped over for a week's visit so we hired a car and went to Fez. We drove through melon fields over the Rif mountains. Fez was amazing. We hired a trusty guide to get around the souk. We saw the dye pits, the brass workers and all sorts of mosques and street scenes. My mother got semi-trampled many times by pushy donkeys. The alleys were so narrow and crowded, it was amazing. It was well worth a visit. The hotel was very oldie worldly colonial style. The problem was my room overlooked a big mosque so I was jolted out of bed by the call for prayer on several occasions. No rest for the wicked, indeed!

I had some amazing experiences over the following years which mentally I could reflect upon later when I was a single mum fleeing from my husband. I worked in Tangiers and it was a really interesting port city. There was the old walled medina and the souk, as well as a cosmopolitan city centre with upmarket colonial hotels, French inspired shops and a wonderful French salon de thé which I frequented every day. There were pavement cafes and bars one of which remained open all night serving alcohol and coffee or tea plus a good chilli con carne at the bar.

I met a man at the salon de thé with a penchant for mille feuilles pastries like me, who became a boyfriend for three years on and off. He came from a large, wealthy family who lived in a twenty bedroomed villa with Italian marble floors and Murano glass chandeliers. We travelled a lot to see his brother, a doctor, in Casablanca and we often hopped over the sea by ferry and stayed in Malaga or near Algeciras. His uncle was the Moroccan ambassador in New York and spoke excellent English. I had an incredible experience there but my time in Morocco ended so I returned temporarily to the UK to interviews with two major travel companies. I was offered both but I chose the job in Tunisia. After nine months I transferred to Estoril in Portugal for three months over Christmas, then after that I went to Italy where I stayed.

Estoril again was very upmarket with a casino and fine hotels. The country was more like North Africa economically speaking. It was underdeveloped and financially struggling. Tourism was starting to expand and it was popular with golfers. My lasting memories are of frequent heavy rain, rough Atlantic seas and men who thought it was socially acceptable to pinch ladies' backsides, that included the male hotel staff. The national football stadium was close to the large and very modern airport and we had several flights in from Scotland when they were playing Portugal. I drew the short straw with another colleague to meet and greet the Scottish team on one day which was pleasant enough but the next day we had to cater for four flights of spectators who were 90% young Scottish males, very inebriated and dressed in kilts. Trying to round them up to get them moving was a challenging task to say the least. Trying to walk up the coach was as pleasant as being mauled by a bunch of raccoons!

Running the gauntlet was not a pleasant experience. Then dealing with the aftermath, i.e., the number who had been easy targets for pick pockets, the hospital visits after brawls often with each other and the rowdiness in the hotels. They were never abusive to us but inebriation does not lend itself to social charms and I had to be so sickly nice to the Police and hotel management to let them off with a vicious warning rather than throw them cuffed in a cell. Getting them all back on those flights home was indeed a miracle.

The week after that was quite a treat. We had NATO in Lisbon on manoeuvres. The top ranking officers in full formal dress from the US and Canada were staying in my hotel. These were impeccably mannered and charming. One man in a uniform is a treat for the eyes, a whole bar full when you are the only young female, is a veritable smorgasbord. Suffice it to say I didn't have to pay for any drinks or snacks and the conversation was civilised and interesting. No raccoons present that week. I was invited to eat my dinner that evening with a table full of thirty senior naval officers in their uniforms, none of whom were ancient or unattractive in any way. In early Spring I left Portugal and I flew to Italy to start my season on the Adriatic as explained in my earlier chapter.

All of these experiences, both good and bad, have helped shape me to become the resilient woman I am today!

SURVIVAL TIPS FROM SOME WHO COULDN'T TAKE PART

(*Expressed in their own words*)

- "If you've had a bad experience in a heterosexual relationship, don't write off all men! I have met a kind and decent man. I'm very careful now not to fall into the trap of expecting to be treated badly, but instead I am with someone who treats me as an individual. We have a respectful, balanced relationship."
- "Sometimes life can turn out better than you anticipated: for example, I didn't think Frank would speak to me again after our relationship ended and I found myself expecting a baby, but he is and although we're not together, he's willing to help. So you can still have a respectful, supportive relationship even if you are co-parenting as opposed to being in a relationship."
- "Believe in yourself. Women have so much shame: I think it's inherent but don't expect to be abused!"
- "I think having a Christian childhood conditioned me to be vulnerable from the start. Even if you've had a difficult start, you're not a doormat for others to walk-over, you have to stand up for yourself."
- "Don't be afraid to leave so-called 'friends' behind and don't make snap judgements about others. Try to pick your friends wisely, but if some turn out to be false, discard them and don't feel guilty and sentimental about doing this but rather, be strong. Start afresh and welcome genuine people into your life!"
- "When you're going through birth and early motherhood, it feels so different because your whole identity's taken away but you're actually forging a new identity that's going to be there forever."
- "If your children come to you with trauma, be sympathetic, don't turn them away as this could be detrimental to them for the rest of their lives."
- "It's absolutely not doom and gloom to become a single mum. Rather it has taught me far more calmness and patience than I had before. I've learnt to breathe slower and deeper and to have coping mechanisms to deal with situations far better."
- "As a single parent you don't have to worry about having a partner around who feels they're being neglected because of the baby."
- "I followed my intuition 100% and it's always been right! For example, I just 'knew' when I was seriously ill and I had my symptoms investigated. You must trust your body, it knows itself and it gives you signs but you're the only person who can recognise when something's wrong with it."

- "Having validation from someone you respect, massively helps."
- "I realise that I am made of steel and even in my darkest moments, that I can do it!"
- "Have a birthing partner who's prepared to defend you and stick up for you if needed! Consider having a Doula."
- "On Instagram, I particularly like the account of Yasminbrooke1 as it's so honest about motherhood. She is trying to cope with everything. I love her honesty. Being able to be genuine is so important. She also features in a podcast called 'Mothering through post-partum depression'. Also I like the Podcast by Deliciously Ella, which is fab and in which she talks about birth, mothering, health and nutrition too."

BS - #0003 - 240223 - C0 - 234/156/20 - PB - 9781780916507 - Gloss Lamination